THE REPORT

OF

THE PRESIDENT'S COMMISSION

ON

CAMPUS UNREST

THE REPORT

OF

THE PRESIDENT'S COMMISSION

ON

CAMPUS UNREST

Including Special Reports:

THE KILLINGS AT JACKSON STATE

THE KENT STATE TRAGEDY

ARNO PRESS · NEW YORK

A Publishing and Library Service of The New York Times

Photographs reprinted with permission.
Photograph 9, 15, 45, 55 by Howard E. Ruffner, Jr. copyright © 1970 Howard E. Ruffner, Jr.
Photograph 47, 53, 54 by John A. Darnell, LIFE Magazine, copyright © 1970 Time, Inc.
Photograph 11, 29, 32, 34, 37, 40, 41, 44 copyright © 1970 Valley Daily News, Tarentum, Pa.
Photograph 21, 58 by Beverly K. Knowles, copyright © 1970 Beverly K. Knowles.
Photograph 23, 24, 25, 27, 43 by Richard C. Harris, Jr. copyright © 1970 Richard C. Harris, Jr.

Reprint Edition 1970 by Arno Press Inc.

LC# 71-139710
ISBN 0-405-01712-X

Manufactured in the United States of America

The Report of
THE PRESIDENT'S COMMISSION ON CAMPUS UNREST

PRESIDENT'S COMMISSION ON CAMPUS UNREST

1717 H STREET, N.W.
WASHINGTON, D.C. 20006

WILLIAM W. SCRANTON, *Chairman*
JAMES F. AHERN
ERWIN D. CANHAM
JAMES E. CHEEK
BENJAMIN O. DAVIS
MARTHA A. DERTHICK
BAYLESS MANNING
REVIUS O. ORTIQUE, JR.
JOSEPH RHODES, JR.

WM. MATTHEW BYRNE, JR.
Executive Director

JOHN J. KIRBY, JR.
Deputy Director

September 26, 1970

The President
The White House
Washington, D.C.

Dear Mr. President:

With this letter, I transmit the report of your Commission on Campus Unrest.

The report is based on three months of work by the Commission and its staff. It explores the history and causes of campus unrest. It also contains recommendations to you, the Congress and state legislatures, university administrators and faculty members, students, the police, and the public at large.

Campus unrest is a fact of life. It is not peculiar to America. It is not new and it will go on. Exaggerations of its scope and seriousness and hysterical reactions to it will not make it disappear. They will only aggravate it.

When campus unrest takes the form of violent and disruptive protest, it must be met with firm and just responses. We make recommendations on what those responses should be.

Much campus unrest is neither violent nor disruptive. It is found on any lively college or university campus. It is an expression of intellectual restlessness, and intellectual restlessness prompts the search for truth. We should resist the efforts of some young people to achieve their goals through force and violence, but we should encourage all young people to seek the truth and participate responsibly in the democratic process.

Our colleges and universities cannot survive as combat zones, but they cannot thrive unless they are receptive to new ideas. They must be prepared to institute needed reforms in their administrative procedures and instructional programs.

Still, the essence of a college or university is not the details of this or that program; it is the school's commitment to teaching, learning, and scholarship. Even in this troubled and confusing time, and precisely because we need knowledge and wisdom in such a time, our colleges and universities must sustain their commitment to the life of the mind.

Respectfully,

William W. Scranton
Chairman

THE PRESIDENT'S COMMISSION ON CAMPUS UNREST

William W. Scranton
CHAIRMAN
Former Governor of Pennsylvania

James F. Ahern
Chief of Police
New Haven, Connecticut

Erwin D. Canham
Editor-In-Chief
Christian Science Monitor

James E. Cheek
President
Howard University

Lt. Gen. Benjamin O. Davis, USAF (Ret.)
Director, Civil Aviation Security
U. S. Department of Transportation

Martha A. Derthick
Associate Professor
Boston College

Bayless Manning
Dean, School of Law
Stanford University

Revius O. Ortique, Jr.
Attorney-at-Law
New Orleans, Louisiana

Joseph Rhodes, Jr.
Junior Fellow
Harvard University

STAFF OF
THE PRESIDENT'S COMMISSION ON CAMPUS UNREST

Wm. Matthew Byrne, Jr.
Executive Director

John J. Kirby, Jr.
Deputy Director

Paul A. Brest
Erwin A. Glikes
John R. Labovitz
Associate Editors

Peter W. Blackman
Special Assistant to the
Executive Director

Richard McCormack
Special Assistant to the
Chairman

Paul H. Weaver
Editor

James D. Arthur
Administrative Officer

Christopher Cross, Director
Abby L. Chapkis, Deputy
Office of Public Affairs

W. Samuel Pickens
Production Manager

FIELD OPERATIONS

Kent State	General Investigations	Jackson State
Kenneth G. McIntyre Coordinator	James O'Toole Coordinator	Charles Quaintance, Jr. Coordinator
James Strazzella Chief Counsel	Morey M. Myers Coordinator	Peter J. Nickles Chief Counsel
Terry W. Baker	Wick Allison	Douglas Dalton Director of Investigations
Urbane Bass	Gerald A. Fill	
Steven L. Friedman	Leslie I. Gaines, Jr.	Richard T. Andrews
Jacquelyn M. Howard	Michael S. Garet	Jack Bass
Charles Stine	John P. Gaventa	Tyrone Brown
George V. Warren	Gerald P. Grant	Mary K. Doar
M. Lee Winfrey	Dale G. Higer	Walter Grebe
Lloyd R. Ziff	John R. Loch	Gene G. Livingston
	Roland D. Patzer	D. Robert Owen Advisor
	Edward Sanders-bey	
	Samuel J. Wallace	
	Steven M. Woodside	

WRITING AND EDITORIAL STAFF

PERSONAL ASSISTANTS

Phyllis Bonanno (William W. Scranton)
Ann Hope (Wm. Matthew Byrne, Jr.)
Ann Wyatt (John J. Kirby, Jr.)

PRODUCTION

Ronald D. Beidler
Lloyd P. Boucree
Yvonne Erikkson
Mary E. Kay
Ruth J. Novick
Letitia Walker

CONSULTANTS AND CONTRIBUTORS

William Beall	John Heaphy	Robert Rice
E. Howard Brooks	Lewis B. Kaden	Leonard Ross
Charles J. Creasy, Jr.	William Keisling	Joseph Sahid
Jack D. Douglas	Martin Kilson	Ralph Salerno
James Fisk	Neal Kozodoy	Elmer Schiller
Owen Fiss	Joseph Laitin	John R. Searle
Harley Frankel	Seymour M. Lipset	Irwin Jay Talbot
Raymond Galvin	Norman J. McKenzie	Martin Trow
Nathan Glazer	Thomas Milstein	Fred M. Vinson, Jr.
Erwin A. Glikes	George J. Nolfi, Jr.	Paul H. Weaver
Charles V. Hamilton	John R. Powell	James Q. Wilson
	A. James Reichley, Jr.	

The Commission expresses its appreciation to the Federal Bureau
of Investigation and to Robert Haynes of FBI liaison.

Preface

The President established this Commission on June 13, 1970, in the wake of the great tragedies at Kent State University in Ohio and Jackson State College in Mississippi.

The Commission held its first meeting on June 25, 1970. During the next three months it conducted 13 days of public hearings in Washington, D.C.; Los Angeles, California; Jackson, Mississippi; and Kent, Ohio; and met 15 times in executive session.

The Commission staff conducted intensive investigations in Jackson, Kent, and Lawrence, Kansas, and visited for shorter periods many other colleges and universities throughout the country. These staff teams interviewed students, faculty members, and administrators. The Commission examined the available material on the subject of its mandate and commissioned a number of scholarly papers. The Commission also benefited from the services of a number of consultants.

This report is the result of all these efforts.

One of the major barriers to rational discussion of the subject of campus unrest is that the term means many things to many people. Indeed, the term has become so general that it now embraces not only the intellectual ferment which should exist in the university but also all forms of protest, both peaceful and otherwise. The use of the term "campus unrest" in its present undifferentiated meaning is unfortunate because it blurs the distinction between the desirable and the abhorrent, between activities which the university and society should encourage or must tolerate, and those which they must seek to prevent and must deal with firmly.

As a result of the muddling of the term "unrest," the university and law enforcement agencies find themselves under pressures to stifle even peaceful and legitimate forms of unrest and to condone its violent and illegitimate forms Pressures of this sort can lead only to confusion and injustice. Throughout this report we stress that campus unrest is in fact a complex phenomenon that is manifested in many kinds of protest activity. Most protests, even today, are entirely peaceful and orderly manifestations of dissent, such as holding meetings, picketing, vigils, demonstrations, and marches—all of which are protected by the First Amendment.

Other protest is disorderly, that is, disruptive, violent, or terroristic. Campus unrest has taken each of these forms. Protest is disruptive when it interferes with the normal activities of the university, or the right of others to carry on their affairs. Obstructive sit-ins, interference with classroom teaching, blockading recruiters, and preventing others from speaking or hearing speakers are further examples of disruptive protest.

Violent protest involves physical injury to people, ranging from bloodied noses and cracked heads to actual death. It involves the willful destruction of property by vandalism, burning, and bombing.

A small but highly publicized number of student protests can be called terroristic. Terrorism involves the careful planning and deliberate use of violence in a systematic way in order to create an atmosphere of fear to obtain revolutionary political change.

Each manifestation of campus unrest calls for a different response. Peaceful, orderly, and lawful protest must be protected. Violent and terroristic protest must be dealt with under the law by law enforcement agencies. Disruptive protest is in the first instance the responsibility of the university.

We will return to these distinctions over and over again in this report.

CONTENTS

To The
American People

The crisis on American campuses has no parallel in the history of the nation. This crisis has roots in divisions of American society as deep as any since the Civil War. The divisions are reflected in violent acts and harsh rhetoric, and in the enmity of those Americans who see themselves as occupying opposing camps. Campus unrest reflects and increases a more profound crisis in the nation as a whole.

This crisis has two components: a crisis of violence and a crisis of understanding. We fear new violence and growing enmity.

Crisis of Violence

On the nation's campuses, and in their neighboring communities, the level of violence has been steadily rising. Students have been killed and injured; civil authorities have been killed and injured; bystanders have been killed and injured. Valuable public and private property and scholarly products have been burned.

Too many Americans have begun to justify violence as a means of effecting change or safeguarding traditions. Too many have forgotten the values and sense of shared humanity that unite us. Campus violence reflects this national condition.

Much of the nation is so polarized that on many campuses a major domestic conflict or an unpopular initiative in foreign policy could trigger further violent protest and, in its wake, counterviolence and repression.

The Constitution protects the freedom of all citizens to dissent and to engage in nonviolent protest. Dissent is a healthy sign of freedom and a protection against stagnation. But the right to dissent is not the right to resort to violence.

Equally, to respond to peaceful protest with repression and brutal tactics is dangerously unwise. It makes extremists of moderates, deepens the divisions in the nation, and increases the chances that future protest will be violent.

We believe it urgent that Americans of all convictions draw back from the brink. We must recognize even our bitter opponents as fellow Americans with rights upon which we cannot morally or legally encroach and as fellow human beings whom we must not club, stone, shoot, or bomb.

We utterly condemn violence. Students who bomb and burn are criminals. Police and National Guardsmen who needlessly shoot or assault students are criminals. All who applaud these criminal acts share in their evil. We must declare a national cease-fire.

There can be no more "trashing," no more rock-throwing, no more arson, no more bombing by protestors. No grievance, philosophy, or political idea can justify the destruction and killing we have witnessed. There can be no sanctuary or immunity from prosecution on the campus. If our society is to survive, criminal acts by students must be treated as such wherever they occur and whatever their purpose.

Crimes committed by one do not justify crimes committed by another. We condemn brutality and excessive force by officers and troops called to maintain order. The use of force by police is sometimes necessary and legal, but every unnecessary resort to violence is wrong, criminal, and feeds the hostility of the disaffected.

Our universities as centers of free inquiry are particularly vulnerable to violence. We condemn those groups which are openly seeking to destroy them.

We especially condemn bombing and political terrorism.

The full resources of society must be employed to bring to justice those who commit terroristic acts. Anyone who aids or protects terrorists, on or off campus, must share the moral and legal responsibilities for the crimes they commit.

We find ominous and shocking reports that students are laying in supplies of weapons, and that others are preparing to take the law into their hands against protestors and minorities they dislike. There can be no place in our society for vigilantes, night riders, or militants who would bring destruction and death upon their opponents. No one serves the law by breaking it.

Violence must stop because it is wrong. It destroys human life and the products of human effort. It undermines the foundations of a just social order. No progress is possible in a society where lawlessness prevails.

Violence must stop because the sounds of violence drown out all words of reason. When students and officials resort to force and violence, no one can hear and the nation is denied a vital call to conscience. It must stop because no nation will long tolerate violence without repression. History offers grim proof that repression once started is almost impossible to contain.

Crisis of Understanding

Campus protest has been focused on three major questions: racial injustice, war, and the university itself.

The first issue is the unfulfilled promise of full justice and dignity for Blacks and other minorities. Blacks, like many others of different races and ethnic origins, are demanding today that the pledges of the Declaration of Independence and the Emancipation Proclamation be fulfilled now. Full social justice and dignity—an end to racism in all its human, social, and cultural forms—is a central demand of today's students—black, brown, and white.

A great majority of students and a majority of their elders oppose the Indochina war. Many believe it entirely immoral. And if the war is wrong, students insist, then so are all policies and practices that support it, from the draft to military research, from ROTC to recruiting for defense industry. This opposition has led to an ever-widening wave of student protests.

The shortcomings of the American university are the third target of student protest. The goals, values, administration, and curriculum of the modern university have been sharply criticized by many students. Students complain that their studies are irrelevant to the social problems that concern them. They want to shape their own personal and common lives, but find the university restrictive. They seek a community of companions and scholars, but find an impersonal multiversity. And they denounce the university's relationship to the war and to discriminatory racial practices.

Behind the student protest on these issues and the crisis of violence to which they have contributed lies the more basic crisis of understanding.

Americans have never shared a single culture, a single philosophy, or a single religion. But in most periods of our history, we have shared many common values, common sympathies, and a common dedication to a system of government which protects our diversity.

We are now in grave danger of losing what is common among us through growing intolerance of opposing views on issues and of diversity itself.

A "new" culture is emerging primarily among students. Membership is often manifested by differences in dress and life style. Most of its members have high ideals and great fears. They stress the need for humanity, equality, and the sacredness of life. They fear that nuclear war will make them the last generation in history. They see their elders as entrapped by materialism and competition, and as prisoners of outdated social forms. They believe their own country has lost its sense of human purpose. They see the Indochina war as an onslaught by a technological giant upon the peasant people of a small, harmless, and backward nation. The war is seen as draining resources from the urgent needs of social and racial justice. They argue that we are the first nation with sufficient resources to create not only decent lives for some, but a decent society for all, and that we are failing to do so. They feel they must remake America in its own image.

But among the members of this new student culture, there is a growing lack of tolerance, a growing insistence that their own views must govern, an impatience with the slow procedures of liberal democracy, a growing denial of the humanity and good will of those who urge patience and restraint, and particularly of those whose duty it is to enforce the law. A small number of students have turned to violence; an increasing number, not terrorists themselves, would not turn even arsonists and bombers over to law enforcement officials.

At the same time, many Americans have reacted to this emerging culture with an intolerance of their own. They reject not only that which is impatient, unrestrained, and intolerant in the new culture of the young, but even that which is good. Worse, they reject the individual members of the student culture themselves. Distinctive dress alone is enough to draw insult and abuse. Increasing numbers of citizens believe that students who dissent or protest—even those who protest peacefully—deserve to be treated harshly. Some even say that when dissenters are killed, they have brought death upon themselves. Less and less do students and the larger community seek to understand or respect the viewpoint and motivations of others.

If this trend continues, if this crisis of understanding endures, the very survival of the nation will be threatened. A nation driven to use the weapons of war upon its youth is a nation on the edge of chaos. A nation that has lost the allegiance of part of its youth is a nation that has lost part of its future. A nation whose young have become intolerant of diversity, intolerant of the rest of its citizenry, and intolerant of all traditional values simply because they are traditional has no generation worthy or capable of assuming leadership in the years to come.

✻ ✻ ✻ ✻ ✻

We urgently call for reconciliation. Tolerance and understanding on all sides must reemerge from the fundamental decency of Americans, from our shared aspirations as Americans, from our traditional tolerance of diversity, and from our common humanity. We must regain our compassion for one another and our mutual respect.

There is a deep continuity between all Americans, young and old, a continuity that is being obscured in our growing polarization. Most dissenting youth are striving toward the ultimate values and dreams of their elders and their forefathers. In all Americans there has always been latent respect for the idealism of the young. The whole object of a free government is to allow the nation to redefine its purposes in the light of new needs without sacrificing the accumulated wisdom of its living traditions. We cannot do this without each other.

Despite the differences among us, powerful values and sympathies unite us. The very motto of our nation calls for both unity and diversity: from many, one. Out of our divisions, we must now recreate understanding and respect for those different from ourselves.

Violence must end.

Understanding must be renewed.

All Americans must come to see each other not as symbols or stereotypes but as human beings.

Reconciliation must begin.

We share the impatience of those who call for change. We believe there is still time and opportunity to achieve change. We believe we can still fulfill our shared national commitment to peace, justice, decency, equality, and the celebration of human life.

We must start. All of us.

Our recommendations are directed toward this end.

Recommendations

Far more important than the particular recommendations of this Commission are the underlying themes that are common to all:

* Most student protestors are neither violent nor extremist. But a small minority of politically extreme students and faculty members and a small group of dedicated agitators are bent on destruction of the university through violence in order to gain their own political ends. Perpetrators of violence must be identified, removed from the university as swiftly as possible, and prosecuted vigorously by the appropriate agencies of law enforcement.

* Dissent and peaceful protest are a valued part of this nation's way of governing itself. Violence and disorder are the antithesis of democratic processes and cannot be tolerated either on the nation's campuses or anywhere else.

* The roots of student activism lie in unresolved conflicts in our national life, but the many defects of the universities have also fueled campus unrest. Universities have not adequately prepared themselves to respond to disruption. They have been without suitable plans, rules, or sanctions. Some administrators and faculty members have responded irreso-

lutely. Frequently, announced sanctions have not been applied. Even more frequently, the lack of appropriate organization within the university has rendered its response ineffective. The university's own house must be placed in order.

* Too many students have acted irresponsibly and even dangerously in pursuing their stated goals and expressing their dissent. Too many law enforcement officers have responded with unwarranted harshness and force in seeking to control disorder.

* Actions—and inactions—of government at all levels have contributed to campus unrest. The words of some political leaders have helped to inflame it. Law enforcement officers have too often reacted ineptly or overreacted. At times, their response has degenerated into uncontrolled violence.

* The nation has been slow to resolve the issues of war and race, which exacerbate divisions within American society and which have contributed to the escalation of student protest and disorder.

* All of us must act to prevent violence, to create understanding, and to reduce the bitterness and hostility that divide both the campus and the country. We must establish respect for the processes of law and tolerance for the exercise of dissent on our campuses and in the nation.

We advance our recommendations not as cure-alls but as rational and responsive steps that should be taken. We summarize here our major recommendations, addressed to those who have the power to carry them out.

For the President

We urge that the President exercise his reconciling moral leadership as the first step to prevent violence and create understanding. It is imperative that the President bring us together before more lives are lost and more property destroyed and more universities disrupted.

We recommend that the President seek to convince public officials and protestors alike that divisive and insulting rhetoric is dangerous. In the current political campaign and throughout the years ahead, the President should insist that no one play irresponsible politics with the issue of "campus unrest."

We recommend that the President take the lead in explaining to the American people the underlying causes of campus unrest and the urgency of our present situation. We recommend that he articulate and emphasize those values all Americans hold in common. At the same time we urge him to point out the importance of diversity and coexistence to the nation's health.

To this end, nothing is more important than an end to the war in Indochina. Disaffected students see the war as a symbol of moral crisis in the nation which, in their eyes, deprives even law of its legitimacy. Their dramatic reaction to the Cambodian invasion was a measure of the intensity of their moral recoil.

We urge the President to renew the national commitment to full social justice, and to be aware of increasing charges of repression. We recommend that he take steps to see to it that the words and deeds of government do not encourage belief in those charges.

We recommend that the President lend his personal support and assistance to American universities to accomplish the changes and reforms suggested in this report.

We recommend that the President take steps to assure that he be continuously informed of the views of students and Blacks, important constituencies in this nation.

We recommend that the President call a series of national meetings designed to foster understanding among those who are now divided. He should meet with the governors of the states, with university leaders, with law enforcement officers, and with black and student leaders. Each participant in these meetings should be urged to bring with him practical suggestions for restoring trust and responsibility among those whom he represents, and commit himself to continue this process of national reconciliation in frequent meetings throughout the school year.

For Government

We strongly urge public officials at all levels of government to recognize that their public statements can either heal or divide. Harsh and bitter rhetoric can set citizen against citizen, exacerbate tension, and encourage violence.

Just as the President must offer reconciling leadership to reunite the nation, so all government officials—at all levels—must work to bring our hostile factions together.

Like the President, the governors of the states should hold meetings and develop contacts throughout the school year to further the cause of reconciliation. Like the President, other federal, state, and local officials must be sensitive to the charge of repression and fashion their words and deeds in a manner designed to refute it.

We urge state and local officials to make plans for handling campus disorders in full cooperation with one another and with the universities. We urge the states to establish guidelines setting forth more precisely the circumstances that justify ordering the Guard to intervene in a campus disorder.

We recommend that the federal government review all its current policies affecting students and universities to assure that neither the policies nor administration of them threatens the independence or quality of American higher education. At the same time government should increase its financial support of higher education.

We urge public officials to reject demands that entire universities be punished because of the ideas or excesses of some members and to honor their responsibility to help preserve academic freedom.

We recommend that the Department of Defense establish alternatives to ROTC so that officer education is available to students whose universities choose to terminate on-campus ROTC programs.

We recommend greatly increased financial aid for black colleges and universities. All agencies of government that support such institutions should massively increase their grants to enable these colleges to overcome past short-comings.

We support the continuing efforts of formerly all-white universities to recruit Black, Mexican-American, Puerto Rican, and other minority students, and we urge that adequate government-sponsored student aid be made available to them. We recommend that in the process of becoming more representative of the society at large, universities make the adjustments necessary to permit those from minority backgrounds to take maximum advantage of their university experience.

Bombing and arson pose an increasing threat to lives and property on campus. We urge prompt enactment of strict controls over the sale, transfer, and possession of explosive materials. Such statutes are needed at both the federal and the state level.

For Law Enforcement

We have deep sympathy for peace officers—local and state police, National Guardsmen, and campus security officers—who must deal with all types of campus disorder. Much depends on their judgment, courage, and professionalism.

We commend those thousands of law enforcement officers who have endured taunts and assaults without reacting violently and whose careful conduct has prevented violence and saved lives.

At the same time, we recognize that there have been dangerous and sometimes fatal instances of unnecessary harshness and illegal violence by law enforcement officers.

We therefore urge that peace officers be trained and equipped to deal with campus disorders firmly, justly, and humanely. They must avoid both uncontrolled and excessive response.

Too frequently, local police forces have been under-manned, improperly equipped, poorly trained, and unprepared for campus disturbances. We therefore urge police forces, especially those in smaller communities, to improve their capacity to respond to civil disorders.

We recommend the development of joint contingency plans among law enforcement agencies. They should specify which law enforcement official is to be in command when several forces are operating together.

Sending civil authorities on to a college campus armed as if for war—armed only to kill—has brought tragedy in the past. If this practice is not changed, tragedy will come again. Shoulder weapons (except for tear gas launchers) are very rarely needed on the college campus; they should not be used except as emergency equipment in the face of sniper fire or armed resistance.

We recommend that National Guardsmen receive much more training in controlling civil disturbances. During the last three years, the Guard has played almost no role in Southeast Asia but has been called to intervene in civil disorders at home more than 200 times.

We urge that the National Guard be issued special protection equipment appropriate for use in controlling civil disorders. We urge that it have sufficient tactical capability and nonlethal weaponry so that it will use deadly force only as the absolute last resort.

For the University

Every university must improve its capability for responding effectively to disorder. Students, faculty, and trustees must support these efforts. Universities must pull themselves together.

The university should be an open forum where speakers of every point of view can be heard. The area of permitted speech and conduct should be at least as broad as that protected by the First Amendment.

The university should promulgate a code making clear the

limits of permissible conduct and announce in advance what measures it is willing to employ in response to impermissible conduct. It should strengthen its disciplinary process. It should assess the capabilities of its security force and determine what role, if any, that force should play in responding to disorder.

When criminal violence occurs on the campus, university officials should promptly call for the assistance of law enforcement agencies.

When faced with disruptive but nonviolent conduct, the university should be prepared to respond initially with internal measures. It must clearly understand the options available to it and be prepared to move from one to another if it is reasonably obvious that an earlier tactic has failed.

Faculty members who engage in or lead disruptive conduct have no place in the university community.

The university, and particularly the faculty, must recognize that the expansion of higher education and the emergence of the new youth culture have changed the makeup and concerns of today's student population. The university should adapt itself to these new conditions. We urge that the university make its teaching programs, degree structure, and transfer and leave policies more flexible and more varied in order to enhance the quality and voluntariness of university study.

We call upon all members of the university to reaffirm that the proper functions of the university are teaching and learning, research and scholarship. An academic community best serves itself, the country, and every principle to which it is devoted by concentrating on these tasks.

Academic institutions must be free—free from outside interference, and free from internal intimidation. Far too many people who should know better—both within university communities and outside them—have forgotten this first principle of academic freedom. The pursuit of knowledge cannot continue without the free exchange of ideas.

Obviously, all members of the academic community, as individuals, should be free to participate actively in whatever campaigns or causes they choose. But universities as institutions must remain politically neutral except in those rare cases in which their own integrity, educational purpose, or preservation is at stake.

One of the most valid criticisms of many universities is that their faculties have become so involved in outside research that their commitment to teaching seems compromised. We urge universities and faculty members to reduce their outside service commitments. We recognize that alternative sources of university funding will have to be developed to take the place of the money attached to these outside commitments. Realistically, this will mean more unrestricted government aid to higher education.

Large universities should take steps to decentralize or reorganize to make possible a more human scale.

University governance systems should be reformed to increase participation of students and faculty in the formulation of university policies that affect them. But universities cannot be run on a one man, one vote basis with participation of all members on all issues.

Universities must become true communities whose members share a sense of respect, tolerance, and responsibility for one another.

For Students

Students must accept the responsibility of presenting their ideas in a reasonable and persuasive manner. They must recognize that they are citizens of a nation which was founded on tolerance and diversity, and they must become more understanding of those with whom they differ.

Students must protect the right of all speakers to be heard even when they disagree with the point of view expressed. Heckling speakers is not only bad manners but is inimical to all the values that a university stands for.

Students must face the fact that giving moral support to those who are planning violent action is morally despicable.

Students should be reminded that language that offends

will seldom persuade. Their words have sometimes been as offensive to many Americans as the words of some public officials have been to them.

Students should not expect their own views, even if held with great moral intensity, automatically and immediately to determine national policy. The rhetorical commitment to democracy by students must be matched by an awareness of the central role of majority rule in a democratic society and by an equal commitment to techniques of persuasion within the political process.

The Commission has been impressed and moved by the idealism and commitment of American youth. But this extraordinary commitment brings with it extraordinary obligations: to learn from our nation's past experience, to recognize the humanity of those with whom they disagree, and to maintain their respect for the rule of law. The fight for change and justice is the good fight; to drop out or strike out at the first sign of failure is to insure that change will never come.

This Commission is only too aware of America's short-comings. Yet we are also a nation of enduring strength. Millions of Americans—generations past and present—have given their vision, their energy, and their patient labor to make us a more just nation and a more humane people. We who seek to change America today build on their accomplishments and enjoy the freedoms they won for us. It is a considerable inheritance; we must not squander or destroy it.

1

Student Protest In The 1960'S

On April 30, 1970, President Nixon announced that American and South Vietnamese forces were moving against enemy sanctuaries in Cambodia. Minutes after this announcement, student-organized protest demonstrations were under way at Princeton and Oberlin College. Within a few days, strikes and other protests had taken place at scores of colleges and universities throughout the country.

The expanding wave of strikes brought with it some serious disturbances. One of these was at Kent State University in Ohio, and approximately 750 Ohio National Guardsmen were sent to quell the disorders there.

On May 2, the ROTC building at Kent State was set afire. On May 4, Kent State students congregated on the university Commons and defied an order by the Guard to disperse. Guardsmen proceeded to disperse the crowd. The students then began to taunt Guard units and to throw rocks. The guardsmen fired tear gas into the crowd, and then some fired their weapons. Four students were killed, and nine were wounded.

During the six days after the President's announcement of the Cambodian incursion, but prior to the deaths at Kent State, some twenty new student strikes had begun each day. During the four days that followed the Kent killings, there were a hundred or more strikes each day. A student strike center located at Brandeis University reported that, by the 10th of May, 448 campuses were either still affected by some sort of strike or completely closed down.

Ten days after the events at Kent State there were disturbances at Jackson State College, a black school in Jackson, Mississippi. On the night of May 14, students threw bricks and bottles at passing white motorists, a truck was set ablaze, and city and state police, called to protect firemen, were harassed by the crowd. Some policemen fired a fusillade into a girls' dormitory. Two Blacks were killed, and at least twelve were wounded.

Other schools joined the student strike, and many temporarily suspended classes in memory of those killed at Jackson State. By the end of May, according to statistics compiled by the Urban Research Corporation, nearly one third of the approximately 2,500 colleges and universities in America had experienced some kind of protest activity. The high point of the strikes was during the week following the deaths at Kent State.

As the summer neared its end, the University of Wisconsin's mathematics research center at Madison was destroyed by a bomb. A researcher was killed, and four other people were injured. A revolutionary group calling itself "the New Year's Gang" took credit for the bombing and warned that, unless certain demands were met, there would be more bombings. The FBI was called into the case, and it launched a nationwide manhunt for four youthful suspects.

In this chapter, we trace the development of American student protest during the decade of the 1960's, from the peaceful demonstrations of the civil rights movement to the terrorist bombing in Madison. When the decade began, the American public was impressed with the courage, idealism, and restraint of student civil rights workers; as the decade ends, public opinion is fearful, angry, and confused over the escalation of student protest. When the decade began, the vast majority of American students were either apolitical or dedicated to working peacefully for change within the existing system; as it ends, ever-increasing numbers of students accept a radical analysis of American society and despair of the possibilities of peaceful social change. How did this shift occur in just ten years?

We must begin this inquiry into the development of campus unrest in the 1960's by drawing some preliminary distinctions. "Campus unrest" is too simple a term for the complex phenomenon it attempts to describe or for the many different kinds of protest activity it usually denotes. In our preface we have stressed the importance of distinguishing between lawful protest and disorderly protest, the latter of which can take the forms of disruption, violence, or terrorism.

Just as there are many kinds of protests, so are there many kinds of students involved in protests. We must distinguish, too, between the political objectives of protestors and their tactics. Students seeking the same objective may adopt different tactics, just as students may employ the same tactic in pursuit of quite different goals.

With regard to objectives, American students today occupy the full political spectrum that runs from radical to conservative. Radicals generally reject the prevailing institutions and policies of American society and seek to establish a new kind of society. Liberals desire social change but believe it can be accomplished through reforms within the existing political system. Conservative students believe that American society is basically sound and wish to preserve its prevailing values and institutions.

Cutting across this spectrum of objectives are fundamental differences in political tactics. A substantial majority of American students are tactical moderates, who rely on persuasion and reject force or violence as methods of political action. Some students, however, are tactical extremists and advocate or use force, violence, intimidation, and coercion as means of attaining their objectives.

Public discussion of campus unrest often begins with the assumption that all students who protest are radical, that all radicals are extremists, and that all campus unrest is disruptive or violent. The facts are that the overwhelming majority of American students still are liberal or conservative, not radical, that only a minority of the students involved in most campus protests are tactical extremists, and that the vast majority of student protests, even in 1970, have been well within the American tradition of lawful protest.

Nonetheless, the history of the last decade clearly shows a gradual movement toward more disruptive, violent, and even terrorist tactics in campus protest and a steady and significant growth in the number of radical students and tactical extremists.

The Background of Student Protest

Student discontent in America did not begin at Berkeley in 1964, or with the civil rights movement in the early 1960's. The history of American colleges during the early 19th century is filled with incidents of disorder, turmoil, and riot. These disturbances generally arose over poor food, primitive living conditions, and harsh regulations. Even today, such traditional complaints still spark many more campus protests than is generally realized. But though 19th century campus turbulence occasionally reflected a rebellion against the dominant Puritan religious ethic of the colleges of the time, student discontent here, unlike that in Europe, was largely apolitical.

This pattern began to change during the early years of the 20th century, when the first important radical political movement among American college students—the Intercollegiate Socialist Society—emerged. When the ISS flourished, it had more members, measured as a proprotion of the total student population, than the Students for a Democratic Society (SDS) had in the late 1960's. During the 1920's, there were campus protests against ROTC, denunciations of the currriculum for its alleged support of the established system, and attacks on America's "imperialistic" foreign policy. During the Depression, there was still greater student discontent. Polls taken during the 1930's showed that a quarter of college students were sympathetic to socialism and that almost 40 per cent said they would refuse to take part in war. There were many student strikes against war, a few disruptions, and some expulsions.

Thus, it is not so much the unrest of the past half-dozen years that is exceptional as it is the quiet of the 20 years which preceded them. From the early 1940's to the early 1960's, American colleges and universities were uncharacteristically calm, radical student movements were almost non-existent, and disruptions were rare. The existence of this "silent generation" was in part a reflection of the Cold War. But as the tensions of the Cold War lessened, students felt less obliged to defend Western democracy and more free to take a critical look at their own society. Once again the American campus became a center of protest.

In its early phases, this reemerging campus activism was reformist in its aims and nonviolent in its tactics and pursued its goals by means of moral and political persuasion. But it did not persist in this form. For in the autumn of 1964, a critical series of events at the University of California at Berkeley tranformed campus activism into the complex, changing phenomenon it is today.

The Berkeley revolt did not explode in a vacuum. It was preceded by a chain of developments during the late 1950's and early 1960's which helped to revive campus activism.

The most important of these was the civil rights movement. Since protest by black students has many unique features of its own, the distinctive character of black student protest is reviewed separately and at greater length elsewhere in this report. Here we need only emphasize that throughout the sixties, black college students played a central role in the civil rights movement. After four black students from North Carolina Agricultural and Technical College staged an historic sit-in at a segregated lunchcounter in Greensboro, North Carolina, in February 1960, the spread of sit-ins and other civil rights activities aroused the conscience of the nation and encouraged many students to express their support for civil rights through nonviolent direct action.

The peace movement, founded on an abhorrence of nuclear weapons, added another important element to the background of student activism. And in 1962, in Port Huron, Michigan, the Students for a Democratic Society reorganized itself with a statement that called on students to work for a society where all men would more fully control their own lives and social institutions. Under the banner of "participatory democracy," the SDS launched its early efforts to organize slum dwellers in northern cities.

Local events in the San Francisco Bay Area further prepared the way for the Berkeley revolt. In 1960 there had been a tumultuous demonstration, in which Berkeley students took part, against the House Un-American Activities Committee. Later, University of California students participated in a series of sit-ins, sleep-ins, shop-ins, and other actions to persuade Bay Area employers to hire Blacks. Like the HUAC demonstration, many of these involved off-campus confrontations with the police. And on campus, growing student and faculty dissatisfaction with higher education led to a movement to reform the university curriculum.

Thus by the autumn of 1964, there was growing student concern on the Berkeley campus that expressed itself both in protest demonstrations and in community service. Its focus was on the unresolved issues of war and peace, on civil rights, on the quality of education, and on the plight of the poor. Within this context of opinion and activity the Berkeley revolt broke out.

THE BERKELEY INVENTION

What happened at Berkeley was more than the sum of its parts. The events on that campus in the autumn of 1964 defined an authentic political invention—a new and complex mixture of issues, tactics, emotions, and setting—that became the prototype for student protest throughout the decade. Nothing quite like it had ever before appeared in America, and it is with the nature and evolution of this long-lived invention, in all its variations, that this Commission is concerned.

In brief, the events at Berkeley were these: In the late summer of 1964, the university administration began enforcing an old rule which prohibited political groups from collecting money or soliciting memberships on campus. Until then, such activity had been allowed in one well-defined area at the edge of the campus. Campus activists now found themselves deprived of their familiar turf. Incensed, they decided to violate this new prohibition, and university officials summarily suspended eight of them.

Shortly thereafter, on October 1, campus police arrested a nonstudent activist for trespassing. When they attempted to remove him in a campus police car, students spontaneously formed a sit-in which prevented the car and its occupants from moving for 32 hours. The crowd broke up when the university agreed not to press charges; but for the next two months, the issue of what political activity would be permitted on campus remained unsettled. So did the matter of university discipline. After a series of hearings, the university announced on November 20 that six of the eight suspended students would be penalized only by suspension up to that time, and that the other two would be placed on probation for the remainder of the semester. A week later, these same two students were informed that new disciplinary actions had been initiated because of their activities on October 1.

After the Thanksgiving vacation, protest resumed. Leaders of the Free Speech Movement (FSM), which was formed by campus groups of all political persuasions to defend their right to organize on campus, began a large, two-day sit-in at the administration building. The sit-in came to an end when Governor Edmund G. Brown called in the police. There were hundreds of arrests and many charges of police brutality.

Before the police intervention, the FSM actions were supported by only a small fraction of the Berkeley student population—perhaps a total of 2,500. That quickly changed. The police action and mass arrests mobilized huge numbers of students and faculty in support of the FSM goals. Classes and other normal activities came to a halt in an unprecedented strike against the university.

In many respects, the FSM succeeded. By January, the Chancellor had taken a "leave of absence," and the rules governing student political activity on campus had been greatly liberalized. The campus slowly returned to its normal routine. Yet beneath the appearance of normalcy, some things were no longer the same. What happened at Berkeley had altered the character of American student activism in a fundamental way.

The events at Berkeley proved exceptionally difficult to interpret with balance and candor. What was essentially a complex phenomenon quickly came to be interpreted in two grossly oversimplified ways. According to one interpretation, what happened at Berkeley was the mischievous work of a small cadre of dedicated revolutionaries, outside the mainstream of American life, who exploited issues to which they actually were indifferent as a convenient means of mobilizing and manipulating large numbers of students. Whatever their higher self-justifications, it was claimed, these nihilists were capable of nothing but havoc, destruction, and violence and should be ignored or, if necessary, punished.

The other interpretation was that, regardless of who and how many started them, the FSM protests never would have succeeded without the support of many liberal, nonextremist students. Such students supported protest demonstrations because the issues at stake pointed to genuine deficiencies in the university and in American society. Student protest thus reflected not a desire to destroy, but rather a sincere and constructive idealism. If its tactics were violent, that was either the consequence of students' indignation at injustice or the direct result of police violence. The appropriate response to student protest was to support it without reservation—not to suppress it.

These interpretations were inadequate because they did not reflect the complexity and the novelty of the protest scenario that Berkeley activists had acted out for the first time. We call this scenario the Berkeley invention, and it involved the following elements:

* The protest was initiated by a small group of student activists. As the protest proceeded, the most radical students assumed leadership.

* The issue was in fact a dual issue, combining on-campus and off-campus matters. At one level, it was a civil liberties issue, involving intense feelings and high moral values. But at a second level, it was a university issue, for it raised the question of what kinds of political activity would be permissible on campus. The FSM itself did not attack off-campus foes of civil liberties and free speech. Neither did it attack those who discriminated against blacks or prevented them from voting. Its target was instead a liberal university administration, which it cast—which had cast itself—in a repressive role.

This combination of major social and political issues with local university issues turned out to be extremely difficult for a university administration to deal with. For although administrators were faced with a specific, university-related demand—one which was within their power to grant—the demand was put forward with a fervor and moral intensity aroused by a transcendent social cause that was not within their jurisdiction. Yielding to the protestors' university-related demand—the right to organize on campus—could never entirely dispel their underlying fervor and discontent.

* The activists introduced into campus protest new tactics that disrupted the university and denied others their fundamental civil liberties. These tactics included blocking of university officials carrying out their duties, harassing of university officials, and sit-ins in university buildings. The origin of these tactics, which had not been used by radical groups on

campus before, was the civil rights movement, in which several FSM leaders had taken part. These tactics required some university response. At Berkeley, the administration chose to call in the police.

The administration's response to disruption was decisive in determining what would follow. At Berkeley, the police intervention was interpreted as a confirmation of the radicals' original claim that the university was unjust and repressive, especially toward those working for civil rights.

* Police action produced a strong reaction. Previously, only a small minority had actually demonstrated; now, vast numbers of indignant students and faculty joined the widening protest. Classes came to a halt, and a wave of politicking, protesting, and speech-making swept the campus. This response demonstrated the extraordinary power of the dual issue at Berkeley. It became clear that more students would demonstrate against an administration which punished students for on-campus infractions committed in the pursuit of valued social objectives than would join other sorts of political action. Strong feelings of generational loyalty were aroused as students watched their classmates being dragged off limp, resisting, and sometimes bloodied, to jail.

* By these means, the Berkeley invention enlisted large numbers of liberals and tactical moderates, who contributed their own distinctive style to campus protest. At first, the concern of the liberals focused upon the university's stance toward political activities on campus, but soon it widened to encompass a new range of issues. The liberals now demanded participation in university governance and reform of curriculum. The radicals, who were primarily interested in political action on larger social issues, were for the

most part indifferent to such campus reforms but aligned themselves with the liberals in return for support that helped legitimate the radicals' demands. New liberal and "moderate" leaders emerged.

* The radical and liberal leaders were linked to the mass of demonstrators not by organizational ties or formal mechanisms but rather by common participation in a movement. Unlike traditional campus political organizations, but like the civil rights movement, the FSM emphasized reaching decisions by group consensus and mass meetings and avoided bureaucratic organization. At the same time, key tactical decisions were made at critical moments by a small group of leaders who directed the movement.

* Few concrete changes resulted from all this effort. By midwinter, most of the excitement had died down, the strike against classes had ended, and the campus began, slowly, to return to normal. As calm returned, widespread efforts were under way to implement a broad range of university reforms—of disciplinary procedures, governance, the conditions of student life, rules concerning political activity, and curriculum. A series of reports were issued; some reforms were instituted. But despite the time and energy that went into these efforts, the university's formal programs remained essentially unchanged. Four years after the FSM, the average Berkeley faculty member spent *less* time in the classroom than he had in 1964. Thus, although the Berkeley invention stimulated broad demands for university reform, its aftermath offered little hope that any such reform would be achieved. And there was cause for concern that the extended turmoil had so upset the fragile balance of a large and complicated university that it was less capable than before of coherent self-improvement.

* Perhaps the most distinctive aspect of the Berkeley

invention was its success in combining two impulses that previously had been separate in student disruption. The high spirits and defiance of authority that had characterized the traditional school riot were now joined to youthful idealism and to social objectives of the highest importance. This combination moved the participants to intense feeling and vigorous political activism and provoked from state or university officials reactions and overreactions that promised to keep the whole movement alive.

THE BERKELEY INVENTION EXPANDS

The mass media gave intensive coverage to the Berkeley events, and Americans were exposed for the first time to a new sort of news story—the tumultuous campus disruption. It was news in a traditional sense because it involved conflict and controversy. It was especially suitable for television because it was colorful and visually interesting. Night after night, television film of events on one campus carried the methods and spirit of protest to every other campus in the country.

Most student protestors, like advocates of all ages and points of view, welcomed television coverage. Many of them grew sophisticated in inviting it, and some of them undoubtedly played to it. Television news crews obliged them, occasionally in an irresponsible fashion. But of far greater importance was the selective nature of the television medium itself, with its tendency to emphasize the most emotionally and visually exciting aspects of stories. Again and again, the cameras focused on whatever was most bizarre, dramatic, active, or violent. Few television or radio and newspaper reporters had the time or knowledge to explore the causes and complexity of campus protests.

The public reacted to Berkeley with concern and anger. In California and throughout the nation, campus events became controversial political issues. Many citizens believed that students had no reason to protest. Many were deeply opposed to the protestors' disruptive tactics. Many also criticized the faculty and administration for not taking a sufficiently "hard line." As student protest spread to more campuses and as its tactics became more disruptive or violent, citizens and political leaders called for action to prevent further campus disturbances.

Even in 1964-65, the year of the Berkeley disturbance, there was much more turmoil on campus than the media reported or the public knew of. Of 849 four-year colleges responding to a national survey that year, the great majority reported some kind of protest. But almost all of these protests were of the pre-Berkeley variety—traditional, single-issue protests, many of them conducted off-campus. More than a third of the campuses reported off-campus civil rights activities, and just over one fifth had on-campus protests against the Vietnam War. A variety of other issues stimulated protests on campus, including the quality of food, dress requirements, dormitory regulations, controversies over faculty members, censorship of publications, rules about campus speakers, and the desire for more student participation in university governance.

This early pattern of campus protest, then, reflected a high level of concern and activism diffused among a large number and broad range of distinct issues, which students rarely lumped together in criticisms of "the system." The university usually was subject to protest only over matters that were within its own control.

After 1964-65, however, this pattern began to change, and students increasingly related campus issues to broader political and social issues, and these broader issues to one another. As they did, the Berkeley invention began to spread to other campuses.

The growing frequency with which campus protest reflected the Berkeley scenario was largely the result of the emergence and development of three issues: American involvement in the war in Southeast Asia, the slow progress of American society toward racial equality, and charges of "unresponsiveness" against the federal government and the university and against their "repressive" reaction to student demands. These three issues gave campus protests their unifying theme. They were defined by protesting students as fundamentally moral issues, and this definition gave a tone of passion, fervor, and impatience to student protest.

The rapid escalation of American military efforts in Vietnam in 1965 made the Vietnam War one of the bitterest issues of the decade. This issue gave student activists an ever-increasing self-assurance and solidarity, for growing public concern over the constant escalation of the war seemed to legitimate the activists' early opposition. They redoubled their efforts; the Vietnam issue came to dominate their thoughts; and the previously scattered pattern of campus protest began to alter accordingly.

The war was strenuously debated among students and faculty. At first there were considerable differences of opinion on the subject. During this early period, students and faculty at the University of Michigan created a new method for discussing the war: the teach-in. When it began, the teach-in was a balanced affair that took the form of an extended debate, rather than a vehicle for antiwar protest. But it did not last in this form. When the teach-in reached Berkeley, it was simply a mass demonstration in which no supporters of the war were heard. Soon, government spokesmen who went to campuses to explain or defend American foreign policy were shouted down and, at times, physically attacked. In some cases, the students responsible were never disciplined.

This transformation of the teach-in suggests one consequence of growing opposition to the war and of the rising tide of campus unrest that was to persist and expand through the rest of the decade.

The moral sentiments and passions aroused by the war had a chilling effect on rational academic discourse. Faculty members who met to discuss university policy while thousands of students waited outside or listened to their debates on the radio were at times unwilling to speak their minds on the issues or to speak out against student extremists. Rational debate and critical analysis were replaced by impassioned rhetoric and intense political feeling.

As opposition to the war grew and the war continued to escalate, explanations of America's involvement in it became more radical. From having been a "mistake," the war was soon interpreted by radical students as a logical outcome of the American political system. They argued that what was most objectionable was not the war itself, but rather "the system" that had entered, justified, and pursued it. According to this logic, the appropriate target of protest was "the system" itself, and especially those parts of it that were involved in the war. The university, too, came to be seen as a part of "the system," and therefore it became a target—as distinct from an accidental arena—of antiwar protest. As it did, the Berkeley invention, with its dual issues, increasingly dominated the pattern of campus protest.

The escalation of the war in Southeast Asia produced an increasing demand for military manpower that resulted in larger draft calls. In 1965, the federal government decided to defer college students from the draft on the basis of their academic standing. Draft boards asked universities to provide such information, and students and faculty passionately debated the propriety of compliance. In the end, the issue was usually resolved by agreeing that draft data would continue to be divulged only at the student's request. There were major student demonstrations over the question, and some of them borrowed directly from the Berkeley scenario. One of the most notable of these demonstrations occurred at the University of Chicago, where the administration building was occupied and many demonstrators were later suspended.

When disciplinary actions followed such disruptions, a new issue arose—the demand for amnesty. Students who faced punishment for disruptive actions taken in the name of high moral principles felt they should be exempt from the rules applied to other students. Increasingly, radical groups charged that university attempts to impose disciplinary sanctions were only further evidence of the university's larger complicity in the evils of American society and the war effort.

These groups—particularly the SDS—actively sought information, sometimes by illegal means, concerning all connections between the university and the war. Their research provided a constant flow of information and misinformation. Sometimes it yielded dramatic findings, for in fact there were many links between the university and the defense establishment. For example, it was revealed in 1967 that a "research center" at Michigan State University was a conduit for the funding of a CIA operation in Southeast Asia. Many other research centers were accused, often justly, of receiving military money and, less justly, of conducting "imperialist" research. In some cases student aid programs that were tied to defense spending were cited as proof of the university's involvement in the war. Campus recruiters from the military and from war-materiel corporations were harassed, and some found it necessary to conduct interviews with students and other prospective employees off campus.

As the escalation of the war in Vietnam proceeded and as a radical analysis of the wider society evolved, few campus issues were seen as *not* related to the basic problems of the nation.

Anger and despair over persistent racial injustice in American society provided a second and equally important focus for student protest. Racial prejudice—especially against Blacks but in some parts of the country equally cruel in its effect upon Mexican-Americans, Puerto Ricans, and other minorities—became increasingly unacceptable to many students. For many young Blacks in the mid-1960's the drive for equality and justice took a new form, symbolized by the concepts of Black power and Black pride. Young whites, even those who feared Black separatism, could not deny the justice of demands for equality.

Just as the Vietnam War was escalating, the civil rights movement underwent a fundamental change. The summer of 1964 was the last in which black and white students, liberals and radicals, worked together in a spirit of cooperation and nonviolence. But urban riots in Harlem, in Rochester, and in Watts divided many white liberals and moderates from those white and black militants who considered the riots legitimate rebellions. In 1965, Stokely Carmichael helped establish an all-black political party in Lowndes County, Alabama. During the next spring, he led those who were no longer committed to nonviolence in taking control of the Student Nonviolent Coordinating Committee. Subsequently, whites were expelled from the organization. In the summer of 1966, the cry of "Black Power" was first heard, and Huey Newton and Bobby Seale founded the Black Panther Party in Oakland, California.

These events marked a rapid erosion of the commitment by civil rights activists to nonviolence and to interracial political action—and had important consequences for campus protest. Militancy on southern black campuses increased during 1966 and 1967. In May 1967, students at Jackson State College in Mississippi fought with police for two nights. The National Guard was called out, and one person was killed. Militant actions by students at Howard University established a pattern that was to be repeated at black colleges and would spread to northern campuses as well.

Whereas earlier civil rights activism had generally attacked off-campus targets, the protests of black militants now were usually directed against the university itself. The university, they claimed, had helped to perpetuate black oppression through its admissions policies, its "white-oriented" curriculum, and its overwhelmingly white teaching staff. Black students found their cultural heritage slighted or ignored altogether. Their critique of the university intensified in the late 1960's, as predominantly white institutions began to admit black students in larger numbers. At Harvard, at San Francisco State, and elsewhere, black students organized groups dedicated to serving the larger black community. Their aim was to establish for Blacks an equal place in all parts of the university. Their attention thus focused not only on curriculum, faculty appointments, and student living conditions, but also on nonacademic matters like the university's hiring practices and its impact on local housing conditions.

The escalating war in Vietnam and the unresolved problem of racism helped push radicals toward an increasingly political view of the university. By 1968, radicals were almost unanimous in viewing the university not as a center of teaching and scholarship but rather as an institution guilty of "complicity" with a "system" charged with being immoral, unresponsive, and repressive. In an attempt to undermine the war effort, more students began to demand that the university eliminate ROTC and end defense research. Increasingly, the stated purpose of radical demands was the transformation of the university into a political weapon— their own weapon—for putting an end to the war, racism, and the political system they considered responsible for both. The demands of some black student groups had a similar thrust.

In addition to war and racism, a third issue—the issue of "repression"—began to emerge. The charge that the American system is basically "repressive" originated with radicals. But moderates began to give it credence as student protest encountered official force. Many students were "radicalized" by excessive police reactions to disorderly demonstrations. Although major property damage in campus disruptions between 1960 and 1970 was almost entirely perpetrated by students, and although injuries to students occurred largely during confrontations which they themselves had provoked, students suffered more deaths than their adversaries. A growing number of students came to see themselves as "victimized" by law enforcement officials.

Events at the Democratic National Convention in 1968 had a particularly strong impact. Student protest at the convention was often disruptive, provocative, and violent, and it was met by a police reaction so brutal that the Walker Report called it a "police riot." Some students perceive "repression" also in the harassment of young persons with distinctive clothing or long hair and in police enforcement, which they believe to be selective, of the laws against marijuana and other drugs.

Whether or not they accept the radical slogan of "repression," many students have come to believe that the American political system is unresponsive and must be fundamentally reformed. They have been bitterly disappointed by the failure of a national majority and the national government to accept, and quickly to act upon, political positions that they find morally compelling. Like most Americans, they were profoundly disheartened by the murders of Martin Luther King, Jr., and Senator Robert F. Kennedy, the more so because these murders followed a moment of high hope for the end of the war, when President Johnson announced that he would limit the bombing of North Vietnam and also that he would not run again for the Presidency.

These experiences, events, and feelings tended to make radicals of liberal students and tactical extremists of moderates. But the vast majority continued to believe in the American system of government, and thousands worked within it for change, notably in the primary campaigns of Robert Kennedy and Eugene McCarthy in 1968. And although they were dismayed and disappointed by Kennedy's death and by McCarthy's defeat, the fact is that their work had helped bring about change in national leadership and in policies toward the war. Still, the gradual nature of that change in policy and the refusal of the government to disengage itself from Vietnam quickly and completely left many students convinced that "the system" was unresponsive to their best efforts to work within it.

COLUMBIA: THE BERKELEY INVENTION REVISED

At Columbia University in the spring of 1968, students participated in a tumultuous series of demonstrations, sit-ins, and disruptions. The Columbia revolt was important because it illustrated the spread of the Berkeley invention and the rising tide of student opposition to war and racial injustice. It was important also because the differences between it and the Berkeley revolt four years earlier indicated the growing disillusionment of many American students with the possibilities of change within the existing political system, their diminishing commitment to nondisruptive forms of protest, and the consequent evolution of the Berkeley scenario.

Throughout the academic year 1967-68, Columbia had experienced continuing SDS agitation and occasional demonstrations. In April, five campus buildings were occupied by members and supporters of SDS and the Students Afro-American Society. The announced issues of the disruption were a plan by Columbia to build a gymnasium in a park between the campus on Morningside Heights and Harlem, and the university's affiliation with the Institute for Defense Analyses, a consortium of eastern universities for defense research. Underlying these specific issues were Columbia's relations with the surrounding black community and the university's links with American foreign policy. SDS leader Mark Rudd later said that the announced issues were simply pretexts for protest; if they had not existed, he implied, others would have been substituted. Yet these issues were meaningful and plausible to the more moderate students, who constituted a majority of those in the occupied buildings.

With the police "bust"—the movement, since Berkeley, had developed its own jargon—the classic Berkeley scenario was reenacted in many respects: occupation, faculty and administration confusion, police intervention and student injuries, indignation of the moderate students and faculty, a major strike, and, finally, endless consideration of reforms in administration, governance, and disciplinary procedures. In these respects, Columbia was like Berkeley four years earlier.

There also were significant differences that highlight the escalation of campus unrest in the intervening years. The Berkeley protest had been started by a sudden change in the enforcement of campus rules governing political organizing, and the activists' objections had been couched in civil-libertarian terms. Their underlying demand had been for a more open campus and for the removal of restrictions on speech and political activity imposed by administrators and university regents.

At Columbia, however, the demands of radicals suggested that they viewed the university largely as a political instrument. The goal of the SDS leaders was not to make Columbia more neutral politically and more open intellectually, but rather to transform it into a revolutionary political weapon with which they could attack the system. Furthermore, violence by students was greater at Columbia: considerable property damage was done, and some students forcibly resisted arrest. For their part, the police reacted to the Columbia disturbances with excessive force and violence of their own.

The Berkeley invention, then, was substantially modified at Columbia and after. In its new form, it involved:

* Destruction of property, papers, and records. At Columbia, university officials estimated that the 1968 incidents resulted in hundreds of thousands of dollars of property damage. On a number of campuses, ROTC buildings became popular targets for arson. Threats were made to destroy other university facilities unless the radicals' demands were met. At Columbia, the notes of an historian, the result of years of work, were destroyed by a fire that some alleged was maliciously set by student protestors. The rifling and copying of files became a more common occurrence in student-occupied buildings.

* Counterviolence against protesting students by law enforcement officers. There were charges of police brutality at Columbia, and many of them had a basis in fact. Both before and after Columbia, every police bust gave rise to brutality charges. Far too often, they were true.

* University unpreparedness. In spite of the increase in the number and intensity of student protests since Berkeley, university administrators rarely had formulated plans to deal with them. Convinced that their own campuses were immune to disruptive or violent

protests, administrators were unprepared to cope with them when they occurred. In the midst of a crisis, some administrators believed that their only options were to do nothing or to call in the police. If they did nothing, they would allow the extremists to take over the campus; if they called in the police, they could not be sure the police would act properly.

* Threats against university officials. In April 1968, black students at Trinity College in Hartford, Connecticut, held the school's trustees captive until their demands were accepted. In November 1968, students at San Fernando Valley State College in Los Angeles held officials at knife point. Anonymous threats against university officials and faculty members critical of student activities became more frequent.

* Acts of terrorism. In February 1969, a secretary at Pomona College in California was severely injured by a bomb. In March 1969, a student at San Francisco State College was critically injured while attempting to place a bomb in a classroom building. On another occasion, a bomb was placed near the office of a liberal faculty member who opposed the "Third World" strike there. Later that year, a custodian at the University of California at Santa Barbara was killed by a bomb in the faculty club. The underground press proclaimed that the bombing in Madison, Wisconsin, on August 24, 1970, was part of a terrorist strategy. Earlier this summer, Assistant Secretary of the Treasury Eugene T. Rossides reported that, between January 1, 1969, and April 15, 1970, almost 41,000 bombings, attempted bombings, and bomb threats were recorded in the nation as a whole. Most could not be attributed to any specific cause. Of those that could be attributed to some cause, more than half—over 8,200—were attributable to "campus disturbances and student unrest."

* University disciplinary action. Faced with increasingly disruptive or violent demonstrations, university officials began to take stronger disciplinary actions against disruptive and violent students. In 1969, for example, one study of disciplinary measures at 28 campuses reported that more than 900 students had been expelled or suspended, while more than 850 others were given reprimands. In a statement to this Commission, J. Edgar Hoover reported that disruptive and violent protests resulted in over 4,000 arrests during the 1968-69 academic year and about 7,200 arrests during 1969-70. At the University of Chicago, Harvard, and elsewhere, students were expelled from the university because of their involvement in building occupations. Others were suspended or placed on probation.

* The influence of a new youth culture. Student unrest was increasingly reinforced by a youthful "counter-culture" that expressed itself in new kinds of art and music, in the use of drugs, and in unorthodox dress and personal relations. Students were receptive to this culture's accent on authenticity and alienation. Many university communities began to attract nonstudents who also participated in the new youth culture. These "street people" in turn played a prominent part in some student demonstrations, violence, and riots, and complicated responses to campus unrest.

* The growth of militancy and of political and cultural self-consciousness among minority group students other than Blacks, particularly among Puerto Ricans in the East and among Chicanos in the West and Southwest. Chicano and Puerto Rican student activists increasingly formed cohesive groups dedicated to asserting the claims of their communities upon the resources, curriculum, admissions policies, and concern of the university. While maintaining its separate identity, the movement of Spanish-speaking

students sometimes made common cause with black and other minority students in a "Third World" coalition, as at San Francisco State and elsewhere.

* Public backlash against campus unrest. The great majority of Americans were outraged by violence on American campuses. Such reactions against campus unrest were often intensified by a more general revulsion against the distinctive dress, life style, behavior, or speech adopted by some young people. Concerned over what they saw as an erosion of standards, a loss of morality, and a turn toward violence, many Americans came to believe that only harsh measures could quell campus disturbances. Many failed to distinguish between peaceful dissent and violent protest and called for the elimination of all campus unrest. Such public backlash made events on campus—in particular, protests, disruptions, and violence—a major political issue, both rationally discussed and irresponsibly exploited.

* Legislative action. As a major political issue, campus unrest has been the subject of much legislation, most of it punitive. By mid-1970, over 30 states had enacted a total of nearly 80 laws dealing with campus unrest. Some laws require expulsion or withdrawal of financial aid from students committing crimes or violating campus rules; others require dismissal or suspension of faculty members for similar offenses. Criminal statutes passed in 12 states so far authorize jail sentences and fines for anyone who willfully denies free use of university property and facilities to members of the university community. The federal Higher Education Act of 1968 and a number of federal acts passed since 1968 bar federal financial aid to students who disrupt campus activities.

* Indirect legislative reactions also became increasingly common. In some states, appropriations for higher

education were delayed or denied; in others, funds were diverted from major universities and colleges to community colleges where there have been fewer protests. Public officials, regents, and trustees intervened far more actively in university decisions on curriculum and faculty appointments.

In the years since Berkeley and Columbia, an ongoing escalation of rhetoric and tactics has taken place. On the students' side, the incidence of violence, destruction of property, and disruption has risen steadily. On the part of civil authorities, the response to student protest has become harsher and at times violent. Some segments of the public also have become increasingly disenchanted with student protests of all kinds—and even with higher education itself.

THE PARADOX OF TACTICS

After intense confrontations such as that at Columbia, it might have been expected that most moderate students would follow the lead of the extremists, adopting their tactics as they had supported their goals. Instead, moderate students often reasserted their commitment to nonviolence and their determination to work within the system.

We call this the paradox of tactics, and it is dramatically apparent in the history of the student movement during the past few years. The more violent the extremists became, the more active many nonviolent moderates became. As the number of violent and terroristic acts increased, so too did the frequency with which moderates would organize large—sometimes enormous—nonviolent protest demonstrations. Whenever a demonstration was planned well in advance and there were grounds to fear that it would be violent, moderates did all they could to assert themselves. They would help plan the demonstration, enlist student marshals to control the crowds, and make transportation and living arrangements for the thousands who would be present. As a rule, such demonstrations proceeded peacefully, thereby vindicating the good intentions and self-discipline of the student protestors.

This gradual escalation of violence and this growing involvement of great numbers of moderates in attempts to provide more acceptable modes of political action recurred in a cycle which repeated itself at many campuses.

In 1964, the year of the Berkeley invention, almost all the tactics used by student protestors were nonviolent. Even the most militant students agreed that the purpose of a demonstration was to mobilize support for reform by appealing to the better nature of the American people. Experience had shown this to be an effective strategy. The sight of young black and white activists enduring with dignity the attacks of southern police inspired many Americans. Public sentiment, especially in the North, was generally favorable.

At Berkeley, and indeed for three years after Berkeley, campus protest generally proceeded in this spirit of non-violence. Demonstrations were generally just that—actions designed primarily to bear witness to the participants' views and depth of concern. At their most extreme, tactics were calculated to provoke officials into an intemperate response and thereby gain sympathy from the previously un-committed. But protestors believed that if they were to win such sympathy, their own conduct had to be nonviolent, and generally it was. Few instances of violent behavior by students, even under provocation, are recorded for student protest from 1964 to 1967.

But after 1967, perhaps influenced by the terrible riots in Newark and Detroit in the summer of that year, some radical students began to employ more extremist tactics. The political views of radical students became ever more extreme, and their commitment to nonviolence was displaced by an increasingly revolutionary impulse. They adopted new tactics designed to shock the American people into a radical perspective on American society. The increasing self-assurance, isolation, and solidarity of these extremists also contributed to this change of tactics. Those who believe their cause is unquestionably right and who act in solidarity with their friends feel that little is impermissible.

During the summer of 1969, the SDS split during its national convention in Chicago. A major issue was the question of tactics. One faction, led by the Progressive Labor Party, wanted to organize the working class to make a revolution; it insisted on strict discipline, careful control of tactics, and opposition to terrorism. The other major faction, which believed American workers were corrupted by America's capitalist system, wanted immediate revolution, involving action in the streets. Out of this second faction came the Weathermen, who advocated violence both against property ("trashing") and against people. Weathermen sponsored the "days of rage" in Chicago, during which they destroyed property and fought with police. Soon they were charged with various crimes and went underground. Three of their number were killed when their dynamite accidentally exploded in New York City in 1970.

There are more than seven million college students in America today. Of these, only a handful practice terrorism. Indeed, some of the violence for which students are blamed is in fact perpetrated by nonstudents. Yet despite their small number, those students who have adopted violence as a tactic have caused much destruction and have evoked considerable sympathy from other students. In a few major campus areas—the San Francisco Bay Area, Madison, and Cambridge—they have done great damage. At Stanford, in April 1970, bands of "guerrillas" systematically terrorized the campus over a period of several nights, throwing rocks, breaking windows, and setting fire to buildings. After the August 1970 explosion at the University of Wisconsin, which killed a postdoctoral researcher and did $6 million worth of damage, underground newspapers all over the country gleefully reported that another blow had been struck against the "pig nation." Students at Madison expressed regret at the death of the young researcher—but some refused to condemn the bombing of the Army Mathematics Center which caused it.

Increasingly, the argument was heard that the use of

violence is justified, whether to promote social change or to suppress campus unrest. Many Americans, confused and indignant over student unrest, concluded that only harsh and punitive measures could control students. Some Americans openly applauded police violence against students, arguing that they had only themselves to blame if they were killed by police during disruptive or violent protests. Such public attitudes clearly encouraged violent responses by civil authorities.

Violent and terroristic incidents naturally received wide publicity, whereas the peaceful protests and constructive efforts of the majority of student activists have received less exposure. College and university disciplinary actions against disruptive or violent protestors have not been publicized. The appearance of a group of nonviolent students, liberals and radicals, who have actively countered the violent style of the tactical extremists has also received little public attention.

A central theme, then, in the current history of student activism is the emergence of an ever larger and more active group of students who, reacting against the extremist tactics of other students, were moved to press for change—which they insisted must come through peaceful, nonviolent means.

An example of the new role of moderates occurred on May 1, 1970, when 12,000 people gathered on the New Haven Green in support of a group of Black Panthers on trial for murder. The precautions of police officials, the cooperation of Yale University administrators, and the careful plans of Yale students and faculty helped prevent all but minor disturbances. Moderates retained control, too, of the 1969 April and October moratoriums against the Vietnam War. Indeed, on many campuses, these events were the perfect expression of the moderates' style and strength.

The moderates had also brought this style to the campaign for Eugene McCarthy's presidential candidacy in 1968, to a number of marches on Washington—and, above all, to the spontaneous demonstrations for peace in May 1970.

Most of the activities during the student strike in May 1970 were peaceful, although there were some cases of disruption and violence. In many cases, state authorities took measures to avert violence. In California, Governor Ronald Reagan shut down for four days all 28 campuses of the University and State College systems. Guardsmen were sent onto the campuses of the Universities of Kentucky, South Carolina, Illinois at Urbana, and Wisconsin at Madison. There was trouble at Stanford, Berkeley, the University of Maryland at College Park, and other places. At Fresno State College in California a firebomb destroyed a million-dollar computer center.

But overall, violence by protestors was limited. University opposition to the combined issues of Cambodia, Kent State, and Jackson State had become so widespread that moderate protestors far outnumbered extremists, and the vast majority of protests remained peaceful. While nearly 30 per cent of U.S. campuses were involved in some degree of strike activity, only 5 per cent experienced violence.

The main reason for the general nonviolence is again to be found in the paradox of tactics: the massive number of moderates who had joined the protest, partly because of violent acts against students, then guaranteed by their involvement that the protests would be largely nonviolent. In part, moderates were able to do this because they out-numbered extremists. But more important were their decisions: on campus after campus, students, faculty, and administrators set up programs of action designed to provide politically viable alternatives to violent action.

Princeton University, for example, decided to reschedule its fall classes to allow students to work in political campaigns for the two weeks before election day. The Movement for a New Congress, an effort to elect antiwar candidates, spread from Princeton to other campuses. At scores of colleges, academic requirements were changed to give students time for political activities. These students canvassed homes, churches, and service clubs to present their views and gather signatures on antiwar petitions.

On May 9, 1970, more than 60,000 people, most of them students, assembled on the Ellipse in Washington for a peaceful antiwar demonstration. Thousands more went to Washington to lobby Congressmen, Senators, Cabinet officers, and even the President himself. For example, on May 11, over a thousand students and faculty members from Yale, led by President Kingman Brewster, Jr., talked with more than three hundred members of Congress or their aides.

Large delegations headed for the Capitol from Brandeis, from the University of North Carolina, from Haverford College, and from many other colleges.

Although all this nonviolent political activity indicated that the moderates had generally prevailed over extremists on the question of tactics, it is clear in retrospect that, on the question of ends, it was the radicals who were victorious. For years, radicals had been working to politicize universities, and in May 1970 entire universities were, in effect, mobilized against the policies of the present national administration. Students, faculty members, and administrators united to turn their attention away from scholarship to what seemed to them the far more urgent demands of politics and of keeping protest activities nonviolent. In May 1970, students did not strike against their universities; they succeeded in making their universities strike against national policy.

Furthermore, the May 1970 strike movement revealed how much the meaning of tactical "moderation" had changed since the events at Berkeley in 1964. In the early 1960's, few moderates would have imagined themselves participating in a student strike, much less in a disruptive sit-in. But as extremist tactics became more extreme and violent, moderate tactics became less moderate and began to include strikes and disruptions. Thus, in May 1970, moderate students and faculty members at hundreds of colleges and universities interrupted their normal academic activity—in some cases, with official university sanction—in order to devote their time and effort to political work against the war. In some places, university property was used for political activity and classes and exams were postponed or cancelled.

For the most part, violence was avoided. But some universities had been politicized for at least a few weeks; and, perhaps most important in the long run, there was growing public concern, anger, indignation, and outrage at the spread of campus unrest.

CAMPUS OPINION IN MAY 1970

This account has summarized the development of contemporary American campus unrest from its beginnings in the civil rights movement in 1960 to the introduction of the Berkeley invention in 1964 and its elaboration in the Columbia disruption of 1968, and finally to the tragic events at Kent State, Jackson State, and the University of Wisconsin in the spring and summer of 1970. The overall trend of the past decade has clearly been toward more widespread and more violent protest. Issues that in the first half of the decade preoccupied only a few students had become, by 1970, the concern of the great majority of students. Tactics once considered outrageous and immoral by almost all students were justified and encouraged by some, and tolerated by many more. The university, once regarded as a bastion of academic freedom, was increasingly viewed by radical students as an instrument of a repressive and immoral society. And the confidence of an influential minority of American students in the ability of existing social and political institutions to effect meaningful change had diminished.

Describing the trends of the last decade still leaves the question: What are the attitudes and opinions of American college students today? How deep and how widespread were the effects of the rising tide of student protest?

On the whole, American students are not as politically radical as some press reports might suggest. Only three years ago, in the spring of 1967, a Gallup poll of college students found that 49 per cent classified themselves as "hawks" on the war in Vietnam. Since that time, there has been a dramatic shift of students' attitudes toward the war. A Gallup poll published in December 1969 found that only 20 per cent of the students classified themselves as "hawks" while 69 per cent classified themselves as "doves." At the same time, 50 per cent—as compared to 64 per cent of the adult public—approved of the way President Nixon was handling the situation in Vietnam. In 1965, one poll reported that only 6 per cent of American students favored immediate withdrawal from Vietnam. In May 1970, a special Harris survey, commissioned by the American Council on Education and conducted after the Cambodian incursion and the events at Kent State and Jackson State, found that 54 per cent favored an end to the fighting in Vietnam and bringing American troops home as soon as possible.

Student opinions on other controversial issues have not been particularly radical either. The special Harris survey found that only 25 per cent felt that ROTC should be completely removed from campus, while 37 per cent felt that it should be permitted on campus and receive academic credit. The same survey reported that 72 per cent believed that companies doing defense business should be allowed to recruit on campus; 70 per cent agreed that "school authorities are right" to call in police when students occupy a building or threaten violence; and, even after the tragic killings at Kent State, 42 per cent of the students felt that "the National Guard has acted responsibly in most cases" when it has been called onto college campuses.

Although these survey data indicate the persistence of liberal, and even conservative, attitudes among college students, other data indicate growing student radicalism. In 1968, the Harris organization found that 4 per cent of American students identified themselves as "radical or far left"; by 1970, 11 per cent identified themselves in this way.

Although only a small percentage of students identify themselves as "radicals," a large proportion of students have come to hold radical opinions. The 1970 special Harris survey revealed that 76 per cent believed that "basic changes in the system" will be necessary to improve the quality of life in America, and 44 per cent thought that social progress in America was more likely to come about through "radical pressure from outside the system" than the actions of major established institutions.

The growth of political radicalism among students has been accompanied by an extension of student protest and a greater willingness on the part of some students to engage in—or at least condone—disruptive and violent protests. On the basis of student responses, the special Harris survey reported that 80 per cent of the respondents' schools experienced protests or demonstrations in May 1970. At these schools, 75 per cent of the students favored the goals of the protests and 58 per cent actually participated in the protests.

Most surveys indicate that the majority of students are not tactical extremists. For example, the special Harris survey found that 68 per cent still do not accept violence as an effective means of change. But tactical extremism has become acceptable to some students. The same Harris survey revealed that 56 per cent of the students *disagree* with the statement that "since colleges and universities are intended as a place for serious intellectual study and learning, they are too important to our society to be continually disrupted by protests and demonstrations." This September, a group of researchers at the University of California reported that a survey of predominantly white, middle-class graduating college seniors revealed that 80 per cent believed confrontations, ranging from nonviolent mass demonstrations to violent acts, are necessary to achieve social change.

In short, the last decade has witnessed growing disenchantment and alienation among many American college students. More than three quarters today believe that "basic changes in the system" are needed; many argue that their earlier efforts to "work within the system" have proved unsuccessful; a large number accept disruptive tactics; and a tiny but important minority have adopted violent tactics—without clear repudiation by all their teachers and fellow students. Thus, in countless individual instances, what began as an idealistic and hopeful commitment to social change has disintegrated. This is a bleak picture, but an accurate one.

The Causes Of
Student Protest

Our purpose in this chapter is to identify the causes of student protest and to ascertain what these causes reveal about its nature. Our subject is primarily the protest of white students, for although they have much in common with Black, Chicano, and other minority student protest movements, these latter are nevertheless fundamentally different in their goals, their intentions, and their sources. In Chapter 3 we consider the special case of the black student movement.

We find that campus unrest has many causes, that several of these are not within the control of individuals or of government, and that some of these causes have worked their influence in obscure or indirect ways. Identifying them all is difficult, but they do exist and must be sought—not in order to justify or condemn, but rather because no rational response to campus unrest is possible until its nature and causes have been fully understood.

Race, the war, and the defects of the modern university have contributed to the development of campus unrest, have given it specific focus, and continue to lend it a special intensity. But they are neither the only nor even the most important causes of campus unrest.

Of far greater moment have been the advance of American society into the postindustrial era, the increasing affluence of American society, and the expansion and intergenerational evolution of liberal idealism. Together, these have prompted the formation of a new youth culture that defines itself through a passionate attachment to principle and an equally passionate opposition to the larger society. At the center of this culture is a romantic celebration of human life, of the unencumbered individual, of the senses, and of nature. It rejects what it sees to be the operational ideals of American society: materialism, competition, rationalism, technology, consumerism, and militarism. This emerging culture is the deeper cause of student protest against war, racial injustice, and the abuses of the multiversity.

During the past decade, this youth culture has developed rapidly. It has become ever more distinct and has acquired an almost religious fervor through a process of advancing personal commitment. This process has been spurred by the emergence within the larger society of opposition both to the youth culture itself and to its demonstrations of political protest. As such opposition became manifest—and occasionally violently manifest—participants in the youth culture felt challenged, and their commitment to that culture and to the political protest it prompts grew stronger and bolder. Over time, more and more students have moved in the direction of an ever deeper and more inclusive sense of opposition to the larger society. As their alienation became more profound, their willingness to use violence increased.

American student protest, like the student protest which is prevalent around the world, thus signifies a broad and intense reaction against—and a possible future change in—modern Western society and its organizing institutions. It thus appears to define a broad crisis of values with which the American people must now begin to cope.

Given that campus unrest reflects such broad historical forces and causes, it is perhaps not surprising that most Americans find student protest as puzzling as they obviously do.

Most Americans believe that protest comes only from groups which suffer injustice and economic privation: yet white student protestors come predominantly from affluent families, attend the better and the larger universities, and have ready access to the highest rewards and positions that American society can offer. Most Americans believe that protest arises only when the conditions at issue are getting sharply worse: yet the trend of American society, as most Americans see it, is one of progress, albeit sometimes slow, toward the reforms students seek—in personal income, in housing, in health, in equal opportunity, in civil liberties, and even in the national involvement with the war. And finally, most Americans believe that an authentic idealism expresses itself only in peaceful and humane ways: yet although students do manifest a high idealism, some student protest reveals in its tactical behavior a contrary tendency toward intolerance, disruption, criminality, destruction, and violence.

Thus, many Americans consider campus unrest to be an aberration from the moral order of American society. They treat it as a problem that derives from some moral failing on the part of some individual or group. The explanations of campus unrest that they adopt therefore tend to be single-cause explanations that clearly allocate blame and that specify remedies which are within the capacity of individuals, public opinion, or government to provide. Three such explanations enjoy particular popularity today.

One explanation attributes campus unrest to the machinations of outside agitators and subversive propagandists.

It is clear that in some cases of campus disruption, agitators and professional revolutionaries have been on the scene doing whatever they could do to make dangerous situations worse. It also is true that some of the most violent and destructive actions (such, perhaps, as the bombing in Madison, Wisconsin, this summer) are attributable to the influence, if not the actions, of small, trained, and highly mobile groups of revolutionaries. But it is equally clear that such agitators are not "the" cause of most large-scale campus protest and disorders. Agitators take advantage of preexisting tensions and seek to exacerbate them. But except for individual acts of terrorism, agitation and agitators cannot succeed if an atmosphere of tension, frustration, and dissent does not already pervade the campus. If agitation has contributed to campus unrest—and clearly, in various ways, it has—it has done so only because such an atmosphere has existed. What, then, created this atmosphere? The "agitator" theory cannot answer this question.

A second popular school of explanation holds that the atmosphere of dissent and frustration on campuses is the result of the pressing and unresolved issues which deeply concern many students. Clearly such issues do exist and do arouse deep feeling. Yet the conditions to which the issues have reference are in most cases not new ones. Why, then, have these issues recently emerged as objects of student protest and as sources of campus tension? And why has that protest become increasingly disruptive and violent? The "issues" theory does not answer these questions.

The third popular school of explanation argues that campus unrest is caused by an increasing disrespect for law and by a general erosion of all stabilizing institutions—a weakening of family (especially by "permissive" methods of child rearing), church, school, and patriotism. To some degree and in some areas, such an erosion of the stabilizing institutions in American society has indeed taken place. Yet we must ask: Why has this erosion taken place? The "breakdown of law" theory does not have an answer.

The basic difficulty with these explanations is that they begin by assuming that all campus unrest is a problem—a problem whose cause is a moral failure on the part of students or of society or of government, and which therefore has a specifiable solution. The search for causes is thus inseparable from the allocation of blame and the advocacy of some course of public action. As a result, causes which are not within human control or which do not lay the mantle of culpability upon specifiable individuals or groups tend to be ignored. Such "explanations" do not really explain. They only make campus unrest more bewildering—and more polarizing—than it need be.

In and of itself, campus unrest is not a "problem" and

requires no "solution." The existence of dissenting opinion and voices is simply a social condition, a fact of modern life; the right of such opinion to exist is protected by our Constitution. Protest that is violent or disruptive is, of course, a very real problem, and solutions must be found to end such manifestations of it. But when student protest stays within legal bounds, as it typically does, it is not a problem for government to cope with. It is simply a pattern of opinion and expression.

Campus unrest, then, is not a single or uniform thing. Rather it is the aggregate result, or sum, of hundreds and thousands of individual beliefs and discontents, each of them as unique as the individuals who feel them. These individual feelings reflect in turn a series of choices each person makes about what he will believe, what he will say, and what he will do. In the most immediate and operational sense, then, it is these choices—these *commitments*, to use a word in common usage among students—which are the proximate cause of campus unrest and which are the forces at work behind any physical manifestation of dissent.

These acts of individual commitment to certain values and to certain ways of seeing and acting in the world do not occur in a vacuum. They take place within, and are powerfully affected by, the conditions under which students live. We will call these conditions the contributing causes of campus unrest. Five broad orders of such contributing causes have been suggested in testimony before the Commission.

They are:

The pressing problems of American society, particularly the war in Southeast Asia and the conditions of minority groups;

The changing status and attitudes of youth in America;

The distinctive character of the American university during the postwar period;

An escalating spiral of reaction to student protest from public opinion and an escalating spiral of violence; and

Broad evolutionary changes occurring in the culture and structure of modern Western society.

ISSUES AND OPINIONS

The best place to begin any search for the causes of student protest is to consider the reasons which student protestors themselves offer for their activities. There are many such reasons, and students are not reluctant to articulate them. These reasons—these positions on the major national issues of the day—must be taken seriously.

We must recognize, however, that students express a keen interest in a large number of issues. Even in the course of a single reenactment of the Berkeley scenario, the issues which are identified and discussed, and which in some degree are the reasons for student participation, can number in the tens or scores.

For example, a protest against university expansion into the neighboring community and against university complicity in the Vietnam War may lead to university discipline. Discipline or amnesty may then become the issue. On this issue there is a larger and more disruptive protest. The police are called. Police brutality now becomes the issue, and the demand is that the university intercede to get students released. The university says this is a matter for the civil courts. It is now attacked as inhuman and soulless and dominated by the material interests of its trustees, who need police and courts to protect those interests. At this point a building goes up in flames. What was the issue?

One must distinguish therefore between primary issues and secondary issues, which arise from protest actions or from the primary issues themselves. Three great primary issues have been involved in the rising tide of student protest during the past decade.

Both historically and in terms of the relative frequency with which it is the focus of protest, the first great issue is also the central social and political problem of American society: the position of racial minorities, and of black people in particular. It was over this issue that student protest began in 1960.

As the decade passed, the definition of this issue changed. At first, it was defined in the South as the problem of legally enforced or protected patterns of segregation. Later, the focus shifted to the problems of extralegal discrimination against Blacks, in the North as well as in the South—a definition of the issue which later was summarized in the phrase "institutional racism." By the middle of the decade, the issue had shifted again and now was understood as a problem of recovering the Black's self-respect and pride in his cultural heritage.

The targets of protest have shifted accordingly. At first, there was protest against local merchants for not serving Blacks, against local businesses for not employing them, and against the university for tolerating discrimination in sororities and fraternities. Soon there were protests against discrimination in university admissions, and demands that more be done to recruit Blacks and that more be done to assist them once admitted. Black students demanded, too, that the university begin to give assistance to local black communities, that it establish a curriculum in Black studies, and that it recruit more black faculty to teach courses in these and other areas. As the target of protest moved from the society at large to the university, it also widened to represent the aspirations of other minority groups, often in a "Third World" coalition.

The second great issue has been the war in Southeast Asia. The war was almost from the beginning a relatively un-popular war, one which college youth on the whole now consider a mistake and which many of them also consider immoral and evil. It has continued now for more than five years, and it has pressed especially on youth. During the last decade, the war issue was less commonly the object of student protest than were questions of race, but as the years went by it became more and more prominent among student concerns.

This issue has also changed form and has become more inclusive over the years: it moved from protesting American intervention, to protesting the draft, to protesting government and corporate recruiting for jobs related to war, and, increasingly, to protesting university involvement in any aspect of the war, such as releasing information to draft boards, allowing recruiters on campus, conducting defense research, and permitting the presence of ROTC on campus.

A third major protest issue has been the university itself. Though at times this issue has been expressed in protests over curriculum and the nonretention of popular teachers, the overwhelming majority of university-related protests have dealt with school regulations affecting students, with the role of students in making those regulations, and more generally with the quality of student life, living facilities, and food services. The same impulse moves students to denounce what they feel to be the general regimentation of American life by large-scale organizations and their byproducts—impersonal bureaucracy and the anonymous IBM card. University regulation of political activities—the issue at Berkeley in 1964—has also been a prominent issue.

Since 1965 there has been steady liberalization in the rules affecting student living quarters, disciplining of students, rules affecting controversial speakers, and dress rules. Increasingly, universities and colleges have incorporated students into the rulemaking process. Yet the issue has lost none of its power.

What students objected to about discrimination against Blacks and other racial minorities was simple and basic: the unfeeling and unjustifiable deprivation of individual rights, dignity, and self-respect. And the targets of protest were those institutions which routinely deprived Blacks of their rights, or which supported and reinforced such deprivation. These two themes—support for the autonomy, personal dignity, individuality, and life of each person, and bitter opposition to institutions, policies, and rationales which seemed to deprive individuals of those things—could also be seen in the other two main issues of the 1960's: the war in

Southeast Asia, and university regulation of student life. They may also be seen in the emerging student concern over ecology and environmental pollution.

These three issues—racism, war, and the denial of personal freedoms—unquestionably were and still are contributing causes of student protest. Students have reacted strongly to these issues, speak about them with eloquence and passion, and act on them with great energy.

Moreover, students feel that government, the university, and other American institutions have not responded to their analysis of what should be done, or at least not responded rapidly enough. This has led many students to turn their attacks on the decision-making process itself. Thus, we hear slogans such as "power to the people."

And yet, having noted that these issues were causes, we must go on to note two further pertinent facts about student protest over race and war. First, excepting black students, it is impossible to attribute student opposition on these issues to cynical or narrow self-interest alone, as do those Americans who believe that students are against the war because they are cowards, afraid to die for a cause. But in fact, few students have been called upon to risk their lives in the present war. It is true that male students have been subject to the draft. But only a small portion of college youth have actually been drafted and sent to fight in Vietnam, and it is reported that, as compared to the nation's previous wars, relatively few college graduates have been killed in this war. It is *noncollege* youth who fight in Vietnam, and yet it is college youth who oppose the war—while noncollege youth tend to support it more than other segments of the population.

It is the same in the case of race. For black and other minority college youth, it hardly needs explanation why they should find the cruel injustice of American racism a compelling issue, or why they should protest over it. Why it became an issue leading to unrest among *white* college students is less obvious. They are not directly victims of it, and, as compared to other major institutions in the society, the university tends to be more open and more willing to reward achievement regardless of race or ethnicity.

Of course, students have a deep personal interest in these issues and believe that the outcome will make their own individual lives better or worse. Yet their beliefs and their protest clearly are founded on principle and ideology, not on self-interest. The war and the race issues did not arise primarily because they actually and materially affected the day-to-day lives of college youth—black students again excepted. The issues were defined in terms not of interest but of principle, and their emergence was based on what we must infer to have been a fundamental change in the attitudes and principles of American students.

This alteration of student principles cannot be said to have occurred because of racism or Vietnam. Racism was hardly something new to American society in 1960 or 1964—it had, of course, existed since the very beginning of the colonies, and in much more brutal and inhuman forms. Indeed, during the 1950's and 1960's, legally imposed segregation in the South was, at long last, beginning to wane, and the economic condition of the Black American was slowly improving. As for Vietnam, even though America had not been engaged in a significant war for ten years when the major escalation in Vietnam occurred early in 1965, it could hardly be said that war was a new phenomenon in American society, or that most previous American warfare had been less brutal.

If, then, war and racism did not directly and significantly affect the daily lives and self-interest of the vast majority of American students; if war and racism were not new to American society; and if their horrors and injustices were, over time, marginally diminishing rather than increasing—the emergence on campus of these issues as objects of increasingly widespread student protest could only have been the result of some further cause, a change in some factor that intervened between the *conditions* (racism, war) in the country and their emergence as *issues* that led to student protest.

Clearly, whatever it is that transforms a condition into an issue lies in the eyes of the beholder—or, more precisely, in his opinions and perceptions. The emergence of these issues was caused by a change in opinions, perceptions, and values—that is, by a change in the culture of students. Students' basic ways of seeing the world became, during the 1960's, less and less tolerant of war, of racism, and of the things these entail. This shift in student culture is a basic—perhaps *the* basic—contributing cause of campus unrest.

THE NEW YOUTH CULTURE

In early Western societies, the young were traditionally submissive to adults. Largely because adults retained great authority, the only way for the young to achieve wealth, power, and prestige was through a cooperative apprenticeship of some sort to the adult world. Thus, the young learned the traditional adult ways of living, and in time they grew up to become adults of the same sort as their parents, living in the same sort of world.

Advancing industrialism decisively changed this cooperative relationship between the generations. It produced new forms and new sources of wealth, power, and prestige, and these weakened traditional adult controls over the young. It removed production from the home and made it increasingly specialized; as a result, the young were increasingly removed from adult work places and could not directly observe or participate in adult work. Moreover, industrialism hastened the separation of education from the home, in consequence of which the young were concentrated together in places of formal education that were isolated from most adults. Thus, the young spent an increasing amount of time together, apart from their parents' home and work, in activities that were different from those of adults.

This shared and distinct experience among the young led to shared interests and problems, which led, in turn, to the development of distinct subcultures. As those subcultures developed, they provided support for any youth movement that was distinct from—or even directed against—the adult world.

A distinguishing characteristic of young people is their penchant for pure idealism. Society teaches youth to adhere to the basic values of the adult social system—equality, honesty, democracy, or whatever—in absolute terms. Throughout most of American history, the idealism of youth has been formed—and constrained—by the institutions of adult society. But during the 1960's, in response to an accumulation of social changes, the traditional American youth culture developed rapidly in the direction of an oppositional stance toward the institutions and ways of the adult world.

This subculture took its bearings from the notion of the autonomous, self-determining individual whose goal was to live with "authenticity," or in harmony with his inner penchants and instincts. It also found its identity in a rejection of the work ethic, materialism, and conventional social norms and pieties. Indeed, it rejected all institutional disciplines externally imposed upon the individual, and this set it at odds with much in American society.

Its aim was to liberate human consciousness and to enhance the quality of experience; it sought to replace the materialism, the self-denial, and the striving for achievement that characterized the existing society with a new emphasis on the expressive, the creative, the imaginative. The tools of the workaday institutional world—hierarchy, discipline, rules, self-interest, self-defense, power—it considered mad and tyrannical. It proclaimed instead the liberation of the individual to feel, to experience, to express whatever his unique humanity prompted. And its perceptions of the world grew ever more distant from the perceptions of the existing culture: what most called "justice" or "peace" or "accomplishment," the new culture envisioned as "enslavement" or "hysteria" or "meaninglessness." As this divergence of values and of vision proceeded, the new youth culture became increasingly oppositional.

And yet in its commitment to liberty and equality, it was very much in the mainstream of American tradition; what it doubted was that America had managed to live up to its national ideals. Over time, these doubts grew, and the youth culture became increasingly imbued with a sense of alienation and of opposition to the larger society.

No one who lives in contemporary America can be unaware of the surface manifestations of this new youth culture. Dress is highly distinctive; emphasis is placed on heightened color and sound; the enjoyment of flowers and nature is given a high priority. The fullest ranges of sense and sensation are to be enjoyed each day through the cultivation of new experiences, through spiritualism, and through drugs. Life is sought to be made as simple, primitive, and "natural" as possible, as ritualized, for example, by nude bathing.

Social historians can find parallels to this culture in the past. One is reminded of Bacchic cults in ancient Greece, or of the *Wandervoegel,* the wandering bands of German youths in the 19th century, or of primitive Christianity. Confidence is placed in revelation rather than cognition, in sensation rather than analysis, in the personal rather than the institutional. Emphasis is placed on living to the fullest extent, on the sacredness of life itself, and on the common mystery of all living things. The age-old vision of natural man, untrammeled and unscarred by the fetters of institutions, is seen again. It is not necessary to describe such movements as religious, but it is useful to recognize that they have elements in common with the waves of religious fervor that periodically have captivated the minds of men.

It is not difficult to compose a picture of contemporary America as it looks through the eyes of one whose premises are essentially those just described. Human life is all; but women and children are being killed in Vietnam by American forces. All living things are sacred; but American industry and technology are polluting the air and the streams and killing the birds and the fish. The individual should stand as an individual; but American society is organized into vast structures of unions, corporations, multiversities, and government bureaucracies. Personal regard for each human being and for the absolute equality of every human soul is a categorical imperative; but American society continues to be characterized by racial injustice and discrimination. The senses and the instincts are to be trusted first; but American technology and its consequences are a monument to rationalism. Life should be lived in communion with others, and each day's sunrise and sunset enjoyed to the fullest; American society extols competition, the accumulation of goods, and the work ethic. Each man should be free to lead his own life in his own way; American organizations and statute books are filled with regulations governing dress, sex, consumption, and the accreditation of study and of work, and many of these are enforced by armed police.

No coherent political decalogue has yet emerged. Yet in this new youth culture's political discussion there are echoes of Marxism, of peasant communalism, of Thoreau, of Rousseau, of the evangelical fervor of the abolitionists, of Gandhi, and of native American populism.

The new culture adherent believes he sees an America that has failed to achieve its social targets; that no longer cares about achieving them; that is thoroughly hypocritical in pretending to have achieved them and in pretending to care; and that is exporting death and oppression abroad through its military and corporate operations. He wishes desperately to recall America to its great traditional goals of true freedom and justice for every man. As he sees it, he wants to remake America in its own image.

What of the shortcomings of other societies, especially the Soviet Union? Why does the new culture denounce only the United States? On this question, Drs. Heard and Cheek said in a memorandum to the President:

> The apparent insensitivity of students to Soviet actions and to evils in the Soviet system is at least partly explainable by considerations like these: *First*, they feel that by the wrongness of our own policies, such as the war in Vietnam, we have lost our moral standing to condemn other countries. *Second*, there is an obsession with our own problems, a feeling that our own crises should occupy all our attention. *Third*, the fear of Communism is less than existed a decade ago.

Students perceive the Czech invasion as one more evil action by a powerful imperialist government, but they don't perceive it as a threat to the United States. Since the Sino-Soviet split, they see Communism as consisting of different and often competing national governments and styles. The Russians appear to repress their satellite countries, but students see that fact as parallel to American domination in *its* sphere of influence (the Dominican Republic, Guatemala, economic exploitation, etc.). They see the Russians as no better than [ourselves], maybe not as good, but feel more responsibility for our actions than for those of foreign powers.

The dedicated practioners of this emerging culture typically have little regard for the past experience of others. Indeed, they often exhibit a positive antagonism to the study of history. Believing that there is today, or will be tomorrow, a wholly new world, they see no special relevance in the past. Distrusting older generations, they distrust the motives of their historically based advice no less than they distrust the history written by older generations. The antirationalist thread in the new culture resists the careful empirical approach of history and denounces it as fraudulent. Indeed, this antirationalism and the urge for blunt directness often lead those of the new youth culture to view complexity as a disguise, to be impatient with learning the facts, and to demand simplistic solutions in one sentence.

Understandably, the new culture enthusiast has at best a lukewarm interest in free speech, majority opinion, and the rest of the tenets of liberal democracy as they are institutionalized today. He cannot have much regard for these things if he believes that American liberal democracy, with the consent and approval of the vast majority of its citizens, is pursuing values and policies that he sees as fundamentally immoral and apocalyptically destructive. Again in parallel with historical religious movements, the new culture advocate tends to be self-righteous, sanctimonious, contemptuous of those who have not yet shared his vision, and intolerant of their ideals.

Profoundly opposed to any kind of authority structure from within or without the movement and urgently pressing for direct personal participation by each individual, members of this new youth culture have a difficult time making collective decisions. They reveal a distinct intolerance in their refusal to listen to those outside the new culture and in their willingness to force others to their own views. They even show an elitist streak in their premise that the rest of the society must be brought to the policy positions which they believe are right.

At the same time, they try very hard, and with extraordinary patience, to give each of their fellows an opportunity to be heard and to participate directly in decision-making. The new culture decisional style is founded on the endless mass meeting at which there is no chairman and no agenda, and from which the crowd or parts of the crowd melt away or move off into actions. Such crowds are, of course, subject to easy manipulation by skillful agitators and sometimes become mobs. But it must also be recognized that large, loose, floating crowds represent for participants in the new youth culture the normal, friendly, natural way for human beings to come together equally, to communicate, and to decide what to do. Seen from this perspective, the reader may well imagine the general student response at Kent State to the governor's order that the National Guard disperse all assemblies, peaceful or otherwise.

Practitioners of the new youth culture do not announce their program because, at this time at least, the movement is not primarily concerned with programs; it is concerned with how one ought to live and what one ought to consider important in one's daily life. The new youth culture is still in the process of forming its values, programs, and life style; at this point, therefore, it is primarily a *stance*.

A parallel to religious history is again instructive. For many (not all) student activists and protestors, it is not really very important whether the protest tactics employed will actually contribute to the political end allegedly sought. What is important is that a protest be made—that the individual protestor, for his own internal salvation, stand up, declare the purity of his own heart, and take his stand. No student protestor throwing a rock through a laboratory window believes that it will stop the Indochina war, weapons research, or the advance of the feared technology—yet he throws it in a mood of defiant exultation—almost exaltation. He has taken his moral stance.

An important theme of this new culture is its oppositional relationship to the larger society, as is suggested by the fact that one of its leading theorists has called it a "counter-culture." If the rest of the society wears short hair, the member of this youth culture wears his hair long. If others are clean, he is dirty. If others drink alcohol and illegalize marijuana, he denounces alcohol and smokes pot. If others work in large organizations with massively complex technology, he works alone and makes sandals by hand. If others live separated, he lives in a commune. If others are for the police and the judges, he is for the accused and the prisoner. In such ways, he declares himself an alien in a larger society with which he feels himself to be fundamentally at odds.

He will also resist when the forces of the outside society seek to impose its tenets upon him. He is likely to see police as the repressive minions of the outside culture imposing its law on him and on other students by force or death if necessary. He will likely try to urge others to join him in changing the society about him in the conviction that he is seeking to save that society from bringing about its own destruction. He is likely to have apocalyptic visions of impending doom of the whole social structure and the world. He is likely to have lost hope that society can be brought to change through its own procedures. And if his psychological makeup is of a particular kind, he may conclude that the only outlet for his feelings is violence and terrorism.

In recent years, some substantial number of students in the United States and abroad have come to hold views along these lines. It is also true that a very large fraction of American college students, probably a majority, could not be said to be participants in any significant aspect of this cultural posture except for its music. As for the rest of the students, they are distributed over the entire spectrum that ranges from no participation to full participation. A student may feel strongly about any one or more aspects of these views and wholly reject all the others. He may also subscribe wholeheartedly to many of the philosophic assertions implied while occupying any of hundreds of different possible positions on the questions of which tactics, procedures, and actions he considers to be morally justifiable. Generalizations here are more than usually false.

One student may adopt the outward appearance of the new culture and nothing else. Another may be a total devotee, except that he is a serious history scholar. Another student may agree completely on all the issues of war, race, pollution, and the like and participate in protests over those matters, while disagreeing with all aspects of the youth culture life style. A student may agree with the entire life style but be wholly uninterested in politics. Another new culture student who takes very seriously the elements of compassion and of reverence for life may prove to be the best bulwark against resorts to violence. A student who rejects the new youth culture altogether may nevertheless be in the vanguard of those who seek to protect that culture against the outside world. And so forth.

As we have observed elsewhere in this report, to conclude that a student who has a beard is a student who would burn a building, or even sit-in in a building, is wholly unwarranted.

But almost no college student today is unaffected by the new youth culture in some way. If he is not included, his roommate or sister or girlfriend is. If protest breaks out on his campus, he is confronted with a personal decision about his role in it. In the poetry, music, movies, and plays that students encounter, the themes of the new culture are recurrent. Even the student who finds older values more comfortable for himself will nevertheless protect and support vigorously the privilege of other students who prefer the new youth culture.

A vast majority of students are not complete adherents.

But *no* significant group of students would join older generations in condemning those who are. And almost *all* students will condemn repressive efforts by the larger community to restrict or limit the life style, the art forms, and the nonviolent political manifestations of the new youth culture.

To most Americans, the development of the new youth culture is an unpleasant and often frightening phenomenon. And there is no doubt that the emergence of this student perspective has led to confrontations, injuries, and death. It is undeniable, too, that a tiny extreme fringe of fanatical devotees of the new culture have crossed the line over into outlawry and terrorism. There is a fearful and terrible irony here as, in the name of- the law, the police and National Guard have killed students, and some students, under the new youth culture's banner of love and compassion, have turned to burning and bombing.

But the new youth culture itself is not a "problem" to which there is a "solution"; it is a mass social condition, a shift in basic cultural viewpoint. How long this emerging youth culture will last and what course its future development will take are open questions. But it does exist today, and it is the deeper cause of the emergence of the issues of race and war as objects of intense concern on the American campus.

The University Community

This change in the youth subculture derived from major changes in the social functions and internal composition of the American university.

The American university was traditionally a status-conferring institution for middle and upper-middle class families. As such, it was closely integrated with the family and work life of these social groupings, and its subcultures were appropriately cooperative.

The college experience provided an identity moratorium following childhood. Students spent the "best years of their lives" mostly enjoying themselves with good conversation, some study, football, dating, and drinking. The experience ended with a *rite de passage*, graduation, which was then followed by adulthood and entry into the serious world of work. The college was completely controlled by the serious adult world, but the student's experiences there were not seen by him or others as part of that world.

In the past few decades, the university has become increasingly integrated into the meritocratic work world. Grade pressures have grown steadily, and students have come to see the university as a direct extension of the adult world. Indeed, by the 1960's, this trend had moved down into the high schools and in some places even to the junior high schools, as formal education became the primary route to the best jobs in the postindustrial society.

The integration of higher education into the adult world of work was intimately associated with another historic change—the rapid expansion of higher education, and the dramatic increase in the proportion of high school graduates who entered college. In the early 1930's there were about a million and a quarter college students in the United States. In the fall of 1969, there were over seven million. By 1978, we may look forward to ten million, and there will be almost as many graduate students enrolled as there were undergraduates before World War II. The U.S. Office of Education now estimates that, nationally, 62 per cent of all high school graduates will attend institutions of higher education.

As higher education expanded, it also lengthened. More and more students went on to enroll in graduate programs leading to advanced degrees; as they did, the vocational value of the undergraduate degree decreased. Students thus were under pressure to spend an ever longer period of time—well into their twenties and not infrequently into their early thirties—in schools which prepared them for the ever longer deferred work world.

More and more young Americans found themselves in an ambivalent status for an ever longer time. Physically and psychologically, they had long since become adult. As students in the meritocratic system of higher education, they were already integrated into a part of the adult work world. Accordingly, they came to think of themselves as adults and to demand all the rights and privileges of adults. And yet, though in part they were treated as adults, they nevertheless remained financially dependent upon the adult world and were not yet full-fledged participants in adult work. Especially for older students, but increasingly for all students regardless of age, this condition created tensions and frustrations.

Against the background of this ambivalence, two further factors led the college student culture into an increasingly bitter sense of opposition to the larger society. One of these was affluence. Most college students during the past decade have grown up in the greatest affluence and freedom from the discipline of hard and unremitting work of any generation in man's history. Life, at least in its material aspects, has not been difficult for them, and they have thus found a great deal in the larger society, oriented as it is to work and production, that seems needless or strange.

That students increasingly rejected this larger society, and rejected it passionately and in the name of moral principle, was the result of a second factor. The college students among whom the youth culture and campus unrest emerged were principally those from affluent families whose parents were liberals or radicals, and who attended the larger and more selective universities and colleges. They were part of the first generation of middle-class Americans to grow up in the post-Depression American welfare state under the tutelage of a parental generation that embodied the distinctive moral vision of modern liberalism. Insofar as these students learned the lessons that their parents and their experiences taught, they became, inevitably, more liberal than the older generation, which had grown up in a harsher time.

The parental generation's liberalism expressed itself most characteristically in the belief that their greatest personal fulfillment came not from work, income, power, or social status, but rather from the purely nonvocational pursuits of life—the activities of living well, and the rewards of identifying with right principles applicable to the society as a whole. They pictured work, money, discipline, and ambition to their children as having little intrinsic merit and as deserving correspondingly little praise. It was instead the high-minded virtues, such as compassion, learning, love, equality, democracy, and self-expression, which they considered worthy of respect and pursuit.

Not a few among this older generation believed that they managed to live strictly in accord with this hierarchy of values. Considering the decency and comfort of their lives, it is understandable that they could have entertained such hopes. But whether for reasons of modesty or because of aspirations for higher things for their children, they persistently passed over the fact that their own comfort was usually the fruit of hard work and self-discipline.

If the parents held views which did not justify or reflect their personal history of work and self-discipline, the children, brought up in conditions of affluence and freedom from worldly struggle, adopted those views not only as attitudes but also as habits of life. They began to live, in short, what their parents preached but did not entirely act upon. And as they brought their parents' high-minded ideals to bear upon American society in a thoroughgoing way, their vision of that society changed radically.

The parental values were strongly reinforced in the elite universities by the liberal values of faculty members. That faculty members began to have and to transmit such an outlook was the result of another development within the university community—the professionalization of the academy, by which professors became more mobile, more independent of the university administration, more oriented to research and publication, and, as a group, more ethnically diverse. As a result, the student subculture, particularly in the more selective schools, came to be far more liberal than the subcultures of students at other institutions or of the general population.

As higher education expanded, more and more students

took the values of liberal idealism as their code and habit of life. As they did, more and more students found themselves in increasing opposition to the larger society, which did not embody these values nearly so much.

The thoroughgoing idealistic liberalism of the student generation of the 1960's was the ideological beginning point of the student movement and of campus unrest as they exist today. It predisposed many students to oppose the Vietnam War, to react with fury over the use of police power to quell student disturbances, and to enlist themselves in whole-hearted support of civil rights and the movement for Black pride.

The student subculture reflected and, as it coalesced, magnified these changes of perception and value.

THE UNIVERSITY AS AN OBJECT OF PROTEST

As the midpoint of the 1960's was reached, campus unrest became more and more radical in character. Indictments of race discrimination and of the war grew more sweeping and soon encompassed the university, which itself became a major target of political protest. "University complicity" proved to be a powerful issue with which to mobilize students.

Yet despite the large volume of protest against the university, polls of student opinion do not in fact indicate wide-spread discontent with higher education. A winter 1968-69 poll revealed that only 4 per cent of seniors and 9 per cent of freshmen found higher education "basically unsound—needs major overhauling." Fifteen per cent of freshmen and 19 per cent of seniors said, "not too sound—needs many improvements." Fifty-six per cent of seniors and 49 per cent of freshmen found higher education "basically sound—needs some improvement." And 19 per cent of seniors and 32 per cent of freshmen voted for "basically sound—essentially good."

A survey in the spring of 1969 found that only 4 per cent of college students noted strong assent, and 4 per cent moderate assent, in response to the statement, "On the whole, college has been a deep disappointment to me." In response to the statement, "I don't feel I am learning very much in college," again 4 per cent noted strong assent and 13 per cent moderate assent. However, in response to the statement, "American universities have largely abdicated their responsibility to deal with vital moral issues," 9 per cent indicated strong assent and 30 per cent moderate assent.

These surveys suggest that most American students are not fundamentally discontented with their college and university education. But substantial numbers do seem to disapprove of their schools as *moral* institutions.

Those who feel that the universities have failed them in a larger moral sense are often the children of liberal, middle class families, well prepared to do college work, and with the highest expectations of their colleges. Why is it that the university has become the special target of so many of the very students who might be expected to find an institution devoted to the life of the mind particularly worthy of respect?

Partially, the answer may be found in the observation that Americans today have higher expectations of the university than they do of practically any other social institution. It is expected to provide models, methods, and meanings for contemporary life. It is an advisor to government and a vehicle for self-improvement and social mobility. Indeed, since science and critical method are enshrined in the university, it occupies a place in the public imagination that may be compared to that of the church in an earlier day.

It is precisely because of these high expectations that the university has forfeited some of its authority and legitimacy in the eyes of many "moderate" students. For radicals, perhaps, the university, as a part of the established society, may never have had much authority or legitimacy. But without the support of moderates, militant disruption could never have become a nationwide problem. The "moderate" campus majority makes common cause with the militants because student rebellion is not merely a crisis at the university. It is equally a crisis *of* the university itself—of its corporate identity, its purposes, and its justifications.

Despite the sophisticated style of many bright young people today, the freshman still looks forward to the great freedom and variety of college and anticipates the excitement of serious study and personal growth within a community of students and scholars. And if he does not expect it when he arrives, he learns to demand it once he has been there awhile.

According to the professed culture of the university, the principal values against which any activity or vocation are to be measured are justice, compassion, and truth. The rewards of such endeavors are pictured to be intellectual excitement, personal fulfillment, and a sense of having done something worthwhile. As the academy sees itself, these are the rewards of the scholarly life itself and the basis of the sense of community within the university. Thus, the student's expectations are raised even higher as he is integrated into university life and becomes acquainted with its distinctive values.

But it is usually not long before he realizes that college life bears little relation to his expectations, and that the university itself is often quite unlike what it pictures itself to be.

Far from being a "community of scholars," the large university today is much more like a vast and impersonal staging area for professional careers. Anxious to maintain their professional standing and not unresponsive to financial inducements, the professors appear to the freshman more like corporation executives than cloistered scholars. What these professors teach seems less the humane and civilizing liberal education the freshman anticipated than a body of impersonal knowledge amassed and accepted by an anonymous "profession." The student's role in this process of education is largely passive: he sits and listens, he sits and reads, and sometimes he sits and writes. It is an uninspiring experience for many students.

This is especially the case because the contemporary youth culture is so very different in its quality and intentions. For while that culture does value the life of the mind, it also places high value on the truth of feeling and on the cultivation of the whole person. This basic attitude is not easily reconciled with the idea at the heart of the modern university—that a scholar's proper work is the pursuit of probable truth, which is a goal that is thought to lie outside the preferences and tastes of the man who pursues it and to impose a stringent discipline upon him. Because this academic method is the very antithesis of the style of the youth culture, large numbers of students today are ill suited to university life and its academic pursuits.

Student reactions to higher education vary. Radicals increasingly express a desire to reorganize the university in order to have it act upon their own political convictions and programs. Others, less certain of their goals, seem to accept their personal disappointment or disinterest until an issue emerges on campus which symbolizes to them the university's "complicity" in social evils or its "hypocrisy" about its aims and practices.

The moral authority of the university was compromised as a result of its expansion and professionalization after World War II. For as it expanded, higher education in America changed. But these changes had primarily to do with physically accommodating the huge influx of students, with meeting the increasing variety of demands being made upon the university by government and business, and with satisfying the ever increasing appetite of the faculty for freedom, including the freedom to do things other than teaching. By the mid-1950's, universities were permitting faculty to accept research grants which, in some instances, were larger than the operating budget of their entire academic department.

As a result, new men of power walked the campus. Recognition for distinguished teaching and scholarship in the traditional manner, which rewarded knowledge pursued for its own sake, so that a medievalist might be as highly regarded as a chemist, became rarer. Certainly, knowledge for its own sake was still admirable, but scholars now could also hope to achieve wealth and power by proposing technological and political solutions to the problems of industry and government—and this cast doubt upon the university's claim that it was a center for disinterested research and teaching.

Are there any reforms which might solve the problems arising out of the university's loss of moral authority? The question has produced a serious debate in colleges and universities across the country, but no clear answer.

Some suggest the colleges and universities should relate themselves more fully to life around them and thus respond to the demand for "relevance." Others suggest they should withdraw further and thus free themselves from the taint of involvement with an impure society and government.

Some argue strongly that colleges and universities must make every effort to restore as soon as possible a meaningful core curriculum which would socialize youth into society and provide the basic education that any citizen should have. Others assert that it is impossible for any modern university to agree on what such a curriculum should be, and that even the modest efforts of colleges to provide a core curriculum should be abandoned as intellectually and culturally arbitrary.

Some have emphasized that the most serious educational failing of the university was to dilute its teaching function and to disorder its moral priorities by placing too great an emphasis on research and on establishing links to government and business. Others insist that the research emphasis and even consulting improve the university—and specifically improve the quality of teaching—by bringing it in closer touch with the frontiers of knowledge and with the practical needs that occasion research.

The Commission engages in no rhetorical evasion when it places against each interpretation largely contradictory interpretations of just what in the colleges and universities has led to the crisis and what should therefore be reformed. All these positions can be argued persuasively, and specific proposals for reform are as numerous as they are controversial.

Still, without attempting to endorse a particular point of

view, we do think it can be said that some of the causes of student unrest are to be found in certain contemporary features of colleges and universities. It is impressive, for example, that unrest is most prominent in the larger universities, and that it is less common in those in which, by certain measures, greater attention is paid to students and to the needs of education, and where students and faculty seem to form single communities, either because of their size or the shared values of their members.

THE ESCALATION OF COMMITMENT AND REACTION

The emergence of the great issues of our time, the evolution of an oppositional college student subculture, and the changing nature of the university have all contributed to the development of campus unrest. Yet as we emphasized at the outset, these are no more than contributing causes. They explain—at least they suggest—the general direction in which opinion on campus was likely to move. Yet they do not suffice to explain why campus unrest developed at the time it did, or with the speed it did. Neither do they explain why tactics changed as they did.

We also pointed out at the outset that the direct functional cause of campus unrest has been the free existential act of commitment which each member of the student movement has made to a particular political vision, to the practice of expressing that vision publicly, and to particular acts of protest. To say this is to state more than a simple deductive truth, for the choice of an activist mode of expressing political opinion has important consequences for the development of that opinion itself.

Studies of activist youth reveal that in most cases students become activists through an extended process. They encounter others who are politically involved, assimilate their views, reassess their own thinking, engage in some political action, but make no conscious decision about what their politics will be, or how far they will go in pursuing activist modes of political expression. At some point, however, they discover that they have changed in some qualitative way, that they are no longer what they were, and that they now conceive of themselves as "radicals" or "activists."

This discovery often provokes or heightens in the activist a sharp sense of commitment to act in behalf of his vision of a just society. As he pursues such action, and especially as he does so in the face of opposition, his sense of commitment often grows. So, too, do the consciousness and decisiveness with which he chooses to commit himself to specific acts of protest.

These spiraling acts of will and choice lead the activist to reject the society which harbors the evils he commits himself to extirpate. For each act of commitment is a promise to make any sacrifice necessary to demonstrate against social evils and to promote justice. Over time, these acts of commitment amount to a conscious decision to alter one's ways of thinking and acting and to pursue some vision of a good society in an activist way. And thus, over time, they define the activist as one in an adversary relationship to the larger society.

Such acts of commitment may be compared, in their total effect, to sudden and intense religious conversions, through which an individual perceives anew the evil in the world and dedicates himself to the way of righteousness. For there is in the character of radical protest today an almost religious fervor, as there has been in other college movements in other nations in other times. The religious parallel suggests itself, too, for the way it illumines the problem of responding to campus unrest. For just as it has never worked to send guns— or lions—against religious converts, so too has it been un-availing to meet campus activism with force. Force only tests the mettle of the activist's commitment and thus ends not by weakening the movement but by strengthening it.

The idea of commitment is central to an understanding of campus unrest in part because it accurately describes why a demonstration happened when it did. In a very real sense, the answer is that it happened because, for whatever complex or even accidental reasons, somebody or some group decided, against the background of a general vision of the good society and of effective political action, to commit himself or itself to a particular act, in a particular place, at a particular time. Thus, a radical commitment is as much a commitment to the act of protest itself as it is a commitment to certain positions on the issues and to a certain moral vision. Where issues are not compelling, there still may be protests. The upward spiral of protest reflects the intentions of the protestor as much as the circumstances and objects of his protest.

The notion of commitment helps to explain the escalation of tactics that occurred during the 1960's. For the radical commitment contains built-in dynamic processes which, in reaction to resistance, make opinions and tactical actions ever more radical.

Finally, students increasingly discovered that each issue was neither single nor simple. Once a student made the decision to be active, he became aware of the connectedness of all issues; and the more he saw, the more convinced he became that his stance was valid.

The University Environment

A university campus is an especially favorable place for those who wish to make such a commitment, for students and faculty can consider committing themselves in the almost certain knowledge that the act of commitment has no severe personal costs attached to it.

White students generally are freer than black students, nonstudents, and older people to act because they are subject to fewer competing commitments to family and job and because what job requirements they do have can be put aside at relatively little cost. This is also true of professors. But students especially may drop out of school, put off their studies for short or long periods, and delay taking examinations, without paying a great price.

The relative freedom of students to act without fear of immediate serious consequences is reinforced by the partial survival of the custom of treating students as adolescents who may be forgiven their errors. Students also benefit from the historic idea of university sanctuary, which would bar police and civil authority from enforcing law on campus except in extreme circumstances. Such norms, while never having the sanction of law in the United States as they have in other countries, have still had an influence.

Moreover, the erosion of the sense of community on many campuses has meant that fewer informal social controls are at work to deter students from engaging in new or unusual modes of behavior, even ones which may harm the university. There is less traditional school spirit, fewer personal relationships, more anonymity—and, therefore, fewer personal costs involved in the commitment to engage in radical action, or even in the decision to use the university as a means of furthering political ends.

Formal controls within the university—especially university disciplinary systems—have also grown weaker. At many universities today, students encounter little formal deterrence because university administrators and faculties have often failed to punish illegal acts. In part, this has been a result of their sympathy to student causes. It is certainly due as well to the feeling of outrage on the part of faculty members over the use of force against students by the police.

Just how sympathetic faculty members are to student unrest was suggested by a comprehensive survey conducted by the American Council on Education during 1967-68. It found that faculty members were involved in the planning of over half the student protests which occurred. (The vast majority of such protests were, of course, lawful and peaceful.) And in close to two thirds of them, faculty bodies passed resolutions approving of the protest.

The more general reason for the failure of the universities to preserve order and to discipline those who were disruptive or violent was that power in American universities is limited and diffuse. Their disciplinary and control measures were established on the assumption that the vast majority of faculty and students would be reasonable people who would support reasonable actions on common assumptions of what is reasonable, and that this majority would accept and support the specific goals of the university. These assumptions have become increasingly unrealistic.

Finally, the campus is a favorable environment for the growth of commitment and protest because the physical situation of the university makes it relatively easy to mobilize students with common sentiments and with a common predisposition to take direct political action. Their numbers serve to protect them from the isolation and criticism they would experience if they were dispersed throughout the larger society.

The increase in sheer numbers of students in the United States has magnified the significance of this fact. Only a small percentage of students on a campus of 20,000 or more are needed to create a very large demonstration. Thus, in 1965-66, although opinion polls indicated that the great majority of students still supported the Vietnam War and that antiwar sentiment was not more widespread among students than among the population as a whole, opposition on campus was able to have a disproportionate public impact because it was readily mobilized in protest demonstrations. Relatively small percentages of large student bodies have constituted the "masses" occupying administration buildings or bringing great universities to a halt.

Protest itself has become an activity accepted as proper and even honorable by the general student body. Students who are not participants in an act of protest will usually take no step to impede it—except sometimes in cases where violence is involved—and will seldom assist in imposing punishment upon their fellow students.

The Spiral of Commitment and Reaction

Within this unconstraining environment, then, many students freely committed themselves to the student movement. Those who did so were in turn subject to a number of evolutionary forces which tended to move their opinions and protest behavior toward the extreme.

To the extent that audience reaction was the proximate goal of student protest, the activists were at any given moment under a strong incentive to express themselves a little louder and a bit more forcefully than the last time—otherwise there was a possibility that people would become accustomed to acts of protest and begin to ignore them. Thus, the simple passing of time spurred the movement to go farther and farther afield of the tactics and perspectives of instrumentalist, reformist politics, and closer and closer to a thoroughgoing radical strategy.

A second dynamic at work in student activism arose out of frustration. In the struggle for desegregation in the South, activists had many successes. But a few years later, it had become only too clear that doing away with legalized segregation had not brought about genuine equality and integration. As the movement began carrying the fight for equality to the informal bases of discrimination, it met a growing political resistance. Social change of the magnitude in question takes a very long time even when all agree that there should be change. Yet patience has never been a characteristic of the young, and the deferment of gratification is something for which the student subculture has little sympathy.

In addition, there was growing frustration over the Vietnam War. With each instance of student protest, popular opposition to the war seemed to grow, and yet the war itself seemed no closer to an end.

Such frustrations were exasperating to energetic and impatient students. Their seeming failure—and it was only a seeming failure—to influence the course of events led them to adopt an ever more extreme view of the inadequacies of the American political system as a whole, and an ever more extreme way of expressing that view.

And there was a third dynamic operating within the movement. In any ideological group, the more extreme views and the more extremist members tend to wield disproportionate influence. For leaders are usually chosen because they embody and represent the values and qualities to which the group is dedicated. Thus, in activist groups, the leaders, who articulate members' views to the world at large and who interpret events to their followers, tend to be ideological purists.

Moreover, members of groups tend to talk in terms of what their group has uniquely in common, and that, for student activists, is their opposition to American society in its present form. Thus, as the group coalesces, as time passes, and as external hostility increases, that opposition becomes more important as a source of solidarity. As it becomes more important, views become more extreme.

As the student movement grew stronger, bolder, and more extreme, it began to encounter opposition—sometimes from within the university, but more often from outside it, especially in the form of the police or, less often, the National Guard. Often—usually as the result of some failure to control deadly weapons or the men carrying them—there was violence and injury, and on some occasions there was death. This developing opposition and its implementation by law enforcement provided the fourth dynamic at work in the evolution of student opinion and tactics toward the extreme.

The encounters usually had the effect not of intimidating student protestors but rather of angering and emboldening them. They seemed to dramatize the participants' initial commitments and to reinforce their sense of the irreversibility of that commitment.

Most of the deaths have been accidents in the sense that they did not reflect the intention or policy of police and Guard units; and many—but not all—have been accidents in the sense that the policemen and guardsmen immediately involved acted in fear or passion, or through authentic inadvertence. But the operating rules and routines of many police and Guard units have made the probability of accidental death higher. Inadequate or nonexistent programs in attitude training, crowd-control work, and command and control have made it more likely that police or guardsmen would break discipline and, in fear or anger, behave defensively and brutally. Routinely carrying rifles and bayonets and ammunition also increased the chances of an accident. Finally, rising tensions between student protestors and law enforcement officials also contributed to the likelihood of accident. For when students faced police, the confrontation was not only physical but also cultural and attitudinal. Hostilities and fears on both sides could become so great—especially when public rhetoric was growing hotter—that the probability of violence—with whatever weapons were at hand—became extremely high.

To recapitulate then: once the commitment was made, and once the protest organization was established, there were psychological and organizational mechanisms which would almost guarantee that it would persist. And more than persist: it was likely to become stronger. For the movement had its own culture, its solidarity, and its sense of being set apart from and against the outside society. It thus could easily interpret any event and any issue in ways that would contribute to the strengthening of the movement rather than to its weakening. Because the commitment was both for something and against something, either success or opposition was capable of intensifying it. Hostility and violent responses aided the movement, especially when, as often happened, they mobilized moderates. And each such event reinforced the intensifying and expanding student subculture, lent it greater solidarity, and led to a deeper alienation from American society. As the subculture coalesced in this way, student protest became less and less the result of specific issues or events, and more and more the expression of a generalized animus against the larger society.

EVOLUTIONARY CHANGES IN WESTERN SOCIETY

The final body of contributing causes of student unrest is the most difficult to formulate. These are certain broad, evolutionary changes occurring throughout the Western world, which has become a series of ever more complex and interconnected societies, organized in large-scale urban complexes, dependent on an increasingly sophisticated technology, dependent therefore upon education and especially upon the university, and increasingly susceptible to general immobilization or breakdown as a result of even tiny disturbances in any of its many subunits.

These long-range changes in society have created deep disaffection among youth, not only in the United States, but in most other Western countries as well. This wave of unrest has occurred while these societies are engaged in repairing many of the defects and evils for which social critics attacked them in the past. They are withdrawing or have withdrawn from their overseas colonies. They are engaged in extending the welfare features of their societies. They are giving increased attention to the problem of equality in income and in education. Thus, we do not deal with any simple revolt against the "evils of capitalism," as may be indicated by the fact that, in other countries as in this one, it is a revolt of middle-class rather than working-class youth.

What we face is a revolt among educated youth against certain features of liberal democratic capitalism—especially "the affluent society." There is growing opposition to the emphasis on material goods. Thus, French students proclaimed opposition to a "consumer" society, and American students, by their dress, their attitude toward material goods, and their direct statements, also express opposition to their society's emphasis on consumption. This opposition is not yet fully consistent, for critics of consumer society also see as one of its chief defects its failure to supply sufficient consumer goods to some strata of society. Nevertheless, the consumer goods criticism is real and strongly felt.

We may also point to a nascent—if still largely implicit—opposition to democracy which is beginning to receive serious formulation by some political theorists. The youth most active in the unrest now tend to feel that determination of political representation or policies by simple measures such as one man, one vote may be inadequate, and that the human qualities of the representatives and policies thus adopted must play a role in their acceptance. A rather elaborate critique of democracy from the left has been developed by one contemporary radical philosopher, Herbert Marcuse, and he and others have also attacked the virtue of tolerance in the present society.

A third aspect of what we might call Western, capitalist, liberal society to which many young people are now hostile is the emphasis on effort, disciplined work, and the mechanisms that encourage it and reward it. This is seen in the insistence that everyone should do "his own thing" and more that he should not suffer for it.

It would be an illusion to see this as being directed simply against some of the errors of this kind of society. This attack is directed as strongly—even *more* strongly—against those features of this kind of society that most of us consider virtues: its capacity to improve the material condition of people; its dependence on democracy and tolerance; its capacity to evoke work and effort and to reward work and effort.

Thus, the possibility cannot be overlooked that the true causes of the events we today characterize as "campus unrest" lie deep in the social and economic patterns that have been building in Western industrial society for a hundred years or more. It is at least remarkable that so many of the themes of the new international youth culture appear to revolve in one way or another about the human costs of technology and urban life, and how often they seem to echo a yearning to return to an ancient and simpler day.

End Note

Our theme in this chapter has been that the root causes for what we call campus unrest are exceedingly complex, are deeply planted in basic social and philosophic movements, and are not only nationwide but also worldwide.

Given this view of the matter, how should the United States and American society deal with the problems of campus unrest, react to them, respond to them?

First, much good can be done through more understanding and better understanding. Substantive differences divide the proponents of the new culture from those of traditional American society. Superficial differences in style also separate them. But in addition to these differences, unnecessary tensions emerge from simple misunderstanding of one another. A large crowd of students may well appear threatening to others when it is in fact a normal gathering for communication. Language that affronts may have had no such intent. The university administrator who seeks to explain how and why a particular decision was made through a complex series of committee decisions is not by that fact giving a bureaucratic runaround to his inquirer. Understanding does not obliterate differences. But understanding can reduce incidents and clashes and the risks of greater distrust and violence.

Second, teachers, scholars, and parents may well find many of the adherents of the new culture to be inexperienced in affairs, impatient of explanations, uninformed about the world, rude and arrogant in their self-righteousness, and insufficiently alive to the importance of vital principles and ideals that are not central to the new youth culture. The only answer here is to seek to teach, to educate, and to inform. And in turn, the students will be found to have the capacity on some matters to educate and enlarge the perspective of the older generation.

Beyond that, it must be stressed again that much of what is commonly called "campus unrest" is not a problem. It is a condition. If a generation of American students are emerging to full adulthood affected in varying degrees by a different world view and a different set of values, accommodations to their perspectives can be made only over a long period of time and through the operation of the political process. In that case, we can only hope, and try to insure, that the American political system will continue to assist the peaceful coexistence or blending of different life styles.

To the extent that campus unrest is caused by particular governmental policies and university practices, we are, however, presented with operational choices. Movement by the government along the lines suggested in Chapter 7, and reforms by universities along the lines suggested in Chapter 6, would, we believe, have a corresponding mitigating effect in the long run upon campus unrest. In a somewhat different way, adoption of the more particular recommendations set forth in Chapters 4 and 5, concerning the response of universities and civil authorities to campus disorders, would have a salutary effect in reducing levels of tension.

Where campus dissent ignites into illegal disorder, violence, or terrorism, the response must be prompt and effective enforcement of the law, as is fully developed in Chapters 4 and 5.

3

The Black
Student Movement

In the preceding chapter we call attention to the pressing problems of American society as contributing causes of campus unrest. The status of black Americans and other nonwhite minorities is the central social and political problem of American society. As we have noted, student protest began in 1960 over the issue of "racism," and the definition of this issue has passed through several phases during the last decade.

In 1944, Gunnar Myrdal called this nation's race problem an American dilemma. In 1970, many people—black and white—regard this problem as an American crisis.

The mood, attitudes, aspirations, and goals of black students—and of Blacks in general—have changed substantially since the civil rights demonstrations began in 1960. In one decade the basic thrust of black protest, and especially black student protest, has shifted profoundly.

We devote special attention to the black student movement for the purpose of portraying the mood, attitudes, and aspirations of black students.

The Nature of Black Student Protest

If the emergence of a "new culture" has played an

important role in campus unrest and student protest generally, still another cultural strain has played a major role in campus unrest and protest and will continue to be a factor in American higher education and in the larger society. This cultural strain grows out of the black presence in a predominantly white society and is the driving force among black students and, to an increasingly larger extent, among Blacks who are not students.

Blacks have been in America since 1619. They brought with them a culture, a history, an identity, and a perception of the world which were not European but African. The institution of slavery and a variety of customs and practices revolving around race and color valuations attempted to obliterate the cultural roots and historical antecedents of American Blacks over the next three centuries. Not assimilated into the mainstream, but rather segregated and discriminated against, black Americans were largely conditioned to despise their original homeland and to deprecate their color and everything related to Blackness. To be black was to be inferior; in order to overcome inferiority one had to emulate white culture, ape or imitate white society, and embrace Anglo-Saxon values and norms.

In the mid-1960's, this "bondage of the spirit" was broken, and there emerged among black students a deep and intense awareness and consciousness that a Black culture existed. They came to realize that Africa was not a savage land of ignorant people without a civilization; and that black people in America possessed in their own right a history, a life experience, and a world view peculiarly American, but with roots in Africa rather than in Europe—a culture that could be called "Afro-American."

This discovery has largely shaped the black student movement today, but that movement has also been shaped by the reaction and response of white America to the discovery.

Black pride, Black identity, Black unity, Black power, Black self-determination, and Black survival are not idealistic and romantic notions to black students. Rather, they are fundamentally existential expressions which give meaning, direction, purpose, and vitality to the contemporary Black struggle.

With the heightened awareness and consciousness of being black, students and others have also become increasingly aware of white racism and have begun to react more militantly against it.

Racism, in all of its varied institutionalized forms, was not a new discovery by Blacks. Its existence in America has been pervasive and has shaped and governed the American experience since even before the founding of the Republic. But in the mid-1960's, with the dawn of Black consciousness, a new generation of young Blacks began the pursuit of social justice—the pursuit of equity and parity in the American society. They began to demand access to, and participation in, all of the opportunities, rewards, benefits, and powers of America—not on the basis of race or even of citizenship, but on the basis of their very humanity. In the movement for civil rights, one could say that the battle was fought largely in terms of being American citizens, but in the new and developing struggle for social justice, it is regarded as being waged in terms of being human beings.

Black student unrest is, therefore, not identical with white student unrest, and cannot be seen as simply "campus unrest." It extends beyond the college and university campus and, in varying degrees, involves the total black population of America.

It is for this reason that one black educator has written:

"Campus unrest" among black students has its genesis in and is related to the total socioeconomic situation of Black Americans in 1970.

It represents in microcosm the macrocosm of opinion, feelings and attitudes of the black communities in general across the country. The frustration, anger, outrage, fears and anxieties of black students are expressive of the same feelings and emotions which exist among a large spectrum of the black population—

"moderate" as well as "militant." Today there is not an appreciable difference between the feelings and attitudes of these generalized categories; the principal difference may lie in the degree of faith each has in the ability and willingness of the [federal] government to be responsive to the legitimate goals and aspirations of Black Americans.

Black students and black institutions of higher learning also must be understood and seen in the context of the overall contemporary struggle of Black Americans.

Members of the Commission have been exposed to a wide spectrum of opinions and convictions from black students and other black Americans. We believe the above assessment to be essentially correct, and we are compelled to warn the nation that what is at stake is the stability of our social order, the fulfillment of the American promise, and the realization of the American possibility. This promise must be fulfilled and this possibility realized not just for some Americans, but for all Americans.

The National Advisory Commission on Civil Disorders sought to direct our nation's attention to the prospect of our nation moving toward two societies: one dominant and superior, the other subordinate and inferior.

We wish to call attention to the fact that, as a nation, we are now and always have been two societies. Segregation and discrimination, whether *de facto* or *de jure*, have served to keep America's black citizens in a condition of economic disadvantage, cultural exclusion, social ostracism, political disenfranchisement, and educational inequality.

Few white Americans understand the depth of alienation and bitterness among black students, including those who are considered moderate. A group of 22 Congressmen who visited more than 50 universities across the nation in 1969 found a depth of bitterness among black students at black institutions that surpassed anything found among white students:

The black student expresses bitterness about our system from personal experience. Many white students expressed concern about problems such as discrimination, poverty and hunger, but unlike the black students, most of them stated they had not personally experienced these problems. As more than one black student said—"You have to be black to understand."

A substantial number of black students at predominately black institutions stated that they have lost faith in our political system, which over the years has promised them much, but in their opinion, delivered little. They say there "are political wolves in the South and political foxes in the North." Many of the blacks want desperately to believe in the system, but can see no real progress being made. Their problem is more external than internal. They are concerned about non-college problems which they identified as discrimination, economic oppression, loss of identity, poverty, hunger and racism. They ask to be respected and desire true economic opportunity. Words and promises will no longer suffice.

. . . The main goal of the majority of black students seems to be service to their "black brothers and sisters." Some said that they would rather die for their people in the streets of the United States than in Vietnam.

. . . The primary concern of minority students is to acquire the kind of education they perceive as essential to being able to return to their communities and better the conditions of their people. They want their education to provide the training they need to deal with the problems of minority groups in America, and they see higher education as the best avenue to their personal development.

. . . It is important to make a clear distinction between the purposes and goals of black militant students and white revolutionaries. Aside from similarities in tactics, there are substantial differences. Without doubt, the alienation and bitterness among some black students is so great that they have completely lost faith in the ability of the nation to remove obstacles to full equality . . . . Many black student activists on predominantly white campuses, however, appear to be seeking to reform the university, to make it better suited to serve their needs and desires, to create the mechanism for training students from minority groups to go back into their communities to deal with major social and economic problems, and not to destroy the university. This is in contrast to the goal of destroying the institution held by some white and black revolutionaries. Thus black student militants have held the white revolutionaries at arm's length—forming alliances when useful but preserving their separate identity and independence. By the same token, the formal involvement of black student groups in issues not directly related to minority student problems has been, in most cases, limited.

One black student on a campus visited by members of the Commission staff explained that most black students did not participate in the strike at his college in May after the deaths at Kent State because they felt that, "although it was relevant, it wasn't as relevant as some other things." As he stated it:

They feel stuff like this had been happening to black people for God knows how long. So, it wasn't anything new to them.

I'm positive that like what happens on the college scene is not separable from what happens in the community . . . . Since coming to college, I'm becoming more enlightened, more conscious of problems outside the problems right here on campus . . . .

I kind of feel like if you're black, no matter where you

go, no matter what you do, you're going to run into problems that are common to Blacks everywhere. It's something you just can't forget. I know I can't forget it and I don't want to forget it. I have visions of trying to do something to help improve conditions of black people here in this country.

Following the deaths of two black youths at Jackson State last May, the president, faculty, and students of a prominent, predominantly black university in the South issued a public statement in which they stated that in a time of grave social turmoil, "the image of a university as an ivy-covered refuge is a luxury neither institutions of higher learning nor the nation itself can afford." The statement asserted that a fundamental aspect of the present crisis in which the nation is embroiled is "racism with its evils of oppression of minorities and their consequent alienation." And the statement went on to declare:

... This university recognizes its responsibility in helping the nation understand the implications of racism and in encouraging men of reason and goodwill to marshal their resources in defense of human dignity.

... The history of Black people in the United States has been marked by organized terror and violence perpetrated upon them by whites acting both on behalf of the government and as private citizens. The arrival of Black people on these shores as parcels of white men's property was in a real sense the beginning of a series of well calculated measures designed to exploit and oppress them. This exploitation and oppression, characterized by violence and terror, has continued virtually unabated, varying only in intensity.

Events of recent months suggest that a rapid intensification of the violence and terror directed against Black people is occurring. Governmental authorities, nationally and locally, are using their powers to thwart the legitimate aspirations of Black people, and this, in turn, precipitates greater violence directed against them by private individuals and groups.

. . . In the current era of systematic repression of Black people, police authorities are wantonly shooting down Black men, women, and children while elected officials both national and local, by their outrageously false and inflammatory public utterances, fan the fires of hatred and bigotry. Black people are being heinously murdered, as in the Algiers Motel in Detroit, at South Carolina State College in Orangeburg, in Augusta, Georgia, and at Jackson State College in Mississippi. The Black Panther Party is being deliberately persecuted by state and national forces acting in tandem: a Federal grand jury has confirmed the summary execution of Panthers by police in Chicago.

The conclusion is obvious. In the face of an apparent incompatibility of Black aspirations for political and economic liberation and the maintenance of a capitalistic system grounded in the doctrine of white supremacy, white governments and individuals have resorted to organized coercion to suppress the Black community. This is genocide. Victims of this oppression, wherever they may be, along with other men of goodwill must join together to halt this brutal assault. We, the students, faculty, and administration . . . urge strongly that action be taken immediately.

On May 20, fifteen black college presidents met with the President of the United States and expressed their feelings and those of their students to him in a formal statement, subsequently made public, that stated in part:

We come to express the anger, outrage and frustration of the Black people of this nation. We wish to convey to you the disenchantment of Blacks, especially Black youth, with our society and with the Federal Government.

This feeling is engendered by a number of longstanding conditions: manifestations of racism in all areas of

American life, inadequate educational opportunities for Blacks and other disadvantaged minorities; widespread poverty and hunger in this affluent nation; high unemployment rates among the Blacks and racial discrimination in employment; racial differentials in law enforcement procedures; and deplorable housing conditions. While there has been improvement in many of these areas over the years, progress has been all too slow.

On July 3, 1970, a group of 50 prominent black clergymen representing a variety of denominations, diverse affiliations, and various parts of the country, published a full-page advertisement in *The New York Times*, entitled a "Black Declaration of Independence." It began by calling attention to the conditions under which Blacks were brought to America and recited the essential Black experience over a period of 351 years. It declared:

Whenever any form of government, or any variety of established traditions and systems of the Majority becomes destructive of Freedom and of legitimate Human Rights, it is the Right of the Minorities to use every necessary and accessible means to protest and to disrupt the machinery of oppression, and so to bring such general distress and discomfort upon the oppressor as to the offended Minorities shall seem most appropriate and most likely to effect a proper adjustment of the society.

Their statement concluded with these words:

We, therefore, the Black People of the United States of America, in all parts of this Nation, appealing to the Supreme Judge of the World for the Rectitude of our Intentions, do, in the Name of our good People and our own Black Heroes—Richard Allen, James Varick, Absalom Jones, Nat Turner, Frederick Douglass, Marcus Garvey, Malcolm X, Martin Luther King, Jr., and all Black People past and present, great and small—

Solemnly Publish and Declare, that we shall be, and of Right ought to be, FREE AND INDEPENDENT FROM THE INJUSTICE, EXPLOITATIVE CONTROL, INSTITUTIONALIZED VIOLENCE AND RACISM OF WHITE AMERICA, that unless we receive full Redress and Relief from these Inhumanities we will move to renounce all Allegiance to this Nation, and will refuse, in every way, to cooperate with the Evil which is Perpetrated upon ourselves and our Communities. And for the support of this Declaration, with a firm Reliance on the Protection of divine Providence, we mutually pledge to each other our Lives, our Fortunes and our sacred Honor.

Increasing numbers of white Americans have recognized and expressed these sentiments. As Robert Rankin of the Danforth Foundation testified before the Commission:

No group in America, I dare say, knows the truth . . . regarding student discontent and despair about our society, better than the black students of this country who [are] suffering the continuing humiliation of racism, a beast in our midst whose claws create incalculable damage to the souls, bodies and minds of men, black and white.

When one examines black protests on campus throughout the past two years, the main target of those protests—nearly always precise and concrete in objective contrast to the cosmic scope of white radical protest—is our persistently racist society. In some instances it has become the object of such unbridled hatred and rage among young persons who have lost all of their patience waiting for fair treatment, that black students are perfectly prepared to risk their security and their lives to destroy its dreadful presence. America's hypocrisies and contradictions in race relations must be designated as one of the major causes of violence on the campus.

. . . The American people have not experienced repression before. The German people have. We have not.

Suddenly we find ourselves in a situation where a new factor has entered into the cultural and historical mix, a new fear which we don't comprehend, and which may be deeply damaging to the soul of this nation. I think, yes, it is new rather than old and I would appeal to this Commission to do its utmost to cope with a force which could be ravishing to the American spirit.

And Dr. Margaret Walker Alexander—poet, novelist, a native black Mississippian—expressed to the Commission how she felt:

I believe that it is no secret in this country that our society in the last few years has become largely a polarized society, and our people feel that we are further apart insofar as races are concerned than ever before. And I feel young people especially are aware of this and that our young people feel that we have reached a point of no return, a kind of impasse, that unless something happens to remedy the situation—and remedy isn't going to be enough to give black people in the country a real sense of relief not only of oppression, but repression.

I am afraid that I am hopeless, too. I think it is almost like a farce that we are going through. We black people—I don't speak for anyone, I am speaking personally and in my personal opinion; I don't represent any particular group—but as a black woman observing the conditions in the country, it would seem to me that we are in a terrible state. It goes beyond my understanding, it goes beyond a sense of enmity. We are in a state of crisis, of tremendous crisis in this country. And we are observing a crisis in every phase of the so-called American way of life and as such, black people feel it more keenly because we are the ones who suffer most under it.

Our history indicates that we have the problems of education and housing and living, jobs, employment, everything. We feel these things, the problems, much more keenly than others.

I am afraid to say that—in fact, I do not see it is any better. As a matter of fact, it is a tragic situation for us and the incidents we see around us, the problem, sporadic spurts of violence everywhere, not just in our own state and in our own community, indicate that there is real trouble, that this country is in real trouble. If we go back into the history of the problem of race in this country—and I could go back as far back or as recently as one would desire—everything has conspired to lead us to a more tragic condition than we have already witnessed . . . .

I thought a few years ago, I thought during the sixties when we were making the strong push towards civil rights, I thought in the days of Dr. Martin Luther King and some of the others, that the conscience of America had been aroused and there might be hope. I thought then that if there were changes in the country, if you looked for better housing, or if you looked for schools being built, over a period of 35 years, it looked as if the South were getting better and the North was getting worse, as they looked at the big northern cities and looked at the southern states.

But I have come to the conclusion today that the whole country is in the same boat. I don't think things are getting better for us now, no.

We cite these examples of diverse representations to illustrate the gravity of the racial crisis. The testimony is voluminous. Numerous letters, faculty and student position papers, books, articles, and other published materials stating the same basic theme have come to the Commission's attention. The language that is used is sharp and cutting. These are words most Americans do not wish to hear.

Although these attitudes may not represent the attitudes of all the nation's black citizens, they are sufficiently widespread among black students, black leaders, and others to give us concern and to lead us to urge that appropriate remedies be enacted immediately.

The conditions in America that provide the context in which black student unrest exists, and against which black students protest, were described by the National Advisory Commission on Civil Disorders in its report of 1968. That Commission found conditions resulting from white racism to be the essential cause of urban disorders. These conditions—"massive concentration of impoverished Negroes," "pervasive discrimination and segregation," and intersection of "segregation and poverty" within "teeming racial ghettos"—are still a vivid and harsh reality to black students and the black masses. In the judgment of that Commission, a number of forces, including "frustrated hopes," "legitimation of violence," and "powerlessness," catalyzed these conditions to produce the disruptions during the summer of 1967. The effects of these disorders and the conditions underlying them have created a new mood among Blacks, especially among black youth.

The new mood among Blacks is revealed most clearly in a *Time*-Louis Harris poll conducted this year and published in *Time* on April 6, 1970.

The poll revealed that black people's "pride in themselves and in their culture" is now a pervasive reality. Eighty-five per cent of those surveyed strongly endorsed Black Studies programs in high schools and colleges, and regarded such programs as an "important sign of Black identity and pride." Among the high-priority steps that Blacks felt were necessary to achieve full equality in the next ten years were: "achieving equal educational opportunities with whites," "greater unity among Blacks," and "continuing to push and fight."

In the first part of 1970, as this poll revealed, the mood of Blacks generally could be described as "more militant, more hopeful and more determined." Most black students do have tremendous faith in the federal government, but they also are deeply frustrated over what they sense to be government's unwillingness to attack social conditions that divide the nation and deprive a significant segment of its population of full and equal participation in all aspects of American life.

Among Blacks, a strong feeling of identification with Africa, with Africans, and with people of African descent all over the world, is emerging. Under the concept of "Pan-Africanism," this identification is being explored in many forms: dress; hair styles; learning African languages; learning and appreciating African art, music, and other artistic expression; attending Pan-African Conferences; and developing new methods to express their African goals and aspirations.

But overall, the greatest emphasis is being given to building the black community through strengthening and developing black institutions. Many black students say that the days of marching in the street singing "We Shall Overcome" are over, that such "civil rights" styles of protest and demonstration in 1970 have no purpose or function in achieving the ends black people seek.

There is no student organization today comparable to the Student Nonviolent Coordinating Committee in the 1960's. But there does exist a developing spiritual and ethnic identity that gives black students a sense of unity and oneness among themselves and with other Blacks.

No one can predict what form student protest may take among black students. But in terms of achieving equity in all areas of American life, black students and their parents are emphasizing more and more the value and significance of acquiring an education, and the necessity for that education to be relevant to the life situation and needs of black people.

It would appear, therefore, that colleges and universities will increasingly be at the center and not on the periphery of the "Black struggle."

The Status of Blacks in Higher Education

Education, and especially higher education, has served as an instrument of social mobility for every American ethnic group—except for black Americans and other similarly disadvantaged minorities.

Despite the nation's growing commitment to universal access to college education, and the openness of the American system of higher education, the socioeconomic status and inferior schooling of America's Blacks have prevented many Blacks from attending college. As in other areas of American life, the status of Blacks in higher education remains one of inequity and disprivilege.

The critical importance of higher education for Blacks in their struggle for social justice is revealed by the fact that almost all recent surveys indicate that "getting an education" or "going to college" is given the first priority as the surest and most secure route for changing the economic, social, political, and cultural status of Blacks in the society.

The *Time*-Louis Harris survey conducted in April 1970 revealed that 97 per cent of young Blacks planned to complete high school and 67 per cent expected to go to college.

Despite the strong faith in education and the extraordinary desire or expectation of young Blacks to attend college, current data indicate that only 58 per cent of black school children complete the eighth grade while 73 per cent of white school children do so. Only about 40 per cent of black teenagers complete high school, compared to 62 per cent of white teenagers; and only 22 per cent of black young people of college age are enrolled in college, compared to 38 per cent of white youth of college age.

Although black college enrollment has doubled since 1964, the proportion of Blacks among college students has not significantly increased: in 1964, black students constituted approximately 5 per cent of the total national enrollment; by 1969, the proportion of black students had grown to 6 per cent. And from 1940 through 1969, the percentage of black men and women in the age group 25-34 with four or more years of college increased less than the percentage of whites of the same age group. The gap between the level of higher education for Blacks and whites, so wide at the beginning of the thirty-year period, has grown even wider. That fact is more significant than the numerical increase in black college enrollment.

This gap is underscored by data in the *Manpower Report of the President* which show that between 1964 and 1968 the total of nonwhite college-trained males in the labor force rose by 13,000 (from 266,000 to 279,000), a gain of slightly less than 5 per cent. In the same period the number of college-trained working white males increased by almost one million (from 5.158 million to 6.076 million), or nearly 18 per cent.

Additional evidence of the educational disparity between Blacks and whites comes from the joint publication of the U.S. Census Bureau and the Bureau of Labor Statistics, *The Social and Economic Status of Negroes in the United States, 1969.* It indicates that in 1969 about one black male in fourteen in the age group 25-34 claimed a college education as compared to one in five among white males of the same age group.

At the graduate level, in 1969 the nation's Blacks accounted for less than 1 per cent of doctoral candidates, only 2 per cent of the law students, and 2.5 per cent of medical students.

The general situation is this: Although Blacks made up 12 per cent of the college-eligible age group in 1969, only 6 per cent of the students enrolled in colleges were black. When one considers the future, it must also be kept in mind that 14 per cent of all children now in elementary and secondary school are black and that approximately 16 per cent of preschool children are black. Almost half of all black Americans are now under the age of 20. Overall, the black population is younger and has a higher fertility rate than the white population. It is likely that this trend will continue, and it is possible that it may increase.

In considering the status of Blacks in higher education, it must also be noted that black students are poorer economically and less well prepared educationally than are white college students, a condition reflecting the economic and educational status of Blacks generally.

We also cannot overlook the fact that in spite of the overwhelming desire and expectation of black youth to attend college, the end result is not equity and parity, but further disprivilege and disparity. In 1968, a black high school graduate earned less on the average ($5,801) than a white male who had completed only grade school ($6,452), and a Black who had completed four or more years of college earned less than a white who had completed only high school.

In sum, the status of Blacks in higher education adds up to one of the most glaring inequities in American life: an inequality of quantity as well as an inequality of quality.

The Nation's Black Colleges and Universities

If the inequality of quantity can be demonstrated by the numbers of Blacks having access and entry into college, the inequality of quality is revealed by the fact that half of the total black college enrollment in 1969-70 was in the nation's 123 predominantly black colleges and universities. Taken collectively, these institutions are among the most impoverished and deprived of any group of American institutions of higher learning. And yet, in 1969, they enrolled approximately 50 per cent of the black college students and, in 1968, accounted for 80 per cent of the degrees awarded to black students.

These colleges and universities have survived economic adversity, neglect, and even hostility to the notion of providing higher learning for Blacks. Their very survival—in some cases for more than a century—is an achievement of significance. In a draft of a preliminary report concerning black colleges prepared by the Carnegie Commission on Higher Education, their importance is aptly summarized:

The colleges founded for Negroes are both a source of pride to blacks who have attended them and a source of hope to black families who want the benefits of higher learning for their children. They have exercised leadership in developing educational opportunities of young blacks at all levels of instruction, and, especially in the South, they are still regarded as key institutions for enhancing the general quality of the lives of black Americans.

This same draft report goes on to highlight their specific accomplishments:

Among their 385,000 alumni are substantial numbers of the country's black government officials, army officers, professors, doctors, lawyers, and members of other professions.

They have prepared most of the teachers employed for the education of many generations of Negro children in the South. One-third of all principals and one-half of all teachers in public schools in Mississippi are graduates of one Negro college—Jackson State.

They have acquired extensive experience in providing higher education for students who come to them underprepared by reason of inadequate prior schooling.

They have an outstanding record of recruiting and educating students from low-income families. Today, the average family income of students in Negro colleges is less than $4,000.

The plight and prospects of black colleges and universities have been well documented. During the 1960's, they were extensively studied by the federal government, special commissions, philanthropic groups, and private consulting firms.

These colleges and universities have a special importance because of their location (the majority are in the South and border states), the student population they serve, and their strategic significance in helping to further accommodate and accelerate the full drive toward social justice and racial equality.

In comparison to many predominantly white institutions, black colleges and universities have been relatively free of student protest leading to disruption or violence. They have been, and continue to be, however, campuses of active ferment and deep unrest.

With the heightened social tension existing in the nation, the exacerbation of feelings on both sides of the racial line, and the militancy and determination of their students, these black colleges and universities demand the attention of all Americans in the 1970's.

Throughout this report we have called attention to the presence of the "Black issue" in campus unrest and protest. A study by the Urban Research Corporation of incidents of student protest on 232 campuses in 1969, reported that "Black recognition" was the principal cause of campus protests. It was an issue on 59 per cent of the campuses and in 49 per cent of the incidents. Specific issues included: "provide more courses on Black studies," 32 per cent; "increase numbers of Black students," 24 per cent; "hire more Black faculty and staff," 23 per cent; "end discrimination and honor Blacks," 15 per cent; "provide more facilities for Black students," 9 per cent; "increase Black representation on general committees," 8 per cent; and "support off-campus Black power" and "hire Black employees," 4 per cent.

Most of the incidents reported by the Urban Research Corporation were at predominantly white institutions in the North. But similar attitudes and issues are also present among black students in black colleges and universities. And the number of incidents of protest on these black campuses is increasing.

We have noted that, with students' heightened awareness of being black, has come an increased sensitivity to the implications and realities of being black in predominantly white America. For a black student in a predominantly black institution, the "Black condition" is thrown into bold relief. Typically, the black student is surrounded by poverty and deprivation—from his own personal situation to the situation of the institution he attends.

The American Council on Education's 1968 survey of the

national college population discloses in capsule form the background of students attending black colleges:

* Freshmen in black colleges are distinctly of nonurban backgrounds; only 19.5 per cent of the men are from large cities, but 38 per cent are from farm or small-town backgrounds and the remainder largely from medium-sized towns.

* About 60 per cent of all freshmen in black colleges have fathers who did not complete high school and 27 per cent have fathers with grammar school education or less. This may be compared with the 25 per cent of white freshmen whose fathers did not complete high school. Fifty per cent of the black freshmen have mothers who did not finish high school while this is true of only 20 per cent of white freshmen.

* The occupational status of fathers of freshmen at black colleges reflects their educational deprivation. The fathers of freshmen at black colleges are overwhelmingly unskilled or semiskilled: 50.6 per cent of the men (43.2 per cent of the women) entering black colleges have fathers in these occupational categories. The fathers of black freshmen are three times as likely to be semiskilled or unskilled as fathers of white freshmen.

* The income of the parents of students at black colleges is, like their education, significantly below that of white students. Thus 62.3 per cent of the freshmen in Negro colleges had parents with less than $6,000 income in 1968, while only 13 per cent of white freshmen had parents in this income bracket.

In addition to their economic deprivation, black students on the whole are less well prepared in basic verbal and quantitative learning skills than white students because of the inferior quality of the public schools they attend. Compounding this problem is the relative impoverishment of the black institutions in financial, physical, and human resources.

Because these institutions draw most of their students from low-income families, their tuition charges are low, their charges for auxiliary services (room and board) are kept at a minimum, and the need to provide financial aid to students is enormously large. The average educational and general expenditure per student is considerably lower than that at white institutions of comparable size and type of control.

Faculty salaries are extremely low. On the rating scale—which ranges from AA (the highest rating) to E (the lowest rating)—used by the American Association of University Professors to measure the average compensation of faculty, only one predominantly black university has achieved a rating as high as B, and only three other black institutions participating in the AAUP survey reported an average compensation as high as $12,000 per year.

Adequate financial resources do not guarantee educational quality, but adequate educational quality cannot be attained and maintained without sufficient financial resources.

Black institutions do not have wealthy alumni; their endowments are extremely small or nonexistent; foundation and corporation support and aid from the federal government are relatively low.

A recent report of the Federal Interagency Committee on Education (FICE) shows that, although the total federal outlay to higher education in 1969 was over $4 billion, only $119 million—representing 3.5 per cent of the total—went to predominantly black colleges and universities.

One hundred colleges and universities received 66 per cent of a federal outlay of $3.4 billion to institutions of higher education in fiscal 1968, according to the National Science Foundation. Only one predominantly black university was among the group of 100, and that university ranked 43rd on the list.

The predominantly black land-grant college suffers discrimination in financing at both the state and federal level. Federal and state aid to predominantly white land-grant institutions totals $650 million a year, while the predominantly black land-grant colleges in the same states receive only slightly more than $70 million. In terms of amount per student, the aid is $2,300 in the predominantly white land-grant colleges, but less than $1,365 in the predominantly black land-grant colleges.

Earl McGrath, in his landmark study, *The Predominantly Negro Colleges and Universities in Transition*, published five years ago, summed up the situation exceedingly well:

> ... anyone who thinks that a significant percentage of [black colleges] can be substantially helped by an expenditure of a few million dollars sadly deludes himself. The presently predominantly Negro colleges will need several hundred million dollars in the next five or ten years merely to keep step with the growing needs of their potential student bodies and the unprecedented advancements in higher education .... Anything less than such efforts will result in continuing restrictions nearly as demeaning and privational as segregation itself.

Recently the question has often been raised as to whether it is a wise social policy to attempt to maintain colleges and universities that have such critical deficiencies in financial, human, and physical resources.

In answer to this question, we must note, first, that these institutions are suffering foremost from the lingering legacy of their history of neglect and deprivation. If young black people are to receive higher education in the same proportion to the number of Blacks in their age group as white people do, these institutions should be enrolling twice the present number of students.

Second, we must observe that, given the increasing demand for higher education on the part of Blacks, predominantly white colleges and universities are not likely to be able to expand their enrollments at a rate sufficient to the need.

Third, we must emphasize the critical importance of strengthening and further developing all institutions and resources related to, identified with, and capable of, serving the needs of black Americans. The predominantly black colleges and universities are among the most promising and strategic of these resources and institutions.

Another question frequently raised is whether the strengthening of predominantly black colleges and universities would, in effect, be supporting and continuing "segregated" higher education.

In response to such a question the following observations are pertinent:

Although most of the black colleges and universities were created to serve the educational needs of black Americans, they have never been segregating institutions. From the beginning, all have had white faculty members and almost all still do. Many have had white presidents. Traditionally they have enrolled proportionately more nonblack students than white colleges and universities enroll nonwhites. Among institutions of higher learning, they are the most open and nondiscriminatory in the appointment of faculty and in the admission of students.

Second, continued inequity in the distribution of financial resources is guaranteed to worsen the deprivation and relative weakness of these institutions. Strengthening them through increased financial support will enable them not only substantially to improve their overall academic quality, but also to develop elements of originality and distinctiveness sufficient to attract students from a diversity of social and ethnic backgrounds.

And third, it must be acknowledged candidly that "integration," by definition and in practice, cannot be allowed to be a process that moves only in one direction—of Blacks integrating with whites. It must also involve whites integrating with Blacks. The latter will occur in higher education only when and if black institutions are made capable of offering quality education on a par with comparable institutions that are predominantly or historically white.

In our judgment, the question of the future usefulness and ability of predominantly black colleges and universities transcends the integration-segregation issue and relates primarily to the question of quality education.

The national interest requires the existence of institutions of higher learning that are excellent by any measure, that are not wedded to any political, nationalistic, or racist ideology, but are identified—unashamedly and without apology—with the black communities, and integrally bound up with the quest and struggle of black Americans to establish themselves as an integral part of America's educational, economic, political, and cultural life.

The success of this quest and the positive outcome of this struggle are possible only through strengthening predominantly black institutions—including the colleges and universities. We therefore recommend that all Americans accept and support such institutions.

If public policy were formulated and executed with the objective of substantially improving the status of black young people in higher education and the condition of predominantly black colleges and universities, the nation would take a giant step toward the ultimate objective of freedom and equality of opportunity necessary for the attainment of the goals of black students and the realization of their aspirations.

The Goals and Aspirations of Black Students and Black Institutions

The contemporary "Black struggle" is diverse in its leadership, and no single strategy or set of tactics has yet emerged to which all black leaders subscribe. Nevertheless, there is a strong commitment among black students and many young black intellectuals to what is referred to as "liberation" and "transformation."

These are relatively new concepts in the vocabulary of the Black movement, and whether they will take roots and help to shape the future course of Black activism cannot now be determined. It is important to underscore, however, that these concepts and their application to the Black struggle appear to be gaining increasing affirmation among many Blacks and are replacing such concepts as "integration" and "assimilation."

Integration, as currently defined and carried out, appears to many young Blacks to be a doctrine and practice of white supremacy. In their view, integration means the destruction of all things Black and the exaltation of all things white, and thus perpetuates the notion that only what is white-controlled, white-determined, and white-led has validity and significance in American society.

Thus when Blacks speak of "liberation" they use the term in its literal sense: to free from domination and oppression. Their aim is to bring about a condition in which all Blacks—without regard to economic status or position—are free to compete on equal terms with all other Americans for access to the opportunities, rewards, benefits, and powers of American society.

For many if not most black students, the integrationist-separatist dichotomy—now prominent in discussions of the historic race problem—is irrelevant to the fundamental issue of whether black Americans will be accorded the same rights and privileges as other Americans and whether they—as a people—will be accorded the rights and privileges due them as human beings.

"Integration" as the ultimate goal for America to pursue is not disavowed, but there is insistence upon the fact that America today is a "pluralistic" society and not a "melting pot" and that equity and parity for black Americans will be achieved not from a position of weakness, but only from a position of strength.

Hence, there is a preoccupation with the strengthening and developing of black institutions and the celebration of Black history and culture—a heritage of which black Americans are proud and which they are prepared to honor and defend.

Many Blacks, and particularly black students, argue that strength and power for black Americans can be achieved only through ''self-determination," "self-sufficiency," "self-respect," and "self-defense."

These were the dominant themes at a recent conference of Blacks from all strata of American society and from more than 35 foreign countries. This conference placed an overall emphasis upon unity and solidarity. Its aim was the gaining of insight and information on the problems facing Africans and their descendants, and solving these problems through the development of power and strength, unity and solidarity. Ultimately, the goal of Black activism and of black student leadership is to transform America into a society characterized by justice, equity, freedom, and fraternity for all Americans.

While black student leaders and young black intellectuals carry on the task of self-definition and the development of group unity and solidarity, black students on the whole—the future leadership—look upon education as one means (perhaps the major one) through which they can acquire the knowledge, skills, appreciation, and understanding that will enable them to function competently and to compete on equal terms within American society.

Predominantly black institutions are regarded by the young Blacks and their leaders as the major resource related to their communities and their people, capable of developing and providing the new programs, new research and knowledge, and new kinds of public services that the nation now needs in coming to grips with its historic race problem.

Because the goals and aspirations of black students (in predominantly black, as well as in predominantly white colleges and universities) are specific, concrete, tangible, and identifiable, they can be met through the appropriate and sufficient response of government at all levels, of college and university administrators, faculties, and boards of trustees.

Specific recommendations to achieve these goals have been made by the Carnegie Commission on Higher Education, the Southern Regional Education Board (in their report on the traditionally Negro College in the South), the United Negro College Fund, and other groups. Implementing them will not by itself eliminate the developing alienation from and disaffection toward the American society felt by growing numbers of black students. But such positive responses will constitute progress toward making possible the vital process of healing the social wounds that 350 years of experience have created.

4

The University's Response to Campus Disorder

An appropriate and effective response to campus protest is impossible without a clear understanding of the distinction between disorder and orderly protest.

Disorderly campus protest is of three general types: disruption, violence, and terrorism.

By disruption we mean any interference with the ability of others to conduct their rightful business. Examples include obstructive sit-ins, interference with academic activities, the blockading of campus recruiters, and interference with the rights of persons to speak or to hear others speak.

Violence includes willful injury to persons or damage to property—for example, physical assault, throwing rocks, shooting, destroying records, burning buildings, and "trashing."

Terrorism is the organized, systematic use of violence by clandestine groups, usually in the pursuit of political objectives. Typical terrorist tactics include bombing and arson.

This chapter concerns the responses to disorder available to the university, short of calling in the police. Our discussion focuses largely on the responses to disruption, for most universities are potentially capable of forestalling or terminating at least some disruptions without resorting to outside law enforcement agencies. Violence and terrorism are generally beyond the university's own power to control, and in dealing with them the university has no choice but to seek police assistance.

Peaceful dissent, in sharp contrast to all forms of disorder, is altogether permissible on a university campus. The university is above all a place for the pursuit of knowledge. As such it must be an open forum in which all members of the university community may freely debate, discuss, and question.

The conflict of ideas within the classroom is familiar and acceptable to most Americans. But many are less capable of accepting the conflict of political ideas expressed in dramatic forms of protest such as marches, parades, picketing, and large assemblies. However, the right to engage in such protest, no less than the purely intellectual challenge to received wisdom, is part and parcel of the freedom without which a university could not exist.

Because there seems to be so much confusion on this point, we cannot emphasize too strongly that dissent and orderly protest on campus are permissible and desirable. American students are American citizens, and a campus—frequently even the campus of a private university—is essentially a public place. Court after court has declared that for most universities the area of permissible expression on campus is at least as broad as that protected by the First Amendment. As the courts have defined free speech, it includes such activities as marching, carrying placards, and passing out handbills. It also includes discourse which is not reasonable or calm or polite.

Revolutionary slogans shouted by hundreds of students doubtless are offensive to many people, but so long as they do not incite a crowd to riot, the offense is not a legal one.

Throwing a picket line around an ROTC building may make some students uncomfortable or even deter them from entering the building, but as long as the deterrence is psychological and not physical, the picketers have every right to march.

Greeting with boos and catcalls the arrival of a prominent citizen on campus may exasperate him and his friends, but no

law protects a citizen from exasperation—though it emphatically does protect his right to speak and his listeners' right to
hear him.

This is not to say that foul, mindless, or hysterical
language and gestures are any more desirable on the campus
than elsewhere. Indeed, they are more reprehensible, for civil
and rational discourse is the lifeblood of the university;
thoughtless and intolerant rhetoric is its poison. Members of
the academic community therefore have a special obligation
to frame their protest in civil terms and to listen tolerantly to
the views of others. But this is largely an intellectual and
social obligation. Except at the extremes, it cannot constitutionally be compelled by law or regulation.

Private as well as public universities should therefore take
the First Amendment as a guide to what is permissible on
their campuses. They should not impose restrictions on
meetings or rallies or marches that almost any court would
strike down, such as bans on "subversive" speakers or on
those "who advocate overthrow of the government by force
and violence," or a recently voided rule denying students the
right "to celebrate, parade or demonstrate on the campus at
any time without the approval of the [college] President."
Above all, universities must staunchly preserve and defend an
atmosphere in which all points of view may be freely
expressed.

Much of the protest on a university campus is directed
toward the university itself—its goals, policies, and programs.
It would be paradoxical if an institution that encouraged its
members to listen and respond to one another did not listen
and respond to its members' grievances.

By being self-critical, responsive to grievances, and
amenable to change, and by understanding and defending a
broad scope of freedom of expression, a university may
remove some of the factors that contribute to campus
disorder. Acting on these principles should make less common the kind of thoughtless and excessive reaction to
student protest that too often has stimulated serious disruption or violence, led to injury and destruction, and divided

campus after campus.

But openness and responsiveness will not end all campus disorder. Many universities are involuntary hosts to small and dedicated groups—not always composed of members of the university itself—that are committed to the use of violence and disruption. In addition, many large universities have become centers of youth communities. The ranks of those who will commit disorder are often swelled by these "street people." And finally, at many universities there are persons for whom disorder is the first or the only answer to dissatisfaction with the university or the nation. Some of these need no issue to justify disruption and regard it as a game to be played for its own sake.

University officials must make their plans accordingly. They must increase their capacity and bolster their will to respond firmly, justly, and humanely to disruption.

The Criteria of Response

We have said that a university's openness may help prevent disorder. But its openness also renders the university peculiarly vulnerable to disorder and constrains its responses to disorder.

Disorder is a problem of rule application, of order maintenance, and of tactics for the university administration. University officials must choose among a wide variety of possible strategies and methods, the effects of which are difficult to predict, and each of which has its distinct advantages and disadvantages. The university's response must be guided by the purposes and values of the institution, which in many cases are in conflict, and what it does must be acceptable, or at least not do injustice, to the various constituencies of the university.

Administrators and the public should therefore be aware that in many cases no entirely successful response to campus disorder is possible.

To some, of course, a good response is one that quickly restores peace to the campus. But important as tranquility may be, it surely cannot be the sole criterion. The absence of disorder is a necessary but not a sufficient condition for teaching, learning, and scholarship.

No response is satisfactory if it purchases order at the cost of physical injury or death. No response is satisfactory if it weakens the independence of the university from external power or the freedom of university members from internal harassment.

Nor is it satisfactory if the preconditions of the life of the mind are met only by the imposition of force—the occupation of the campus by troops or police or the enforcement of court injunctions against lawful assemblies or disturbances of the peace. Measures such as these may be required at times if the university is not to collapse utterly, but the circumstances must be extraordinary and their duration brief.

The free pursuit of learning is a delicate process. For it to survive, it must be based on a degree of mutual forbearance, tolerance, and trust. These qualities cannot be secured by force, nor their absence penalized by law.

These institutional constraints upon the response to disruption flow from the central purposes of the university. Other constraints derive from the composition of the university community and from the way its members will react to what the university administration does in a particular situation.

Campus disorders are likely to involve students with widely disparate attitudes and beliefs. Any large-scale disturbance will invariably include a sizable number of moderate students who are socially concerned, not committed to disorder for its own sake, but sometimes susceptible to mobilization in disruptive activities over an intensely felt concern.

A disturbance is also likely to include more militant students, alienated in some degree from American society and its institutions and quick to resort to unlawful methods to gain immediate ends.

Finally, there are the totally alienated students—few in number, but tactically sophisticated and hence influential beyond their numbers—who are committed to the destruction of the established system, and who try to assist the process by inducing repressive countermeasures against disrupters.

In a situation in which, as Governor John Burns of Hawaii has written, "the mix of the . . . types of dissenting students may vary considerably," it would be "an overwhelming mistake to treat any group of dissenting students as if they were all hard-core radicals—basically unreachable and responsive to force alone. Such a tactic is virtually guaranteed to turn mild dissenters into radicals and to swell the number of protestors to an unmanageable level."

Because of all the constraints operating upon it, a university's response must be extraordinarily sensitive and measured if it is to prevent the escalation of disorder and a corresponding increase in the danger to life and property. The common distinction between "hard" and "soft" attitudes toward student disruption is dangerously misleading. The decisions made by a university administration must depend upon the immediate situation. In the course of any single disruption the administration may need to change its approach frequently: to be flexible when, for example, fruitful negotiations seem possible, and firm when that possibility disappears. Candor and consistency will serve an administration better than adherence to any fixed formula, and are far more likely to win the trust and respect of all members of the university community.

IMPROVING THE UNIVERSITY'S CAPABILITY TO RESPOND TO DISRUPTION

Most American colleges and universities are not prepared to respond to disorder in a manner that satisfies the criteria we have described. In part, as we have said above, the difficulty lies in the nature of the university itself. An institution committed to intellectual freedom, to individuality, and to the toleration of eccentricity is bound to be loosely organized at best, and its internal processes of governance and law are bound to be somewhat uncertain.

But if our universities are to survive the continuing crisis of the coming years, they must develop effective institutional methods for responding to disorder. Never has there been a greater need for universities to pull themselves together.

The Role of Students, Faculty, and Trustees

The administration must accept primary responsibility for the management of the campus in times of crisis. But the best of administrators cannot operate without the support of the university's other major constituencies—the students, faculty, and trustees. This support often has not been forthcoming.

Students form a special, self-contained community in which there is a strong obligation not to betray one's peers, an equally strong inclination to question the legitimacy of adult authority, and a remarkable capacity for immediate action and impromptu organization. The membership of this community changes rapidly, but the fact of its transience does not diminish the sense of solidarity, which has become more intense and self-conscious in recent years. The very term "student" has come to confer, in addition to educational status, a political and moral identity.

Most students tend to be unwilling to agree to organizational or tactical plans that would place them in alliance with conventional sources of adult authority—the faculty or administration—or that would place some of them in the position of reprimanding or punishing other students. This is not to say that all students agree or that students and administrators always disagree. But there are substantial obstacles in the way of a dispassionate, collaborative attempt by administrators and students to define and work toward the common good of the university community.

The typical faculty, on the other hand, is less a community than a collection of highly individualistic scholars and teachers. Few faculty members are well informed about most universitywide issues. Fewer still are concerned with the problems faced by administrators, whom they tend to dismiss as mere housekeepers or public relations men. Faculty turnover is high—and those faculty members who remain do not have to live with or answer for the immediate consequences of most university decisions.

Faculty concerns tend to be ideological in nature. Faculty members may sympathize with student concerns, or fear the politicization of the university, or feel strongly about a particular moral issue. A faculty meeting called to discuss a campus crisis is likely to be heavily attended (unlike most faculty meetings), emotionally charged, rhetorically intense, and wholly unpredictable. Such meetings display both the best and the worst qualities of the old-fashioned town meeting: a high sense of concern and a low order of practicality. However, that sense of concern must be taken seriously, for no university can continue acting in a way that is not consonant with the widely shared opinions of its faculty.

Trustees seldom involve themselves in the everyday affairs of the university. But when disorder occurs they sometimes stride (or are pushed) to the center of the stage to act as intermediaries between the university and the off-campus community. Unfortunately, trustees seldom understand institutional, student, and faculty concerns well enough to be able to perform this role with skill. Indeed, under the pressure of criticism from alumni, citizens, and politicians, they may feel constrained to attack rather than to explain or defend the university's handling of a campus crisis.

If the university is to meet the critical demands of the coming years, all of its members must rededicate themselves to its common purposes.

The trustees must exercise the greatest care in making their most important decision—the choice of the university president. He must possess, in addition to more traditional attributes, the qualities of leadership necessary to steer the institution through crisis and disorder. He must have the courage to tell students clearly and honestly when he cannot meet their demands, and he must have the consideration to explain why the answer must be "No." Having found such a man, the trustees should permit him (and his administration) to administer the university without undue interference and should support him in times of stress.

The trustees—as well as the regents or governing boards of public universities—have a particular responsibility to mediate between their institution and alumni, politicians, and the public. They have a continuing duty to explain the institution's values, goals, complexities, and changes. They should, for example, explain why the nature of a university requires it to condone seemingly untoward conduct, such as the espousal of unpopular views by students, teachers, or guest speakers.

A trusteee who is not prepared to proclaim in public that his unversity is correct when it defends the right of dissent and of orderly protest should ask himself whether he has any business being a trustee.

Students and faculty members, for their part, should be informed about campus issues and should respond to them with the same civility and reasonableness that they are expected to bring to their scholarship. They need not refrain from criticizing what they believe to be bad institutional policies or actions, but their criticisms should reflect knowledge of the facts and comprehension of the complexities of the issues. Equally, they should be willing to support and defend those decisions of which they approve. Few students and faculty members recognize the importance of their moral support to an administration attempting to cope with campus crisis or disorder. There are occasions, moreover, when more than moral support is required—for example, standing "fire watch" when arson is threatened, or acting as observers or marshals at mass assemblies and demonstrations.

Students and faculty should not lend support to those few among them who, for whatever purposes, would subvert and destroy the central values of the university. Sometimes these persons, because they are vocal, assume leadership roles when in fact they speak for scarcely anyone but themselves. By the same token, students should overcome their reluctance to inform authorities of those within their midst whom they know to be plotting or to have committed acts of violence and destruction. This is essential not only to protect lives and property, but also to reduce the need for intelligence activities by law enforcement agencies.

We must also note that administrators are sometimes subjected to intense political pressures which make it difficult, if not impossible, to execute their role responsibly. For example, one president of a big-city college, where a major disruption occurred only a few weeks before a hotly contested mayoral election, told the Commission staff that the mayor telephoned him to demand that he expel a few disruptive students in order to convince the voters that the mayor was not "soft" on students. When the president refused to comply, the mayor replied that he would use his influence to make sure that the college did not obtain an injunction it was seeking against the students. A state institution whose administrators the legislature considered "soft" was the only college of its kind in the state last year not to receive an increased appropriation from the legislature. In another state the legislature singled out by name in an appropriation bill a "soft" dean as being ineligible to receive any salary. Administrators threatened with intervention of these kinds are scarely in a position to act reasonably or responsibly.

Organizing the Administration for Crisis

We recommend that every institution have, as part of its administrative structure, a group that will be responsible for keeping the administration aware of developing campus issues, rumors, and activities that require reply or action; for drawing up plans to deal with disruption; and for putting those plans into effect when necessary.

Naturally, the size of such a group will vary with the size of the university, and its composition with the university's organizational structure. The head of the group, if it is not the university president, should be a high administrative official who possesses the confidence and many of the powers of the president. The team might also include: an administrator responsible for keeping abreast of campus issues and grievances and for making timely reply to charges without basis in fact; the officials who supervise the campus police force and maintain liaison between the university and outside law enforcement authorities; and the persons responsible for initiating proceedings before the campus disciplinary body and in state civil and criminal courts.

The team should consult formally with designated representatives of the university's major constituencies. Institutional arrangements for this must be made in advance; the middle of a crisis is not the time to summon a constitutional convention, hold a mass meeting, or conduct a plebiscite.

The administration should also make physical provision for the functioning of the university during disorder. Confidential files and sensitive areas, such as telephone switchboards and computation centers, can often be made more secure.

Proper contingency planning makes possible a variety of responses to disorder. Without planning, options narrow quickly to capitulation or the use of force.

Defining the Limits of Permissible Conduct

A university should decide and announce in advance what conduct it will not permit on the campus and what measures it is willing to employ in response to such conduct.

We recommend that universities make well known their willingness to file criminal charges in appropriate cases and their intention to cooperate actively with public officials in their prosecution. Students know that serious felonies are prohibited on the campus as elsewhere, but they are often unaware of the broad range of state laws that apply to campus disturbances. Some are under the mistaken impression that the university campus is a sanctuary from most of the laws of civil society. Where this ignorance is widespread, resort to the courts and the use of police carry the risk of sparking further protest and disruption. We agree with the National Commission on the Causes and Prevention of

Violence that members of the university community "cannot argue that of all Americans they are uniquely beyond the reach of the law."

The university's internal disciplinary code should define clearly the limits of lawful protest activity. People must be informed of the university's rules so that they can conduct themselves accordingly; they should be held legally accountable only for conduct that they had reason to know was prohibited. The absence of clear, enforceable, and enforced rules of conduct can produce confusion and turmoil. Further disorder can result from the unexpected imposition of sanctions.

Equally, the university administration needs rules to guide its response to campus situations. The line between orderly protest and disorder is often thin; disorders have frequently begun as entirely peaceful events. The university must protect its member's rights to engage in the full range of legitimate protest activities, but it must also be prepared to respond rapidly when the line is crossed. Clear regulations will help prevent inappropriate or premature responses.

The current disciplinary codes of many universities are inadequate. Some are inconsistent with the university's commitment to the principles of free expression. Others are vague or overbroad: instead of informing students what they may not do, the codes merely proscribe "conduct unbecoming a student." The code should include, among other things, simple and precise regulations governing the time, place, and manner of permissible mass assemblies and demonstrations.

We recommend that every college or university that has not recently done so reexamine its internal rules of conduct with a view toward making them consonant with principles of free speech and due process, as well as more explicit in defining what the university considers to be impermissible conduct.

In this reexamination and reform of a university's disciplinary regulations, the opinions of all segments of the university should be sought. The justification for such openness goes far beyond the need to establish "credibility." Different parts of the university community have different values and interests which can be reconciled in a code of discipline only if all factions have the opportunity to be heard. The extent of direct participation of university members in these processes will vary from one institution to another and will in any event depend on their good faith and willingness to work for the common good of the university. We emphasize that the university cannot allow itself to be paralyzed by the failure of all segments of the university to agree on a disciplinary code. Agreement is desirable, but even in its absence there must be a code.

The Disciplinary System

The code reforms we have proposed may help avoid confusion on the part of students and prevent precipitous action on the part of administrators. But the best of codes is useless if adequate provision is not made for its enforcement.

The political nature of most campus disruptions often has undermined traditional disciplinary procedures and rendered them ineffective. Many students and faculty may sympathize with the broader aims of disrupters even though they disapprove of the tactics employed. This distinction between ends and means, never entirely sharp, can easily become obscured in the aftermath of a campus disturbance. The disciplinary tribunal may be unwilling to impose meaningful sanctions, and if it does it may risk losing broad support within the university. Moreover, because campus tribunals usually lack the sanctions as well as the respect that protect a court of law from disruption, the proceedings themselves can become the focus of mass disturbances. In sum, disciplinary hearings for those involved in disruptions are apt to become political circuses rather than procedures for determining culpability and for imposing appropriate sanctions.

Despite these inherent problems, the university needs an internal disciplinary process to deal with disruption as much as it needs one to deal with cheating on examinations and other academic infractions. The university should have a means by which to express institutional disapproval of harmful conduct. Moreover, a disciplinary system offers a flexibility in the imposition of sanctions that exclusive reliance on the criminal courts does not permit. Finally, the university must have a procedure for removing, temporarily or permanently, those whose presence poses a danger to its members or processes.

We believe that there are several areas in which the university disciplinary process can be strengthened to deal with campus disorder.

First, scrupulous adherence to fair procedures is essential in a situation of mass campus disorder. The disciplinary proceedings will be subject to unusually critical scrutiny, and any perceived arbitrariness will diminish their apparent legitimacy. The Commission endorses, as minimal requisites, the principles of procedural fairness recommended in the *Report of the American Bar Association Commission on Campus Government and Student Dissent* (1970).

Second, universities should reexamine carefully the structure and composition of their disciplinary tribunals. Two simple points, ignored at many institutions, concern the combination of judicial with other, conflicting functions. Entrusting the disciplinary process to the administrative official responsible for handling grievances is likely to deprive the official of legitimacy in both roles. Similarly, the disciplinary process is likely to gain more respect, and in fact be fairer, if serious offenses are tried on an adversary basis, with a clear separation of the role of prosecutor from that of judge.

An increasing number of institutions have retained outside hearing examiners, attorneys, and investigators to handle the disciplinary problems arising out of campus disruptions. The hearing examiner, who determines disputed facts and sometimes recommends penalties, can adjudicate with an impartiality often lacking in the traditional university tribunal. Consequently, his decisions may gain more respect.

The question of student and faculty participation in disciplinary proceedings has been a matter of serious concern on many campuses. In attempting to legitimate student tribunals, some universities have selected members by election. This process facilitates the politicization of tribunals and should be discouraged. A tribunal with a broad base of participation—including both student and faculty members—is more likely to gain the community's consent to the process and to assure the tribunal's freedom from improper influence. On the other hand, students and faculty at some institutions seem unwilling to impose appropriate sanctions against disrupters.

Students and faculty should have a sufficient commitment to the university and to principles of legality to prevent this problem from arising. Such a commitment must be developed and acted upon if members of the university community wish to retain their traditional autonomy and freedom from outside interference and control.

Finally, faculty members should not be able, as they apparently are on many campuses, to perform disruptive acts with impunity. Universities should establish a code and procedures for disciplining faculty members—including those with tenure—who behave impermissibly. We recognize the difficulty of designing appropriate mechanisms for this purpose and of gaining acceptance for them. Nevertheless, we think it essential that efforts be made to rectify a situation that is harmful to the institution and is rightly perceived by students to be unfair.

The University Police Force

The university's police or security force is its ultimate internal resource for preventing and coping with campus disorder. Most universities do not have forces competent for the task. In some cases this is the result of a conscious choice, but in many others the universities have simply not addressed themselves to the problem.

Every institution should examine the capability of its internal force, determine what its role should be, and take the necessary steps to bridge the gap between capability and expected performance.

University forces run a wide range. At one extreme are watchmen or contract guards—typically, untrained personnel whose main duties consist of locking doors and detecting fires, vandalism, and other maintenance problems. At the other pole are the sophisticated forces found at some state universities, often headed by former police officers and organized like a municipal police department, whose officers usually have full police authority and carry sidearms. Between these extremes lies a wide variety of campus forces. most of which are too poorly financed, staffed, equipped, and trained to function effectively in a situation of campus disorder.

We can recommend no single "model" campus police or security force appropriate to all universities. There are too many variables, such as the size and location of the university, the likelihood of serious crime and disorder, the capability of the local police force, and the quality of its relations with the institution. What is suitable for Berkeley may not be suitable for Sweet Briar.

Many universities today have the attributes and managerial problems of civil communities. They are the scene of growing numbers of demonstrations and of an increasing rate and variety of crime. In addition, more nonstudents are present on these campuses than ever before. Chief W. P. Beall, Coordinator of Police Services for the University of California, testified that of 674 persons arrested on the Berkeley campus during the first half of 1970, as many as 587 were nonstudents. The offenses included trespass, disorderly conduct, aggravated assault, burglary, arson, narcotics, and sex crimes.

A fully staffed and trained campus police force at its best can perform the functions of a small municipal police department with respect to campus disorders. It can cooperate with persons planning an assembly or demonstration to structure the event and to develop lines of communication and responsibility, and it can police the event, where necessary, with the assistance of student or faculty marshals. An alert force can deploy officers rapidly to the scene of an incipient disturbance or to a building in danger of being unlawfully occupied. Depending upon its size, training, and expertise, the campus force may be able to deal with some disturbances without calling in outside law enforcement officers. Indeed, since it can keep in close touch with the university's day-to-day issues and events, it may be better able to perform on-campus police functions than the local law enforcement agency.

If a university is to maintain a professional police force, however, it must establish salary levels and recruitment procedures capable of producing a force of men with sufficient emotional control and intelligence to deal with unlawful behavior effectively and without antagonizing members of the university community. The university must also provide proper training for its officers, who should attend a good police training center. Officers must be familiarized with campus problems and university regulations, preferably through a training program supervised by university administrators.

The legislation of many states distinguishes between public universities, whose police have the powers of sworn peace officers, and private institutions, whose personnel have little authority, sometimes no more than that of private citizens. This has impeded a number of large private universities from maintaining their own police forces. Where this problem exists, we recommend that state legislatures consider conferring peace officer status on the personnel of private university police departments that meet state criteria for recruitment, training, and organization. We would, of course, expect a university police force to strive to be a model department, exceeding any minimum standards set by the state.

Police training for officers of the campus security force is an expensive undertaking that may require state and federal subsidies. Some states have already begun to allocate more money to campus police forces and have established regional workshops for campus officers. The Law Enforcement Assistance Administration (LEAA) of the Department of Justice has extended educational benefits under its programs to campus police officers of public institutions. Personnel at private universities who have peace officer status should receive the same benefits.

Many universities place their campus security forces under the direction of a business manager or treasurer. This is appropriate where the force performs only watchman functions, but not where it acts as a police force. The expertise and other duties of business personnel are unrelated to the problems and conflicts that might lead to the involvement of a university force. Universities should place campus forces that perform police functions under the immediate control of a well-trained and experienced chief. He, in turn, should be accountable to a high administrative officer or dean whose other responsibilities put him in close contact with the social and political issues that affect the university's day-to-day life.

Where university police have primary responsibility for maintaining peace on the campus, its uniformed officers may be required to perform conventional law enforcement duties that make it appropriate for them to carry sidearms, batons, or nonlethal chemical weapons. Obviously, only well-trained personnel should be permitted to carry weapons, and strict guidelines should be adopted for their use.

Finally, a university's campus police force should enter into a clear jurisdictional understanding with local law enforcement authorities and should establish a working arrangement and channels for the regular exchange of information.

Maintaining a regular campus police force may be appropriate on a large campus which is, in effect, a community separate from that of any neighboring town. For most colleges and universities, however, the cost of such a force is prohibitive and can seldom be justified if local police are available and if good relations can be established between the locality and the university. The large majority of institutions will be adequately protected by security personnel not enjoying peace officer status, or by the services of regular county or municipal officers. We disagree with those who have suggested that watchman security forces should perform a law enforcement role in situations of disruption. Only a well-trained, professional police force can handle such situations without serious danger to all concerned.

Student and Faculty Marshals

Student and especially faculty marshals can fulfill an important function in maintaining order at peaceful mass demonstrations (for example, by guiding marchers along their designated route), and may also be useful in averting incipient confrontations through peaceful persuasion.

When authority figures—including specifically campus police or administrative officers—are suspect, teaching faculty may retain a greater measure of moral authority. Thus, at a number of campuses this spring, marshals wearing distinctive armbands mingled with angry crowds of students, persuading them to disperse, or to refrain from throwing rocks, or simply to remain calm.

The key to the effectiveness of marshals seems to be their neutrality. The administration should resist the temptation to organize marshals, for the necessary neutrality will vanish if either students or faculty feel the marshals are agents of the administration. The impetus to form a marshal force must come from within student or faculty groups.

We caution those who undertake to help preserve the fabric of order in the university by serving as marshals that they must not attempt to perform pure law enforcement tasks. To do so will place them in personal danger and will impede the functioning of law officers trained specifically for this work.

THE RESPONSE TO DISRUPTION, VIOLENCE, AND TERRORISM

When the university is faced with clear acts of criminal violence, such as arson or bombing, its officials should promptly call for the assistance of outside law enforcement agencies, which have the experience and the expertise to deal with crime. Underreaction to dangerously criminal conduct merely encourages those bent on violence to believe they can get away with it—as, indeed, they sometimes have.

When the conduct is disruptive but not violent, the initial response should generally be internal. The administration must know and understand the range of available choices. It must choose a course of action and pursue it in a measured fashion, with full awareness of the nature of the disorder and the makeup of its participants.

For example, the university's objective in responding to an obstructive sit-in must be to restore the occupied building or classroom to its normal university use. It is often both possible and wise to begin by discussing or even negotiating the protestors' grievances, by calling attention to the applicability of internal disciplinary and external criminal sanctions, and by stating when these will become effective. If persuasion fails and the university cannot "wait it out," it may be necessary to resort to more direct measures—injunctions, for example, or the use of police. Here again, it is almost always desirable to give advance notice of the university's intended action in order to provide the disrupters with the opportunity to desist voluntarily.

Escalation from one step to the next should come only after it has become reasonably obvious to students as well as to the authorities that the earlier tactic definitely did not work. There can be no question, however, that the objective itself—restoring the building to its intended use—must eventually be achieved.

It is impossible to suggest the appropriate response to each and every type of disruption that has occurred on American campuses in the past few years. The range of conduct is too wide and campus situations too varied for such advice to be of much practical use. Nevertheless, some general observations can be made about the options available to universities.

Negotiation

In Chapter 6 we recommend that a university administration stay aware of student issues and grievances, discuss them openly, and respond to them promptly. In general, there is no reason for a university to refuse to discuss grievances with students involved in a disruption—even when the students' request comes in the form of a list of "nonnegotiable demands."

Discussion and negotiation can, with the best of luck, isolate those who engage in disruption for its own sake from those who either honestly seek a solution to a problem or can be persuaded that an issue is not within the university's cognizance. As President Bruce Dearing of the State University of New York at Binghamton stated to the Commission:

> A faculty and administration and student body which can together swallow pride and irritation, can listen for the message behind the shrillness of some demands, and can undertake to redress genuine grievances, to undertake overdue reforms, to justify defensible policies and abandon indefensible ones—can effectively deny a significant constituency to the committed revolutionaries for whom a peaceful solution of a campus problem comes as a defeat.

There are, however, substantial constraints that often render discussions and negotiations ineffective.

First, either students or administrators may be reluctant to compromise. To students, the idea of compromise may seem to be immoral. Administrators may feel that compromise or even discussion with disrupters will have the appearance of capitulation. And they may fear—not without some reason—that by giving in to the demands of today's disrupters they will stimulate a new disruption with different demands tomorrow.

Second, the issues may not be amenable to resolution by those participating in the discussions. Some disruptions are designed to publicize national issues rather than locally resolvable grievances. Issues that may appear to be within the parties' cognizance often are not—the state legislature, a union, or some other unwilling and absent party may be necessary to reach a meaningful agreement. On more than a few occasions, students and administrators have made a settlement only to have it overturned by the university government or the trustees or regents.

Third, the negotiators may not be vested with meaningful decision-making authority by their constituents. A spokesman without authority can frustrate the bargaining process. A faculty member who attempted mediation during the April 1968 disturbances at Columbia University, described this problem:

> The students were organized in such a way that negotiations were impossible. First, proposals would go to the negotiators, then to the headquarters, then to the general membership in the occupied buildings, then back to headquarters, and finally back to the negotiators. They were not willing to break the solidarity and they were constitutionally unable to negotiate.

Finally, negotiation may founder because of lack of sensitivity to personal style and to the use of symbolic gestures. Feelings of fear and defensiveness, the need to save face, styles of dress, and rhetoric can, if they are not understood and allowed for, involve the parties in emotional responses that will effectively prevent resolution of the issues.

Students engaged in an unlawful disruption often have demanded "amnesty" from disciplinary or criminal sanctions as a condition for ceasing their disruptive behavior. We do not state that a university should never negotiate the matter of amnesty, but we do believe that it must take very seriously the long-range implications of such a decision—especially where it means granting amnesty to leaders of a disruption or to persons chargeable with serious offenses. A university that permits the issue of discipline to become a bargaining point risks sacrificing the integrity of its internal judicial processes. Moreover, granting amnesty to one group can subject the administration to the plausible charge of discriminatory enforcement if it invokes sanctions on a subsequent occasion.

Waiting It Out

A university faced with nonviolent disruptive conduct sometimes has the option of waiting for it to lose momentum and dissipate of its own accord. How long, if at all, it can afford to allow such conduct to continue depends upon the severity of the disruption and the atmosphere within the university and the surrounding community.

As UCLA student body president Tom Norminton testified, allowing a nonviolent disruption to continue often minimizes the danger of physical violence on campus and is the least likely of all possible responses to win sympathy and converts for the protestors.

It is, however, no guarantee against violence. On a number of campuses, counterprotestors have sought to force their way into an occupied building or to force dissidents out, and the ensuing battles have ultimately required calling in the police. Conflict of this sort has far greater potential for serious injury and for creating deep hostilities within the campus community than does confrontation between demonstrators and a properly trained, disciplined, and prepared police force.

Universities that have allowed sit-ins to continue have sometimes been denounced by those who demand an immediate, visible, and drastic response. Their criticism has merit if the university is not able or willing to discipline or prosecute any protestors after the disruption has ended. Thus, even when a university chooses to "wait it out," it should take whatever measures are necessary—and they are often costly and cumbersome—to identify the participants and to be prepared to deal with them appropriately.

Obtaining an Injunction

The injunction has qualities that make it an attractive alternative or supplement to the invocation of criminal law. The very occurrence of an unlawful disruption means that the criminal law has failed to deter. This failure may be due to ignorance of the law or to a mistaken belief that the campus is a sanctuary. Just as often it is due to the imbalance between the immediacy of the issue that moves the students to protest and the remoteness of the penalty for unlawful protest.

An injunction, by which the court directly commands the participants to desist, restores the balance. In the words of a student militant:

> The injunction escalates the risk of taking part in a sit-in. It is no longer a question of simply violating university rules, or even of being subjected to charges of criminal trespass, which may later be withdrawn. It brings direct confrontation with the court.

This was reiterated by the District of Columbia Chief of Police Jerry Wilson, who went on to testify that the issuance of injunctions in his jurisdiction had usually terminated sit-ins or building occupations without a police confrontation.

No formula can prescribe whether or when or how to employ an injunction; each disruptive situation is unique. We can only offer these general observations:

* In advance of any disturbance, a university should prepare guidelines specifying the circumstances under which an injunction will be sought. It should determine the court in which to file suit; know what facts are required to maintain the suit; and prepare a contingency file containing the necessary legal forms, leaving only the particulars to be completed in the event of disruption.

* If time permits, the university should make it plain to the disrupters that it intends to seek the injunction and that they are likely to bear the court costs, which may be substantial. This warning may be sufficient to end some disruptions. In other circumstances, the issuance of the injunction, without any further official action, may terminate the disruption.

* Universities frequently have obtained injunctions and then failed to serve or enforce them. This has caused some courts either to refuse to issue injunctions without a guarantee that the university will enforce them or, simply, to send in police to enforce the injunction without the university's consent. Administrators should realize that once they obtain an injunction they may lose control over its enforcement. A university should not seek an injunction unless it is prepared to have it enforced.

* Familiarity breeds contempt. Universities that have gained voluntary compliance with their first injunction seem often to have experienced violations of subsequent ones. This suggests that injunctive relief should be sought sparingly.

* Injunctions have had the greatest success in static situations, such as sit-ins, where the locus is fixed, the leaders and other participants are identified, and the course of future conduct is fairly predictable. The dynamics of an unstable, roving disruption are not conducive to voluntary compliance. In such situations it may be difficult to serve process on named defendants, to notify those acting in concert with them of the injunction, and, more difficult still, to prove that an alleged participant received notice—a fact that must be proved to hold him in contempt.

* It may be charged that the university, as plaintiff, possesses an unfair advantage. For example, in some

states a temporary restraining order, obtained without an adversary hearing, can be kept in effect for an inordinate length of time before the defendants are heard. A university seeking to restore internal order should not be a timid litigant. But it must remain committed to principles of fair play and to the preservation of the freedoms of peaceable assembly and expression.

✳ Exclusive reliance on the injunction to control campus disorder can, as the American Bar Association Commission on Campus Government and Student Dissent suggests, have untoward consequences. It can encourage students to "conclude that they can engage in disruptive activity without fear of arrest or university disciplinary proceedings as long as they are prepared to yield to a court order when the university seeks injunctive relief." The university should be prepared to utilize an appropriate mixture of disciplinary and criminal sanctions even when it also seeks injunctive relief.

Disciplinary and Judicial Sanctions

After a disruption had ended, the university may proceed against the participants under its internal disciplinary procedure and in the state civil and criminal courts. Whether the university chooses to pursue one or more of these processes depends upon a number of factors, including the nature and seriousness of the offense and the effectiveness of its internal disciplinary system.

The university disciplinary system may often be employed instead of the criminal process to deal with those who engage in minor disruptive conduct. The internal sanction is particularly appropriate where the offense is against the academic process—disrupting classes or shouting down speakers, for example—or where the continued presence of the offender on campus threatens the university's welfare. In the latter case especially, the university should not hesitate to proceed both internally and criminally against a student or faculty member who has committed a serious offense. The university usually has no control over the prosecution of those who engage in violence. Such conduct not only endangers the university, but threatens the entire community as well. It clearly is a public offense and is appropriately dealt with in the state courts.

Much nonviolent disruptive conduct violates state criminal laws. Except when the police have been called and arrests made, the university often can exercise discretion to prosecute for such conduct. The chief advantage of the criminal process lies in its power: it is not subject to the constraints that enervate many university disciplinary systems. Its disadvantages are that the stigma of a criminal record may follow the student through his life, that in some areas the local courts may be as unreasonably hostile to the disrupter as the disciplinary tribunal is unreasonably sympathetic, and that once the university files criminal charges it is likely to lose all control over the process.

Administrators should keep in mind that an important function of both the disciplinary and the criminal process is to deter *future* misconduct. This requires, as we stated earlier, that the university make good its intention to prosecute those who violate its rules. An institution that sets a pattern of nonprosecution will find that such announcements soon lose all effectiveness.

Another judicial remedy available to the university is civil action for damages. In most cases, disruptive conduct is tortious under state laws. In some instances—the disruption of classes, for example—the damage is not easily quantifiable; in others—breaking windows, for example—it is. In any case, the university is likely to win at least nominal, and probably punitive, damages. Some students lack the resources to satisfy a civil judgment, but the judgment may be collected in the future. In any event, the prospect of defending a civil action may work as an added deterrent to injurious conduct if the university announces beforehand its intention to sue.

Closing the University

Continued violence or unrelenting and potentially danger-ous nonviolent disruption may force a university to consider the extraordinarily difficult question of whether to close down the institution—for a weekend, or a week, or the remainder of the term.

Closing for a long weekend, as several institutions have done in times of extreme tension, can serve to cool off a disturbance. However, the atmosphere on a campus may become so inimical to scholarship, or the situation so dangerous to life and property, that a brief recess of classes is insufficient.

For example, a university may find itself subjected to constant classroom disruptions, harassment of faculty and students, and dangerous turmoil in its public meeting places. When disruption moves from organized action directed at clearly defined targets to the stage of terrorist activities by small bands acting against particular individuals, the univer-sity—or, for that matter, a police force—loses its capacity to restore order. Anticipating the source or direction of harass-ment is virtually impossible. Identifying those responsible is a difficult and uncertain task. Nor can the university end the disorder by introducing substantive changes in university structure or policy, since the only changes that would restore tranquility are those that would destroy the free intellectual life of the university.

The complications that attend the full-scale closing of a university for any substantial period are severe. To mention only a few: loss of students' class time, jobs, and living quarters; interruption of research; interference with univer-sity service functions; and a significant reduction in the university's income, which may require curtailing the payroll of faculty, researchers, and other staff. In addition, the university may find itself subject to lawsuits seeking a refund of tuition and other fees; several universities that have closed for relatively brief periods are presently facing such suits.

The university should make it known in advance if it is

considering closing the campus. Only in this way can those faculty and students who regard campus disruptions as a form of spectator sport be made to consider seriously the costs of disorder and thus ultimately assume some of the responsibility for reaffirming and supporting the values of academic life.

CONCLUSION

Our remarks in this chapter have been directed to the members of the nation's colleges and universities—to students, faculty, trustees, and administrators.

We repeat: the university must pull itself together. It must develop that sense of community which has often been sadly lacking.

It must face up to the fact that campus disruption will not cease in the foreseeable future. It must recognize its responsibility to protect itself, its values, and human life in the event of disorder.

The university must honestly and forcefully reiterate its first principles and must clearly distinguish between those forms of protest which it will permit and defend and those it will prohibit.

The university must draw up a practical plan of tactics for use when disorder and disruption occur. It must clearly understand its available options and how each option fits into a strategy of measured response.

It must frankly state in advance what range of sanctions it proposes to employ against those who participate in impermissible conduct, and it must adhere to its promise of punishment after the conduct has ceased.

Administrators must bear the central responsibility in preparing for a crisis and in managing the institution in time of crisis. They must act resolutely in the face of disruption and respond firmly and justly to it. In accomplishing this task, they need the support and cooperation of the entire university community.

Students must be worthy of the mature treatment which they rightfully claim as adults. The administration is not always wrong, and more students must be willing to say so. There are values other than student solidarity, and more students must say so. Not every campus "leader" is necessarily worthy of support simply because he is attacking established authorities, and more students must say so.

Students, while still remaining loyal to their fellows, must give their loyalty to the university as well. They must face the fact that giving moral support to those who are planning violent action is as morally despicable as standing by while a criminal beats someone senseless on a street corner.

Faculty members who engage in or lead disruptive conduct have no place in the university. The spectacle of a professor leading a band of marauders into a colleague's lecture bent on disrupting the classroom is abhorrent to anyone who values the university as an institution. By attempting to destroy a fellow faculty member's right to teach, no matter what the content of his course, such individuals have forfeited their right to remain in the university community.

More positively, faculty members must be vigorous supporters as well as responsible critics of their university. They must lend active support to the administrators who are attempting to preserve the university as an institution.

Faculty members must realize that they have a shared interest and responsibility in the university community as a whole. They must act on that responsibility not only when their own work is disrupted, but also whenever any part of the university is threatened.

Above all, the faculty—the chief beneficiary of academic freedom—must be a vigilant defender of this freedom within the university community.

Finally, administrators cannot do their jobs without the support of alumni, citizens, and government leaders. All three of these groups have been guilty of substituting thoughtless criticism for helpful support precisely at a time when the welfare of the nation's institutions of higher education is in grave peril.

Alumni and citizens have criticized administrators, often in an uninformed or even hysterical manner, for being "soft" in the face of unlawful disorder and excessively tolerant of protest—even of peaceful, constitutionally protected protest. Politicians have often been equally virulent in their attacks, and equally ignorant. Some have misled public opinion with regard to the university, whether deliberately or unthinkingly we cannot say. Legislators in a majority of states have passed antistudent and antiuniversity laws that range from the unnecessary and ill-directed to the purely vindictive.

Any academic institution worthy of the name must protect the right of its students and faculty to express themselves freely—outrageously as well as responsibly. The job of administrators in handling campus crises or disorders is a complex and difficult one—all the more so when they face thoughtless pressures from outside as well as the very real constraints from within.

The Law Enforcement Response

Despite its best efforts to prevent disorder or to end disorder after it begins, a university may be compelled to call in law enforcement officers to preserve or restore order on campus. Even under the best of circumstances and with the best of luck, the presence of law enforcement officers on campus is troubling and troublesome. It is troubling because it means that at an institution where reason should prevail, reason has failed; and it is troublesome because a campus occupied by policemen or troops is a spectacle to be regretted by all Americans. We must try to prevent this happening; but we must also be prepared.

Events in the past year have made it clear that the price of being unprepared can be tragically high. Lack of preparation increases the chance of injury and death. Lack of preparation gravely increases the risk of excesses by both police and students in the heat of confrontation. If these excesses occur, after the tumult dies down, we find fewer students who respect the law and its officers, and fewer policemen and citizens who respect universities and their members. The stage is thus set for even worse confrontations in the future.

Despite the painful clarity of this conclusion, the Commission has serious reason to doubt the awareness of universities and law enforcement authorities of the need to prepare themselves for the use of police or the National Guard in situations of campus disorder.

The President's Commission on Law Enforcement and the Administration of Justice, the National Advisory Commission on Civil Disorders, and the National Commission on the Causes and Prevention of Violence have already published careful and detailed recommendations concerning police recruitment, training, advance planning, and command and control, designed to prepare the police to respond effectively to disorders. Some law enforcement agencies have taken substantial steps to implement these recommendations, but too many others are as poorly prepared to cope with mass disorder now as they were five years ago.

At the same time, our investigations indicate that on many campuses that have not yet experienced disorder (and on some that have) university administrators have made no useful preparations for the possibility of disorder. When asked to explain this extraordinary lack of forethought, one administrator after another gave an answer that could be reduced to "It can't happen here" or, equally incredible, "It can't happen here again." University officials who believe this are worse than naive. They are derelict in their responsibilities to the university community and to society at large. No less than the police, universities that are unprepared to cope with serious campus disturbances are properly held accountable when tragic consequences follow.

THE POLICE

Police cannot be barred from university campuses. The police are dutybound to enforce the law on the campus as well as elsewhere within their jurisdiction. When there is personal injury or serious property damage on the campus, the police must enforce the criminal law.

The university has no capacity to deal with bombing, arson, and similar acts of violence or terrorism. It must call the police. Such criminal acts put the entire community in such obvious and immediate danger that the police are obliged not only to discover their perpetrators, but also to take all reasonable steps to prevent their occurrence. More-over, no university security force has the manpower and expertise to deal unaided with mass disorders of the size that dozens of universities have experienced in recent years.

As long as violence and disruption continue, outside policemen must continue to come on campus.

Yet on almost any campus to which policemen are called to deal with disorder, they are threatening and unwelcome to many. Some university members view the police as the repressive arm of the established authorities. Some hold to the notion, often unspoken, that the university is a kind of sanctuary where the laws of civil society do not apply. And for the majority, the massive presence of officers implies—as it would in any community—that something frightening or dangerous is under way or about to happen.

In much the same way, a campus embroiled in disorder is likely to appear threatening to a policeman. He is generally unfamiliar with its geography and its inhabitants. He is there to perform an unpleasant and dangerous task. He will often be treated with hostility by participants and onlookers alike.

So much has already been written about the conflict between policemen's attitudes and students' attitudes that we need not linger over the subject. Many policemen cherish established values and institutions; they often equate uncon-ventionality and eccentricity with disorderliness or even crimi-nality; they believe in the efficacy of punishment; and some think that they do not only serve the law, but also embody it, and that therefore disrespect for them is tantamount to disrespect for law itself. Many students, on the other hand, question established values and institutions, cherish uncon-ventionality and eccentricity as the outward symbols of a free spirit, suspect that society is forever trying to coerce and repress them, believe that if policemen embody the law, that in itself is good reason to disrespect it.

Consequently, when students and policemen confront each other on a troubled campus, the atmosphere is almost invariably hostile. Some students may taunt the police by calling them inferior, uneducated, and brutal; they may deliberately heap ridicule, often obscenely, on the virtues and institutions they feel policemen treasure. Some students may try to provoke the police through sheer juvenile reckless-ness—for deliberately setting out to enrage an armed man is, to say the least, reckless. Other students may taunt the police in the hope of provoking a conflict that will cause hitherto uncommitted students to join them in disaffection.

The way policemen behave during a campus disorder is often the most critical determinant of the course the disorder may take. The job of a law enforcement officer in such a highly charged atmosphere is enormously complex. He must prevent the threatened injury, destruction, or illegal disrup-tion. He must minimize possible injury to the participants and to himself. He must exercise particular care to avoid conduct that can be interpreted as excessive, harassing, or discriminatory. Not only is such conduct unprofessional and sometimes unlawful, but it is also apt to make moderate members of the campus community join with the disrupters against the police.

To do all of this well requires that both the police and the universities take certain steps well in advance of any disorder to prepare for the possibility of the police on campus. We discuss below the critical need for joint planning and consultation. But this presupposes, as do our later tactical recommendations, that policemen have been pro-vided with the resources they need (but too often now lack) to do their duty coolly and expertly and to maintain their discipline under the exceptionally trying circumstances of a campus disorder.

The Need for Professionalism

The most astute advance planning and the most careful tactical preparations for police operations on the campus will not guarantee successful performance unless the policemen are well-trained professionals.

The job of law enforcement is growing in difficulty and complexity. The police bear the brunt of much of the convulsive social upheaval in this country. They are increas-

ingly beleaguered by its grim manifestations—including individual crimes of violence, disorders in the streets and on the
campus, and even violent and deadly attacks on policemen
themselves.

While there have been major improvements in law enforcement in many places in the past few years, police departments all too often have been unable to keep abreast of
increasing crime and increasing public disorder. To make real
headway will require much greater efforts, assistance from
every level of government, and broad public support.

The public and the police themselves must come to realize
that the most serious problems of law enforcement cannot be
solved by providing the police with more manpower and
more weaponry. In many departments, the need is not for
more men but for better men; it is not for more weapons
and equipment but for training that will give policemen
more sophistication, judgment, and restraint in dealing with
the complex situations they face. Police performance cannot
be judged by how much force they can or do show. American
policemen are meant to be peace keepers, not aggressors.

Police professionalism has often been undermined by
politicians who—whether through carelessness or for personal
gain—inflame the atmosphere in which the police must work.
The police should be subject to legitimate control by the
officials of the locality they serve, but those officials in turn
have the obligation to insulate the police from partisan
political influences. We cannot criticize too harshly someone
in a position of authority who in time of crisis gives
impetuous or prejudiced policemen the impression that they
have a license to misbehave with impunity. It is already
difficult enough for policemen to do their jobs in a cool,
professional manner.

Finally, if the police are to maintain the respect and
support of the public, they must deal openly and forcefully
with misconduct within their own ranks whenever it occurs.
The police are greatly harmed by the belief of many citizens
that departmental solidarity shields dishonest or brutal
policemen from punishment. Police departments must dis-

cipline those responsible for misconduct, and prosecutors must bring criminal charges whenever warranted against police officers. In the long run, it is only to the extent that policemen observe the law that they will be able to enforce it.

The Quality of Police Manpower

Law enforcement agencies desperately need better educated and better trained policemen.

The Task Force Report on the Police of the President's Commission on Law Enforcement and the Administration of Justice reported that in 1966 the median education level of police officers was 12.4 years. The Report concluded:

> There is a need for educated police officers. Certainly a liberal arts education should be prerequisite for those police officers who aspire to positions of leadership in the police service. Encouraging educated young men to enter the field of law enforcement is increasingly important. Most intelligent well-adjusted high school graduates now go into college. Unless law enforcement attracts individuals from this group, it will be forced to recruit from among those who lack either the ability or the ambition to further their education.

To recruit this manpower, local governments must provide levels of pay for the police competitive with those of private industry; there should be special monetary incentives for all who enter the police service with college degrees or who obtain degrees while in police service.

Police departments are hampered in their search for better people by limitations on the mobility of police officers among departments. Civil Service regulations require many law enforcement agencies to promote only from their own ranks. As a result, an officer who hopes to be promoted is frozen into the department in which he began, even though his skills may not be fully utilized. In addition, police departments do not permit transfer of retirement credits: officers who move to another department lose the credits they have accrued during their years of service, even though they stay in police work. These barriers to interdepartmental transfers should be removed. Police agencies should permit lateral entry from other police departments. A nationwide retirement system should be created, providing for the transfer or cumulation of retirement credits obtained in different police departments. Such a system could be established either under private auspices like the nationwide college teacher retirement plan or, if necessary, by the federal government.

Better recruitment and transfer policies will, in the long run, permit police departments to obtain more capable officers. But departments can take a simpler and more immediate step—as a growing number are doing— to improve their utilization of manpower. Departments can deploy more officers to perform the law enforcement tasks for which they are trained by relying on civilians to perform logistical and supportive functions. Civilians can serve as record clerks, school-crossing guards, lab technicians, court bailiffs, receptionists, and can perform other clerical and mechanical tasks. Civilians can also perform technical and skilled administrative functions, often more adequately than sworn personnel. Many departments have an acute need for planners, trainers, computer experts, juvenile delinquency caseworkers, and research analysts. We urge police departments to look outside their own ranks and to hire civilian specialists with these skills.

Training. Too many of the nation's law enforcement officers have been deprived of the training required to develop the skills, attitudes, and self-control they need to cope with civil and campus disorders.

The police departments of most towns and cities lack the money and experience necessary to provide such training. Smaller departments, with five or ten recruits entering at a time, cannot economically run adequate recruit or in-service training programs. Even the training programs offered by large departments often do not provide officers with an adequate understanding of the environment in which they work and the complex problems they face.

Better curricula and more skilled instructors are needed. Courses in such subjects as community relations, human relations, minority group history, police ethics, psychology, sociology, and constitutional law are essential for modern police work. And they must be taught well, through sophisticated materials and modern instructional methods.

Too few police departments have taken advantage of the resources of nearby colleges and universities to help develop the curricula and materials they need. Social science departments in these institutions could assist in developing curricula in such fields as intergroup relations and minority group history. Law schools could provide materials on relevant aspects of constitutional law and criminal procedure.

Far too many departments rely exclusively on police officers as trainers, rather than seeking skilled, professional instructors from outside. Many courses, especially those in subjects other than technical police skills, could better be taught by civilian specialists. In some cases, nearby universities would be able to provide these instructors.

The federal government should help bear the cost of expanded and improved police training programs. We recommend that the Law Enforcement Assistance Administration (LEAA) of the Department of Justice actively support a major effort to develop curricula for police training programs; that it develop and fund special programs to train instructors for police training; and that it take the initiative to promote regional or statewide training programs in which smaller departments could participate.

Specialized training in such subjects as leadership, fiscal management, and supervision is essential for those who will administer modern police departments. Here, too, departments should seek the assistance of colleges and universities. We further suggest study of the feasibility of establishing special institutes to train promising policemen and specially selected preservice recruits for supervisory positions, in order to expand the base of law enforcement leadership. These institutes, which might be patterned after the Police College at Bramshill House in Great Britain, should maintain high entrance and performance requirements and should require liberal arts courses as well as training in police administration.

Beyond these programs, however, law enforcement officers should have the opportunity to obtain a broader educational background than can be gained either in police academies or within police departments.

The Office of Academic Assistance of LEAA recently began offering financial assistance, in the form of loans and grants, for policemen and students entering law enforcement careers to pursue full-time or part-time courses related to law enforcement. In the first six months of these programs, some 20,000 students and police officers received financial aid.

Unfortunately, the federal statute limits the loan program to courses directly related to law enforcement. The result has been to foster narrow and unimaginative police science programs. According to testimony before this Commission by Charles Rogovin, former Director of the Law Enforcement Assistance Administration, these programs are "second rate"—"neither good as training nor particularly good as education." We recommend that Congress amend the Safe Streets Act to give individual policemen the opportunity to pursue broader academic interests.

The grant program also needs to be changed. Under the current program, educational assistance grants go to a designated institution rather than directly to individual policemen. We believe the grant procedure should be altered to give the grants directly to policemen and to permit them far greater freedom in choosing where they take their courses.

These changes would enable policemen seeking higher education to avoid the artificial and contrived police education courses now being offered. The changes would also permit the police to gain a better understanding of the campus community as a whole, helping to end the isolation that now so often exists.

Federal responsibility for improving law enforcement. Increasing the effectiveness of law enforcement throughout the nation will be an expensive undertaking for which federal funds are needed. The enactment of the Omnibus Crime Control and Safe Streets Act of 1968 was an initial recognition by the federal government of its responsibility in this area. The Law Enforcement Assistance Administration, established to distribute funds appropriated under Title I of that Act (primarily as block grants to the states), could play a major role in bettering law enforcement. It could provide states and localities with advice and financial assistance for improving police standards, recruiting practices, training programs, and career and educational opportunities for policemen.

To date, however, the Title I program has not fulfilled its intended purposes. The National Urban Coalition, the Conference of Mayors, the National League of Cities, and others have criticized the administration of Title I. The critics allege that LEAA has not provided sufficient leadership in the establishment of priorities for use of the funds, for the structuring of regional and local planning mechanisms, or for the development of sound action programs under Title I.

The states have responsibility for program planning and the internal allocation of block grants under Title I. But those who have studied the program say that many states have not met their responsibility adequately; they claim that grants are being dissipated, both geographically and programmatically, and that the funds are not being used for programs with any real potential to prevent or reduce crime. In some cases, critics say, too much of the money is going to rural areas and too little to urban population centers, where crime problems are far more serious.

The federal government must utilize the leverage its funds provide to encourage excellence in law enforcement. Whatever the merits of the block grant approach in the area of law enforcement, the program can be improved. Minimum performance standards are urgently needed for many aspects of police work, including training, recruiting, personnel evaluation, and administration of police complaint systems. LEAA should work to establish these standards and to ensure that its funds do not support programs which fail to meet them. This may require legislative changes, and Congress should enact any necessary amendments. Even without congressional action, LEAA can—and should—establish a full review process to insure that state plans required to be "innovative" and "comprehensive" are in fact so. It should develop effective program evaluation procedures to assure that its funds are being used to improve the quality of law enforcement.

In addition, LEAA must strengthen its nondiscrimination guidelines and its civil rights compliance machinery to guarantee that no federal funds are used to support segregated law enforcement agencies.

Nationwide professionalization of the police and the need for leadership. The effort to establish truly professional law enforcement throughout the nation could be well served by a professional organization for the police. We believe that a study group, composed primarily of local law enforcement officials, should be organized to determine how such an organization should be established, what its structure should be, and what functions it should undertake. This study group might be appropriately financed by LEAA.

The professional organization for the police, once established, could perform a number of functions to promote police professionalism. It could design and encourage a nationwide retirement system for police officers, as well as other reforms we discussed above. It could provide guidance and support for local police departments.

Most important, this organization could establish standards of conduct and ethics for all policemen just as the bar and medical associations do for lawyers and doctors. It might recommend procedures for investigating abuses and for disciplining those who violate its standards. The organization's efforts could help to insure that improper political influences do not impede professionalism of local police departments or lead to improper police conduct.

The police throughout the nation need assistance and leadership if they are to develop the kind of professional pride that will enable them to provide the public with the most effective and most just service possible.

Consultation and Planning

The police cannot prepare to deal with campus disorder without extensive consultation and joint planning with the university itself. In most cases, the relations between university officials and the police do not extend beyond what is needed to handle minor problems in normal times. This is not enough to meet the problems of a campus disruption. Developing a capacity to deal with disruption requires a continuing relationship between the university and the police. We recommend several measures to help achieve this.

The university and police must consult with one another at the first hint of a threatening situation. University officials generally have been reluctant to consult with the police until very late in the course of a crisis, while the police have often been willing to go into action without serious consultation with university officials. This lack of coordination has made dangerous situations more dangerous and has precipitated troubles that could have been averted.

Beginning consultation when a disorder is impending is, at best, a minimal step. Consultation before a crisis threatens is far better. Police officials can help administrators and campus police officers to control a disturbance with the university's internal resources before it escalates into violence. Where the assistance of outside policemen appears necessary, early consultation enables the police to respond promptly and effectively to the university's request. It gives police the opportunity to mobilize, to prepare a specific tactical plan, and to brief policemen on the roles they will play. Early consultation can familiarize campus administrators with the legal and operational constraints that govern the police response. It can give the university an opportunity to influence the shaping of police tactics. Learning the measures the police plan to use on the campus lessens surprise when those tactics are used.

But even early consultation is not enough. Public agencies and universities must develop relations of a far more regular kind. Long before the threat of a crisis, the highest officials of the university and the city or town in which it is located should arrive at some understanding about law enforcement and protest on the campus: specifically, they should agree upon the circumstances in which the police are to be called onto the campus. Until the highest authorities agree about general principles, those at the operations level cannot begin drawing up specific plans. Through good planning, university officials and the police can develop a long-range strategy for handling protest on the campus that will avoid or minimize violent confrontations.

In some cases, this will take weeks or months of consultation, discussion, and even argument. However difficult reaching such an agreement may be, the result is worth the time spent. It will provide a measure of assurance that, should trouble arise, the campus and the town will not work at cross-purposes. Most important, it may help create an atmosphere in which both university and town residents will respond reasonably rather than viscerally to each other. A policeman who knows that his chief and the mayor are dedicated to the protection of legitimate acts of protest and dissent is less likely to consider everyone with a tie-dye T-shirt and long hair as a potentially violent criminal. It is useful as well for a protesting student to know in advance precisely when his activities will be halted and that illegal conduct will be dealt with as such.

Discussions of this sort need not be formal. However, there is much merit in creating a standing joint committee composed of designated representatives of concerned public agencies and of the university. Such a committee should include the university officials chiefly responsible for dealing with campus crisis; the local chief of police, the district attorney, and the mayor, or their special assistants; and, sometimes (where, for example, a large university is situated in a small town), representatives of the state police and

National Guard, who in any event will be included in the contingency planning we discuss below.

The committee should meet regularly even when no trouble appears to be imminent. It should set general guidelines for the use of law enforcement agencies in situations of campus disorder. In addition, it could serve as a channel through which the campus and off-campus communities keep each other informed and resolve mutual problems.

Beyond this, however, universities and law enforcement agencies need to engage in detailed and technical joint contingency planning in which the state police and the National Guard are also included. Although joint contingency plans must have sufficient flexibility to accommodate the unpredictable specifics of an actual disruption and will vary from campus to campus, we can discuss some of the problems and areas the plans should cover.

A joint contigency plan should identify a university official (and his deputy) responsible for maintaining liaison with the police. It should define the circumstances under which the university is likely to call in the police. It should describe the degree of force and types of weapons likely to be used under different contingencies. It should determine the circumstances in which university observers and student marshals will be used.

The plan should address itself to the question of command among all possible participating law enforcement agencies and the National Guard. In general, local police properly have assumed command of the outside forces on campus. Command relationships may vary, however, and—particularly where National Guard troops are committed—relationships sometimes have been confused. This is why they should be established in advance—by agreement, statute, or executive directive. This will minimize friction, misunderstanding, and loss of time and effectiveness.

Proper command and control requires that the participating law enforcement agencies be able to communicate effectively with one another. Despite the strong recom-

mendations of the National Advisory Committee on Civil
Disorders and the allocation of additional emergency radio
frequencies by the Federal Communications Commission,
cooperating agencies often do not have compatible communications equipment. We found this to be the case in Jackson,
Mississippi, and it is also true in many other areas of the
country.

State governments and the federal government through
the Law Enforcement Assistance Administration should
make funds available to remedy this defect. In small
communities, where the cost of new or modified radio
equipment is not commensurate with the likely need,
participants in the contingency plan should establish procedures whereby the command post can act as a relay for
interagency communications.

As part of a joint plan, a notebook should be prepared for
each university. The notebook should include detailed maps
of the campus and the immediate vicinity, designating the
location of critical on-campus areas, sites for the location of a
command post, staging areas for personnel and equipment,
and power and communications sources.

The joint contingency plan should include arrest policies
and procedures, and it should provide for the presence of the
district attorney or his assistant to give legal guidance. Mass
arrests may require adjustments in traditional booking and
arraignment procedures and may create a need for additional
transportation and detention facilities. This in turn requires
the making of advance arrangements with judges, prosecutors, public defenders, doctors, court administrators, and
those who supply transportation, detention facilities, and
medical facilities. These matters are discussed at length in the
Report of the National Advisory Commission on Civil
Disorders.

In addition to the joint contingency plan, each law
enforcement agency should have its own, more detailed,
internal contingency plan.

The internal plan should provide for the organizational
structure and chain of command necessary to meet a

situation of campus disorder. In their day-to-day activity police officers generally work singly or in two-man teams. Many officers are not accustomed to squad-type operations under the continuous direction of supervisors. As Chief Jerry Wilson of the District of Columbia Police Department testified before the Commission:

> A police officer goes out alone or with a partner and is expected to take action based on his own judgment . . . . But in handling a demonstration you are in a considerably different situation. The police officer who just yesterday was out there more or less his own boss . . . is in a squad with a sergeant directly over him.

Moreover, the organizational structure of the department and channels of communication are oriented toward usual police business. The contigency plan should establish lines of communication that will give a commander access to accurate campus information and enable him to convey orders to the campus clearly and directly.

The agency's internal plan should also provide for the rapid and efficient mobilization of sufficient manpower. An undermanned police effort is ineffective and is likely to be dangerous to police and participants alike. If necessary, mutual assistance agreements and procedures with other law enforcement or supporting agencies should be established to insure that there will be enough manpower to respond adequately with only minimum curtailment of other essential police services. In addition, we should emphasize that contingency plans—no matter how carefully formulated—are practically useless unless they are periodically tested with the participation of all concerned agencies.

After the civil disorders in 1965-68, the Justice Department and the International Association of Chiefs of Police organized conferences involving mayors, city managers, and police officials to focus attention on the lessons learned from the riots. These conferences contributed markedly to the improvement of riot control techniques.

Last year the Law Enforcement Assistance Administration

attempted to bring university and law enforcement officials together to discuss campus disorder problems. Many universities declined this invitation. Whatever may have been the universities' justifications in the past, the events of this year have removed them. We suggest that the President ask LEAA to arrange a series of local and regional training conferences on campus disorders and that he urge top university, law enforcement, and National Guard officials to attend.

Police Tactics on the Campus

It is a truism about police work that a small mistake by an individual policeman can have enormous consequences. Therefore the seemingly trivial details of police tactics in a variety of campus situations are not at all trivial. They are the essence of a measured and appropriate response. We do not purport to provide a manual of police tactics—there are good manuals available. But we do believe it is appropriate to emphasize those tactical matters that are particularly applicable to campus disturbances.

Two points should be stated at the outset. First, with some notable exceptions, campus disorders have usually presented a less serious threat to life, limb, and property than civil disorders generally. To date, moreover, there has been little use of lethal weapons against the police in campus disorders. Second, it should be obvious that a tactic applied successfully to control one disorder may fail utterly in an attempt to control another, even though the two disorder situations may seem identical. No manual or guidelines can substitute for the exercise of sound judgment based upon the sensitive evaluation of the known facts.

Preventing public assemblies from becoming public disturbances. Mass meetings and demonstrations are a part of the everyday life of many campuses. Most of them do not require a police presence. A university which has promulgated clear, specific, and constitutional provisions regulating such events, and which has at its disposal a competent campus security force, should be able to manage most campus assemblies without difficulty.

The police can help protect the right of protestors to assemble peaceably, however. In advance of massive assemblies, or ones that appear to present some risk of violence, university officials should inform the police of the circumstances and seek their advice about how to prepare for them. A foolproof system of rapid communication between police, university officials, and leaders of the demonstration should be set up. Police observers at the demonstration can provide necessary advice and reduce police response time. If it is determined that officers should stand by, the police should establish a command post, organize the officers on a unit rather than an individual basis, and maintain clear lines of command. If deployed to the area of the assembly, the police should show as little strength, in either manpower or weaponry, as is consistent with maintaining order. Although it may occasionally serve to deter violence or disruption, the show of strength is more often counterproductive.

Dispersal of crowds on campus. The police cannot disperse or arrest a crowd simply because the university administration wants them to do so. The police enforce the criminal laws, not the university's internal rules. An assembly which violates campus rules may not be illegal. Where it is not, the police have no authority to intervene. Confusion over this point can result in an improper or ineffective law enforcement response on the campus. Such confusion can be avoided through a clear definition of the limits of the authority of the police and the situations in which the university administration may properly seek their assistance—spelled out in the contingency plan.

If it becomes necessary to restore order on the campus during a massive assembly, and if the police have authority to act, they are more likely to achieve this objective by dispersing the crowd than by attempting mass arrests. As Thomas Reddin, the former police chief of Los Angeles, told the Commission:

> The important thing is to restore order, secure the area . . . not to make arrests. If you dissipate too much

of your strength in making arrests you are going to create further incidents and just make it explode even further.

We recommend the following steps in dispersing a crowd:

(a) Every effort should be made to induce the crowd to disperse on its own. If feasible, a university official rather than a police officer should first appeal to the crowd. The official should notify the crowd that they are participating in an unlawful assembly, order them to disperse, indicate the consequences if the request is not heeded, and indicate acceptable routes of dispersal.

(b) If the crowd refuses to disperse, a police officer should repeat this order and related instructions. The police should then respond in a measured fashion. If the crowd is nonviolent, the use of well-organized police lines, moving slowly but resolutely, is the safest and most effective dispersal method. When it is necessary to arrest demonstrators who refuse to move, teams should be employed to effect methodical arrest and removal. If serious resistance or violence (short of armed resistance) is encountered, the police commander should discontinue the advance and order the use of nonlethal chemical agents, followed once again by the use of police lines. Under no circumstances should the police attempt to disperse a crowd by firing over it.

(c) Escape routes should be left open. Failure to provide avenues of escape increases the risk of injuries and induces members of the crowd to stand and fight. The crowd should always be directed toward areas that facilitate dispersal.

(d) The leaders of unlawful conduct should be arrested at the first reasonable opportunity, but at a time and place selected to minimize adverse reaction from the crowd. Inasmuch as that may require arrests following the dispersal of the crowd, it is helpful for the police to have a photographic record of the disorder for purposes of identification and evidence. The police should employ the minimum force necessary to make arrests and should avoid hasty arrest procedures, unjustified arrests, and other such unprofessional and provocative conduct.

Commanders must recognize that their conduct and attitude can help minimize tensions and confusions. By maintaining a balanced perspective, they encourage their men, and even members of the crowd, to exercise restraint.

Ending sit-ins and occupations of buildings. When the police are asked to regain possession of an occupied building, their goal should be to do it with a minimum of injury to persons and property. These guidelines should increase the likelihood of success:

(a) Before attempting to gain possession, the police should state the nature of their authority and request the occupiers to leave. If possible, this request should be conveyed personally to the leaders.

In rare situations a warning may increase the risk to property or to hostages in a building. In most situations, however, a public announcement provides the occupiers with a last opportunity to avoid arrest. Many may take advantage of the opportunity. But the very existence of this opportunity—even if no one uses it—fixes responsibility for the arrests upon those who persist in staying in the building. The announcement also minimizes the risk that surprise police action will cause a frightened or violent overreaction by the occupiers.

(b) After a brief but reasonable interval, persons remaining in the building should be arrested on a systematic and individual basis by specially detailed arrest teams. These arrest teams should use the minimum force necessary to make the arrests. They should be protected and supported by other officers in the unit. The rapid entry of a large number of officers into a building may lead to a chaotic situation, increasing the likelihood of personal injury.

(c) Police should carefully choose the time when the occupiers are to be removed from the building to reduce the threat of crowd reaction from those outside the building. University officials should be consulted before making the decision.

(d) The police should encourage a small number of students and faculty who are not involved in the occupation or sit-in to observe their action at as close a range as is practical. Observers can have a quieting influence on both the arrestees and the police; they can also refute false charges or confirm true ones against either the police or the protestors.

The control of massive disorders. Certain procedures for the deployment of police are particularly applicable to campus disorders that have become so intensified and widespread as to require large numbers of officers.

(a) Mobilized personnel should report directly to a staging or assembly area where they can be formed into squads or other tactical units before deployment to the scene of the disorder. This will enable commanders to establish early control over the operation, which usually cannot be done if officers report directly to the scene of the incident.

(b) It may often be advisable to seal off all or part of the campus. Such perimeter control limits the numbers of individuals engaged in the disorder, prevents sightseers from exposing themselves to danger or interfering with police activities, and prevents expansion of the disorder from the campus to the neighboring community.

(c) Police should leave the campus rapidly as soon as the need for their presence has ceased. Although too hasty a withdrawal of police can lead to a new outbreak of disorder, the continued appearance of a quasi-military occupation after peace has been restored can be equally inflammatory. When their presence is no longer required, officers should proceed to their off-campus command post, to be available for return to the campus if necessary.

Counteracting violent conduct and gunfire. The prevention and control of violent conduct aimed at destroying property or inflicting serious personal injury require special tactics. Above all, police commanders should make sure that their officers respond to such actions in a coordinated manner. The loss of command and control may result in hasty and precipitous action by individual officers, in the use of excessive force, and in the isolation of officers from their units, all of which increase the risk of serious physical harm.

Participants in campus disorders have very rarely fired

weapons. However, even the inaccurate report of sniper fire presents a difficult test for effective police command and control. Every police agency must develop guidelines and training procedures to insure a disciplined and orderly response whenever sniper fire is reported or observed.

Only specially trained and disciplined teams should be used in antisniper action. The general issuance of shoulder arms, such as shotguns or rifles, is normally not justified, and lethal shoulder weapons should not be carried onto the campus except by these teams. If at all possible, the teams should remain at a command post, out of sight, until ordered to a particular location to respond to reported or observed sniper fire. Only in the event of gunfire beyond the capabilities of these teams should more police be armed with such weapons. They must be subject to the same rigid controls imposed upon the antisniper teams.

The following general procedures should be followed when sniper fire is reported:

(a) The police should take cover and withhold their fire.
(b) The police should determine the validity of the report. If the report is valid, an antisniper team should be called.
(c) Persons in the area should be ordered away, and the area or building should be isolated to prevent escape of the sniper and danger to bystanders.
(d) If, as the last resort, gunfire is needed to respond to sniper fire, it should be limited and controlled by a supervisor or senior officer. Police must never respond to sniper fire with a broad barrage of gunfire.

Some police forces, such as the Mississippi Highway Safety Patrol, have allowed their officers to use a variety of unofficial weapons and ammunition during disorders. This practice can result in undisciplined fire and hinders accountability for deaths and injury. It should be ended immediately. Only through the use of specifically controlled weapons can police commanders ensure that officers are trained in their proper use.

After-action reports. High standards of professional police conduct require after-action reports. These are necessary to investigate and evaluate the disorder, to maintain internal discipline, and to improve training and operating procedures. A useful after-action report should include a log or journal of events, a list of arrests and injuries, and an evaluation of the tactics employed. A thorough investigation and report of the incident must be made, with special attention to all shooting and to complaints received about police misconduct. Those preparing the report should consult other involved law enforcement agencies, individuals witnessing or involved in the events, student and faculty marshals, and campus officials.

Covert crimes of violence. Bombing and arson have increased alarmingly on campuses. This sort of covert and terrorist crime by individuals or small groups presents an extremely difficult police problem. Often it cannot be countered without imposing severe restrictions upon movement and other individual liberties—restrictions particularly alien to an academic community. Expanding police patrols, guarding buildings, inspecting packages brought into buildings, and admitting only persons with identification cards are possible responses to the threat of bombing and arson. But the problem also necessarily involves the police in extensive intelligence-gathering activities.

Intelligence. If the police are to do their job of law enforcement on the campus properly, they need accurate, up-to-date information. Only if they are well-informed can the police know how and when to react and, equally important, when not to react.

Students' intentions are more often publicly announced than surreptitiously plotted; most student grievances are proclaimed rather than concealed. No clandestine intelligence work is necessary to discover what both university and law enforcement officials can easily discover in other ways—by sending policemen to attend open campus meetings, for example, or by making a daily harvest of the leaflets that are distributed on the campus. Surely the university administration can, and should, keep the police informed of significant day-to-day developments. Such information gathering by or for the police hardly merits charges of invasion of privacy or "repression."

But if most information-gathering techniques do not threaten anyone's privacy, some kinds, such as the use of police undercover agents posing as students, do create such dangers. They are sometimes required, but they should not be used unnecessarily. Quite aside from the possibility of abuse, these methods may compromise the openness of the university community, make its members reluctant to express themselves freely, and cause each man to suspect the good faith and integrity of his neighbors. These costs must be weighed against the value of the information gained by such techniques.

Is planting undercover agents in radical groups to keep abreast of possible plans for disorder worth the risk that the campus atmosphere will be poisoned by the suspicion that informants are lurking everywhere? Is collecting the names of the participants in groups that may be involved in such conduct worth the risk that a wave of fear about "dossiers" will sweep the campus? Such questions cannot be answered categorically. They must be answered by those involved when and where they arise.

But, lamentably, there are cases where the decision whether to use informers and undercover agents is not difficult at all. It is an undoubted fact that on some campuses there are men and women who plot, all too often successfully, to burn and bomb, and sometimes to maim and kill.

The police must attempt to determine whether or not such a plot is in progress, and if it is, they must attempt to thwart it. If they are unable to prevent it, they must seek to identify, locate, and apprehend the participants after the fact. The best, and sometimes the only, means the police have to effect these purposes, especially the preventive one, is by clandestine intelligence work. Here the general distastefulness of systematic deception is outweighed by the specific threat to life and limb.

There always is a danger that information acquired clandestinely will be used improperly: to compile dossiers to be used for general or individual intimidation, to compel people to desist from one or another kind of legal activity, to jeopardize the future careers of people who have done nothing to merit official punishment, or even to blackmail people financially.

There is also a danger that a police infiltrator may act as an *agent provocateur*. It is hard to draw very clear lines in this area, for the credibility and therefore the continued effectiveness of an informer or undercover agent may well depend on his willingness to participate in unlawful activity. It is a matter of no great moment if he merely becomes a passive participant in a sit-in. But it becomes deeply troubling when he begins hurling rocks, and it is plainly intolerable when he urges others to engage in violent conduct.

These dangers provide compelling reasons to keep intelligence operations at the lowest possible level consistent with peace and security, to entrust intelligence activities to officers whose sensitivity and integrity are above suspicion, and to allow such activities to be undertaken only under strict guidelines and with close supervision. In the long run, clandestine police work can be no more scrupulous than the departments and men who carry it out.

Finally, we are sure that uninvolved students sometimes become aware that other students are conspiring to commit violent acts, and yet they fail to do anything about it because of the tradition of student "solidarity." If students identified those who plot grave crimes, there would be considerably less need for police intelligence gathering on campus.

The State Police

The discussion and recommendations in this section apply to the state police as well as to local law enforcement agencies. Many campuses are located in medium-sized or small communities whose handfuls of undertrained police cannot begin to deal adequately with even a minor disturbance. The state police force often is capable of providing significant assistance to these local police departments. Its capability could usually be improved significantly with additional civil disorder training and, often, with increased manpower.

We urge each governor to assess the capabilities of the police force of his state, and to prepare that force for a role in controlling campus disorders.

THE NATIONAL GUARD

In recent years the National Guard has been called upon with increasing frequency to intervene in campus disturbances. During May 1970, for example, National Guardsmen were activated on 24 occasions at 21 universities in 16 states, including Kent State University in Ohio. The tragic turn of events at Kent State focused nationwide attention on the Guard—its training, its leadership, and the guidelines under which it operates on campuses. Although it has improved somewhat in response to the criticisms by the National Advisory Commission on Civil Disorders and others of its performance in civil disorders during 1967, we find that the Guard urgenly needs to improve further.

Training

Between September 1967 and June 1970 the National Guard played almost no role in Southeast Asia. During the same period it assisted civil authorities in dealing with urban and campus disorders 221 times. However, the training which National Guardsmen receive still focuses heavily on the primary mission assigned to the Guard—that of augmenting the active military in time of war or national emergency. The six-month basic training for members of the Guard is identical to that received by regular army troops. Only military policemen receive special civil disturbance training.

When guardsmen rejoin their units after basic training, they receive only limited civil disturbance training. Following the 1967 disorders in Newark and Detroit, the Department of

Defense raised the requirement for such training to 33 hours. But since then the requirement has been cut back again to 16 hours of annual refresher training and eight additional hours for new recruits. Moreover, the Department of the Army has instructed the National Guard to carry out this training between January and May, which prevents units from devoting any of their prime training period—the annual two-week summer camp—to learning how to control civil disturbances. All summer camp time is spent in regular combat training.

Guardsmen must receive far more adequate and extensive disorder control training, in recognition of the fact that the National Guard today has a second mission which it performs far more often than wartime duty.

It is not just the lack of technical skill that hampers the Guard when it is called upon to intervene in campus or civil disorders. The Guard is also limited by the dangerous lack of self-confidence that results from inadequate training. The events at Kent State betrayed not merely the Guard's poor preparation, but also the poor morale—indeed, the anxiety— that inevitably accompanies poor preparation.

We recommend that additional training in the control of civil disorders be given National Guardsmen during their six-month basic training program and also during their annual two-week summer training period, and that the federal government provide the states with funds to pay for additional disorder control training.

In some instances the Army has sent senior Guard officers to the Civil Disturbance Orientation Course at Fort Gordon, Georgia, and has established similar courses for junior officers in some states. In a few states the Guard participates in field training exercises with police agencies. We recommend that the Department of the Army ensure that all senior Guard officers attend the Civil Disturbance Orientation Course and that it encourage participation by junior officers in annual field training exercises with police agencies. We also recommend that university administrators be invited to attend the course and observe the exercises.

Protective Equipment

The equipment currently worn by guardsmen is designed for combat use, not for civil or campus disorders. In most states the Guard's protective gear is far inferior to that worn by the police. This lack of defensive equipment—helmets, face masks, flak vests, etc.—subjects guardsmen to the risk of personal injury, which in turn increases the danger that they will overreact to threatened harm.

Proper protective equipment not only wards off rocks and bottles hurled by demonstrators, but also serves an important deterrent function. As Major General Charles L. Southward of the District of Columbia National Guard told the Commission, the use of visible protective equipment impresses demonstrators with the guardsmen's determination. This in itself often obviates the need to employ force.

Some progress has been made since 1967 in supplying the Guard with protective equipment, but guardsmen have arrived on many campuses without it. We recommend that the Department of the Army assign a high priority to the provision of protective equipment for guardsmen detailed to civil disturbance duty.

Nonlethal Weapons

The Department of the Army must ensure that guardsmen have appropriate equipment for campus and civil disorders, as well as combat equipment. The two separate functions of the Guard—and the different equipment needed for each—must not be confused. Rifles designed for combat use have been inappropriately carried onto the campus in the past. Effective nonlethal weapons are urgently needed by the Guard, so that M-1 rifles or other lethal weapons will not be improperly used in campus disorders again.

The Department of the Army, which has the responsibility for outfitting and arming the Guard, should ensure that its members are provided with the tear gas, batons, and other nonlethal equipment generally appropriate for campus and civil disorders.

After the disorders of 1967, the National Advisory Commission on Civil Disorders urged that the federal government undertake a crash program of research to develop improved nonlethal weapons. To date, little has come of this research. The need for something more effective than tear gas and less deadly than bullets is greater than ever before. We recommend that the federal government actively continue its research to develop nonlethal control devices for use in civil and campus disorders.

Lethal Weapons

Issuing lethal weapons to inexperienced or part-time soldiers involved in controlling a campus disorder creates a great and unjustifiable danger. We recommend that the states forbid guardsmen to carry rifles, shotguns, and sidearms on the campus, except as follows:

First, until nonlethal devices and protective gear are available to guardsmen, it may be necessary, as a last resort, to issue unloaded shoulder arms for defensive and crowd control purposes. But we reiterate that nonlethal devices and protective gear must be made available immediately.

Second, squad or detail leaders trained in the use of sidearms should carry them holstered while on the campus. This creates little risk and affords a measure of protection to the squad or detail in the face of an emergency.

Third, if the command officer is convinced there is a risk of sniper fire, he should deploy specially trained antisniper teams operating under guidelines similar to those set forth for the police earlier in this chapter.

Only in the event of armed resistance for which antisniper teams are inadequate is it proper to deploy disciplined fire teams, armed with appropriate weapons. They must operate under controls similar to those imposed on antisniper squads. They should be available for immediate deployment but held until that time at nearby locations.

The Army manual on civil disturbances and disorders used by the Guard should explicitly describe those situations in which the issuance of rifles and ammunition is inappropriate.

The Army and the National Guard Bureau should make every effort to see that these guidelines are adopted.

The provocative appearance of a rifle is multiplied when a bayonet is affixed to it. Using bayonets in a campus situation is unthinkable and should be prohibited. The Department of the Army and the National Guard Bureau guidelines should explicitly forbid it.

Use of Force

The Guard must adopt uniform and restrictive guidelines governing the use of deadly force. The Army guidelines, contained in the manual *Civil Disturbances and Disorders*, specify that only commanders may issue live ammunition to soldiers. The guidelines forbid soldiers to load or fire their weapons without direct orders from an officer. Before such an order can be issued, moreover, the responsible officer must determine that three circumstances exist:

1. Lesser means have been exhausted or are unavailable.
2. The risk of death or serious bodily harm to innocent persons is not increased by its use.
3. The purpose of its use is one or more of the following:
   a. Self-defense to avoid death or serious bodily harm.
   b. Prevention of a crime which involves a substantial risk of death or serious bodily harm (for example, sniping).
   c. Prevention of the destruction of public health or safety.
   d. Detention or prevention of the escape of persons against whom the use of deadly force is authorized in subparagraphs (a), (b), and (c) immediately above.

In almost all states the Guard is nominally committed to adhering to the Army guidelines for the use of force. In actual practice, however, some state units have deviated substantially from the Army guidelines. For example, the Ohio Rules of Engagement provide in part: "In any instance . . . when rioters to whom the riot acts have been read cannot be dispersed by any other reasonable means, then shooting is justified." We recommend that state National Guard organizations adopt and strictly adhere to standards of restraint for the use of deadly force in campus disorders which at a minimum conform to those promulgated by the Department of the Army.

The Decision to Call Up the Guard

During a number of recent campus disorders, the Guard has been sent onto campuses prematurely. Sometimes this has been the result of inadequate information, planning, and coordination. On other occasions, political considerations appear to have contributed to the decision. Premature commitment may worsen a tense situation and reduce the likelihood of a peaceful resolution.

Premature commitment of the Guard must not be confused with early mobilization. There is an inevitable lapse of time between a call for the Guard and its arrival in the vicinity of a disorder. If the threat that a campus situation will get out of hand is great, the National Guard should be mobilized, stationed at a place close to the potential trouble spot where it will attract little attention, and retained there on a standby basis until it is needed or until the threat has subsided.

There are times, moreover, when the very fact of the arrival of the Guard may avert disorder before any has begun. When reliable information indicates that a mass assembly or demonstration threatens to become violent, the presence of the Guard may serve a deterrent function. The Guard successfully played such a preventive role in New Haven in May 1970.

To facilitate the decision as to whether and when the Guard should be committed, every state should adopt a formal set of guidelines, preferably in the form of a statute or an executive order, setting forth the circumstances that justify the use of the Guard.

Such guidelines should provide, for example, that Guard units not be sent onto a campus unless there is serious and widespread violence that cannot be controlled by local and state police. State constitutions often give governors great discretion in activating Guard units, and guidelines cannot restrict this constitutional power. Nevertheless, a definition of the emergency conditions that justify the use of the Guard, prepared well in advance of a crisis, will help a governor faced with this difficult decision.

The power to activate the National Guard must be clearly fixed. It appears that in some situations the state commander of the National Guard has acted without authority, or that the governor has delegated his responsibility to the state commander. In one instance, in May 1970, two squads of the Oregon National Guard appeared on the University of Oregon's campus at the personal request of the police chief of Eugene and without the authorization of the state commander. The state commander and governor were unaware of the deployment and, when informed, ordered immediate withdrawal.

We recommend that each state review its laws concerning Guard call-up, and amend them to give the governor sole authority to activate the Guard. Of course, it is extremely important that the governor consult university, local government, and law enforcement officials before making that decision.

Deployment of the Guard

The Guard should generally be deployed in a manner that supplements rather than supplants the efforts of local and state police agencies. Guard units should be used primarily for tasks that call for large numbers of men and do not require close or frequent supervision. These include such assignments as establishing perimeter control, manning barricades, guarding buildings, riding with fire department vehicles to protect firemen, and guarding prisoners in open areas.

Whenever possible, confronting crowds of disorderly or

violent people should be left to the police. If police need the assistance of guardsmen in these situations, they should assign officers to work with Guard units involved. Such liaison officers can ensure coordination between the Guard's activities and those of the police. The officers also can furnish technical advice and assistance to the Guard, which in most cases has little or no experience with such details of police routine as making arrests.

The command relationship between the Guard and the police often presents complex practical as well as political problems. When the Guard is deployed to assist a large and knowledgeable police force, the local police chief should command. However, we have noted that local police forces are often too small to respond to a disturbance alone, and officers from neighboring towns, from the county sheriff's force, and possibly from the state police are likely to be on the scene.

The Guard's role in this confusing scheme is too important a matter to be decided in the midst of a crisis. It must be determined in advance and tested and confirmed in joint training exercises.

Some states have enacted statutes defining command relationships when the Guard is called up to help the police. We urge the states that have not yet explored this possibility to do so. In any event, the order activating the Guard should spell out clearly the command responsibility if it has not been previously established. Inappropriate or confused command can prolong or intensify a disorder.

State and Federal Responsibility

A governor is the commander-in-chief of the Guard in his state, and he has the authority for directing its activities. Governors must recognize—as apparently not all do—how grave their responsibility is when they call out the Guard to intervene in a civil or campus disorder.

Under existing law, the federal government has little control over how any state Guard conducts its affairs unless the President federalizes it. Nevertheless, the federal government can and should play a major role in improving the Guard. The Army should assign a much higher priority than it does to equipping and training the Guard for duty in civil disturbances.

In addition, we urge the President to use the power of his office to help persuade the states to bring their Guard up to the standard necessary to deal properly with civil disturbances. The President should invite the governors to meet with him to discuss methods for improving the Guard and insuring that it has effective professional leadership and the resources it needs. We urge him to do this at once. One Kent State is far too many.

CONCLUSION

In this chapter we have emphasized steps which should be taken to minimize the dangers of violent overreaction to campus demonstrations by the police and the National Guard. The relation of such overresponse to the escalation of violence on both sides is devastatingly clear. The use of excessive force against students, like the dangerous use of violence by students, is a manifestation of the disturbing trend toward polarization in this country.

We have emphasized what must be done to reverse this trend. But we should not fail to note what has already been done. In May 1970, in literally hundreds of cities, thousands of policemen responded to mass student demonstrations with professional skill. With intelligence and restraint, the police withstood severe verbal and even physical provocation during extended tours of duty. In Washington and New Haven, for example, massive demonstrations, which attracted not only peaceful protestors but also small minorities determined to precipitate disorder, were handled with exemplary sophistication and calm.

While the improper use of force by the police or National Guard may exacerbate campus situations, its proper use can protect the right to protest and prevent the occurrence of violence. Moreover, it is clear to us that, in the face of violent and dangerous conduct, the use of force—at the minimum level necessary—is completely warranted to defend the university and our civil society.

The growing disrespect for police is a sad consequence of our national disunity. It will not disappear until as a nation we agree that the cost of injustice and disorder is too high.

It is essential that those committed to law, order, and justice in these difficult times recognize and commend the high standards of professionalism that an impressive number of law enforcement agencies meet.

Police departments are not the independent masters of their own destiny. Police professionalism cannot be further developed without a recognition of its prerequisites by top civilian officials and their decision to support it and give it room to develop.

The police—and the National Guard—cannot meet the new challenges confronting them without assistance. They need broad public support to perform their enormously difficult tasks skillfully and effectively. The prevention of needless and tragic violence is the shared responsibility of us all.

6

University Reform

The many serious weaknesses in American colleges and universities today have contributed significantly and needlessly to the growth of campus unrest.

In Chapter 4 we have considered remedies for the unpreparedness and inconsistency which often have characterized university responses to specific incidents of disorder.

In this chapter, our concern is with the reform of the structure of the university and of the educational experiences it offers. Recent history has made it only too clear that the failure of the university to pursue effectively its stated goals, let alone to live up to them, has also contributed to student unrest.

The goals of any university reform should be clearly understood at the outset. No college or university should change itself in order to satisfy every demand, no matter how ill-considered or inappropriate, that students may make of it. Any attempt to do so will ultimately fail and is likely in the long run only to weaken the university still more. Nor should a university undertake reforms in the hope that these will guarantee its freedom from disruption and violence. There are many factors which have contributed to the current pattern of student protest, and most of them are not within the university's control. Moreover, even the most perfect university the imagination could conceive would still be an unrestful place. Among other things, it would concentrate on its campus significant numbers of young people, and it would encourage them to entertain novel ideas, to read heterodox books, and to submit all received wisdom to critical scrutiny.

What universities should attempt, however, is to create a climate—a sense of community and of common purpose—in which widely shared agreement on the fundamental mission and values of the university itself will deter the destructive forms of protest. To create such a climate, the university will have to demonstrate, both to students and to the larger society, that its values are worthy of support and that its policies and programs reflect an authentic commitment to those values.

The last few decades have witnessed a serious erosion of any clear sense of mission in American higher education. Students, faculty, and the larger society are increasingly in agreement that the university has failed to give priority and meaning to its central purposes. In our view, this failure—and it is primarily a failure of commitment—has occurred in four major ways:

* Academic freedom has been threatened by increasing political pressure within the university and from the larger society.

* The university's core functions—teaching and research—have suffered as increasing involvement in peripheral service activities has drained vital resources from them and compromised the university's commitment to them.

* Few new and academically sound programs have been developed; educational reform has been too slow at some institutions and excessively rapid at others.

* Traditional assumptions about university governance have become invalid as the minimal but essential sense

of community once shared by most faculty, students, and administrators has eroded.

ACADEMIC FREEDOM AND THE MISSION OF THE UNIVERSITY

When we say that universities have failed to adapt themselves to contemporary conditions, we have in mind a historic definition of the central purposes of higher education that should be restated. The key functions of the university are two: first, teaching and learning; second, research and scholarship.

Teaching and learning should involve all parts of a university community. Faculty members, though defined primarily as teachers, are also expected to be learners. Students, though formally cast in the role of learners, have much to teach, as many professors can attest. And administrators and trustees should be both learners and teachers, open to new ideas and ready to share their understanding of the university with students, faculty, and the public.

Research and scholarship are no less essential to higher education. The contribution of a university to society lies not merely in the imparting of knowledge, but also in the search for new knowledge and in a constant reexamination of traditional widsom. It should be noted in this context that a major part of the renewal of our society's wisdom, of its vision of itself, and of its moral canons occurs in undergraduate teaching, where the confrontation of experience and imagination, of the old and the young, takes place.

In emphasizing the centrality of teaching and research, we have omitted that commitment to "service" often included as a separate university function. "Service" has too often covered activities that are at odds with the central function of the university and that the university is ill equipped to perform.

Teaching and research are themselves the major services higher education renders. More than any other institution in modern society, the university serves the community through its capacity to examine and analyze and to provide each generation with the best skills, understanding, and knowledge available. The university at its best is and must be a "service organization," not by attempting to be something other than a university, but rather by fulfilling its own basic mission as well as it can for its own place and time.

When we stress the importance of research and teaching in the university, we are reiterating traditional principles. Yet in this time of rapid change, growing polarization, and pressing social problems, these ancient principles must be applied in new ways. In 1970, to insist that the university concern itself with teaching and research is also to insist that it teach and learn in and for today's world.

For the university to function adequately—for it to be a true university—it must create an atmosphere of openness, lively debate, critical discussion, generosity, freedom from intimidation, and mutual respect and tolerance. These are the components of academic freedom, and its defense requires resistance to pressures toward conformity and the presence of a forum in which diverse views are respected, frank exchanges of opinion and fact are encouraged, and no view honestly presented and defended is held to be beyond the pale.

If academic freedom is to be maintained, the public must understand the long-term benefits it offers to society at large. Such understanding has not always existed. There is a long history of efforts, often successful, by those outside the academic community to prevent the discussion of controversial views, the appearance of controversial speakers, or the advocacy of unpopular positions on university campuses.

In this time of rapid cultural, social, and technological change, the expansion of knowledge through free inquiry and debate is more important to society than ever before. Yet today, both external and internal threats to academic freedom have increased as the nation has become more sharply divided.

The revelation that research or teaching has often directly or indirectly supported controversial public policies has led many (rightly, we believe) to question the claim that

American higher education is "institutionally neutral." Yet some students and faculty have reacted not by insisting that the university strive for greater neutrality, but rather by urging that the university become more one-sided and more openly political. Experience clearly demonstrates, however, that if the university is to hold the public support it must have to exist, it must be steadfast in its commitment to combat dogmatism, intolerance, and condescension, as well as attempts to suppress divergent opinions among its members.

The Question of Politicization

One of the most widespread fears of many faculty members, administrators, and students, as well as of the general public, is that the current wave of campus unrest has resulted in, or will lead to, "politicization" of the university.

In a narrow sense, universities are inevitably political institutions. They both affect and are affected by local, state, and national politics. Their decisions about admissions policies and educational programs may have direct or indirect political impact. The various service projects which they undertake for government, industry, and local communities frequently have political implications. Finally, universities often act politically when the interests of higher education itself are directly at stake. Institutional positions in favor of increased financial support, in opposition to government policies that directly and adversely affect higher education, or in defense of institutional autonomy and academic freedom, are widely regarded as both political and legitimate.

In the end, it rests with individual institutions to decide which political issues have direct bearing on higher education and warrant taking institutional positions. We recommend, in general, that such institutional positions be taken infrequently: only when there is clear evidence concerning the direct effects of government policies on higher education; only after considering other possible actions short of taking institutional positions; and only following a full appraisal of the consequences for academic freedom which could flow from taking such a stand. Even then, institutional positions should be taken, when possible, by many institutions acting in concert, rather than by single universities acting alone.

As a practical matter, it would be naive for universities that frequently or intensely involve themselves in controversial political issues to expect to retain the full financial and attitudinal support of a society to which they may seem to be laying political siege.

Even more important, the frequent assumption of political positions by universities as institutions reduces their ability to pursue their central missions. As Professor Kenneth Keniston has stated:

> The main task of the university is to maintain a climate in which, among other things, the critical spirit can flourish. If individual universities as organizations were to align themselves officially with specifically political positions, their ability to defend the critical function would be undermined. Acting as a lobby or pressure group for some particular judgment or proposal, a university in effect closes its doors to those whose critical sense leads them to disagree.

Political involvement of the *members* of universities is quite another matter, of course. Students, faculty members, and administrators may participate as individuals in the full range of peaceful political activities.

The university is often held responsible for the actions of individuals or groups who are its members. Sometimes this happens even when these political actions are obviously unrepresentative and clearly do not have the support of the institutions involved. We urge everyone—alumni, legislators, and the public at large—to understand that such individual actions are just that, and to refrain from condemning a university or withholding support from it because it protects its members' rights as citizens.

Universities, for their part, have an obligation to assure that the rights of students and faculty are not abridged from within the university community and to see to it that institutional supplies and services are not used for the direct political activities of students and faculty.

Some universities have recently considered holding a formal recess for several days or for one or two weeks immediately prior to the general election in November. On some campuses, this proposal has the apparent support of a majority of students. The most widely publicized of these proposals, the Princeton Plan, was developed in May 1970, partly in response to opposition to the Cambodian incursion. Some argue that adoption of this plan would necessarily involve politicization of the university. Others maintain, however, that as long as members of the university are free to support whatever candidates they wish (or none if they choose), and as long as the plan is intended as a permanent university program to encourage involvement in campaigns and in issues in general—for its own sake, and not as a unique response to a specific issue—an election recess is not a partisan political act.

Proponents of the plan note that a fall recess to allow students to participate in the political process of a democratic nation may make as much sense in 1970 as the summer recess, whose origins lie in the distant agricultural past. Opponents of the plan counter that most political activity takes place during the summer and early fall before primary elections, that during those periods most students and faculty are completely free to participate, and that even during the academic year they are generally more free to participate than are most Americans, whose job and other responsibilities are not so easily put off as those of students and faculty members.

Undoubtedly, different universities will resolve this issue in different ways in accord with their own intentions and interests.

SERVICE ACTIVITIES

The service activities of American universities are relevant to a discussion of campus unrest for at least three reasons.

First, university services that entail direct or indirect support for controversial policies have been the primary target of many student protests. Second, student activists often urge that the university should become a service agency promoting social change. Finally, involvement of faculty members in outside consulting and research activities diverts the scarce resources of the university from its primary missions of teaching and research.

American higher education has a long tradition of providing direct services. Since the second half of the 19th century, many American colleges and universities have provided a variety of agricultural and engineering services. Such efforts have frequently enhanced teaching and research and have usually created no intense political controversies.

During World War II many universities developed new service commitments to defense-related research. Most of the conditions that made earlier kinds of service feasible still applied. Since World War II, however, government and industry have turned to the universities for both advice and research in an ever-growing variety of tasks, while students, faculty, and some citizens have urged direct university programs to deal with racism, housing, unemployment, crime, water and air pollution, hunger, and overpopulation.

These new kinds of service activities differ from the traditional kinds in two major ways. First, many of the new service projects bear little natural relation to research and teaching. Second, the services, and the methods of performing them, are sometimes highly controversial. The various constituencies—from students to taxpayers—that are essential to the financial support and academic freedom of the universities tend to react sharply when the university engages in services whose political purposes or consequences they oppose.

Some universities—particularly in recent years—have tried to solve this problem by performing services for practically every constituency that requested it. Their assumption was that, out of gratitude for the services it received, each would ignore the university's close ties with opposing groups and organizations. Many other universities expanded their service commitments in a more random, less conscious, fashion. In both cases, major pressures were generated by faculty members in quest of research and service grants and the prestige, promotion, and mobility their capture brought. But whatever their origins, these service relationships are now a major source of income in many universities and provide the bulk of the operating budgets for teaching and pure research as well as for applied research of some departments and divisions. As a result of these developments, a major problem now confronts universities attempting to conserve scarce resources and to redirect them toward teaching and research: What to do about existing and proposed service relationships?

In general, we recommend reduction of outside service commitments. But this recommendation is tempered by our earlier insistence that teaching and research are forms of service. And today it must be accompanied by a second recommendation: As universities reduce their extraneous service commitments, they must also search for new ways to serve by relating their policies, programs, and expertise to pressing local and national problems.

Service to the Local Community

American universities have special—and sometimes neglected—responsibilities to the communities in which they are located. Especially when they are in or near areas of major economic and social deprivation, universities should carefully examine their existing policies in the light of the following suggestions:

* Universities should avoid actions that will aggravate existing local problems or create new problems.

* Plans for university expansion should be implemented only after consultation with the community.

* In light of existing teaching and research programs,

colleges and universities should search for service projects that strengthen the university's basic purposes. Medical education is an example of the fruitful union of direct health services with medical teaching and research.

* Universities should also consider providing field work and other "real world" experience in conjunction with regular academic work in the social sciences and the arts. A model for such a program—a multidisciplinary graduate school of applied behavioral sciences—has been proposed recently by the National Academy of Sciences and the Social Science Research Council.

* Universities should make available to members of the local community as many educational and cultural programs as possible within the constraints of their other commitments and responsibilities.

* Outside practitioners should be more frequently involved in regular academic courses, especially in the social sciences, in order to provide students with the opportunity to compare the practitioner's perspective on the world and on his experience of it with that of the academician.

* In making decisions, universities should consider giving weight to broad social aims and to specific community needs. For example, some institutions are already acting—although not without considerable complications—as sponsors for federally subsidized housing, while others are developing practices to guarantee equal opportunity to minority group workers and businesses.

* Universities should set an example of nondiscriminatory practices in all areas.

While urging universities to accept increased responsibilities vis-a-vis their local communities, we recognize that university resources should not be spread too thin. Furthermore, a key criterion for judging service proposals must be the extent to which they allow the university to do what it can do best. The experience of the last decades indicates that when higher education undertakes service projects that are not consonant with its basic mission of teaching and research, it is incapable of performing either that mission or the services well.

Services to the Federal Government

Defense research on the campus generally is under vigorous attack from many students and faculty members. Much of this research, however, has academic merit; the fact that the money supporting it comes from the Pentagon is hardly evidence that it does not enhance academic programs. For such research to be academically productive, however, it must be readily available and subject to use and criticism by other scholars. Because classified research does not meet this crucial criterion, we recommend that universities avoid acceptance of new classified projects and terminate existing classified projects unless it is clear that the undesirable results of undertaking such a project are outweighed by compelling advantages.

Besides performing military research, many American universities—particularly state-supported land-grant institutions—have housed and given credit for ROTC programs. These programs, which now involve 212,000 students on 353 campuses, provided over two fifths of the officers commissioned in the armed forces in fiscal year 1970.

Advocates of ROTC argue that officers trained in civilian universities rather than the service academies provide a valuable civilian dimension to a professional military officer corps. The need for college trained officers would become all the more important, they claim, with an all-volunteer, professional military force. The armed services prefer ROTC to expanded service academies because ROTC is less expensive, and they believe that it produces more capable officers than officer candidate schools.

On the other hand, ROTC is a form of vocational training which is different from the rest of the curriculum at many institutions. It involves courses designed by the services, not by the faculty, and taught by instructors not chosen by normal faculty selection procedures. Moreover, opponents of ROTC contend that it aligns a university with controversial federal defense policies.

In Chapter 7 we recommend development of non-college-based military training programs and improvement of existing ROTC programs on the campus. Many schools will continue to find ROTC compatible with their other activities, while others will choose to terminate their ROTC contracts. Each college or university must determine for itself whether continuation of such programs is appropriate in its particular setting.

Faculty Service Commitments

Some professors have extensive outside service and consulting jobs. We believe that professors who are preoccupied with such outside work can have a damaging effect on teaching and scholarship. The conglomerate university may have service-oriented departments but still maintain a community of scholars as one of its divisions. But the entrepreneurial professor cannot so easily claim that his outside activities have no effect on his academic role.

Naturally, as with the institution, the question is one of degree: not all outside activities detract from scholarship, and some enhance it.

But some scholars are so heavily engaged in outside research that they have become virtually inaccessible to students and colleagues. In students' eyes, they are compromised by their dependence on nonacademic patronage and by their attachment to rewards more tangible than the discovery of truth. But most important, the existence of substantial outside commitments means that faculty members do not give to teaching and research a fair share of time, energy, or care.

We recommend that universities establish general guidelines governing both the acceptance of outside commitments by the institution and the outside activities of individual faculty members. The guidelines should restrict outside service activities—whether for government, industry, or the local community—that drain energies away from teaching and research. Such guidelines should be sensitive both to the individual rights of faculty members and to the differences between teachers in various disciplines. They should be developed and enforced by committees of faculty members and administrators.

As Professor Jacques Barzun has suggested, the members of such committees

must be intelligent, scrupulous, puritanical, and must carry heavy life insurance. Logrolling has to be suppressed, as well as temperamental attachment to the "tried-and-true" and "good enough." The committee members must work for the university—for themselves through its preservation—and they must see its salvation not in prestige but in performance . . . not "every full professor is entitled to his sideshow"; rather "what will this sidewhow contribute to teaching? To knowledge? How many of its size can we carry at one time?"

IMPROVING HIGHER EDUCATION

Several changes in curriculum and degree requirements seem likely to improve the climate, quality, and cohesiveness of the university.

A university that made such changes would become a university whose students would be more likely to be there because they genuinely wanted to be. It would offer students a variety of different learning styles and educational programs, an environment in some reasonable human scale, and academic work and teaching both educationally sound and relevant. It would certainly not be a university without dissent, controversy, or protest. But it would be a university whose members were more committed to its central purposes. We believe that recent experience demonstrates the urgent need for a renewed sense of shared commitment and community within American higher education.

One major step in this direction would be to encourage what has been called the voluntary university. As we have noted earlier, general pressures in American society, aided by government largesse, have led to a vast expansion of college and university enrollments in the past three decades. Many students are now enrolled in higher education largely for the sake either of being enrolled and certified or of being draft-deferred, and not for the sake of obtaining an education. The presence of such unwilling students at the university seriously undermines its morale, for understandably they demand kinds of experience and instruction that universities are ill equipped to provide.

To alleviate this condition, universities should consider ways to reduce the flexible scheduling of most present degree programs, as well as ways to eliminate the stigma attached to "dropping out." Students who have doubts about their higher education, or who are preoccupied with personal or political matters, should be given every opportunity to take extended leaves of absence, with guarantees of readmission and renewal of financial aid.

It should also become easier to gain access to nondegree programs; the process of transferring from one institution to another should be simplified; and universities and colleges which are near each other should permit extensive reciprocal registration in courses. The value of residency requirements for graduate students should be reconsidered.

Universities might also consider establishing work-study programs, which can offer meaningful experiences for some students, better financial arrangements for others, and, perhaps, better use of scarce resources and facilities for the university as a whole.

Another general way of improving the morale in American colleges and universities is to increase the variety of teaching styles and learning environments. Many students who are capable of taking advantage of the opportunities of higher education are not stimulated, or are even repelled, by the uniform approach to teaching which prevails at many American universities. Such exclusive reliance upon either narrative-memorization styles or abstract conceptual styles may deter many students from learning. Colleges and universities should experiment with and, where feasible, adopt additional styles of teaching and learning. The predominance of departmentalized courses also needs to be reexamined, as does the educational value of heavy reliance upon lectures, examinations, grades, and even degrees.

No one educational system will suit the needs of all students. Greater diversity in teaching approaches and educational programs should be made available within the framework of single universities and throughout higher education. If universities offered more diverse programs, more students might find greater challenge and excitement in their work, and their commitment to the purposes of the institution might be correspondingly greater.

Still another way for universities to improve their cohesiveness is to limit their size. A major factor contributing to the loss of a sense of community in American higher education has been the development of huge universities with as many as thirty thousand, forty thousand, or more students on a single campus. As size increases, effective communication becomes difficult, governance becomes unwieldy, and students have less sense of involvement with the institution as a whole.

We recommend that government should avoid—and educators should resist—further increasing the size of existing campuses. Additional growth should be achieved by starting new branches under separate systems of governance.

Very large universities should seriously consider decentralization at their current sites or geographic dispersal of some of their units. As Bruce Dearing, President of the State University of New York at Binghamton, testified before the

Commission, "Human scale may be developed or recreated through sub-colleges, house plans, various living-learning facility groupings, language, ethnic or common interest corridors."

The idea of cluster colleges—small units whose definition of purpose is shared by students and faculty members with common interests—seems particularly promising. It is worth noting in this connection that in California cluster-college institutions have experienced less violence and disruption these past few years than have multiversities.

Another common student complaint about American higher education is the charge of "irrelevance." Often this charge comes from students whose presence at the university is not entirely voluntary. In some cases, the remedy for their discontent will be a more voluntary university, with freer entry and exit. But in other cases, we believe that the remedy will be a reform of curriculum to include subjects and courses which students find more "relevant." There have been too few careful attempts to relate past experience, traditional knowledge, and academic methods to the problems and conditions of modern society in ways that are educationally sound.

In the search for greater relevance, subjects that are esoteric, traditional, or highly abstract should not be neglected or eliminated, but there must also be course offerings which focus directly and concretely upon the contemporary world. Students demand and deserve an education that will provide them with the knowledge needed to be effective and responsible members of society.

Finally, and of major importance, many students complain that the quality of the teaching they receive is poor. They generally blame excessive outside faculty commitments, university reward systems biased in favor of research and publication, and faculty indifference.

We believe these charges often have a basis in fact. Many universities have developed no systematic way of assessing teaching performance through consultation with students.

Students should be provided with regular means for evaluating courses and the teaching effectiveness of faculty members. Faculty committees should be enpowered to act upon the information gathered and to make recommendations for improvement.

As one means of improving the quality of teaching in higher education, we urge reconsideration of the practice of tenure. Tenure has strong justifications because of its role in protecting the academic freedom of senior faculty members. But it also can protect practices that detract from the institution's primary functions, that are unjust to students, and that grant faculty members a freedom from accountability that would be unacceptable for any other profession.

At all levels of the university, excellence in teaching should be recognized, along with excellence in scholarly work, as a criterion for hiring, salary increases, and promotion. In the case of nontenured faculty, clear evaluation procedures emphasizing both teaching and research should be developed, publicized, and used.

For the same reasons, the role of graduate teaching assistants should be reconsidered. The present system of undergraduate education at many universities relies heavily upon graduate students to do much of the teaching. These teaching assistants are necessarily inexperienced, often distracted by the demands of their own degree program, not infrequently unprepared to give even minimally adequate instruction, and in some cases deeply disillusioned. They often have little choice over whether to be a teaching assistant and are generally underpaid and overworked. No college or university can do justice either to its undergraduates or to its graduate students as long as it continues the current system of graduate teaching assistantships. We would strongly recommend eliminating the "TA" were it not for the fact that universities cannot presently afford to do so. At a minimum, however, they can and should take steps to improve the teaching skills and working conditions of these assistants.

CAMPUS GOVERNANCE

One of the most hotly disputed topics on American campuses today is that of governance—who shall have the power to make organizational and educational decisions? A major complaint of student protestors is their lack of formal power in this process. Few major campus disturbances have been without demands for a "restructuring" of university governance in order to expand the role of students.

Until the last decade, the nation's academic institutions devoted little attention to the allocation of decision-making powers to students. It seemed natural to most faculty members, administrators, and trustees that each had distinct privileges and responsibilities—although these varied greatly from institution to institution and were often bitterly disputed. Students rarely if ever participated in the process of governance. Most institutions assumed—largely correctly—that controversies about campus matters could be readily resolved because of the prevailing sense of community among the interested parties.

Unfortunately, the importance of this sense of community to the process of university governance was little appreciated until it had seriously eroded. And few institutions have yet developed more effective means to compensate for its loss. Recent campus disorders have revealed startling weaknesses in the systems of governance at most universities.

Most current debate and experimentation revolve around questions of student participation in university decisions on academic matters, general policy issues, and the regulation of student life. Evidence has been produced both for and against various participatory models of governance. Unfortunately, there is too little experience to date with participatory university government to permit conclusive judgments about the merits of any of the particular models being tried, or of the idea of participation in general.

In any case, no single method of governance will suit all institutions of higher education equally well. In keeping with their individual purposes and traditions, universities will and should continue to differ in their internal organization and administration. It is therefore possible to offer only very general guidelines to be considered in the process of reform of governance.

* Increased participation of students, faculty, and staff in the formulation of university policies is desirable.

* However, universities are not institutions that can be run on a one man, one vote basis or with the participation of all members on all issues.

* Competence should be a major criterion in determining involvement in the university decision-making process.

* Another criterion for involvement in decision-making should be the degree to which decisions affect any given group. Changes in regulations concerning student life should be made with the involvement of students; changes in faculty policies should obviously be made with faculty involvement.

* Procedures for electing representatives of university constituencies should be carefully designed to guarantee true representativeness, perhaps by having representatives elected by small departmental or residential units, or by establishing quorum requirements to encourage participation and to enhance the legitimacy of the election result.

* Reforms of governance should not undermine administrative leadership. On the contrary, they should be designed to produce policies and leaders who will have the broad support of the community, especially in times of campus crisis.

* Once basic policy decisions are made, their execution should be left to expert administrative hands. Administrators must, of course, remain ultimately accountable to the various constituencies of the university—

trustees, students, faculty, alumni, and the general public. But their actions should not be constantly overseen by any of these groups. The involvement of nonadministrators in the daily operations and minor policy decisions of the university erodes the effectiveness and sense of responsibility of administrators.

Creation of procedures for dealing with grievances is an aspect of university governance that deserves special attention. Few American colleges and universities have done enough to improve communications—to assure that grievances are promptly heard, fairly considered, and, if necessary, acted upon. Often administrators and faculty have been taken by surprise by the intensity of student feeling over issues. And often, those charged with university decision-making have been unresponsive or condescending toward student criticisms and suggestions.

Students do not typically conceal their grievances. If an administrator and his aides take the time to talk to students and faculty, to read the student paper and student handbills, and to attend occasional student meetings and rallies, they will find it easier to understand what students are thinking. The reasons for doing this are clear enough. Many grievances are legitimate and correctable, but even when they are not—even when they are nothing but a pretext for disruption—they often arouse emotions that are more than ephemeral. Within the limits of practicality, every student complaint should be investigated and answered.

This can be an extremely informal process. But it requires a willingness to admit mistakes and propose accommodations. And it means keeping the mimeograph machine in the front office whirring in order to repudiate charges that are unwarranted, explain policies that are misunderstood, dispel rumors that are unfounded, and provide facts that are unknown. Doubtless, many administrators will find it humiliating to be called upon to respond to allegations made from the steps of the library or in a leaflet, but the fact is that, for good or ill, leafleteering and mass meetings have become conventional modes of communication among students in most universities and therefore, in the minds of students, appropriate ways of addressing the administration.

Several kinds of formal grievance procedures have been tried on campuses across the country. The most common are grievance committees, which vary widely in membership from campus to campus. Problems with such committees have included the polarization of their members, a tendency to handle grievances on the basis of politics instead of merit, and the slowness with which they respond.

Grievance petition systems have also been established on many campuses. While these assure that grievances are heard by the relevant officials or bodies, they have also tended to create new problems. The process of soliciting signatures for petitions tends to inflate artificially both the issues and the number of aggrieved students.

A third approach is the so-called ombudsman method. The ombudsman is an individual who acts as a mediator and fact-finder for students, faculty members, and administrators. To be successful, the ombudsman must have both great autonomy and the support of the university president. He must not be penalized by the college administration if his findings and recommendations embarrass university leaders.

Some universities have appointed special student affairs administrators to act as liaison between students and the administration. These men and women are sometimes recent graduates. For example, a young, independent, black administrator often serves in the role of spokesman, mediator, and advisor for black students. Because these administrators have the confidence of the students, they can suggest practical modifications of student demands without being automatically branded as "sell-outs." They can formalize complaints or proposals and bring them to the attention of appropriate faculty members and administrators.

Conditions and personalities at particular campuses will dictate what kind of grievance system should be established. We can urge only that each university recognize the necessity of establishing such procedures and the channels of communication that they require.

Reforms in governance are not a panacea for university problems, but they are necessary to assure that campus decisions are made with the greatest possible involvement of those who are competent to make them and of those who are affected by them. They can strengthen the authority and capacity for decisive action of university leadership. Above all, they are necessary to create a context in which the university community can be united and strengthened through frank discussion and reasoned deliberation.

THE RESPONSIBILITIES OF UNIVERSITY MEMBERS

The manifestations of the current campus crisis include conflicts both within and between the various constituencies of the university: some students have turned against other students; faculties have been divided; and, especially in times of crisis, college presidents have too often found themselves unsupported by their faculties or by the trustees and regents to whom they are responsible. Differences of opinion on univeristy matters are inevitable and desirable, but in the current situation these differences are so deep and often so irresponsibly expressed that the survival of higher education itself is threatened. It is therefore essential that everyone involved in American higher education accept greater responsibility for the well-being and revitalization of the university.

We have addressed recommendations to various parts of the university community in Chapter 4. But members of the university have responsibilities even when there is no disorder on the campus. Meeting these responsibilities should make disorder less likely.

Students in particular have too often failed to accept responsibility for the well-being and integrity of their universities. Herdlike generational solidarity has prevented some students from acting in support of the very values of peace, justice, and freedom in whose name they frequently speak.

We believe that:

✳ As members of an academic community, students must deal with controversial issues in a reasonable, civil, and tolerant manner. They should not refrain from criticism or from expressions of their views. But their criticisms should reflect knowledge of the facts and comprehension of the complexities of the issues. Their expressions should be designed to persuade, not to offend.

✳ Students must recognize that the university's central missions are teaching and research. They have the right and obligation to demand excellent academic programs, but those students who are not prepared to participate seriously in these programs should leave the university.

✳ Students should not underestimate, as they have tended to in recent years, their great actual effectiveness in changing American society. They have played a major role in many historic developments of the 1960's: the movement for civil rights, the growing opposition to the war in Indochina, and the movement for university reform.

✳ Students should not expect their own views—even when held with great moral intensity—automatically and immediately to determine national policy. Their rhetorical commitment to democracy must be matched by an awareness of the crucial role of majority rule in a democratic society and by an equal commitment to the techniques of persuasion within the political process.

Faculty members, both as members of the academic community and as professionals, have an obligation to act in a responsible and even exemplary way. Yet faculty members have been reluctant to enforce codes of behavior other than those governing scholarship. They have generally assumed that a minimum of regulation would lead to a maximum of academic freedom.

Recent events have cast doubt on this assumption. In some campus disturbances, some faculty members have acted improperly, irresponsibly, and even illegally. Too little self-regulation by faculty members has often resulted in reduction of academic freedom. The irresponsible political actions of some faculty members have infringed upon the rights of others and prompted regents, trustees, and politicians to take actions that limit academic freedom generally.

We therefore recommend that faculty members assume much greater responsibility for self-regulation and for the welfare of their university community in the following ways:

* Many faculty members know very little about the operation of their universities. They should inform themselves about the principles, mechanisms, and constraints that are involved in decision-making, rather than simply demand dramatic changes without demonstrating how they can be achieved.

* Faculty committees should be established to evaluate and guide the teaching performance of faculty members.

* Limitations on the outside service commitments of faculty members should be made explicit and should be enforced by faculty committees.

* Faculty members, if they engage in political activities, have an obligation to make it clear that they act as individuals, not as representatives of their institutions.

* Faculty members should always insist that students and colleagues exhibit an awareness of the full complexities of controversial issues.

Administrators are in the business of being leaders. Since an academic community is not a battleship, academic leadership is a subtle as well as a demanding task. No dean or president can lay a claim to real leadership unless his voice is the authentic voice of the entire institution. To be an effective academic leader, the administrator must grasp the realities of his institution: its traditions, its strengths, its weaknesses, and, above all, the aspirations and interests of its members.

We believe that:

* Because faculties are often wedded to the status quo, university administrators must provide much of the leadership for reform.

* Administrators, principally the president, must bear most of the burden of defending the university against attacks from the outside and of articulating the university's needs and purposes to the public.

* Above all, the administrator must keep open every possible channel of talk with students. He must have an open mind, for much that students say is valuable; he must have a cryptographer's mind, for much that they say comes in code words and postures; he must have an honest mind, for the worst crime in dealing with the young is to lie to them; he must have a tough mind, for he will frequently, for reasons either invisible or simply unintelligible to his hearers, have to say "No." Above all he must have a compassionate spirit—for youth is neither a disease nor a crime, though to its elders it may be one of the world's major puzzles.

Trustees occupy a critical position between their institutions and alumni, politicians, and the public. This position is especially difficult and important today, when public anxiety threatens the integrity of the university, and when the convictions of university members often run counter to those of many members of the general public.

We believe that:

＊ Trustees have a particular responsibility to interpret and explain their institution to the larger society. They should attempt to inform the public about the institution's values, goals, complexities, and changes. They should defend academic freedom and the right of students, teachers, and guest speakers to espouse unpopular views. They should attempt to help the public understand the underlying causes of student unrest and to prevent punitive or counterproductive public policies toward higher education.

＊ Trustees have an equally important responsibility to assure that their university maintains its central commitments to teaching, to research, and to the preservation of academic freedom against internal erosion. Specifically, this means discouraging excessive service commitments by the university, resisting internal politicization of the university, supporting academic reform, and encouraging improvement in university governance.

＊ To be effective in these difficult roles, trustees must be familiar with the institution they oversee and with the concerns of its constituents. They should read campus publications and be in contact with students, faculty members, and administrators. Those unable to find time for these activities will be unable to perform their role well.

Alumni have their own distinctive responsibilities to the institutions at which they were educated:

* Alumni should refrain from hasty judgments on complex university problems and should avoid stereotyping entire groups because of the actions of a few of their members.

* Alumni should support improvements of American higher education. They should not insist that universities remain changeless or be surprised if their institutions are not the same as they were when the alumni were students.

* Constructive criticism and sustained financial support from alumni are essential to the vitality of American colleges and universities. Many of the nation's universities and colleges are in an unprecedented financial squeeze. Disagreement with specific university policies or actions should not lead alumni to withdraw their general support from higher education.

Obviously, not all of the reforms we have discussed can be undertaken at once. We believe, however, that some reforms involving the regulation of outside service commitments, changes in governance, and new emphases in academic programs can be achieved at relatively little cost.

Moreover, if the universities and colleges can demonstrate a restored sense of purpose and willingness to reform, aid from both private and public sources may become more plentiful. For although Americans have begun to question the authority of those running universities and colleges, they have not yet abandoned their commitment to higher education itself. To the extent that American universities and colleges can be true to their basic missions, to the extent that they can be a progressive force in the future as they have been in the past, and to the extent that they can create a community whose members respect the moral authority of its leaders, campus unrest may become less a threat—and more an opportunity—for the nation. We are hopeful that students, alumni, and the public at large will recognize anew the importance of the university and will foster rather than oppose its reform.

7

Government and Campus Unrest

Campus unrest is a varied pattern of opinion, deeply held, passionately expressed, and highly critical of American policies and social structure. So long as such opinion is not manifested in disruptive, violent, or terrorist conduct, it is not a "problem" to be "solved." In a free society, it is every man's right to hold whatever opinions he chooses and to advance them as the basis of public policy. Other citizens and government itself should listen to, consider, and then accept or reject these opinions, but they should not—they cannot—"solve" them.

Illegal forms of protest are a problem—a problem for law enforcement, which must be dealt with firmly, promptly, and justly, primarily on the level of local and state government.

Government often can solve the social problems and evils which many students and other citizens point to. We emphatically believe that many problems exist in American society and that government must address itself to their solution with urgency and commitment. We believe, too, that only if America pursues such reforms can it redeem its historic promise of life, liberty, and the pursuit of happiness.

We support the positions that many students and other citizens now urge. Racial equality must be achieved. Social justice must be realized. The Indochina war must end.

Pollution, hunger, inadequate housing must be attended to. National priorities must be reassessed.

But we also believe that these things must be done because they are right and good in themselves, not because this or that group demands them. Campus unrest, together with the unrest that exists throughout our society, frames issues that the American people cannot ignore. But the response must be to the issues themselves, considered on their merits and in light of the public interest.

In making public policy the President and other officials must take into account the views of all citizens, as well as many factors that fall outside this Commission's purview. The level of disruption on the campus cannot be treated as an indicator of what is politically or morally acceptable. But neither can the concerns of America's university communities be ignored. In determining the wisdom of decisions, officials must henceforth take into account the impact of their choices on the nation's campuses.

Campus unrest is not itself a social problem. It therefore cannot be solved by vast government programs or billions of dollars. But clearly it has become an urgent political problem. It has helped to create deep and bitter division within the country. As that division has grown deeper, tensions have risen, hostility has surfaced, trust among citizens has waned, political violence has increased, and the legitimacy of government has eroded. As a result, the lives and rights of individuals have become less secure, and the ability of government to maintain harmony and lasting progress has declined.

Democratic societies are especially vulnerable to conflicts of cultures and values such as that which exists today. For when hostilities emerge, each group attempts to attack its opponents by wielding the powers of government against them. Each group therefore confronts not only opposing groups, but also the threat of government oppression. Matters can reach a point at which government is seen by all sides as repressive and illegitimate. Hostilities then intensify, the likelihood of violence and death increases, and civil society can disintegrate into a brutal war of each against all.

We emphasize that this nation is not now in any such condition, but we must also warn that it could come to that if the escalation of hostility and fear does not stop.

Because these divisions are in large part based upon disagreements over public policy and over the direction of American society, they cannot be healed simply by adopting the policies and values of one side or the other. Indeed, this could easily make them worse. For these divisions are political problems, and they can only be resolved politically, by reconciliation and accommodation. Of course, reform must also be a part of the healing process. But it cannot contribute to a lessening of hostilities until a considerable measure of accommodation has already taken place. Such reconciliation, then, must be the first operational priority of government in responding to the divisions within American society, and it cannot come about without leadership, especially Presidential leadership.

In this chapter, we address ourselves to the question of how government should respond to campus unrest. We believe that its principal contribution must be in bringing about a reconciliation of this nation's increasingly divided population. To that end, we urge the President to bring all the moral authority of his office to bear upon the task. We also urge officials and government at all levels to avoid actions or statements that stigmatize or that are arbitrary and punitive, for these will only increase tensions and reduce trust among citizens.

THE RESTORATION OF LEGITIMACY

The most urgent task for government must be to restore the faith of Americans in their government, in their fellow citizens, and in their capacity to live together in harmony and progress.

In this task, the President must take the lead. For as President Nixon has said, it is the responsibility of a President to "articulate the nation's values, define its goals, and marshal its will." The Presidency is a symbol of national unity and values, and effective Presidential leadership—particularly in times of internal division—can be an incomparable force for unity and reconciliation.

The President must seek to create an atmosphere of mutual trust and respect where mutual suspicion and anger now reside. He must articulate and reemphasize the values —liberty, equality, democracy—that all Americans hold in common. Equally, he must seek out and illumine for the American people those new areas of common ground between the emerging youth culture and the older American cultures. By doing these things, and by avoiding invidious speech that destroys trust and increases polarization, the President can enhance the legitimacy of his own office and of the government, and impart a renewed sense of confidence to the nation.

We will not pretend that it is easy for a President to inspire a diverse people or to set the tone for a nation: it is not. Yet he must strive to do just that. Especially in this time of division, every American must find in the President's leadership some reflection of what he believes and respects. We therefore urge the President to reassert his administration's openness to all views, including the voices of student protest. And although it may not be easy for the President to communicate with some students, we are strongly of the opinion that the effort to do so will be of great benefit.

Specifically, we urge the President to take the following steps:

* Convey his understanding of the seriousness of the divisions in this country to its citizens and particularly to students. The forthcoming White House Conference on Youth might be an appropriate occasion for a major address on this subject.

* Use the moral authority of his office to convince all Americans of the need to confront candidly the serious and continuing problems of the nation.

* Deliver a major address reaffirming the nation's and his administration's commitment to realizing the

long-denied birthright of Black Americans.

✳ Urge members of his administration and Americans of all parties and persuasions to resist the temptation to capitalize upon the divisions within the country for partisan political gain. Political leaders—of whatever party or movement—who use the "student issue" in this manner contribute nothing but further bitterness and polarization to an already divided republic.

✳ Deal with students, and young people generally, as constituents and citizens. The President should meet on a regular basis with representatives of student groups of varying ideological persuasions, as well as with faculty and administrators from the nation's institutions of higher education. The White House staff should maintain lines of communication with students and the academic community. We do not, however, recommend creation of positions for "youth representatives" within the executive branch. Young people are politically more diverse than any other group in American life; the impossibility of finding a single "representative" young person is obvious; and it is in any case doubtful that formal recognition should be granted to groups defined merely by age.

The Question of Repression

A Harris survey conducted in May 1970 revealed that 58 per cent of American students believed that the United States had become "a highly repressive society, intolerant of dissent." To most Americans the charge of student activists that American society is repressive is not only untrue but incredible.

For them, repression means concentration camps, political trials, mass police violence, and rule by official terror. They neither see nor experience such things in their own lives, and they continue to believe that America remains a liberal and democratic society. They would probably agree with the portrait drawn by a university official of a campus convulsed by major disruption:

> When I look out my window, when I try to carry on my job, I would simply have to break into hysterical laughter if someone came in and told me that what was happening in that school right then was that the students were being repressed. The fact of the matter is they have got me locked in the room; the rocks are coming through the window; nobody has been punished for anything; the whole judicial process has collapsed; whatever standard you think is important in any area of drugs or law or sex or clothes or anything else has been abandoned; and just under my door has been slipped a copy of an openly published newspaper which says things no newspaper has ever before dared to say. A howling mob is outside and nobody is going to do anything about it and I am supposed to believe that students are repressed?

We believe, however, that the charge of repression cannot be dismissed that lightly, for there is at least a possibility that in a society in which the forces of repression were in a considerable majority and in which those subject to repression constituted a small minority, most of the nation could be unaware of the fact that they and their public institutions were seen to be, or were in fact, acting in a repressive fashion.

It is unquestioned that systematic injustice exists in parts of this country. Blacks in the South and in urban ghettos know it and live with it. Many Blacks have stated that they fear for their lives. Sometimes repression of Blacks is hidden, perhaps even unrecognized by those responsible for it. At other times it is overt, as it was so shamelessly at Jackson State College last May.

There is also a great deal of intolerance in this country. This intolerance of diversity in ideas, in dress, in life style, and in aspirations has given rise to actions which have denied student protestors and others their just rights. This was the case in New York last May when construction workers fought with student protestors, and in Isla Vista in June when sheriff's deputies dealt harshly with students.

But these actions and intolerant attitudes, which do in fact exist, do not exhaust the meaning of the word "repression." The term "repression" denotes a wider variety of actions. It includes attempts by hostile forces, including public opinion and especially government, to ignore some political views or to weaken or eliminate a political or cultural movement. In this context, repression is a part of the struggle for political power and can express itself in many ways. Criminal statutes which are seen to have been enacted to allow police to harass or discredit student activists are seen as repressive. Police who shoot peaceful protestors are guilty of repression. The fact that 52 per cent of the American people, according to a Harris survey, believe that students should not have the right to protest peacefully or otherwise, indicates an intolerance of dissent which is repression. Official rhetoric which slanders student activists or subtly encourages law enforcement officers to treat students harshly is repressive. Misuse of undercover agents on campus and of injunctions that prohibit student protests is another form of repression. Legislation which deprives students of financial aid if they have participated in a disruptive or violent demonstration is a repressive effort to deprive students of political power.

We cannot deny the fact that students use the word "repression" in this manner, nor can we deny the existence of injustice and intolerance in this country. We have been impressed by the deep fears of repression expressed by many college students. We nevertheless caution against exaggeration of the extent of repression in America.

In the last 15 years freedom of expression has greatly increased in this country. Constitutional standards that protect the rights of all Americans have become more, not less, exacting.

The fear of repression, as well as the fact of repression where it exists, is another force for division with which government at every level should deal. Obviously, government cannot end repression where it does not exist or eliminate fears of it that are pathological. But it can help eliminate abuses that are repressive or that suggest repression, and it can make certain that its own actions do not contribute to an atmosphere of repression. National leaders must recognize that what they say is also an implicit statement of the premises upon which government will act. When they seem insensitive to individual rights, they appear to imply that government will act insensitively. It is not easy to address issues forcefully without creating suspicion among at least some youthful dissenters, but awareness of their fears should influence political rhetoric as well as official action.

Government leaders from the President on down should also recognize that their words and actions influence the conduct of public officials at all levels. One can never determine the precise extent of that influence—to what degree, for example, the actions of local police are affected by what political leaders say—but it is clear that high government officials help set the climate for law enforcement. They are therefore under a particular responsibility to display awareness of the right of dissident and even disruptive members of society to be treated fairly before the law.

Finally, to help reduce actual instances of injustice, the federal government must continue its insistence that law enforcement everywhere be evenhanded. Additionally, it should encourage and give financial assistance to the effort to reform the nation's system of criminal justice. Detailed recommendations in these areas have been made by the President's Commission on Law Enforcement and the Administration of Justice, the National Advisory Commission on Civil Disorders, and the National Commission on the Causes and Prevention of Violence.

Government and Campus Disruption

The American people are concerned about violent and disruptive campus protest, and it is natural that they should look to government to do something about it. Yet in most circumstances the federal government is all but powerless to deal tactically with individual acts of campus violence and disruption. Moreover, government intervention could readily suggest repression to many students without bringing about results that could not be obtained by other means. Among faculty and administrators, such intervention could erode their sense of responsibility for affairs within the university. It is true that, in several ways, federal interests are specifically affected by campus disruptions. Federal funds are spent on the campus to aid students, including those who engage in violent or disruptive acts, and to support activities that violent protest may disrupt. Campus disorder sometimes interferes with individual constitutional rights, which the federal government has a special obligation to protect.

We believe, however, that the primary role of the federal government in responding to disruption should be to provide the forms of assistance to campus administrators and local authorities described in Chapter 5 of this report. It should resist demands that it enact punitive legislation. And beyond that it should attempt to conduct itself with compassion and to manifest concern for the rights—and the lives—of all Americans, whatever their views or their condition.

In particular, we recommend:

(1) New laws requiring termination of federally funded financial aid to those involved in campus disruption should not be enacted; similar provisions in existing federal law should be repealed or allowed to expire.

In ten separate authorization and appropriation acts effective prior to the beginning of fiscal year 1971, Congress included provisions requiring institutions of higher education to terminate federally funded financial assistance to students or employees involved in disruptive activities. Additional provisions of this type may be enacted during the current session.

Few of the provisions already enacted clearly define the conditions and conduct that justify withdrawing an individual's financial aid. Each creates substantial administrative difficulties, and the interplay of inconsistent provisions, sometimes applicable to the same student, makes it almost impossible to establish workable guidelines. In many cases, it is unclear whether the termination of financial assistance is automatic (upon conviction of a crime, for example) or at the discretion of the institution. Due process requirements under these statutes, and the duration of the ineligibility they impose, are insufficiently defined. The statutes discriminate against students who receive financial aid because they have no effect on those, often from wealthy families, who do not. Finally, these laws have completely failed to deter campus disruptions. They have only complicated campus disciplinary procedures and, by providing another student grievance, sometimes helped to provoke further disruption.

We also oppose legislation that would terminate federal aid to institutions where disruption or violence occurred. In its report on the Military Procurement Authorization Act for fiscal year 1971, the House Armed Services Committee warned that it will "consider restrictive legislation in the next year's authorization act unless the Secretary of Defense can implement a procedure by which defense research funds are denied to those colleges and universities where complete academic freedom is not permitted" as a result of student disruption. Such legislation would be an invitation to students who hope to oust defense research from the campus. By discontinuing defense research where disruption occurs, it would reward rather than put an end to disruption.

(2) Those federal laws which restrict political activities on the campus should not be interpreted or enforced in such a way that the university will not be able to remain a forum for the free expression of ideas.

Several existing laws, while not especially aimed at institutions of higher education, have the indirect effect of limiting partisan political activities on the campus. The Federal Corrupt Practices Act and its state analogues forbid corporations—including colleges and universities—from making contributions or expenditures in connection with an election. The government also prohibits organizations that receive special tax benefits from becoming involved in partisan politics, and it prevents taxpayers from using these organizations as conduits to contribute tax-deductible funds to political candidates. Thus, the Internal Revenue Code does not permit a private nonprofit institution of higher education to "participate in, or intervene in (including the publishing or distributing of statements), any political campaign on behalf of any candidate for public office." The penalty is loss of its income tax exemption and eligibility to receive tax-deductible contributions.

We raise no question with regard to the application of these laws in clear circumstances. We are concerned, however, with the possible application of these laws to what we regard as indirect instances of university political involvement. For example, the guidelines of the American Council on Education (formulated as a guide to the tax law and concurred in by the Internal Revenue Service) acknowledge the educational service performed by partisan political groups on campus, but caution that "to the extent that such organizations extend their activities beyond the campus, intervene or participate in campaigns on behalf of candidates . . . an institution should, in good faith, make certain that proper and appropriate charges are made and collected for all facilities and services provided."

Universities as institutions should not take political positions. We support the continuation of a ban on direct institutional involvement in partisan politics. But we feel that provision of university facilities to members of the university on an impartial and reasonable basis should be permitted activity for the university. This is not "politicizing the university"—it is merely recognizing that the university is a community in which the expression of political ideas should not be hampered.

(3) The federal government should not attempt to mediate campus disputes or bring legal action to enjoin campus disruption.

Campus officials are well advised to consider using the services of a mediator in resolving campus disputes. But federally sponsored mediation could easily be viewed as unwarranted and even "repressive" government intervention in the university's affairs. Private mediation services now available to universities should be as useful, and they do not have the disadvantages of government mediation.

POLICIES TOWARD YOUTH AND
HIGHER EDUCATION

In important respects, government education policies have been immensely beneficial: they have provided more young people with the opportunity to go to college and helped to improve the quality of higher education.

By making higher education more widely available, government policies (state as well as federal) have helped foster broad public expectations that all young people go directly from high school to college. They have reinforced the reliance on college and advanced degrees as a prerequisite for many kinds of employment. And government policies toward higher education often have had the effect of transforming the university from an authentic community of scholars into a clearinghouse for academic entrepreneurs.

Policies Toward Youth

We believe that government policies affecting youth must be reviewed. Young people should have a wide range of life choices when they graduate from high school, and government should help in the search for respected and viable alternatives. The subject of federal policy to promote this objective can usefully be addressed by the forthcoming White House Conference on Youth. And we recommend that specific programs be drawn up in a number of areas:

First, national service projects, enlisting youth in a variety of civilian public service activities, should be tested. Whether in the form of pilot projects or a full-scale program, national service should be voluntary and not, as some have proposed before this Commission and elsewhere, compulsory. In addition to its enormous cost, a compulsory national service program would be an unwarranted infringement on individual freedom of choice. Nor should national service be considered as a method for reforming or replacing the draft. Proposals to make civilian service available as an alternative to the draft fail to resolve compelling problems of equity that plague any attempt to compare civilian programs with military service.

Participating in a national service program will not be an acceptable or practical alternative for all young people who do not want to attend college. Direct federal sponsorship limits the activities of voluntary service programs and of volunteers participating in them. Existing federal volunteer programs—VISTA, the Peace Corps, and the Teacher Corps—will continue to attract substantial numbers of young people. These programs should be expanded if that is necessary to permit more qualified volunteers to serve, but the purposes of these programs should not be changed merely to suit the volunteers' preferences. Many young people interested in serving society will prefer to do so in some other way; such other ways should be provided without altering existing forms of service, which should remain as long as they serve some useful purpose.

Some might be more attracted to programs in which the federal role was less direct or obtrusive, limited perhaps to providing financial assistance or to establishing a central clearinghouse for volunteer placement. The feasibility of such a federal role should be studied.

Second, action should be taken to find job opportunities for the young. Many find valuable experience outside the framework of formal career training. Alternatives should be made available that require neither commitment to dramatic social change nor reliance on formal education. We do not, it should be emphasized, propose a public subsidy to keep the young from being bored. All publicly supported alternatives should involve a commitment to responsible work. The federal government should encourage private employers to hire high school graduates who are undecided as to when or whether they should go to college.

Third, the federal government should expand the range of

its internship programs and encourage state and local governments and private employers to do the same. Some of these programs—such as the present Federal Cooperative Education Program—might combine undergraduate education with jobs in government agencies or private industry. Other programs should concentrate on internship or apprenticeship without relation to college education.

Programs of this sort will require adoption of new hiring standards by government and private industry so that appropriate work experience and on-the-job training are given greater recognition. The federal government should take the lead here by reviewing its own hiring policies. It should also support the development of more effective college equivalency examinations by private institutions.

We note that the President's Commission on an All-Volunteer Armed Force has recommended that the Selective Service System be replaced by an all-volunteer army. It is clear that one cost of the draft is increased tension on the campus. As long as there are undergraduate deferments, college serves as a haven for young men. As long as there is a draft at all, young men are obviously limited in the choice they can make. And it is also clear that none of the federal programs we have proposed to widen the range of choice for young people will work if our society continues to expect all young people to attend college and to penalize those who do not meet that expectation.

Policies Toward Higher Education

Government policies have had a profound impact on the size and shape of American higher education. Federal and state funds have become increasingly important in promoting the rapid expansion of institutions of higher education; today, approximately one half of the current income of the nation's colleges and universities comes from government sources.

It is not surprising that massive infusions of federal money have tended to strengthen university capabilities in fields of particular interest to the federal government. Proportionately little of this money has been given in the form of general unrestricted aid, and federal funding has consequently influenced the decisions of institutions about the functions they will perform and the areas in which they will expand. The inducements federal research funds have offered and the pressure they have created to emphasize research (especially in the sciences) have contributed to the increasing complexity and impersonality of institutions of higher education.

By encouraging universities to become actively involved in classified defense research and by subsidizing the education and training of ROTC officers, the federal government has increased the likelihood that institutions of higher education will be the object of protest by those opposed to American foreign policy.

We do not propose that the federal government end, or even reduce, its financial support of American colleges and universities. Indeed, we think federal support must be increased. We do say, however, that the government should carefully weigh the effect of its policies on institutions of higher education. When calling upon these institutions to help meet pressing national needs, government should measure probable gain against the extent to which its demands distort the primary functions of these institutions. We recognize that Congress and federal officials have a responsibility to demand the best possible uses of public funds. However, policies that distort the primary functions of our nation's institutions of higher education are a disservice not only to these institutions but to the nation itself. The federal government can help improve the existing situation by reducing its claims upon the universities and concentrating on the development of alternative sources of expertise and research while still funding less particularized university programs.

Government aid to higher education has been directed primarily to institutions rather than to students; whatever the consequences of this strategy may have been, they have not included an increase in student influence over the growth and priorities of the university. Federal financial aid programs should be reformed to give a much larger proportion of aid directly to students in order to redress this imbalance. Institutional aid should emphasize grants for especially innovative educational programs, including aid to stimulate improved teaching techniques, and for institutions especially deserving of direct federal support, such as the predominantly black colleges in the South.

The Commission also believes government student aid policies should emphasize aid for students from low-income families. The student aid provisions of the Higher Education Opportunity Act of 1970 proposed by the current administration have this objective, and we therefore support this legislation. The potential of the income contingent loan plan, originally suggested by Milton Friedman and elaborated by Jerrold Zacharias and others, as a more comprehensive solution to the serious problem of financing higher education, deserves careful consideration.

Defense-Related Research

For some students, defense-related research at colleges and universities symbolizes complicity in the war in Southeast Asia. But university involvement in military research had been called into question long before the escalation of America's military involvement. Paradoxically, student protest against defense research increased as defense spending for academic research decreased. By the end of the 1969-70 academic year, a substantial amount of military research had been removed from university campuses. Following the early lead of Harvard, the administrations of Columbia, the University of Michigan, MIT, the University of Pennsylvania, and other schools reduced or ended university involvement in classified research. Study committees at some schools recommended greater academic control over laboratories engaged primarily in military research.

Congress has reacted to the controversy over defense-related research by passing legislation that further complicates the matter. The Military Procurement Authorization Act of 1970 provides that:

None of the funds authorized to be appropriated by this Act may be used to carry out any research project or study unless such project or study has a direct and apparent relationship to a specific military function or operation.

The announced purpose of the section (the "Mansfield amendment") was to make defense-funded research honest and to curtail large expenditures for research that was not related to immediate military needs. Yet the result has been to place faculty researchers in an awkward position. In order to continue with research in progress, they—or the Pentagon—must certify that the research has a direct military application. Having satisfied the legal requirement, the researchers then must contend with student militants whose accusation that the researchers are "working for the war machine" has now been officially confirmed by the Pentagon.

There is no obvious formula for resolving the tension between the values and priorities of government and those of the university. To maintain its defenses, the nation will require research on military matters, and it will turn to universities to do a part of that research. We do not advocate termination of either defense-funded or government-funded research in general, but we urge that such research be planned so as to interfere as little as possible with the normal functions of the schools at which it takes place.

There is much to be said for continuing to support opportunities for students to participate in research. The National Science Foundation has started a modest student research program; it and other government sources of research funds should also attempt to assure that their policies and practices at least do not curtail—and, at best, increase—existing opportunities for students who are interested in research.

ROTC

As noted in Chapter 6, the issue of ROTC programs on campus should be considered in any reevaluation of university life. But the government also has a role to play in this matter. We believe that the Department of Defense should establish alternatives to ROTC that would make officer education available to students without imposing an officer training program on universities that do not find it compatible with their other activities. In urban areas, a "metropolitan center plan" could provide training programs for students at schools that do not participate in ROTC as well as for those at schools that do. Under this plan, there would be no on-campus instruction. During the academic year, training would be conducted at a central facility used by students from all institutions in the metropolitan area.

The armed services should make improvements in ROTC, even at those colleges that want to keep it as an on-campus program. Greater emphasis should be placed on summer and postcommission training. Military instruction in military subjects on the campus should be kept to a minimum, and the question of academic degree credit for these courses should be subject to negotation between the services and the university. Where credit is given, courses and instruction should meet the institution's normal academic standards. Student aid should be increased and offered in the form of loans as well as scholarships, with provision for forgiveness of the indebtedness upon completion of a minimum period of service as a commissioned officer. Punitive clauses, which threaten those who withdraw from ROTC with immediate active duty, would be unnecessary in loan contracts and should be eliminated from scholarship agreements. Recruitment literature for officer education should be candid about requirements and expectations.

CONCLUSION

To promote freedom and to prevent disruption and violence on America's campuses, the Commission finds that there are specific policies and programs the government should not pursue.

But we find that there are even more important things it should do.

There must be continued progress toward the national goals of ending the war and of achieving racial and social justice, and the Commission observes once again that so great is the concern of many university communities about these matters that failure even to appear to be pursuing them could provoke further campus protest.

Additionally, we urge the federal government to champion everyone's right to dissent nonviolently and to promote the evenhanded enforcement of the law everywhere.

We urge governments at all levels to increase the options available to young people—to encourage work and service and internship opportunities—so that those who do not want to attend college will not feel forced to do so.

We recommend massive financial aid for black colleges and universities, increased aid for higher education generally, and expanded programs of student financial aid, particularly for those from low-income families.

But the most important aspect of the overall effort to prevent further campus disorder—indeed, the most important of all the Commission's recommendations—rests with the President. As the leader of all Americans, only the President can offer the compassionate, reconciling moral leadership that can bring the country together again. Only the President has the platform and prestige to urge all Americans, at once, to step back from the battlelines into which they are forming. Only the President, by example and by instruction, can effectively calm the rhetoric of both public officials and protestors whose words in the past have too often helped further divide the country, rather than reunite it.

Kent State

Blanket Hill is a grassy knoll in the center of the campus of Kent State University, named by students who use it as a place to sun themselves in the day and to romance at night. From here, shortly after noon on a sunny spring day, a detachment of Ohio National Guardsmen, armed with World War II-vintage army rifles, fired a volley of at least 61 shots killing four college students and wounding nine.

All of the young people who were shot that day were students in good standing at Kent State University.

The National Guardsmen were there under orders from both civilian and military authorities. Duty at Kent State had not been pleasant: they had been cursed and stoned, and some feared physical injury.

Stones were thrown, then bullets fired.

The events at Kent State over the long May weekend were tragic. They need not and should not have occurred. The Commission has drawn on the lessons learned from Kent State in making its report. This special report is made to give an explicit context to the recommendations made there.

The Commission staff spent several weeks studying reports of other investigations of the May 1970 events at Kent State, including 8,000 pages of reports by the Federal Bureau of Investigation. Three weeks were spent in Ohio interviewing hundreds of witnesses, including students, faculty, university administrators, law enforcement personnel, National Guardsmen, townspeople, and others in possession of relevant information. Special efforts were made to gather contemporaneous photographic and audio evidence from all available sources. The Commission was able to study motion picture films and tape recordings of parts of the events and hundreds of photographs taken by persons present at the scene. The Commission held hearings at Kent State University in Kent, Ohio, on August 19, 20, and 21, 1970.

The Commission's task at Kent State was especially sensitive. At the outset of the investigation, the Kent incidents had not been placed before any grand jury, either county, state, or federal. During our investigation, the Attorney General of Ohio announced the convening of a state grand jury. The grand jury began proceedings in September as this report was being written.

We deem it of paramount importance that the Commission do nothing to interfere with the process of criminal justice. We therefore have not sought to establish and report the names of persons who might be guilty of city, state, or federal offenses—persons who fired weapons or who may have caused property destruction or personal injury by rock-throwing, arson, or other means. The Commission has not attempted to assess guilt or innocence but has sought to learn only what happened and why.

THE SETTING

Kent State University is a state-supported school with some 20,000 students, more than four fifths of them graduates of Ohio high schools. Its main gate is only four blocks from the center of the business district of Kent, a city of some 30,000.

Compared with other American universities of its size, Kent State had enjoyed relative tranquility prior to May 1970, and its student population had generally been conservative or apolitical. Under state law, the university must accept any graduate of an accredited Ohio high school, and five out of six Kent State students are from Ohio, mostly from Cleveland and Akron, from the steel towns of Lorain and Youngstown, and from small rural towns. They are predominantly the children of middle class families, both white collar and blue collar, and in the main go on to careers as teachers and as middle-level management in industry.

Two sizable disturbances had occurred prior to May 1970, however, and were widely remembered.

On November 13, 1968, members of the Black United Students (BUS) and the Kent State chapter of the Students for a Democratic Society (SDS) participated in a five-hour sit-in to protest the appearance on campus of recruiters from the Oakland, California, police department. When the university announced that it planned disciplinary action, 250 black students walked off the campus and demanded amnesty. Kent State President Robert I. White consulted university attorneys and, two days after the walk-out began, announced no charges would be brought, whereupon the black students returned.

The university established an Institute of African-American Affairs several months later. Blacks pressed for further changes, including enrollment of more black students and the addition of more Black-oriented courses. No further race-related disturbances occurred, and black students played virtually no part in the turmoil at Kent State last May. But Blacks at Kent State remained less than content, and after the sit-in, relations between them and the administration were uneasy.

In the spring of 1969, SDS launched a campaign centered around four demands which remain today as campus issues. In this campaign, the Kent State chapter followed tactics used elsewhere by the SDS: finding issues that attract mass support, demanding that action be taken, and then attempting to organize a confrontation to push for the demands. At Kent State these demands were: abolition of the campus ROTC training program; removal of the Liquid Crystals Institute, a university research center funded partly by the

Department of Defense; removal of a state crime laboratory from campus; and abolition of the university's degree program in law enforcement.

On April 8, 1969, a group of about 50 white students, including SDS leaders, went to the administration building planning to post these demands on an office door. Campus police met them outside, pushing and shoving ensued, and some officers were struck. Several students were charged with assault and battery and summarily suspended. In addition, the university revoked the SDS charter; that revocation is still in effect.

A disciplinary hearing for two of the students involved in the April 8 incident was set for the Music and Speech Building eight days later. The university said it scheduled a private hearing at the request of one of the students, but about 100 supporters of the suspended students demanded that the hearing be public. Fist fights broke out between the demonstrators and about 200 counterdemonstrators, including conservative fraternity men and campus athletes. The demonstrators entered the building and broke open a door on the third floor. Campus police sealed exits and called the Ohio State Highway Patrol, which arrested 58 persons. Some students complained that they were permitted to enter and then held inside for arrest.

In autumn 1969, four SDS leaders were prosecuted for their part in the April incidents. Each was convicted (after a jury trial) of assault and battery and pleaded guilty (without trial) to a charge of inciting to riot. The "Kent State 4" served six months each in Portage County jail. They were released April 29, 1970—two days before Kent State's disruptions of May 1970 began.

After these incidents of April 8 and April 16, some students charged that the university had deviated from its own student conduct code in its handling of the disruptions. On the day after the second incident, an organization called the Concerned Citizens of the KSU Community (CCC) was formed to protest the university's suspension of some demonstrators without a hearing and before they were convicted of criminal charges. One week later, the CCC lost a campuswide referendum on this issue and others, including reinstatement of the SDS charter.

There was high campus interest in the referendum, which drew the largest vote ever cast in a campus election. Some tactics employed by the university and student leaders left many CCC supporters resentful. These tactics included a rare extra edition of the campus newspaper, the *Daily Kent Stater*, featuring a front-page editorial headlined, "Evidence Links SDS, 3-C." Some CCC supporters who characterized themselves as liberal or moderate felt that this extra edition, plus an anonymous leaflet circulated about the same time, was an unfair effort to paint them as either dupes or agents of the SDS.

Five months after the April 1969 events, the Kent State chapter of the American Association of University Professors (AAUP) published the findings of a Special Committee of Inquiry. In general, the report was critical of the university administration's handling of the April incidents. It failed, however, to resolve several questions, including divergent views of the Music and Speech Building incident. Administration supporters generally felt that the persons who had been arrested had tried to disrupt or to take over a building. Many radicals and activists felt that police tactics used at that time constituted entrapment.

After the April incidents, the administration maintained its position that national politics and foreign policy were not issues on which the university as an institution should take a formal stand.

The university did take several steps in the late 1960's to liberalize university regulations. Women's curfew hours were abolished, visits by the opposite sex to dormitory rooms were permitted, and the sale of beer on campus was allowed.

A year of quiet followed the April 1969 disturbances. On April 10, 1970, for example, Yippie leader Jerry Rubin spoke at Kent State but drew only a tepid response when he urged students to join "the revolution."

In retrospect, however, the absence of major disturbances

between April 1969 and May 1970 appears to have been deceptive. Interviews with black students show clearly that they were discontented during this time. Many activists, militants, and radicals believe that the university was not only opposed to them but also ready to use any tactics necessary to suppress them.

Present on the Kent State campus during the period 1968-70 were six organizations considered by some to be radical. Almost all were comparatively small, ranging down to the Young Socialist Alliance with only eight to twelve members. The most prominent of these organizations was the Students for a Democratic Society.

The Kent State chapter of SDS was organized in the spring of 1968. In the beginning it drew poor support, with less than 10 persons attending most of its meetings. By autumn, however, attendance grew to about 50 or 60 per meeting.

In October 1968, Mark Rudd, a leader of the SDS at Columbia University, addressed the Kent State chapter. The next month, a regional conference of SDS chapters in northeastern Ohio was held at Kent State, with a speech on that occasion from Rennie Davis, one of the founders of the SDS.

Davis asked for local cooperation in demonstrations in January 1969 against the inauguration of Richard M. Nixon as President. Subsequently 45 Kent State students participated in this demonstration in Washington, including all of the Kent State 4.

After the SDS was banned from Kent State in April 1969, the group held no open meetings and sponsored no demonstrations on campus.

Nationally, in June 1969, the SDS divided into three factions: Revolutionary Youth Movement I, generally called Weatherman; Revolutionary Youth Movement II, often called the RYM II; and the Progressive Labor Party, commonly called the PLP. All espouse some variety of Marxist doctrine and view the United States as an imperialist nation. The Weatherman faction is considered the most prone to violence. RYM II petitioned for official recognition at Kent State in the autumn of 1969 and was active in limited ways. Neither Weatherman nor the PLP has ever been recognized as a campus organization at Kent State.

FBI reports do not indicate that any of the disturbances at Kent State during May 1-4, 1970, were planned by members of the SDS.

The campus is patrolled by a 30-man security force. Downtown, the 22-man Kent Police Department is normally at its busiest on weekends patrolling North Water Street, where many bars draw a heavy student patronage. The two police agencies have had a loose agreement to help each other when severe trouble develops, but clearly, even at combined strength, they have too few officers to handle any assemblage of more than a few hundred.

Also available if trouble comes are the Portage County sheriff's department, with 29 full-time employees and 83 part-time deputies, and the highway patrol, with a statewide force of 1,075 men.

If civilian authorities were not enough, two regiments of the Ohio National Guard—the 107th Armored Cavalry and the 145th Infantry—called to active duty on April 29, 1970, as a result of a truckers' strike, were in nearby Akron.

Such was the situation when on the night of Thursday, April 30, President Richard M. Nixon announced that United States troops were being ordered into Cambodia.

Kent State President White did not hear President Nixon's speech. When his wife told him about it later, he had a "sinking feeling," he said. Downtown, in the North Water Street bar area, slogans denouncing the Cambodian action were being painted on walls. Many students viewed the move as a shocking reversal of President Nixon's announced policy of withdrawal from Vietnam and as an aggressive action which flouted widespread antiwar sentiment in the United States.

FRIDAY, MAY 1

Friday, at noon, a small group of history graduate students calling themselves World Historians Opposed to

Racism and Exploitation (WHORE) held an antiwar rally on the Commons, a grassy field in the center of the campus and a traditional site for student rallies and outdoor meetings. The New University Conference, an organization of younger faculty members and graduate students considered radical by some, also sponsored this rally.

Near the Victory Bell, an old railroad bell normally rung to celebrate Kent football victories, rally leaders buried a copy of the United States Constitution, declaring that it had been "murdered" when troops had been sent into Cambodia without a declaration of war or consultation with Congress. A sign asking, "Why is the ROTC building still standing?" was hanging on a tree nearby.

The ROTC building, a small wooden barracks officially named East Hall, stood at the northwestern corner of the Commons overlooking the rally site.

About 500 persons attended the rally and no disorder occurred. The meeting closed with a call for another rally at noon Monday to discuss the attitude of the university administration toward the Cambodian incursion and toward other student demands, including abolition of the ROTC program.

Few if any Blacks were present at the Friday noon rally, having been urged by their leaders to avoid white rallies and to concentrate on Black concerns. Throughout the weekend, virtually all black students remained apart from the student demonstrations. Many black students stated later that, after the National Guard had arrived, they feared physical violence at the hands of the Guard. At 3:00 p.m. on Friday, the Black United Students held a rally to hear black students from Ohio State University discuss the campus disturbances which had recently occurred there. This rally, which drew about 400 persons, ended peacefully at 3:45 p.m.

Late Friday afternoon, after receiving reports on the two peaceful rallies, President White decided that the situation was sufficiently calm for him to go to Iowa for a long-planned visit with his sister-in-law and a Sunday meeting of the American College Testing Program. He did not return to

Kent until Sunday noon, after the city and campus had experienced two nights of turmoil.

The first disturbance began Friday evening on North Water Street, a downtown area where six bars, popular with young people, are located. Some of these bars feature rock bands. The sale of 3.2 beer to persons 18 or older, and of liquor to 21 year olds, is legal in Kent. Because several surrounding counties prohibit the sale of beer or liquor, the Kent bars draw young people from as far as 50 miles away in addition to Kent State students.

May 1 was one of the first warm Friday nights of the spring. A sizable crowd of young people, some of whom were discussing Cambodia, gathered in and around the bars. About 11:00 p.m., they began to jeer passing police cars.

Kent's small police force had fewer than 10 men on duty when the disturbance began. Four of these men in two patrol cars were specifically assigned to North Water Street.

The crowd grew increasingly boisterous. They began to chant slogans, and a motorcycle gang called the "Chosen Few" performed some tricks with their bikes. Shortly before 11:30 p.m., someone threw a bottle at a passing police car. The Kent city police ceased efforts to patrol the street and waited for reinforcements from the day shift and from other law enforcement agencies.

Some of the crowd, which had grown to about 500, started a bonfire in the street. Soon the crowd blocked the street and began to stop motorists to ask their opinion about Cambodia.

One motorist accelerated when approached, narrowly missing people standing in the street. This incident, according to witnesses, angered bystanders. Shortly thereafter a false rumor that black students were "trashing" on campus circulated among the crowd.

Some demonstrators began to break store windows with rocks. A few items were stolen from the display windows of a shoe store and a jewelry store. A fertilizer spreader was taken from a hardware store and thrown through the window of a bank. In all, 47 windows in 15 establishments were broken, and two police officers were cut by thrown missiles.

At 12:30 a.m., after the trashing had begun, Kent Mayor LeRoy M. Satrom declared a state of emergency and ordered the bars closed. The assembled force of city police and sheriff's deputies then moved to clear the street, which became even more crowded as evicted patrons poured out of the bars.

Mayor Satrom initially estimated the damage to property at $50,000, a figure he subsequently reduced to $15,000. Still later, a study by the Kent Chamber of Commerce placed maximum damage at $10,000.

At 12:47 a.m., Mayor Satrom telephoned the office of Governor James A. Rhodes in Columbus and spoke to John McElroy, the governor's administrative assistant. Satrom reported that SDS students had taken over a portion of Kent. A few minutes later, McElroy phoned the Ohio Adjutant General, Major General Sylvester T. Del Corso, and Del Corso sent a National Guard liaison officer to Kent to assess the situation.

Between 1:00 and 2:00 a.m., a force composed of 15 Kent city police and 15 Portage County deputies used tear gas to force the student crowd out of the downtown area, up East Main Street for several blocks, and back onto the campus through the main gate at Lincoln and East Main Streets. The city police were annoyed when Kent State University police officers did not arrive at the gate to take over from there. City police did not know that students were simultaneously congregating on campus and that the University Police Chief Donald L. Schwartzmiller had decided to use his men to guard campus buildings. That night, a small amount of property damage, including a broken window at the ROTC building, was done on campus.

City police, who would not enter the campus, and students faced each other over the border of the campus, and a virtual stand-off developed. A freak automobile accident on Main Street is generally credited with dispersing the crowd.

An electrical repairman was standing on his truck repairing a traffic light in front of Prentice Gate. A car hit the truck, knocking the scaffold from beneath the repairman and leaving him hanging onto the traffic light above the pavement. His odd predicament completely captured the attention of the crowd. They drifted away quietly after he was rescued.

Fifteen persons, all with Ohio addresses, were arrested that night, most of them on charges of disorderly conduct.

The disturbance on North Water Street angered and frightened many merchants and left the city administration fearful that it did not have enough manpower available to keep order. On the next day, these circumstances were to lead to the calling of the Ohio National Guard.

Some city and university officials suspected that the disturbances had been fomented by the Kent State 4, who had been released from jail two days earlier after serving sentences for their actions during the campus uproar in April 1969. The FBI uncovered no evidence that the Kent State 4 were involved in planning or directing any of the events of the May 1-4 weekend. The presence of at least one of the Kent State 4, who was seen on the street downtown early Friday evening, has been confirmed.

Many of the students who were in the crowd on North Water Street were there only because the bars were closed. Some were disgruntled because they had paid cover charges to hear rock bands and then had to leave before they felt they had had their money's worth.

The pattern established on Friday night was to recur throughout the weekend: There were disorderly incidents; authorities could not or did not respond in time to apprehend those responsible or to stop the incidents in their early stages; the disorder grew; the police action, when it came, involved bystanders as well as participants; and, finally, the students drew together in the conviction that they were being arbitrarily harassed.

SATURDAY, MAY 2

Against the background of Friday night's activities, rumors proliferated.

When 40 uniformed ROTC cadets gathered early Saturday morning at the ROTC building to be transported to a rifle range, students who saw them spread a report that the National Guard was on campus. At this time, only one guardsman—liaison officer Lt. Charles J. Barnette—was actually in Kent. In midafternoon, as cadets returned from the range, some students heckled them, and one student told an officer, "You'd better watch your building. It would make a pretty fire."

Some Kent State students helped downtown merchants clean up Friday night's rubble. In the minds of many merchants and the mayor, however, their good deeds were outweighed by threats which a few merchants said they received from young people whom they presumed to be Kent State students. The owners of a shoe store and a music store were among those who said they were told to put an antiwar sign in their window with "Out of Cambodia" or "Get Out of Vietnam," or some such message, unless they wanted to run the risk of having their shops burned or damaged.

Troubled by these reports and fearful that he did not have enough policemen to protect his city, Satrom began efforts to secure a force of 75 auxiliary deputies from Portage County Sheriff Joseph G. Hegedus. Satrom could not call on the Ohio State Highway Patrol because its jurisdiction is limited to state highways and to property either owned or leased by the state.

Early Saturday, Mayor Satrom formalized his proclamation of civil emergency. He banned the sale of liquor and beer, firearms, and gasoline unless pumped directly into the tank of a car. He established an 8:00 p.m. to 6:00 a.m. curfew in Kent which was to take effect Saturday night.

In the wake of Friday night's window-breaking in Kent, the university administration launched a strenuous effort to restore order among students. Chester A. Williams, Kent State's Director of Safety and Public Services, attended five separate meetings with university and civic officials.

In the first of these meetings, held at 8:30 a.m., university officials (including Robert E. Matson, vice president for student affairs, and Williams) decided to seek an injunction barring further property damage on campus. The name of a male student arrested Friday night on charges of breaking a window in the ROTC building, together with 500 "John Does," was placed on the court order, which enjoined anyone from "breaking any windows, defacing any buildings with paint, starting any fires on campus, and damaging and destroying any property. . . ." The injunction did not include a ban on rallies.

In a meeting at city hall at 11:00 a.m., Mayor Satrom agreed to exempt the university from his 8:00 p.m. curfew. He set the curfew on the campus to begin at 1:00 a.m.

At a 1:00 p.m. meeting, Lt. Barnette told university officials that if the National Guard were called, it would make no distinction between city and campus and would assume complete control of the entire area. University officials were still hoping that if trouble arose on campus they could secure help from the Highway Patrol, whose handling of the Music and Speech Building disturbance in 1969 had been widely praised.

At a 3:00 p.m. meeting, university officials reviewed the special steps they planned to take to entertain students who would be prevented by the curfew from visiting the downtown area. They had arranged for special late hours for the cafeterias and for bands to play at dormitory dances. The university had also activated its rumor control center and its emergency operations center. Vice President Matson and student body president Frank Frisina prepared and distributed a leaflet that informed students of the injunction and of the 8:00 p.m. curfew in Kent but failed to mention the 1:00 a.m. curfew on campus. The leaflet said specifically that peaceful campus assemblies were not banned.

The administration was aware of rumors that a rally was to be held on the Commons that evening, and during the day an informal corps of faculty marshals assembled. The original suggestion for faculty marshals had come the previous year from Vice President Matson in response to criticism by some faculty members of the handling of the Music and Speech

Building incident. Matson discussed the role of the marshals on this Saturday with Professor Glenn W. Frank, a faculty leader. That evening, Frank related the discussion to the marshals. Many of them nevertheless continued to be confused about their exact role. Ultimately, most of the marshals decided that they would not physically intervene in case of disturbances but would confine their activities to discussion and persuasion, fact-finding, and reporting events to the university emergency operations center. Frank purchased armbands and gave them to the marshals, who stationed themselves in groups of two or three around the campus, where they circulated among students and distributed the informational leaflets.

The final meeting of the day was held at 5:00 p.m. in Mayor Satrom's office in city hall. Several times during the day, Lt. Barnette told the mayor that 5:00 p.m. was the deadline for calling the National Guard, which would need some time to assemble and move. The mayor continued to defer a decision, hoping he could secure the sheriff's deputies instead. Campus Safety Director Williams and the university were holding to their position that Kent State would prefer the presence of the Highway Patrol if severe trouble developed.

Satrom felt strongly that help was needed. Rumors, reports, and complaints had been pouring into city hall all day. Kent Police Chief Roy Thompson said a usually reliable campus informant had told him that plans were afoot to destroy the ROTC building, the local U. S. Army recruiting station, and the Kent Post Office that night. He had forwarded this information to the university police.

Satrom told the group at the meeting that he had learned that the sheriff's deputies would not be available. He asked Williams if Kent State officers could help downtown. Williams replied that his men were needed on campus, and Satrom left the room with Lt. Barnette to ask for National Guard assistance. Williams and university Vice President for Financial Affairs Richard E. Dunn, who supervises the campus police, then left the meeting; they were under the impression that the National Guard was being requested for duty only in Kent, not on the Kent State campus.

Mayor Satrom spoke to John McElroy in the governor's office and requested that the Guard be sent to Kent.

McElroy believed that Governor Rhodes' proclamation of April 29, which called out the Guard to control disturbances resulting from a Teamsters' strike, was sufficient to cover the Kent case because it authorized the Guard to "take action necessary for the restoration of order throughout the state of Ohio . . . ." He telephoned General Del Corso and told him to inform Mayor Satrom that troops would be available. Then McElroy telephoned Governor Rhodes and told him about the situation. Governor Rhodes authorized the commitment of guardsmen to Kent.

At 5:35 p.m., General Del Corso, following McElroy's instructions, phoned Mayor Satrom and told him that troops would be available that evening. Del Corso then called Colonel John Simmons, the duty officer at National Guard headquarters near Columbus at Fort Hayes. He ordered guardsmen bivouacked in the Akron area, about 10 miles from Kent, to be placed on standby.

At 6:15 p.m. Del Corso notified Simmons that he and the Assistant Adjutant General, Brigadier General Robert H. Canterbury, were leaving for Kent. Should Simmons receive an urgent request for help while Del Corso and Canterbury were en route, he was to dispatch troops to Kent, the general said. But, Del Corso added, the commander in Akron should be told that no troops were to be committed to the Kent streets until Del Corso and Canterbury arrived. The troops were to assemble on the grounds of Wall Elementary School, on the west side of Kent, and wait until the generals arrived.

At the university, a crowd had assembled on the Commons around the Victory Bell by 7:30 p.m. The group appeared to be an idle collection of students whom the curfew had prevented from going downtown. As a precaution, Kent State Police Chief Schwartzmiller called the Highway Patrol for assistance, but the patrol said that unless arrests were necessary, they would not come to the campus. Schwartzmiller stated that there was no basis for arrests at that time.

On the Commons, a young man is reported to have jumped up on the brick structure from which the Victory Bell is suspended and to have said, "They're trying to keep the kids penned up in the dorms. Let's go."

The crowd soon moved off toward Tri-Towers, a complex of dormitories where one of the specially arranged dances was being held. Faculty marshals observed them as they followed the usual student parade route around the dormitories, picking up new recruits as they went. By the time they headed back toward the Commons, the crowd had grown to around 1,000, and some were chanting, "Ho, Ho, Ho Chi Minh," and "One, two, three, four, we don't want your fucking war." As they crossed the Commons near the ROTC building, some shouted, "Get it," "Burn it," and "ROTC has to go."

The ROTC building was an obvious target. It was a two-story wooden structure—an old World War II-type Army barracks—and it looked easy to ignite. Many students saw it as evidence that the university supported the Vietnam war effort by maintaining a military training program on campus.

About 8:10 p.m., a few students began to throw rocks at the ROTC building. In a short while, flying rocks had broken some of the building's windows. A few in the crowd appeared to have brought bags of rocks to the scene. A group used an ash can as a battering ram to break in a window; some started throwing lighted railroad flares into and onto the building. A curtain caught fire. In the crowd, someone burned a miniature American flag. A student taking pictures was attacked and wrestled to the ground, and his film was taken and exposed. Professor Frank said that when he intervened in the student's behalf, he was grabbed from behind. Frank was saved from further attack only when recognized by one of his students. Finally, a young man dipped a cloth into the gasoline tank of a parked motorcycle. Another young man ignited it and set the building afire. The building began to burn about 8:45 p.m.

The mood of the part of the crowd nearest the ROTC

building was one of anger. "I have never in my 17 years of teaching," said Frank, "seen a group of students as threatening or as arrogant or as bent on destruction as I saw and talked to that night." Faculty marshals did not intervene.

Many spectators behaved around the ROTC fire as though they were at a carnival. Only a dozen or so persons appeared to have made active efforts to set the building afire, and another two or three dozen threw stones, but many others cheered and shouted with glee as the building was destroyed and sat on the hills surrounding the Commons to watch the conflagration.

One student protested the burning of the ROTC building, telling his fellows, "You can't do this." He was shouted down. A faculty marshal who feared that the student was in danger of physical injury led him from the area.

About 9:00 p.m., a truck from the Kent fire department arrived. No police protection was provided. Members of the mob grabbed the hose from the firemen. They slashed and stabbed the hose with pocket knives, an ice pick, and a machete. They threw rocks at the firemen, who then withdrew. At this point, the fire seemed to subside.

Yet the fire quickly began to grow again. When the building was burning furiously and live ammunition was exploding inside, the campus police appeared. Their headquarters were only 200 yards from the ROTC building.

Kent State Safety Director Williams explained later that he and Schwartzmiller had decided not to commit their men to the threatened building promptly because, given the size and mood of the crowd, they feared for the lives of some of their men. Security Chief Schwartzmiller had asked Kent police for help but had been told that almost the entire force had been mobilized and stationed to protect the downtown area. Schwartzmiller said later he received the impression that the Kent police department was "getting even" with him for his failure to dispatch his men to Prentice Gate to disperse the crowd there on Friday night.

As the campus police marched up in riot gear, someone shouted, "Here come the pigs." The police fired tear gas at the crowd, which then left the ROTC building area and moved across the Commons to the tennis courts. Some students bent down the strong metal fence around the courts.

About 9:30 p.m., near the tennis courts, a small shed which was used to store archery equipment was set afire. Flames shot up from the shed and threatened nearby trees. Students hurried into buildings, filled wastebaskets with water, and put out the fire.

Aware of the turmoil on campus, Mayor Satrom had called General Del Corso's office at 8:35 p.m. to renew his request for troops. He spoke to Colonel Simmons. Acting under the directions left him by General Del Corso, Simmons called the Akron bivouac and ordered the troops to Kent.

At 9:30 p.m., Generals Del Corso and Canterbury arrived in Kent. As their troops were pulling into town, the flames from the burning ROTC building lit up the horizon.

The generals went to city hall and were briefed by Mayor Satrom. Del Corso then dispatched one detachment of guardsmen to prevent students from entering downtown Kent and sent another detachment to protect firemen who were returning to the burning building. As a Guard unit rode down East Main Street, it was stoned by persons hiding among trees. Specialist 4th Class Ronald West of Troop G of the 2nd Squadron, 107th Armored Cavalry Regiment, was cut in the mouth by glass when a rock broke the windshield of a jeep in which he was riding, and several other guardsmen in the unit reported they were hit by stones or pieces of brick.

Neither Del Corso nor Canterbury requested permission of any university official before sending troops onto campus. General Canterbury said later that because the building was located on state property, the Guard needed no specific invitation to enter the campus.

At the same time that Del Corso was ordering troops to the ROTC fire, an unidentified guardsman called Matson at the emergency operation center in the administration building to inquire if the Guard was needed at the fire. Matson asked the advice of Vice President Dunn, who supervises campus police and who was at the Kent State police station at this time. Dunn in turn asked Williams and Schwartzmiller if they needed the Guard at the ROTC fire. The Highway Patrol had been called a second time by Schwartzmiller after the fire had been set. Now that there was a basis for arrests, they agreed to come. But Williams and Schwartzmiller had by then abandoned hope that the Highway Patrol would arrive in time and agreed that they needed the Guard. They communicated this to Dunn, who in turn advised Matson. Unknown to them, the Guard was already en route.

Part of the crowd had already left the Commons and was heading for town. Matson was informed of this fact at the same time he heard from Dunn. Matson said later that he told the Guard that the matter was no longer in his hands because the crowd was now off campus and in the town. Guardsmen previously dispatched by Del Corso intercepted the students before they got downtown.

At about this time, campus police, sheriff's deputies, highway patrolmen, and National Guardsmen had assembled on campus. The patrolmen deployed to patrol the campus. The Guard and campus police gave protection to firemen, who now came on campus in a second attempt to put out the fire in the ROTC building. The building could not be saved and soon burned to rubble. The university set the loss of building and contents at $86,000.

Information developed by an FBI investigation of the ROTC building fire indicates that, of those who participated actively, a significant proportion were not Kent State students. There is also evidence to suggest that the burning was planned beforehand: railroad flares, a machete, and ice picks are not customarily carried to peaceful rallies.

Students continued to roam about. A faculty marshal dissuaded half a dozen persons from setting fire to a small information booth at the edge of the campus. Along East Main Street, just off campus, a group of about ten wrecked a telephone booth and tried to uproot a bus stop sign. Others dragged an air compressor from a construction site into the street, piled up sawhorses and debris, and built a bonfire. Still other students followed along trying to prevent damage and put fires out.

At 9:50 p.m., Del Corso telephoned McElroy and reported that he had already sent troops onto the campus and into downtown Kent. McElroy relayed this information to Governor Rhodes.

The Guard set up a campus headquarters in the meeting room of the Board of Trustees in the administration building. The next day, Sunday, they moved their headquarters to Wills Gymnasium, near the administration building.

The National Guard cleared the campus with dispatch, using tear gas freely. Some students had to spend the night in dormitories other than their own because the cleanup was so quick and emphatic. At 11:55 p.m., General Canterbury phoned his staff at Fort Hayes and reported that the situation was under control.

Antagonism toward law enforcement personnel already was evident among many students. A faculty marshal reported seeing a young woman trying to dissuade a young man from throwing a rock toward officers and guardsmen near the ROTC building. She said, "Hey, don't throw that. You might hurt somebody." "That's all right," the young man replied, "they all have helmets on." He threw the rock and ran.

When a group of faculty marshals wearing blue armbands attempted to identify themselves as guardsmen approached, the guardsmen knelt in a skirmish line and pointed rifles at them. Abandoning explanations, the marshals fled.

The university had made no effort beforehand to prepare the students for the possibility that the Guard might come to the campus. Administration officials had met with student leaders several times during the day, but the discussions were confined to the subject of dances and other diversionary social events. There was no discussion of what might happen if another disorder occurred—a subject administrators discussed only among themselves or with city officials.

President White and his wife were at the home of his sister-in-law in Mason City, Iowa, all day Saturday. After repeated telephone conversations Saturday morning with his aides in Kent, he called for the Kent State airplane to be sent to bring him back to his troubled campus. He took off for Ohio early Sunday morning.

As the ROTC building burned, the pattern of the previous night was repeated—authorities arrived at the scene of an incident too late to apprehend the participants, then swept up the bystanders and the participants together in their response. Students who had nothing to do with burning the building—who were not even in the area at the time of the fire—resented being gassed and ordered about by armed men. Many students returning to the campus on Sunday after a weekend at home were first surprised at the Guard's presence, then irritated when its orders interfered with their activities. Student resentment of the Guard continued to grow during the next two days.

SUNDAY, MAY 3

At 10:00 a.m. Sunday, while Kent State President White was on his way home from Iowa by plane, Governor Rhodes arrived in Kent and held a news conference. Among those present to hear Rhodes were his chief aide McElroy, General Del Corso, Mayor Satrom, KSU Vice President Matson, Ohio Highway Patrol Superintendent Robert N. Chiaramonte, Portage County Prosecutor Ronald J. Kane, U.S. Attorney Robert Krupansky, and Kent Fire Chief Fred Miller.

Governor Rhodes called the Kent disturbances "probably the most vicious form of campus-oriented violence yet perpetrated by dissident groups and their allies in the state of Ohio" and told his listeners that "we are going to employ every force of law that we have under our authority." Rhodes alluded to information that he seemed to suggest indicated that the Kent State 4 were involved in the Kent disorders.

After referring to recent disturbances at two other Ohio universities, Governor Rhodes said:

We have the same groups going from one campus to the other and they use the universities state-supported by the state of Ohio as a sanctuary. And in this, they make definite plans of burning, destroying, and throwing rocks at police and at the National Guard and at the Highway Patrol.

"We are going to eradicate the problem," Governor Rhodes said. "We are not going to treat the symptoms."
Rhodes described the troublemakers as

worse than the brown shirts and the communist element, and also the night-riders and the vigilantes. They are the worst type of people that we harbor in America. And I want to say this—they are not going to take over the campus and the campus now is going to be part of the county and the state of Ohio. It is no sanctuary for these people to burn buildings down of private citizens of businesses, in the community, then run into a sanctuary. It is over with in the state of Ohio.

Other officials commented at this point. Highway Patrol Superintendent Chiaramonte said, "We have men that are well trained, but they are not trained to receive bricks; they won't take it. The next phase that we have encountered elsewhere is where they start sniping. They can expect us to return fire." Mayor Satrom said, "We will take all necessary, and I repeat, all necessary action to maintain order."

After the news conference, Governor Rhodes met briefly in private with Prosecutor Kane. Kane reported that he had suggested that the university be closed. Rhodes declined, saying that would be "playing into the hands of the Weathermen." A university official tried to attend this meeting, but he was excluded.

Many persons felt that the governor had spoken firmly and forthrightly. Others felt that his remarks were inflammatory and worsened an already tense situation. Some, including many Kent students, believed the governor was hoping that his words and actions at Kent would win him additional votes in the primary election, to be held two days later, for nomination to the United States Senate.

Governor Rhodes delayed his departure until noon so that he could meet and talk briefly at the university airport with President White as he arrived from Iowa. White later stated that the governor told him, "Bob, you have 400 of the worst riffraff in the state from all of the campuses. They are trying to close you down. Don't give in. Keep open." White said he was told by Chiaramonte, who was with the governor, that the State Highway Patrol had supplied this information.

After the governor departed, widespread uncertainty regarding rules, prohibitions, and proclamations remained. Many people were unsure about what was to be legal and what not, particularly with respect to rallies and demonstrations.

Governor Rhodes had told his news conference, "We are going to ask for an injunction . . . equivalent to a state of emergency," and added that "we're trying to work on it right now." There is no official record that such an injunction was ever sought or obtained. The rules Governor Rhodes intended to apply were never precisely defined. Mayor Satrom had placed Kent under a state of civil emergency but had not banned peaceful rallies.

After Rhodes' news conference, university officials spent several hours trying to define the precise meaning of the "state of emergency" to which the governor had referred. Finally, John Huffman, Matson's executive assistant, talked with a Guard officer, and received the impression that the state of emergency permitted "no gatherings or rallies at all."

Based on this discussion, the university prepared and distributed 12,000 leaflets, again signed by Matson and Frisina. The leaflet listed curfew hours; said the governor through the National Guard had assumed legal control of the campus; stated that all outdoor demonstrations and rallies, peaceful or otherwise, were prohibited by the state of emergency; and said the Guard was empowered to make arrests. Canterbury later cited this leaflet, which was based on an interpretation given to a university administrator by one of his officers, as one source of his authority for banning rallies.

White broadcast a statement of his own, indicating the university had no control over when the Guard might depart, declaring, "Events have taken decisions out of university hands."

Some students disregarded the informational leaflet distributed Sunday when they saw the names of Matson and Frisina on it. Many students disliked the roles these two had played in opposing the old CCC during April 1969.

Many students remained confused all day Sunday about the rules governing the campus and what they permitted.

About noon, the National Guard asked Schwartzmiller for a bullhorn to use in dispersing sightseers at the ROTC ruins. Schwartzmiller complied, although he believed the Guard was being overzealous. In the afternoon, a group of 23 faculty members issued a statement deploring the Guard's presence on campus and student rock-throwing and violence during the previous two days. But the statement also suggested that the building burning should be viewed in the context of the war in Vietnam and the American move into Cambodia. A group of about 60 teachers asked White to call a full faculty meeting immediately. He declined—permission of the Guard would have been required for such an assembly, and in any case the request did not come from the proper body.

Generals Del Corso and Canterbury had left Kent that morning, leaving Colonel Harold Finley in charge of the Guard.

On Sunday afternoon, the campus was generally quiet, and many students felt the worst was over. Sightseers visited the ruins of the ROTC building, and some students conversed with guardsmen.

Students began gathering on the Commons about 8:00 p.m. The crowd was peaceful and included a group of coeds kicking a soccer ball around. But by 8:45 p.m., it had grown so large that campus police and the Highway Patrol suggested to Colonel Finley that the 1:00 a.m. campus curfew be cancelled and an immediate curfew imposed. As a result, shortly before 9:00 p.m., Major Jones read the Ohio Riot Act to the crowd on the Commons and gave them five minutes to disperse. When they did not, police proceeded to disperse them with tear gas. One group headed toward President White's house, another toward Prentice Gate.

The students were driven away from White's home by tear gas. At Prentice Gate, there was a more serious confrontation. A sizable crowd sat down in the intersection of Lincoln and Main, next to the gate, and asked to speak with Satrom and White about six demands: abolition of ROTC; removal of the Guard from campus by Monday night; lifting of the curfew; full amnesty for all persons arrested Saturday night; lower student tuition; and granting of any demand made by the BUS.

Matson and Ronald Roskens, vice president for administration, were at the administration building when a police officer told them the crowd wanted to talk to White. Matson and Roskens rejected the idea. They felt that the Guard was in charge of the campus and that there was no point in negotiating in the streets.

Matson said he contacted White, who agreed with his decision. White's recollection is that he was not personally contacted about the students' request. Matson himself was asked to go to the gathering, but he declined.

Mayor Satrom was informed of the situation at Prentice Gate and left for the scene; before he arrived, the Guard dispersed the crowd.

A tape recording made at the scene was helpful in reconstructing the following account:

An unidentified young man who was permitted to use the police public address system told the crowd that Mayor Satrom was coming to discuss their demands and that efforts were being made to contact President White. (John Huffman, Matson's executive assistant, later said he had just told the young man specifically that White was not coming.) The young man said that if the students would move out of the street, the guardsmen at the scene would reciprocate by moving off campus. Both the Guard and the students did in fact withdraw slightly.

At 11:00 p.m., police were told that the two officials would not talk to the demonstrators. The Riot Act was read to the crowd, and Colonel Finley told them the curfew was in effect as of 11:00 p.m.

The students, previously nonviolent, became hostile. They felt that they had been double-crossed. They cursed the guardsmen and police and threw rocks at them. Tear gas was fired and the crowd ran back from the gate across the campus lawn.

During the confusion of the dispersal, two students were bayoneted and sustained minor cuts. Three guardsmen received cuts and bruises from thrown stones and a wrench.

With tear gas, guardsmen drove one group of about 300 young persons across the campus to the Tri-Towers dormitory area. A helicopter had been hovering over the Prentice Gate sit-in. Its spotlight illuminated the scene, following the students as they ran. Its wash increased the effectiveness of the gas along the ground. Among the fleeing Kent State students was Allison Krause.

Another group of students ran to the Rockwell Memorial Library, the building closest to the gate, and climbed through windows to get inside. A coed was reportedly bayoneted as she attempted to climb through a window. Some of the library windows were broken by rocks. The night guard locked the doors, sealing the students inside. They were later given a 45-minute grace period to leave the building and return to their dormitories.

Fifty-one persons were arrested Sunday night, most of them for curfew violations. This brought the total of arrests to more than 100 since the disturbances had begun.

By the time General Canterbury returned to Kent at 11:40 p.m., the campus was quiet. He called a meeting of law enforcement and other officials for 10:00 a.m. Monday. He was concerned about the lack of coordination and wanted to resolve the confusion over the applicable curfew hours.

Despite the day's promising start, the situation at Kent

State had appreciably worsened by Sunday night. Students were more resentful of the Guard as a result of what they considered to be broken promises at Prentice Gate. The university was anxious to restore normal conditions, and law enforcement officers and guardsmen seemed to be growing more impatient with student curses, stones, and refusals to obey.

MONDAY, MAY 4

As they lined up opposite students on the Commons shortly before noon, the three National Guard units involved in the Kent State shooting had had an average of three hours of sleep the night before.

Company C of the First Battalion, 145th Infantry Regiment, went off duty at 2:00 a.m. Monday morning. At 5:30 a.m., the company commander, Capt. James R. Snyder, received orders to return to patrol on city streets near Kent State.

At 6:00 a.m., Troop G of the Second Squadron, 107th Armored Cavalry Regiment, relieved Company A of the First Battalion, 145th Infantry, which had been on duty all night. Company A then had to move their bivouac area, however, and the company commander, Capt. John E. Martin, said none got to bed before 9:00 a.m. At about 11:30 a.m., they were roused to return to duty on the campus.

Troop G had gone off duty at 6:00 p.m. Sunday, according to the troop commander, Capt. Raymond J. Srp. But they had just lined up for their first hot meal of the day when they were sent back to duty on campus. They served until between midnight and 1:00 a.m. Monday and then were awakened between 4:00 and 4:30 a.m. to prepare to relieve Company A.

Kent State President White met at 7:00 a.m. with his cabinet. At an 8:00 a.m. meeting with the executive committee of the faculty senate, he agreed to attend the senate's regular Monday meeting and to hold an afternoon meeting for the full faculty.

The Education Building was closed at 7:45 a.m., before classes began, because of a bomb threat. Several other Monday classes were cancelled by bomb threats. In many of the classes that did meet, the events of the weekend were the chief topic of discussion.

A call for a noon rally on the Commons was passed around the campus by word of mouth and by announcements chalked on classroom blackboards. The precise purpose was not made clear, but most students assumed it was to protest the presence of the National Guard, which by now was resented by many students, even by many who held no deep political beliefs.

General Canterbury called a meeting for 10:00 a.m. Monday to discuss plans for the day and to reduce confusion over the curfew hours. He attended the meeting in civilian clothes to avoid attracting attention. He did not have time later to change into his uniform. President White, Vice President Matson, Mayor Satrom, Paul Hershey, the Kent city safety director, Major Donald E. Manly of the Ohio State Highway Patrol, and Major William R. Shimp, legal officer of the Ohio National Guard, were also in attendance. They decided to apply the city's 8:00 p.m. to 6:00 a.m. curfew to the campus. The proclamation of civil emergency which Satrom had issued on Saturday was amended accordingly.

Thereafter the major topic of the meeting was what to do about the rally planned for the Commons at noon. A university official phoned Matson at the meeting and asked him about the status of the noon rally. Matson's reaction was that the rally was forbidden by the Guard's rules. He returned to the meeting and raised the issue of how the noon rally was to be handled. Participants in the meeting give differing accounts of this discussion.

Canterbury testified before the Commission that he first learned about the rally during this meeting. When he asked White if it should be permitted, White replied, "No, it would be highly dangerous."

White testified that during this meeting "it became apparent that any noon rallies or any rally would not be

permitted . . . ." Asked what part he played in banning the
noon rally, White testified, "None at all." In a statement
after Canterbury testified, White denied making the statement attributed to him by the general and added, "From past
history, all know that my response would have been
affirmative to a rally."

Satrom, Hershey, and Major Manly do not recall that
White asked that the rally be prevented, but each of them
came away with the belief it was banned.

Matson said he thought it was "more or less assumed" by
all present that Governor Rhodes' declaration of emergency
on Sunday prohibited all rallies. Matson recalled that
Canterbury told the group that the rally would not be
allowed unless he heard strong objections to its prohibition.

After the meeting, Canterbury returned to Guard headquarters in the administration building at Kent State about
11:30 a.m. Two Guard officers present recall that, upon his
return, he stated that the noon rally on the Commons would
not be permitted. Major John Simons, chaplain of the 107th
Armored Cavalry Regiment, expressed concern that the
students might be unaware that the noon rally had been
prohibited. He said a campus official told him that the
university radio station would "spread the word."

Throughout the morning, guardsmen patrolled the campus
without notable incident.

About 11:00 a.m., students began gathering on the
Commons, apparently for a variety of reasons. Some had
heard vaguely that a rally would be held. Some came to
protest the presence of the Guard. Some were simply curious,
or had free time because their classes had been cancelled.
Some students stopped by on their way to or from lunch or
class. The Commons is a crossroads between several major
university buildings.

Many students who described themselves as "straight," or
conservative, later attributed their presence at the rally to a
desire to protest against the National Guard. This attitude
was reflected in the testimony of one Kent State coed before
the Commission:

Q What were your feelings at the time when you saw them [the Guard on May 3]?

A I just really couldn't believe it. It was a very unreal feeling to walk up on your Front Campus and see these armed troops. You know, like you had been invaded, in a way.

Q Did you go back on the campus on Monday, May 4?

A Yes, I did. I have an 11 o'clock class in the Education Building . . . . After that time, I have a 12 o'clock class which is around this side complex, so I had to cross the campus and I went the usual way and found I couldn't get across campus because the Guards were blocking the campus, across the Commons.

Q Had you heard of the rally down on the Commons before you left your class at the Education Building?

A Yes. One of the boys in the class had heard about it and mentioned that there was a rally. And that Governor Rhodes was taking hard lines about the rally.

Q Did you plan to go to the rally?

A No, I had my books with me and I had a report due in the next hour and I intended to go to class. It was when I found I couldn't go across campus, I decided to go to the rally.

Q Had you been to any rallies before?

A Just one, on October 15 [the war moratorium] was the first time I had gone to any kind of a rally.

Q Why did you stay at this particular rally after you got there . . . ?

A Well, I just couldn't believe the Guards were on campus. It was mostly, just outrage and disgust and fear, and all sorts of crazy things. I just couldn't believe that my campus had been taken over by Guards. You know, they said I couldn't cross the campus, they said we can't assemble on the campus. I stood on the Commons. I was watching the Guards and thinking, they are telling us to leave, but this is

> our campus, we belong here and they don't. That is
> why I stayed mostly.

This coed was gassed on the Commons, moved back over Blanket Hill to the Prentice Hall parking lot, and was within three feet of Allison Krause when Miss Krause was killed.

General Canterbury reached the Commons between 11:30 and 11:40 a.m. with Lt. Col. Charles R. Fassinger, commander of the Second Squadron of the 107th Armored Cavalry. Canterbury told a Commission investigator he did not feel that the crowd represented a significant threat at that time.

Fassinger estimated that by 11:45 the crowd had grown to more than 500. The principal group gathered around the Victory Bell about 170 yards across the Commons from the burned-out ROTC building, where the guardsmen were stationed. Canterbury ordered the crowd dispersed.

Fassinger then ordered troops to form up by the ruins of the ROTC building. Some 40 to 50 men from Company A, about 35 to 45 men from Company C, and 18 men from Troop G were hurriedly assembled. Those who had not already done so were ordered to "lock and load" their weapons. By this process an M-1 rifle is loaded with an eight-round clip of .30 caliber ball ammunition, and one bullet is moved up into the chamber ready to fire. The weapon will then fire immediately after the safety mechanism is disengaged and the trigger is pulled. Throughout the weekend, whenever guardsmen were on duty, their weapons were locked and loaded.

A Kent State policeman, Harold E. Rice, stood near the ROTC ruins and, using a bullhorn, ordered the students to disperse. It is doubtful that Rice was heard over the noise of the crowd. A jeep was brought up. Rice, a driver, and two Guard riflemen drove out across the Commons toward the crowd. Rice gave the dispersal order again.

The students responded with curses and stones. Some chanted "Pigs off campus" and "One, two, three, four, we don't want your fucking war." Rocks bounced off the jeep, and Rice said the occupants were hit several times.

Specialist Fifth Class Gordon R. Bedall, who was in the jeep, said Rice saw a student in the crowd who, Rice believed, was one of the instigators of the weekend disturbances. Rice asked the driver to direct the jeep into the crowd so that he could pick up this young man and take him back. According to the driver, a shower of rocks from several students forced the jeep back twice. Major Jones was dispatched from the Guard lines to order the jeep to return.

At 11:58 a.m., as the jeep returned, Canterbury ordered the 96 men and seven officers to form a skirmish line, shoulder to shoulder, and to move out across the Commons toward the students. Each man's weapon was locked and loaded. Canterbury estimated the size of the crowd on the Commons at about 800; another 1,000 or more persons were sitting or milling about on the hills surrounding the Commons. His goal as he moved out was to disperse the crowd.

After the event, Canterbury was asked several times to indicate the authority under which he had issued his order to disperse the crowd.

On May 8, 1970, he told an FBI agent that his order was based on the proclamation of Governor Rhodes on April 29 mobilizing the Guard for a Teamsters' strike. Canterbury contended that the proclamation incorporated the Ohio Riot Act even though it did not explicitly mention that Act.

On August 4, 1970, Canterbury told a Commission investigator that his authority was based on Governor Rhodes' April 29 proclamation, and also on the Ohio Riot Act, which permits an officer to order dispersal of a crowd when it is engaged in "violent or tumultuous conduct which creates clear and present danger to the safety of persons or property."

On August 20, 1970, Canterbury testified before the Commission:

> The assemblies were not to be permitted because of the previous two days of rioting and to permit an assembly at this point would have been dangerous. This was my assessment, as well as the assessment of the President of the University, and the other authorities present.

Shortly before noon, students began to ring the Victory Bell. Two generalized emotions seem to have prevailed among the 2,000 or so young persons who were now on or near the Commons. One was a vague feeling that something worth watching or participating in would occur, that something was going to happen and that the Guard would respond. The other was antipathy to the Guard, bitter in some cases, accompanied by the feeling that the Guard, although fully backed by official pronouncements, was somehow "trespassing" on the students' own territory.

A majority of the crowd was watching the tableau from the patio of Taylor Hall and from the slopes around the adjacent buildings of Prentice, Johnson, and Stopher Halls. The hills made a natural amphitheater from which students could watch events on the Commons floor. Most of the onlooking students could not be described as neutral: in almost any quarrel between students and guardsmen, they would take the side of their fellow students.

The troops lined up with fixed bayonets across the northwestern corner of the Commons. On orders from Canterbury relayed by Fassinger, eight to ten grenadiers with M-79 grenade launchers fired two volleys of tear gas canisters at the crowd, which began to scatter.

Canterbury, in civilian clothes and unarmed, was in command. At the age of 55, he had 23 years of military experience behind him and had served during many previous civil disturbances in Ohio, including ones in Akron and in the Hough section of Cleveland. The Ohio National Guard units Canterbury commanded were also experienced in dealing with disorders. General Del Corso testified that since his appointment as adjutant general on April 1, 1968, the Guard has been mobilized by Governor Rhodes approximately 30 times for civil disturbances. "Twelve or thirteen" of these occasions, said Del Corso, had involved disturbances in the northeastern zone of the state, the location of Kent State University.

The day was bright and sunny, and a 14-mile-an-hour breeze was blowing. The tear gas did not at first scatter all the students: the wind blew some of the gas away; the aim of some of the grenadiers was poor, causing many who were only spectators to be gassed; and some of the students picked up the tear gas canisters and threw them back. Canterbury ordered the troops to move out.

The guardsmen were wearing gas masks. Company A was on the right flank, Company C was on the left flank, and Troop G was in the middle. Moving out with the men were Canterbury, Fassinger, and the third in command, Major Harry D. Jones, battalion staff officer of the 145th.

The guardsmen marched across the flat Commons, the students scattering before them up a steep hill beyond the Victory Bell. Canterbury's original plan was to march to the crest of Blanket Hill, a knoll beyond the bell, between the northern end of Johnson Hall and southern end of Taylor Hall. When some of the students ran to the north end of Taylor Hall, he sent a contingent of men around there to disperse them. He had hoped, after clearing the Commons, to withdraw his troops to the ROTC building.

When Canterbury reached the crest of Blanket Hill, however, he concluded that it would be necessary to push the students beyond a football practice field which lay about 80 yards below the crest of Blanket Hill.

By this time the crowd seemed more united in mood. The feeling had spread among students that they were being harassed as a group, that state and civic officials had united against them, and that the university had either cooperated or acquiesced in their suppression. They reacted to the guardsmen's march with substantial solidarity. They shouted, "Pigs off campus," and called the guardsmen "green pigs" and "fascist bastards."

Rocks flew as the guardsmen marched across the Commons. Capt. Snyder, the C Company commander, said a young man near Taylor Hall struck him twice with stones. When the young man refused Snyder's order to put the rocks down, Snyder knocked him down with his baton. The youth scrambled to his feet and ran away.

The antagonism between guardsmen and students increased. The guardsmen generally felt that the students, who had disobeyed numerous orders to disperse, were clearly in the wrong. The razing of the ROTC building had shown them that these noisy youths were capable of considerable destruction.

Many students felt that the campus was their "turf." Unclear about the authority vested in the Guard by the governor, or indifferent to it, some also felt that their constitutional right to free assembly was being infringed upon. As they saw it, they had been ordered to disperse at a time when no rocks had been thrown and no other violence had been committed. Many told interviewers later, "We weren't doing anything."

The guardsmen marched down the east slope of Blanket Hill, across an access road, and onto the football practice field, which is fenced in on three sides. The crowd parted to let them down the hill to the field and then reformed in two loose groups—one on Blanket Hill, above the football field, and the other in the Prentice Hall parking lot at the north end of the field. The crowd on the parking lot was unruly and threw many missiles at guardsmen on the football field. It was at this point that the shower of stones apparently became heaviest. Nearby construction projects provided an ample supply of rocks.

Tear gas canisters were still flying back and forth; after the Guard would shoot a canister, students sometimes would pick it up and lob it back at the guardsmen. In some cases, guardsmen would pick up the same canister and throw it at the students. Some among the crowd came to regard the situation as a game—"a tennis match" one called it—and cheered each exchange of tear gas canisters. Only a few students participated in this game, however. One of them was Jeffrey Glenn Miller. A few minutes later, Miller was fatally shot.

As the confrontation worsened, some students left the scene. Among those who departed was a student who had gone to the rally with a classmate, William Schroeder. Subsequently, Schroeder was killed.

While on the football field, about a dozen guardsmen knelt and pointed their weapons at the students in the Prentice Hall parking lot, apparently as a warning or a threatening gesture. Whether any shot was fired on the field is in dispute.

Richard A. Schreiber, an assistant professor of journalism at Kent State, said he was watching the action through binoculars from the balcony of Taylor Hall when he saw an officer fire one shot from a .45 caliber automatic pistol at a 45-degree angle over the heads of rock-throwers in a nearby parking lot. Sgt. James W. Fariss of Company A said an officer whom he did not know fired one shot from a .45 caliber pistol while on the field.

The next day, Tuesday, Specialist Fourth Class Gerald Lee Scalf found a spent .22 caliber shell casing near the edge of the football field. Major Jones was the only officer on the field with a .22 caliber pistol, a Beretta automatic. He said he did not fire this pistol on the football field or at any time on Monday.

After the guardsmen had been on the football field for about 10 minutes, Canterbury concluded that his dispersal mission had been sufficiently accomplished. He ordered his troops to retrace their steps back up Blanket Hill. He also thought—wrongly—that his men had exhausted their supply of tear gas. Capt. Srp, commander of Troop G, ordered a tear gas launcher prepared for possible use as his unit marched back up Blanket Hill. One grenadier, Specialist Fourth Class Russell Repp, still had four unused tear gas grenades. Canterbury made no check to determine if tear gas was still available before the order to move out was given.

Later, in discussing his order to move off the field, Canterbury said, "My purpose was to make it clear beyond any doubt to the mob that our posture was now defensive and that we were clearly returning to the Commons, thus reducing the possibility of injury to either soldiers or students."

The Guard's march from Blanket Hill to the football field and back did not disperse the crowd and seems to have done little else than increase tension, subject guardsmen to

needless abuse, and encourage the most violent and irresponsible elements in the crowd to harass the Guard further.

As the guardsmen withdrew from the field, many students
thought either that they had run out of tear gas or that there
was nothing more they could do in their strategically weak
position. Many felt a sense of relief, believing all danger was
over. Most expected the Guard to march back over Blanket
Hill to the ROTC building.

Some students grew more aggressive. A small group of two
to four dozen followed the Guard closely. Some came as
close as 20 yards, shouting and jeering and darting back and
forth. One Guard officer said some students approached as
close as six inches from the end of the guardsmen's bayonets.
None of the many photographs examined by Commission
investigators show any students to have been this close.

Many witnesses said that during the Guard's return march
the intensity of rock-throwing appeared to diminish. The
witnesses also said that most rock-throwers remained so far
away from the guardsmen that most of their stones fell short,
but several guardsmen were hit and some rocks bounced off
their helmets. Other student witnesses said the rock-throwing
never slackened, and some say it grew heavier as the Guard
mounted the hill.

The movements of the crowd in the last minute or two
before the firing are the subject of considerable dispute.
General Canterbury, in a statement to a Commission investigator on August 25, gave this description:

> As the troop formation reached the area of the Pagoda
> near Taylor Hall, the mob located on the right flank in
> front of Taylor Hall and in the Prentice Hall parking lot
> charged our right flank, throwing rocks, yelling obsceni-
> ties and threats, "Kill the pigs," "Stick the pigs." The
> attitude of the crowd at this point was menacing and
> vicious.
> The troops were being hit by rocks. I saw Major Jones
> hit in the stomach by a large brick, a guardsman to the
> right and rear of my position was hit by a large rock and

fell to the ground. During this movement, practically all of the guardsmen were hit by missiles of various kinds. Guardsmen on the right flank were in serious danger of bodily harm and death as the mob continued to charge. I felt that, in view of the extreme danger to the troops at this point, that they were justified in firing.

General Canterbury also testified that the closest students were within four to five yards of the Guard. In the direction the Guard fired, however, photographs show an open space in front of the guardsmen of at least 20 yards. To their side, the nearest student, one of several on the terrace of Taylor Hall, was at least 15 yards away. The nearest person wounded, Joseph Lewis, Jr., who was 20 yards away, said there was no one between him and the Guard. The closest person killed, Jeffrey Glenn Miller, was at least 85 yards away.

An 8-millimeter motion picture film, taken by an amateur cameraman from a point approximately 500 yards northeast of the firing line, indicates that the main body of aggressive students was about 60 to 75 yards away, at the foot of the hill near the corner of the Prentice Hall parking lot.

The crowd's movements can be reconstructed from testimony, photographs, and investigation.

As the guardsmen left the practice field on their way back up Blanket Hill, they encountered a crowd of several hundred students fanned around in a broad parabola from Memorial Gymnasium and Lake Hall on their left to Taylor and Prentice Halls on their right. The crowd divided to let the Guard through.

A small gathering of 25 to 50 persons stood on the crest of Blanket Hill. As the Guard approached them, they retreated down the west slope of the hill and away from the scene of action.

About 100 persons stood on the east terrace of Taylor Hall, watching the guardsmen approach the adjacent hill. They are not known to have thrown any rocks and seem to have been spectators throughout. Perhaps another 100 persons withdrew from the edge of the practice field to a slope just below the east side of the hall. They threw some rocks.

A crowd of about 200 persons near Johnson Hall had generally watched the guardsmen pass by and had not followed them to the football field and back.

As the Guard crossed the road that lies between the football field and the foot of Blanket Hill, perhaps 200 persons moved off to the left of the troops through the trees toward Lake Hall. Among them was student James D. Russell, subsequently wounded as he stood more than 100 yards from the firing line on Blanket Hill.

In the Prentice Hall parking lot, to one side of the withdrawing Guard, were some 100 to 200 students, some throwing rocks, others carrying books. At the time of the firing, some thought the action was over and had started away toward classes, including student Douglas Wrentmore, whose back was toward the guardsmen when the firing began.

About 20 to 50 persons formed the most conspicuous part of the crowd, moving first along the guardsmen's right flank and then behind them. In this group were those most active in throwing rocks. It is not known precisely how many of this group threw rocks, but perhaps half of them threw rocks at one time or another. Included in this group of 20 to 50 were two young men, one carrying a red flag and the other a black flag. This group was particularly aggressive, cursing and jeering the guardsmen, following and pursuing them at a range varying from about 20 to 80 yards. At the time of the firing, most of this group were just south of the Prentice Hall parking lot, just below the eastern side of Taylor Hall.

Movie film and testimony indicate that as guardsmen reached the top of the hill, some students surged from the east face of Taylor Hall and the southern end of the parking lot up toward the guardsmen on Blanket Hill. The film is too indistinct to tell how many of the students involved in this movement were throwing rocks. The leading edge of this crowd appears to have advanced to a point no closer than 20 yards from the guardsmen, with the main body 60 to 75 yards away, before the gunfire began and they reversed their direction. It is possible that some of them had no aggressive intent but instead began running up the hill in the direction of the Guard to get a good vantage point on Blanket Hill after, as they expected, the guardsmen retreated down the far side of the slope.

Near the crest of Blanket Hill stands the Pagoda, a square bench made of 4-by-4 wooden beams and shaded by a concrete umbrella. The events which occurred as the Guard reached the Pagoda, turned, and fired on the students, are in bitter dispute.

Many guardsmen said they had hard going as they withdrew up the hill. Fassinger said he was hit six times by stones, once on the shoulder so hard that he stumbled.

Fassinger had removed his gas mask to see more clearly. He said the guardsmen had reached a point between the Pagoda and Taylor Hall, and he was attempting to maintain them in a reasonably orderly formation, when he heard a sound like a shot, which was immediately followed by a volley of shots. He saw the troops on the Taylor Hall end of the line shooting. He yelled, "Cease fire!" and ran along the line repeating the command.

Major Jones said he first heard an explosion which he thought was a firecracker. As he turned to his left, he heard another explosion which he knew to be an M-1 rifle shot. As he turned to his right, toward Taylor Hall, he said he saw guardsmen kneeling (photographs show some crouching) and bringing their rifles to their shoulders. He heard another M-1 shot, and then a volley of them. He yelled, "Cease fire!" several times, and rushed down the line shoving rifle barrels up and away from the crowd. He hit several guardsmen on their helmets with his swagger stick to stop them from firing.

General Canterbury stated that he first heard a single shot, which he thought was fired from some distance away on his left and which in his opinion did not come from a military weapon. Immediately afterward, he heard a volley of M-1 fire from his right, the Taylor Hall end of the line. The Guard's fire was directed away from the direction from which

Canterbury thought the initial, nonmilitary shot came. His first reaction, like that of Fassinger and Jones, was to stop the firing.

Canterbury, Fassinger, and Jones—the three ranking officers on the hill—all said no order to fire was given.

Twenty-eight guardsmen have acknowledged firing from Blanket Hill. Of these, 25 fired 55 shots from rifles, two fired five shots from .45 caliber pistols, and one fired a single blast from a shotgun. Sound tracks indicate that the firing of these 61 shots lasted approximately 13 seconds. The time of the shooting was approximately 12:25 p.m.

Four persons were killed and nine were wounded. As determined by the FBI, their distances from the firing line and the types of wounds they received were as follows:

1. Joseph Lewis, Jr., 20 yards, wounded in the right abdomen and the left lower leg.

2. Thomas V. Grace, 20 yards, wounded in the left ankle.

3. John R. Cleary, 37 yards, wounded in the left upper chest.

4. Allen Michael Canfora, 75 yards, wounded in the right wrist.

5. Jeffrey Glenn Miller, 85 to 90 yards, killed by a shot in the mouth.

6. Dean R. Kahler, 95 to 100 yards, wounded in the left side of the small of his back. A bullet fragment lodged in his spine, and he is paralyzed from the waist down.

7. Douglas Alan Wrentmore, 110 yards, wounded in the right knee.

8. Allison B. Krause, 110 yards, killed by a bullet that passed through her left upper arm and into her left side.

9. James Dennis Russell, 125 to 130 yards, wounded in the right thigh and right forehead.

10. William K. Schroeder, 130 yards, killed by a shot in the left back at the seventh rib.

11. Sandra Lee Scheuer, 130 yards, killed by a shot through the left front side of the neck.

12. Robert Follis Stamps, 165 yards, wounded in the right buttock.

13. Donald Scott Mackenzie, 245 to 250 yards, wounded in the left rear of the neck.

Of the casualties, two were shot in the front, seven from the side, and four from the rear. All 13 were students at Kent State University.

Schroeder and Kahler were hit while lying prone. MacKenzie and Canfora were wounded while running away from the line of fire. Russell and Stamps were apparently hit by ricochets. Two of the casualties, Lewis and Russell, were wounded twice.

Of the 25 riflemen who admitted firing, 21 said they fired their 41 shots either into the air or into the ground. Four riflemen acknowledged firing nine of their total of 14 shots into the crowd.

Two men fired pistols: one said he fired two shots into the crowd and the other said he fired three shots into the air.

The guardsman who fired a shotgun said he fired a single blast into the air. Russell was wounded by shotgun pellets believed to have ricocheted off nearby trees.

The guardsmen admit firing a total of only 11 rounds into the crowd. Besides the 15 wounds sustained by the casualties, however, a number of parked cars in the Prentice Hall parking lot afterward showed bullet holes.

Guardsmen have claimed that they were under an increasingly heavy barrage of rocks and other objects as they advanced back up Blanket Hill and that students rushed toward them threateningly. Many indicated that they began firing when they heard one or some of their fellow guardsmen open fire.

Although General Canterbury said his men were "not panic stricken," it is clear that many of them were frightened. Many suffered bruises and abrasions from stones, although only one guardsman, Sgt. Dennis L. Breckenridge, required overnight hospitalization. He passed out from hyperventilation and was removed from the field in an ambulance.

A few students and a few guardsmen claim to have heard something like an order to fire. One student testified to the Commission that he saw an officer raise and lower his pistol just before the firing, possibly as a signal to shoot. The weight of the evidence indicates, however, that no command to fire was given, either by word or by gesture.

As the shooting began, students scattered and ran. In the parking lot behind Prentice Hall, where two were killed and two were wounded, students dove behind parked cars and attempted to flatten themselves on the pavement. On the slope east of Taylor Hall, where four were wounded, students scrambled behind a metal sculpture, rolled down the incline, or sought cover behind trees. The scene was one of pell-mell disorder and fright.

Many thought the guardsmen were firing blanks. When the shooting stopped and they rose and saw students bleeding, the first reaction of most was shock. Jeffrey Miller lay on the pavement of an access road, blood streaming from his mouth.

Then the crowd grew angry. They screamed and some called the guardsmen "murderers." Some tried to give first aid. One vainly attempted mouth-to-mouth resuscitation on Sandra Lee Scheuer, one of the fatalities. Knots of students gathered around those who had fallen.

Sandra Lee Scheuer, 20, a junior, is believed to have been on her way to a 1:10 p.m. class in the Music and Speech Building when she was struck. She has not been identified in any available photographs as having attended the prohibited noon rally on the Commons.

Allison B. Krause, 19, a freshman, was among the group of students gathered on the Commons by the Victory Bell shortly before noon. After her death, small fragments of concrete and cinder block were found in the pockets of her jacket.

Jeffrey Glenn Miller, 20, a junior, was present in the crowd on the Commons when the dispersal order was given and made obscene gestures with his middle fingers at guardsmen. He also threw back a tear gas canister at the Guard while it was on the football practice field.

William K. Schroeder, 19, a sophomore, was an ROTC cadet. A photograph shows him retreating up Blanket Hill from the rally on the Commons, but he is not shown taking part in any of the harassment of the Guard.

No evidence was found to establish that any of the casualties were under the influence of drugs at the time of the confrontation. A marijuana cigarette was found in a pocket of the jacket used to cover one of the wounded students, Cleary, after he was injured. Cleary's father said, however, that the jacket did not belong to Cleary.

At the moment of the firing, most of the nine wounded students were far beyond a range at which they could have presented any immediate physical threat to the Guard.

The closest casualties—Lewis, Grace, and Cleary—were all within 20 to 40 yards. At the moment shooting began, Lewis was standing between Taylor Hall and the metal sculpture, making obscene gestures at guardsmen with the middle finger of his right hand. Cleary was standing on the other side of the sculpture, which was perforated by a bullet. Grace was near them, but a little farther away from Taylor Hall. His actions are not known.

Canfora, who said he had been chanting antiwar slogans earlier, had started to run for cover behind cars in Prentice Hall parking lot when he was hit.

Kahler was standing at the northwest corner of the football field, beyond stone-throwing range, when the firing began. He dropped to the ground and was hit while prone.

Wrentmore was in the Prentice Hall parking lot and said he was walking away to a class when he heard the firing begin, turned, and was wounded.

Russell, apparently hit by a ricochet, was standing far away from all the other casualties, near Lake Hall and Memorial Gymnasium.

Stamps, tear gassed on the Commons, had just left Prentice Hall after washing tear gas off his face. He was wounded in Prentice Hall parking lot as he tried to run away from the firing.

Mackenzie, the casualty most distant from the Guard, said

he heard the firing begin and had turned to run when he was hit. The entire length of Prentice Hall parking lot and the east slope of Blanket Hill lay between him and the Guard.

After the shooting, students ran to Taylor, Prentice, and Dunbar Halls to telephone for ambulances. Others ran down to the Commons screaming for ambulances. Several minutes passed before the ambulances came. Students linked their arms and formed rings around the bodies to keep them from further injury. Some students wept. Others wandered around dazed.

The shooting on Blanket Hill was done principally by members of Troop G and Company A. Company C, except for two members who went down to the football field and returned to Blanket Hill with the main body of troops, remained at the northern end of Taylor Hall where they had been dispatched by General Canterbury. The C Company members at that position, which is at the opposite end of Taylor Hall from Blanket Hill, did not fire their weapons.

After the firing, the C Company commander, Capt. Snyder, took seven men down to the Prentice Hall parking lot to render first aid. He looked at two young men who had fallen, probably Miller and Schroeder, but concluded both were dead. While the detachment was in the vicinity of the body of Jeffrey Miller, enraged students began to scream at them. The guardsmen responded by throwing a tear gas pellet at the student group. Capt. Snyder withdrew his unit to its original position and then back across the Commons, leaving the casualties where they had fallen. Many students subsequently believed that no guardsmen made any effort to render first aid after the shootings and added this to their catalogue of charges against the troops.

The scene after the shooting was tense, and there was a possibility of further trouble. After an ambulance removed Miller's body, a demonstrator who had carried a black flag during the confrontation dipped the flag into the pool of Miller's blood and waved it at nearby students in an apparent effort to inflame them further.

Canterbury withdrew his troops to the Commons almost

immediately. He ordered a weapons check to determine how many guardsmen fired how many rounds. He also ordered that no more rounds be fired except at a specified target and upon an officer's order.

After the casualties were removed, students began to gather again on the hills overlooking the Commons. The largest concentration, varying from 200 to 300, congregated on the slope below Johnson Hall at one corner of the Commons. Many of them would later have trouble describing their emotions.

Professor Glenn W. Frank obtained permission from General Canterbury to allow faculty marshals to attempt to persuade this crowd to leave without further military action. Frank and Dr. Seymour H. Baron, who had a bullhorn, persuaded the students to sit down instead of milling around. Baron warned the students they might be shot if they approached the guardsmen again. "They're scared to death," he said of the guardsmen, "a bunch of summertime soldiers. They're not professionals. They're scared kids."

"I'm a faculty member," said Baron, who is chairman of the Kent State psychology department. "I want you to understand the faculty is with you with regard to this Vietnam thing . . . . We're with you all the way."

Major Jones of the National Guard approached. Aware of the crowd's volatile mood, Frank told him, "For God's sake, don't come any closer." Jones said, "My orders are to move ahead." Frank replied, "Over my dead body."

Jones withdrew, but soon a detachment of guardsmen appeared along the hill behind the students. Frank pleaded with the students to leave. "I am begging you right now," he said, "if you don't disperse right now, they're going to move in, and there can only be a slaughter. Jesus Christ, I don't want to be a part of this."

When the guardsmen appeared behind the students, some of the students felt surrounded. Some panicked and ran. Others adamantly refused to leave and had to be physically carried away by faculty marshals and graduate students. The entreaties of Baron and Frank induced others to walk away.

Slightly more than an hour after the shooting, the Commons and the hills around it were clear.

Major Simons, chaplain of the 107th, was one of the officers who checked weapons among the guardsmen. He said when he asked the first guardsman how many rounds he fired and in what direction, the guardsman told him he had fired twice "right down the gully." Simons said the guardsman was tired, angry, and disgusted.

Lt. Stevenson said he felt like he was "swallowing dry lumps" as he checked weapons. He said he saw tears in a number of the guardsmen's eyes and described their mood as "having a lump in your throat and, although your lips are wet, you swallow dry." Stevenson said he felt it was psychologically a bad time for a weapons check and decided to make only mental notes of who fired and to write down the information later. Fifteen guardsmen told him that they had fired into the air, but he never established how many rounds each man fired and made no physical check of weapons or ammunition.

An investigation officer was appointed one hour after the shooting. Guardsmen who fired were instructed to fill out an incident report.

After the shooting, some Guard officers (including Generals Del Corso and Canterbury) said that the guardsmen were responding to a sniper shot. The FBI conducted an extensive investigation for evidence of a sniper, including a search of the Blanket Hill area with a metal detector in an attempt to find nonmilitary bullets. Nothing was found to indicate that anyone other than a guardsman discharged a firearm during the incident. The Ohio State Highway Patrol investigation found no evidence to support conclusively the presence of sniper fire or shooting from the crowd. General Del Corso testified on behalf of the Guard: "We never identified a sniper as such, as defined in the military."

The activities of two persons at the scene may have given rise to the belief that a sniper was present.

Terry Norman, a free-lance photographer, was taking

pictures of the demonstration and was seen with a pistol after the Guard fired. Several civilians chased him from Taylor Hall into the Guard line, where he surrendered a .38 caliber revolver. The gun was immediately examined by a campus policeman, who found that it had not been fired.

Jerome P. Stoklas, a photographer for the campus newspaper, the *Daily Kent Stater*, was taking pictures of the demonstration from the roof of Taylor Hall with a camera equipped with a telephoto lens. Most of the camera, lens, and tripod were painted black and might have given the impression from a distance that Stoklas had a rifle. Stoklas had no firearm.

Dr. Joseph W. Ewing, an Akron plastic surgeon who has both military and civilian experience treating gunshot wounds, was called to St. Thomas Hospital in Akron at about 3:00 p.m. to examine the wound of Donald S. Mackenzie. Dr. Ewing was surprised to see that the bullet had gone completely through Mackenzie's neck and cheek without doing extensive damage. The bullet had entered approximately one inch left of the spinal column, making a small entrance wound, then had shattered part of the jawbone and exited through the left cheek, leaving a wound the approximate size of a five-cent piece.

Dr. Ewing told FBI agents he believed the wound could not have been made by an M-1 rifle or a .45 caliber pistol because either of these would have caused more extensive damage to Mackenzie's neck and face.

A Commission investigator showed photographs of Mackenzie's wound to Lt. Col. Norman Rich, an Army doctor at Walter Reed Army Medical Center in Washington, and to two physicians on his staff. All three physicians agreed with Dr. Ewing's conclusions.

The Walter Reed physicians also indicated their belief that the bullet which struck Mackenzie was not a ricochet or a deflected round, since it still had enough velocity to pierce his neck and cheek. They stated, however, that the velocity of a .30 caliber M-1 bullet could have been considerably reduced if the ammunition were defective. They concluded that the wound was more likely caused by a smaller caliber weapon, possibly a carbine.

General Canterbury said he did not believe that any of the guardsmen on Blanket Hill were carrying any long-barreled weapons other than M-1 rifles, M-79 grenade launchers, and the single shotgun.

A Commission investigator showed photographs of Mackenzie's wound and hospital records on his case to Dr. Milton Helpern, chief medical examiner of the City of New York. Dr. Helpern was told that MacKenzie had been located 245 to 250 yards from the position of men known to have fired .30 caliber M-1 rifles and .45 caliber pistols. Dr. Helpern said the wound definitely could have been caused by .30 caliber ammunition and that he could not rule out that it had been caused by .45 caliber ammunition.

Helpern said that, in his opinion, the entry wound in Mackenzie's neck and the exit wound in his cheek indicated that the bullet struck him on a direct line of fire without deflection or ricochet. He said the bullet had travelled a great distance and that it definitely was not a close-range shot.

Dr. Helpern said that in view of the many variables of gunshot wounds, he would like to see photographs of the other casualties in order to verify his opinion. He was shown the photographs of other victims, which he felt confirmed his initial judgment.

Mackenzie himself told a Commission investigator he believes he was shot by the Guard. He said he heard several shots and ran several steps before he was hit, and then heard shots after he was wounded.

The bullet that wounded Mackenzie was not recovered. No fragments from it were found in his jaw. He was wounded at the same time that the guardsmen fired, and the trajectory of the bullet which wounded him is in the line of fire from Blanket Hill. Since Mackenzie had time to turn and run after the first shot, he plainly was not hit by that initial shot. Listeners who said they distinctly heard a first shot said the

Guard's volley immediately followed it. To conclude that Mackenzie was struck by a sniper's bullet would indicate— unless a sniper stood between him and the Guard—that a sniper fired while the Guard fired and from behind and above them, missed them, and struck Mackenzie. There is no convincing evidence that this happened. And no guardsman who fired indicates he fired in the direction of a sniper.

Generals Del Corso and Canterbury stated that the guardsmen were well-trained in riot procedures and were seasoned veterans of previous civil disorders. Ohio guardsmen receive the same basic training as regular Army recruits and 16 hours of riot training each year they remain in the Guard. Of the 28 men who admit firing, 22 had seen action in previous Ohio disorders.

Ohio Guard procedures require that a portion of the riot training manual be read verbatim to each guardsman at the outset of civil disorder duty. Included in this reading is the following:

ANNEX F (PRE-EMPLOYMENT BRIEFING) TO OPLAN 2 (AID TO CIVIL AUTHORITIES)

RULES OF ENGAGEMENT: In any action that you are required to take, use only the minimum force necessary. When the Riot Act has been read within hearing, it is unlawful for any group of three or more people to remain unlawfully or riotously assembled and you may use necessary and proper means to disperse or apprehend them. Keeping groups from assembling prevents crowds which may become unruly and take mob action. Your use of force should be in the sequence listed below:

a.   Issue a military request to disperse.

   (1) Insure that an avenue of dispersal is available.

   (2) Allow ample time for them to obey the order.

(3) Remain in area for sufficient time to prevent re-assembly.

b. Riot information - show of force. Instructions in a. (1) (2) (3) above apply.

c. Simple physical force, if feasible.

d. Rifle butt and bayonet: If people do not respond to request, direction and order, and if simple physical force is not feasible, you have the rifle butt and bayonet which may be used in that order, using only such force as is necessary.

e. Chemical. If people fail to respond to requests or orders, and riot information and rifle butts or bayonets prove ineffective, chemicals (baseball grenades or jumping grenades) will be used on order when available. When large demands for chemicals are required, a chemical squad will be dispatched to assist you upon request.

f. Weapons. When all other means have failed or chemicals are not readily available, you are armed with the rifle and have been issued live ammunition. The following rules apply in the use of firearms:

(1) Rifles will be carried with a round in the chamber in the safe position. Exercise care and be safety-minded at all times.

(2) Indiscriminate firing of weapons is forbidden. Only single aimed shots at confirmed targets will be employed. Potential targets are:

(a) Sniper—(Determined by his firing upon, or in the direction of friendly forces or civilians) will be fired upon when clearly observed and it is determined that an attempt to apprehend would be hazardous or other means of neutralization are impractical . . . .

(c) Other. In any instance where human life is endangered by the forcible, violent actions of a rioter, or when rioters to whom the Riot Act has been read cannot be dispersed by any other reasonable means, then shooting is justified.

SUMMARY . . .

b. If there is absolute or apparent necessity and all other means of preventing the crimes of murder (such as sniper fire), robbery, burglary, rape, or arson (fire bombing of inhabited building or structure) have been exhausted, then life may be taken to prevent these forcible and atrocious crimes . . . .

c. When the Riot Act has been read within hearing and you are engaged in dispersing or apprehending rioters, using necessary and proper means, then you are declared by Ohio Statute (RC 3761.15) to be guiltless if any of the persons unlawfully or violently assembled is killed, maimed, or otherwise injured in consequence of resisting.

With specific reference to the discharge of weapons, another Ohio Guard training manual states:

I will fire when required to save my life or when returning fire.

A sniper being an individual who fires a small caliber weapon from a concealed location represents a dangerous adversary to civilians and Guardsmen alike.

The following is a recommended method of eliminating or capturing a sniper: On coming under fire, the patrol take cover immediately. No fire is returned unless the sniper's location is definitely pinpointed, in which case, single aimed shots are fired as necessary.

Precisely how much of this training material was read to or discussed with the 28 men who acknowledge firing on May 4 is not known. Although General Canterbury speculated that the first shot may have touched off a chain reaction, he told a Commission investigator that the men who fired did not do so in panic.

During its investigation, the FBI collected rocks from the Blanket Hill area and the football practice field. Rocks collected by the National Guard and the Kent State police department were also turned over to the FBI. The FBI laboratory reported the gross weight of all of the rocks to be approximately 175 pounds and the number of rocks to be about 340. The rocks ranged in weight up to 7 1/2 pounds. FBI agents collected 10 pounds of rocks from the Blanket Hill area. The National Guard and the Kent State police also collected rocks, but it is not known how many of them came from the hill. Also collected from the areas where the Guard marched were a whole brick, two pieces of brick, five broken pieces of tile, a Vaseline jar containing rocks, a 2-by-2 stick 22 inches long, and a tree limb 2 1/2 inches in diameter and 20 inches long.

It is not known how many of these rocks and other objects were thrown and how many hit guardsmen.

At the time of the shooting, Kent State President White was at a luncheon meeting at a restuarant one mile from the campus. His assistant, Ronald S. Beer, was called to the telephone and told about it. The group returned immediately to the campus and White ordered the university closed for the rest of the week.

The Portage County Prosecutor, Ronald J. Kane, superseded White's directive. Kane heard about the shooting over the radio in his office and immediately attempted to telephone Governor Rhodes to tell him he intended to seek an injunction to close the university indefinitely.

Unable to reach Rhodes immediately, Kane told an assistant to begin preparing the appropriate papers. When Kane reached Rhodes about 3:00 p.m., Rhodes told him to confer with John McElroy, the governor's chief assistant. When McElroy questioned Kane's authority to close the school, Kane said he would worry about the legalities later. Rhodes asked Kane to delay for one hour. When Kane did not hear further from Rhodes, he obtained an injunction in late afternoon from Common Pleas Court Judge Albert S. Caris.

Under this injunction, the university was closed the day of the shooting and remained shut down for more than five weeks. It did not reopen until the beginning of summer school on June 13, 1970. During this period, the university improvised with correspondence courses and classes held in the homes of faculty and in churches.

On the day after the shooting, May 5, McElroy drafted a proclamation keyed to Governor Rhodes' April 29 proclamation which called out the National Guard for the Teamsters' strike. The new proclamation provided written authorization for the commitment of National Guard troops to the city of Kent.

CONCLUSION

Kent State was a national tragedy. It was not, however, a unique tragedy. Only the magnitude of the student disorder and the extent of student deaths and injuries set it apart from similar occurrences on numerous other American campuses during the past few years. We must learn from the particular horror of Kent State and insure that it is never repeated.

The conduct of many students and nonstudent protestors at Kent State on the first four days of May 1970 was plainly intolerable. We have said in our report, and we repeat: Violence by students on or off the campus can never be justified by any grievance, philosophy, or political idea. There can be no sanctuary or immunity from prosecution on the campus. Criminal acts by students must be treated as such wherever they occur and whatever their purpose. Those who wrought havoc on the town of Kent, those who burned the ROTC building, those who attacked and stoned National Guardsmen, and all those who urged them on and applauded their deeds share the responsibility for the deaths and injuries of May 4.

The widespread student opposition to the Cambodian action and their general resentment of the National Guardsmen's presence on the campus cannot justify the violent and irresponsible actions of many students during the long weekend.

The Cambodian invasion defined a watershed in the attitude of Kent students toward American policy in the Indochina war.

Kent State had experienced no major turmoil during the preceding year, and no disturbances comparable in scope to the events of May had ever occurred on the campus. Some students thought the Cambodian action was an unacceptable contradiction of the announced policy of gradual withdrawal from Vietnam, or that the action constituted invasion of a neutral country, or that if would prolong rather than shorten the war. Opposition to the war appears to have been the principal issue around which students rallied during the first two days of May.

Thereafter, the presence of the National Guard on campus was the focus of discontent. The Guard's presence appears to have been the main attraction and the main issue for most students who came to the May 4 rally. For students deeply opposed to the war, the Guard was a living symbol of the military system they opposed. For other students, the Guard was an outsider on their campus, prohibiting all their rallies, even peaceful ones, ordering them about, and tear gassing them when they refused to obey.

The May 4 rally began as a peaceful assembly on the Commons—the traditional site of student assemblies. Even if the Guard had authority to prohibit a peaceful gathering—a question that is at least debatable—the decision to disperse the noon rally was a serious error. The timing and manner of the dispersal were disastrous. Many students were legitimately in the area as they went to and from class. The rally was held during the crowded noontime luncheon period. The rally was peaceful, and there was no apparent impending violence. Only when the Guard attempted to disperse the rally did some students react violently.

Under these circumstances, the Guard's decision to march through the crowd for hundreds of yards up and down a hill was highly questionable. The crowd simply swirled around them and reformed again after they had passed. The Guard found itself on a football practice field far removed from its supply base and running out of tear gas. Guardsmen had been subjected to harassment and assault, were hot and tired, and felt dangerously vulnerable by the time they returned to the top of Blanket Hill.

When they confronted the students, it was only too easy for a single shot to trigger a general fusillade.

Many students considered the Guard's march from the ROTC ruins across the Commons up Blanket Hill, down to the football practice field, and back to Blanket Hill as a kind of charade. Tear gas canisters were tossed back and forth to the cheers of the crowd, many of whom acted as if they were watching a game.

Lt. Alexander D. Stevenson, a platoon leader of Troop G, described the crowd in these words:

> At the time of the firing, the crowd was acting like this whole thing was a circus. The crowd must have thought that the National Guard was harmless. They were having fun with the Guard. The circus was in town.

The actions of some students were violent and criminal and those of some others were dangerous, reckless, and irresponsible. The indiscriminate firing of rifles into a crowd of students and the deaths that followed were unnecessary, unwarranted, and inexcusable.

The National Guardsmen on the Kent State campus were armed with loaded M-1 rifles, high-velocity weapons with a horizontal range of almost two miles. As they confronted the students, all that stood between a guardsman and firing was the flick of a thumb on the safety mechanism, and the pull of an index finger on the trigger. When firing began, the toll taken by these lethal weapons was disastrous.

The Guard fired amidst great turmoil and confusion, engendered in part by their own activities. But the guardsmen should not have been able to kill so easily in the first place. The general issuance of loaded weapons to law enforcement officers engaged in controlling disorders is never justified except in the case of armed resistance that trained sniper teams are unable to handle. This was not the case at Kent State, yet each guardsman carried a loaded M-1 rifle.

This lesson is not new. The National Advisory Commission on Civil Disorders and the guidelines of the Department of the Army set it out explicitly.

No one would have died at Kent State if this lesson had been learned by the Ohio National Guard.

Even if the guardsmen faced danger, it was not a danger that called for lethal force. The 61 shots by 28 guardsmen certainly cannot be justified. Apparently, no order to fire was given, and there was inadequate fire control discipline on

Blanket Hill. The Kent State tragedy must mark the last time that, as a matter of course, loaded rifles are issued to guardsmen confronting student demonstrators.

Our entire report attempts to define the lessons of Kent State, lessons that the Guard, police, students, faculty, administrators, government at all levels, and the American people must learn—and begin, at once, to act upon. We commend it to their attention.

Kent State Photographs

PHOTO 1

The first disturbance in Kent State's weekend of disruption. Shown here is North Water Street in Kent, a trash fire burning in the middle of the pavement, shortly before police arrived on Friday night, May 1, 1970.

AKRON BEACON JOURNAL

PHOTO 2

The National Guard arrives Saturday night, May 2, at the Kent State ROTC building, which by then was burning out of control.

AKRON BEACON JOURNAL

PHOTO 3

Students sat down Sunday night, May 3, in the intersection of East Main and Lincoln Streets and were subsequently dispersed with tear gas. Prentice Gate, the main entrance to the KSU campus, is visible at right.

AKRON BEACON JOURNAL

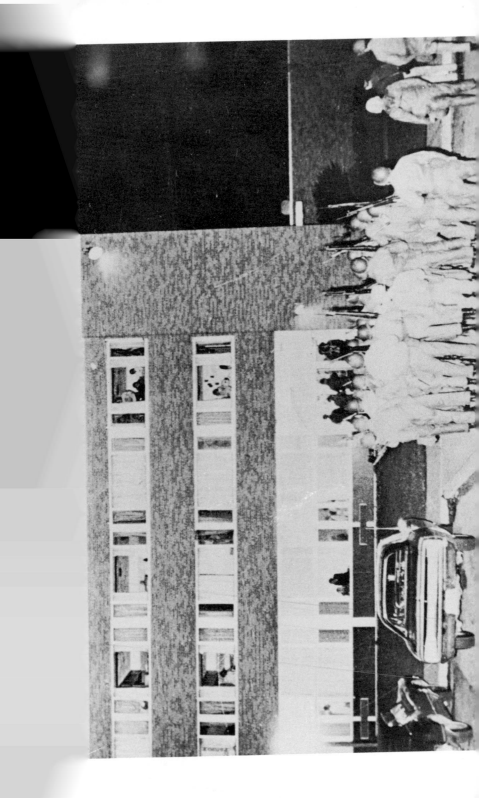

PHOTO 4

On Sunday night, after students were dispersed from Prentice Gate, some were chased to Kent State dormitories as guardsmen cleared the campus.

AKRON BEACON JOURNAL

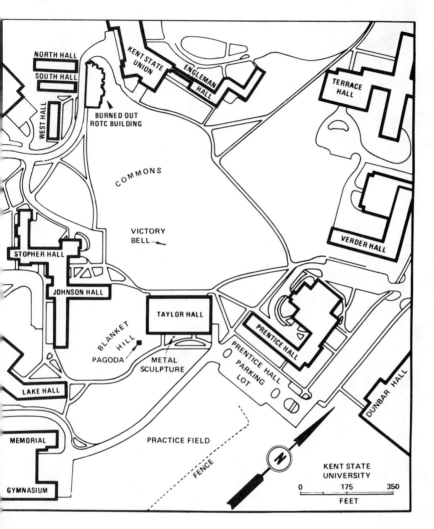

MAP 1

Diagram of KSU campus area around Taylor Hall, showing
Commons area, Blanket Hill, the Pagoda, and football practice field
area.

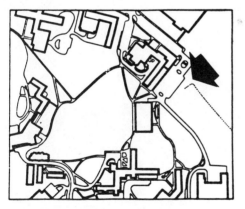

PHOTO 5

An aerial view of the Kent State campus. The large white building at the upper right is Taylor Hall. In right center is the Prentice Hall parking lot. To the left of the parking lot is the football practice field. This photograph was made in August 1970, with trees in fuller leaf than at the time of the shooting.

KENT STATE UNIVERSITY NEWS SERVICE

PHOTO 6

Students congregate on the Commons around noon Monday, May 4, 1970. The brick housing of the Victory Bell is visible at left. The girl at top center, with her pony tail flying, is Allison Krause, later a fatality.

SANDRA MARTIN BULLOCK

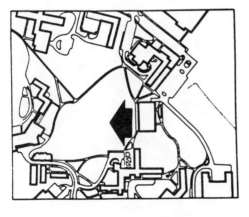

PHOTO 7

Students on the Commons taunt guardsmen. At far left, in the front row, wearing a two-tone shirt and headband, and with both middle fingers upraised, is Jeffrey Glenn Miller, subsequently a fatality.

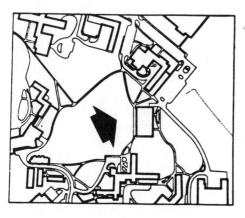

KENT STATE UNIVERSITY NEWS SERVICE

PHOTO 8

A campus policeman in a National Guard jeep rides out across the Commons to give the students dispersal orders at close range.

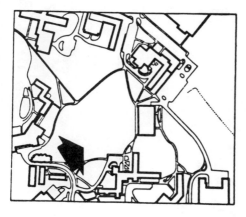

KENT STATE UNIVERSITY NEWS SERVICE

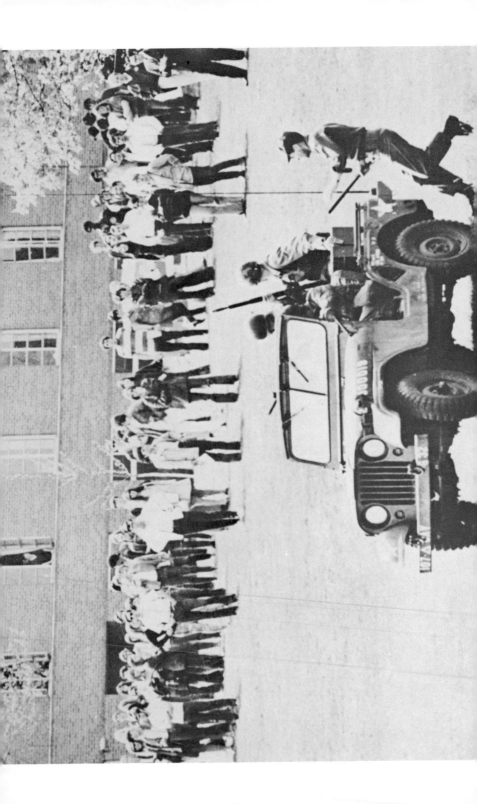

PHOTO 9

Major Harry Jones, shown on foot with a baton in his right hand, instructs the jeep occupants, who had been stoned, to return to National Guard lines by the ROTC building.

HOWARD E. RUFFNER

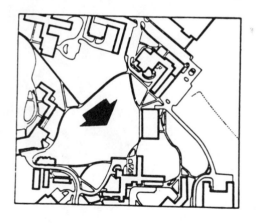

PHOTO 10

Guardsmen move out across the Commons to disperse students gathered on the field.

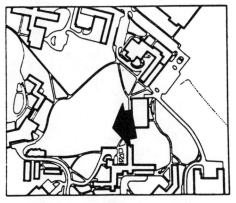

AKRON BEACON JOURNAL

PHOTO 11.

Students retreat up Blanket Hill, away from the guardsmen. The young man in the center of this picture, carrying a manuscript in his left hand, is William Schroeder, who was later killed.

VALLEY DAILY NEWS—TARENTUM, PENN.

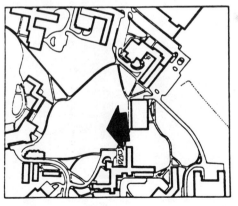

PHOTO 12
Guardsmen march across the Commons, firing tear gas as they go.

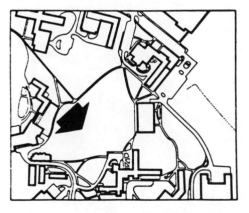

AKRON BEACON JOURNAL

PHOTO 13

Tear gas billows in the ranks of the students as the guardsmen continue their march across the Commons. The building behind the students is Taylor Hall.

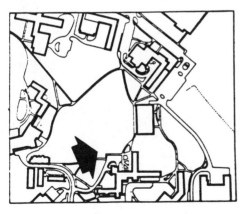

KENT STATE UNIVERSITY NEWS SERVICE

PHOTO 14
Another photo of the Guard's advance across the Commons, the tear gas thicker now.

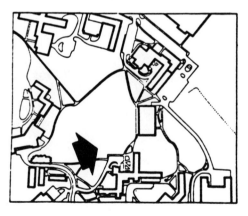

KENT STATE UNIVERSITY NEWS SERVICE

PHOTO 15

Guardsmen begin to climb Blanket Hill. Later their firing line was between the Pagoda, which can be seen here on the crest of the hill, and the adjacent end of Taylor Hall, visible here at left. The coed to the immediate right of the Pagoda is believed to be Allison Krause.

HOWARD E. RUFFNER

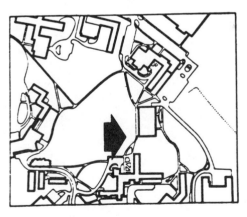

PHOTO 16

After topping Blanket Hill, guardsmen march down its eastern slope, away from the Commons. Taylor Hall is the building at right. Also at right, partially obscured here by a tree, is the Pagoda.

TIM OLECKI

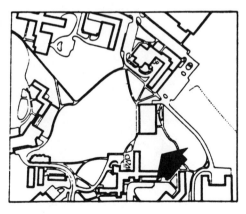

PHOTO 17

The Guardsmen have now marched some 80 yards past Blanket Hill to reach a football practice field which lies below it. The three large buildings in the background are the Tri-Towers dormitory complex.

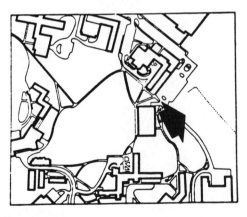

AKRON BEACON JOURNAL

PHOTO 18

With guardsmen on the football field at right, students move toward them from the Prentice Hall parking lot at left.

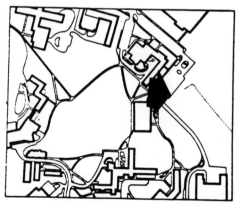

AKRON BEACON JOURNAL

PHOTO 19

The person in the center is shown in the act of throwing a missile of some type at the guardsmen, who are off to the right of this picture. The building in the background is Taylor Hall.

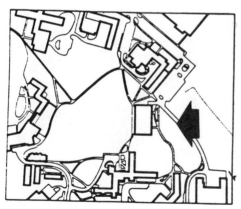

AKRON BEACON JOURNAL

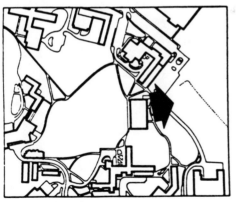

PHOTO 20

Guardsmen on the football field kneel and point their weapons at the students in the parking lot, which is off to the left of this picture. This was apparently an admonitory gesture by the Guard, and these men did not fire at this point.

HAROLD C. WALKER

PHOTO 21

The guardsmen are on the football field at upper left. In the foreground is Prentice Hall parking lot. The building in the left background is Memorial Gymnasium.

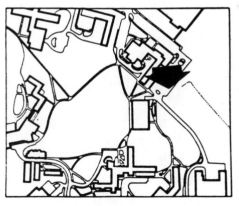

BEVERLY K. KNOWLES

PHOTO 22

A guardsman on the football field hurls a tear gas canister back at the crowd. The building in the background is Dunbar Hall.

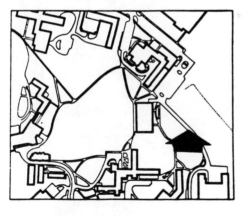

AKRON BEACON JOURNAL

PHOTO 23

Students in the Prentice Hall parking lot watch guardsmen on the football field in the left background. Near the center of this picture, wearing a two-tone shirt and a headband, is Jeffrey Miller, who was later killed.

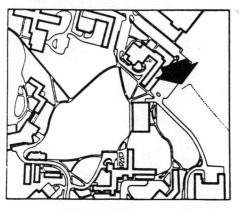

RICHARD C. HARRIS JR.

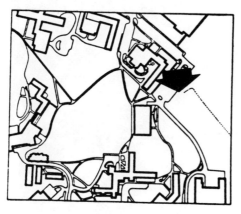

PHOTO 24

The Guard is still on the football field. At left center, jsut off the edge of the Prentice Hall parking lot, Jeffrey Miller in his two-tone shirt is seen throwing a tear gas canister back at the Guard.

RICHARD C. HARRIS JR.

PHOTO 25

Another view of the Prentice Hall parking lot. Guardsmen are visible in left back-ground.

RICHARD C. HARRIS JR.

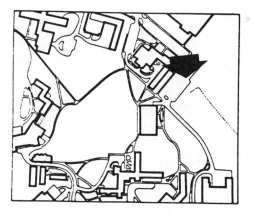

PHOTO 26
Guardsmen begin to leave the football practice field.

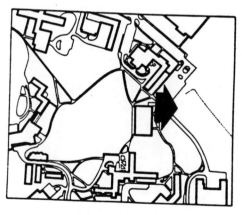

HAROLD C. WALKER

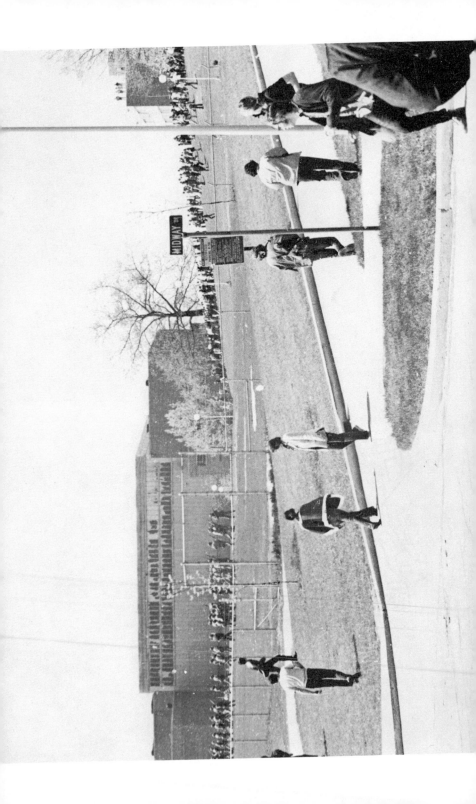

PHOTO 27

Another view of the Guard leaving the football field, with some students in the parking lot moving to follow them while the crowd on the hillside retreats.

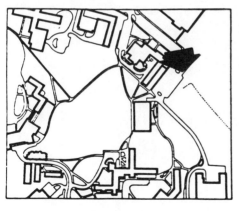

RICHARD C. HARRIS JR.

PHOTO 28

From behind a fence which borders the football field, students watch the departing guardsmen retrace their steps toward Blanket Hill. The student on the field appears to be throwing an object at the Guard.

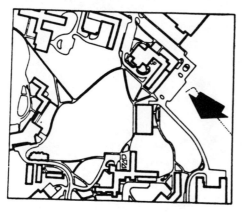

RICHARD G. BOEHME

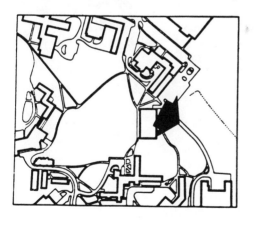

PHOTO 29

Guardsmen assume a V formation as they march from the field toward the Pagoda. The man inside the V, wearing civilian clothes, is Brigadier General Robert H. Canterbury, Ohio Assistant Adjutant General.

VALLEY DAILY NEWS—TARENTUM, PENN.

PHOTO 30

Another view of the Guard's departure from the field. General Canterbury is visible behind them in the center. Directly behind, running to catch up with the formation, is Major Jones.

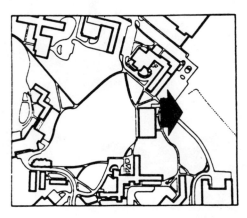

HAROLD C. WALKER

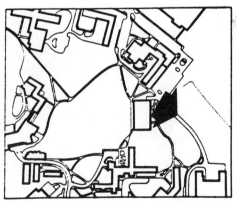

PHOTO 31

A young man throws an object at the retreating Guard. Another youth is wearing a handkerchief over his face to try to protect himself from tear gas.

KENT STATE UNIVERSITY NEWS SERVICE

PHOTO 32

The withdrawing guardsmen reach the access road which borders the football field.

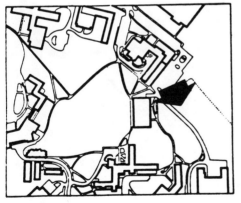

VALLEY DAILY NEWS—TARENTUM, PENN.

PHOTO 33

A view from the side as the guardsmen cross the access road. In the right background is Prentice Hall and in the left background is Taylor Hall. (The black markings in front of the guardsmen are photographic imperfections.)

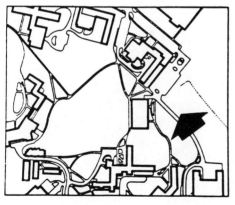

RONALD P. McNEES

PHOTO 34

The guardsmen begin to climb Blanket Hill. Memorial Gymnasium is in the background.

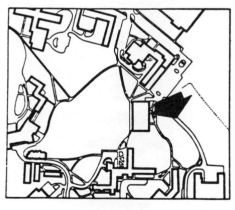

VALLEY DAILY NEWS—TARENTUM, PENN.

PHOTO 35

The guardsmen continue to ascend the hill.

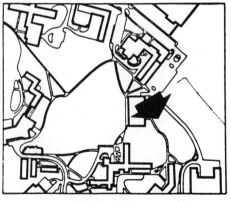

HAROLD C. WALKER

PHOTO 36

The guardsmen near the crest of the hill.

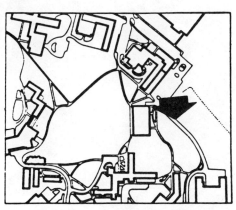

DAVE EADS

PHOTO 37

As the guardsmen march up the hill, a young man in the center of this picture, wearing a handkerchief over his face, draws back his arm to throw something at them. In the center foreground, wearing a white shirt and dark jacket and carrying a cylindrical object in his pocket, is John Cleary, a student who was later wounded.

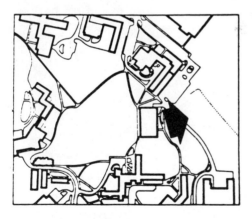

VALLEY DAILY NEWS—TARENTUM, PENN.

PHOTO 38

The Guard is off to the right of this picture, ascending the hill. Some students seem to be hurling objects, some are watching, some are moving away from the Guard.

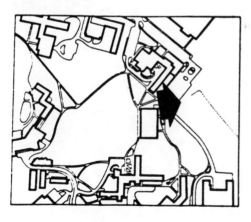

KENT STATE UNIVERSITY NEWS SERVICE

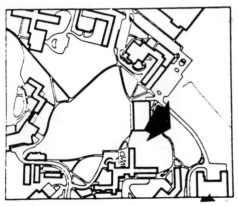

PHOTO 39

The Guard climbs the hill. Visible at right is the edge of an abstract metal sculpture which stands behind Taylor Hall. The dots visible in the sky are photographic imperfections.

AKRON BEACON JOURNAL

PHOTO 40

Here are three views of the guardsmen as they near the crest of the hill.

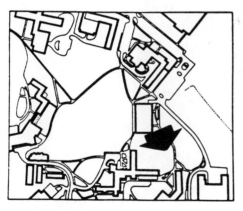

VALLEY DAILY NEWS—TARENTUM, PENN.

PHOTO 41

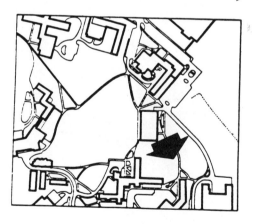

VALLEY DAILY NEWS—TARENTUM, PENN.

PHOTO 42

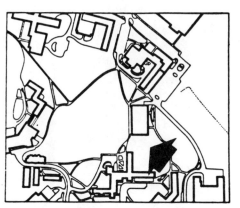

RONALD P. McNEES

377

PHOTO 43

Only moments away from the shooting, the Guard nears the Pagoda in left background.

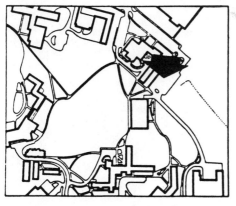

RICHARD C. HARRIS JR.

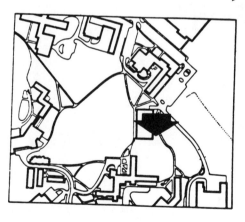

PHOTO 44

The Guard arrives at the Pagoda. The second guardsman from the left, striding along, is Major Jones. The metal sculpture at right and the tree directly behind the Taylor Hall sign were pierced by bullets only a few seconds after this picture was taken.

VALLEY DAILY NEWS—TARENTUM, PENN.

PHOTO 45

The guardsmen turn to face the students, and some of them move toward firing position. A split second later, the volley began.

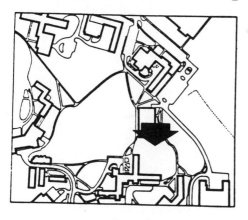

HOWARD E. RUFFNER

PHOTO 46

This picture was taken at virtually the same moment as the preceding one, as indicated by the arm position of a left-handed guardsman with a pistol who is visible in both pictures.

AKRON BEACON JOURNAL

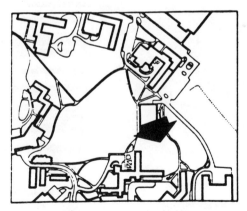

PHOTO 47

Here the guardsmen are shooting. General Canterbury moves forward from extreme right of picture.

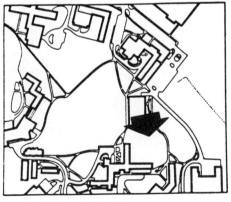

JOHN A. DARNELL

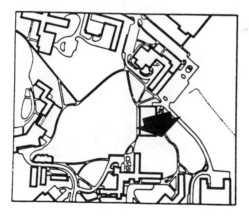

PHOTO 48

On the patio of Taylor Hall, students scatter for cover as the shooting begins. On the grass beyond the rail, visible just over the head of the student nearest the camera, is Joseph Lewis, gesturing at the guardsmen with an upraised middle finger just before he was wounded.

AKRON BEACON JOURNAL

PHOTO 49

This is a view of the students who were behind the guardsmen, on the Commons side of Blanket Hill, at the moment the firing occurred. The guardsmen are at the top of the hill around the Pagoda.

TIM NIGHSWANDER

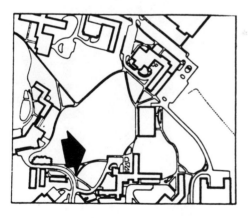

PHOTO 50

The guardsmen photographed from behind while they were shooting.

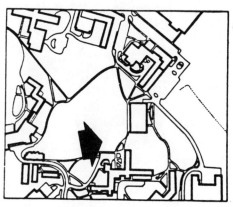

VICTOR J. SLOAN

PHOTO 51

As the firing begins, students in and around the Prentice Hall parking lot scatter for cover.

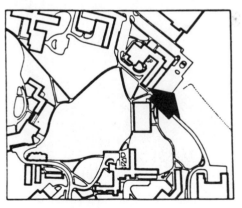

KENT STATE UNIVERSITY NEWS SERVICE

PHOTO 52

Now most of the firing has ceased, although the rifleman just to the left of the large tree still seems to be shooting or aiming his rifle.

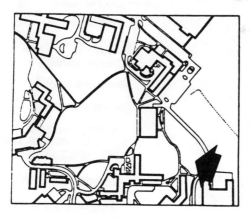

RONALD P. McNEES

PHOTO 53

General Canterbury, wearing a gas mask atop his head, has moved just behind the front rank of shooters as he orders them to cease fire. At far left, the left-handed guardsman with the pistol appears to be ejecting shells from his weapon.

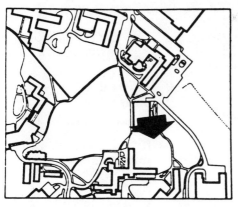

JOHN A. DARNELL

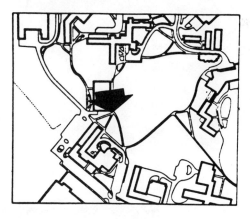

PHOTO 54

Major Jones, wearing a soft cap and carrying a baton, has moved in front of the guardsmen as he orders them to cease firing. In the middle of the group of guardsmen is General Canterbury, distinguishable here by his white collar and dark tie.

JOHN A. DARNELL

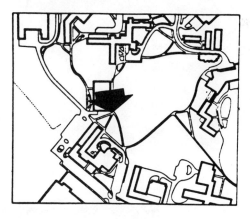

PHOTO 55

Seconds after the shooting, students remain crouched for protection behind a metal sculpture.

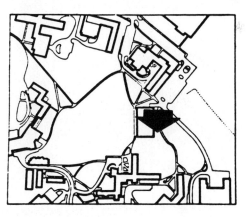

HOWARD E. RUFFNER

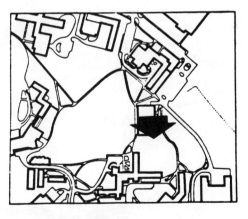

PHOTO 56

Four students gather around wounded Joseph Lewis, Jr. Lewis was the closest casualty to the firing line, about 20 yards away as this photograph verifies.

KENT STATE UNIVERSITY NEWS SERVICE

PHOTO 57

Leaving the scene of the shooting, the guardsmen start down on the western side of Blanket Hill on their way back to the ROTC building. The building at right is Johnson Hall.

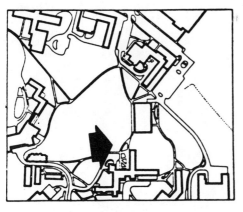

KENT STATE UNIVERSITY NEWS SERVICE

PHOTO 58

The positions of three of the students who were killed are indicated on this photograph of the Prentice Hall parking lot taken seconds after the shooting. Of the three bodies numbered here, No. 1 is William Schroeder, No. 2 is Sandra Lee Scheuer, and No. 3 is Jeffrey Glenn Miller. The Pagoda and guardsmen beside it are visible at upper right.

BEVERLY K. KNOWLES

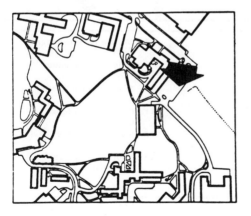

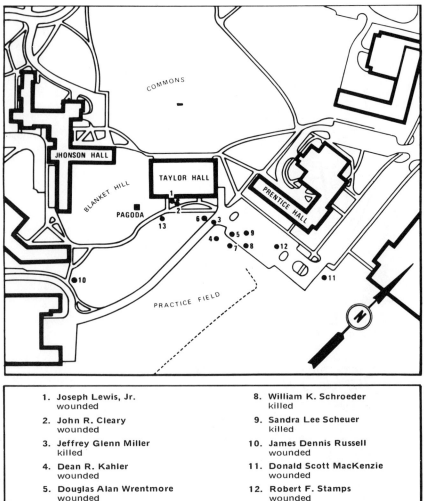

1. Joseph Lewis, Jr. wounded	8. William K. Schroeder killed
2. John R. Cleary wounded	9. Sandra Lee Scheuer killed
3. Jeffrey Glenn Miller killed	10. James Dennis Russell wounded
4. Dean R. Kahler wounded	11. Donald Scott MacKenzie wounded
5. Douglas Alan Wrentmore wounded	12. Robert F. Stamps wounded
6. Allen Michael Canfora wounded	13. Thomas M. Grace wounded
7. Allison B. Krause killed	

MAP 2

This map of the Kent State campus shows the Blanket Hill firing area and the location of all the casualties at the time they were hit. Casualties No. 1 and 13 are each about 20 yards from the firing line, and casualty No. 11 is 245 to 250 yards away.

Jackson State

Two nights of campus demonstrations at Jackson State College in May 1970 ended in violent confrontation and tragedy. After 28 seconds of gunfire by Mississippi Highway Safety Patrolmen and Jackson city policemen, two black youths lay dying and 12 others were wounded.

The Commission's investigators at Jackson conducted nearly 300 interviews. Those interviewed included state and city officials, Mississippi National Guardsmen, state and city police who were on the scene (including officers who fired their weapons), scores of student witnesses (some of whom were injured), college officials, FBI agents, and private citizens. In addition, Commission investigators had full access to the multivolumed reports of the Federal Bureau of Investigation, the Hinds County grand jury, and the biracial lawers' committee appointed by the mayor of Jackson.

The Commission held three days of open hearings in Jackson on August 11, 12, and 13, 1970.

The Commission has not attempted to assess guilt or innocence but has sought to learn what happened and why. We include in this report a statement of the undisputed facts, an examination of facts that are in dispute, an analysis of causes of the violence, confrontation, and death, and recommendations to prevent similar incidents in the future.

THE SETTING

Jackson State College is and always has been a black school. The 1970 spring enrollment of roughly 4,300 students included only five whites. The faculty, integrated in 1967, is 80 per cent black.

Historical marker at Jackson State College, Jackson, Mississippi. On the left is Roberts Dining Hall. On the right is Lynch Street.

The college was founded in 1877 as Natchez Seminary by the American Baptist Home Mission Society to train Negro teachers and ministers. The institution moved to Jackson five years later. Today its location is in one of the city's major black residential areas. The school lost denominational financial aid during the Depression, in 1930. It remained a private school until 1940, when it became a state college. The State Board of Trustees for Institutions of Higher Learning has jurisdiction over the college. The governor appoints the trustees, all of whom are white.

All but a few hundred of the students at Jackson State College are Mississippians, most of them from rural backgrounds. Many are forced to live off campus because the school's enrollment has increased faster than its physical facilities. Jackson State has almost doubled in size in the past four years and is the most rapidly growing institution of higher learning in the state of Mississippi and one of the fastest growing in the nation.

In 1967, Dr. John A. Peoples, Jr., a graduate of Jackson State College and the University of Chicago, became president of the college. Dr. Peoples testified before the Commission that he has encouraged free expression on the part of students and faculty members and has made major institutional reforms. He eliminated compulsory attendance at religious services and liberalized dormitory restrictions. He maintains an "open door" policy so any student with a grievance can see him. While students at Jackson State are concerned about racial justice and the war in Vietnam, Dr. Peoples told the Commission, there are no civil rights or antiwar organizations at the college.

Prior Incidents

Since 1965 there has been trouble every spring at Jackson State. Each time, it has begun on Lynch Street, a major four-lane thoroughfare that bisects the campus.

Beginning one block east of the campus, bars and pool halls dot a three-block area along Lynch Street known as "the corner." At night, black youths referred to locally as "corner boys" loiter in the area, mingling with and sometimes fighting students. There is a long history of friction between Jackson State students and corner boys; Dr. Peoples testified that he had been involved as a student in a gang fight with corner boys in 1950.

Alexander Hall (the largest women's dormitory), Stewart Hall (a men's dormitory), and the campus union all front on the north side of Lynch Street. During the day, pedestrian traffic by students is heavy on Lynch Street. At night, the Lynch Street area is a center of student activity.

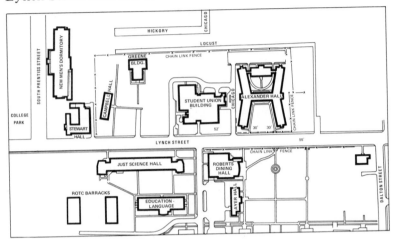

Jackson State College campus.

Lynch Street connects downtown Jackson, which is to the east, with white neighborhoods farther west. For years, college authorities have urged closing to automobile traffic the portion of Lynch Street that passes through the campus. Publicly, the problem of safety to pedestrians has been cited as the reason for the request. Privately, members of the college community maintain that closing off Lynch Street would reduce friction by halting the flow of white policemen and white motorists through the campus.

Incidents at the college in recent years have often begun with students and corner boys throwing rocks at passing white motorists or white policemen.

In 1965, rock-throwing began after a Jackson State College coed was struck on Lynch Street by a white male hit-and-run motorist and received serious injuries. The driver of the car was never apprehended.

Another minor rock-throwing incident occurred on Lynch Street in the spring of 1966.

In 1967, Jackson City Police were pelted with rocks the

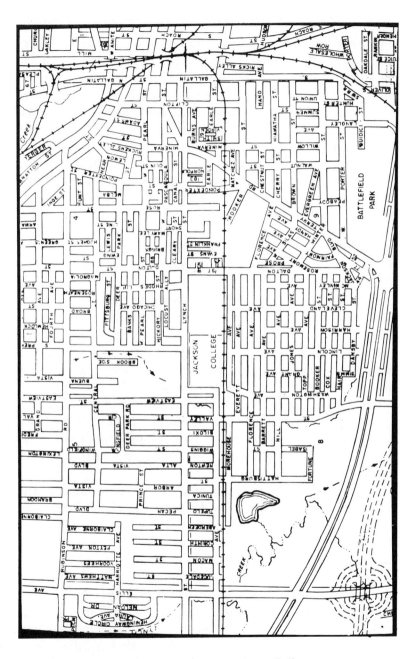

Street map of area surrounding Jackson State College

evening of May 10 after chasing a student and stopping him on campus for an alleged traffic violation. A band of angry students and nonstudents roamed the Lynch Street area and set small fires, broke windows, looted stores, and threw rocks and concrete blocks at passing cars. Lynch Street was sealed off in the disturbance area. The next night rocks were thrown at policemen who manned a barricade near a Lynch Street intersection several blocks from the campus. An officer received a serious cut on the neck after being hit by a thrown bottle. Reinforcements from the Jackson City Police and Mississippi Highway Safety Patrol were brought into the area. Some officers fired shotguns when a group of students and others advanced toward the barricade. One black youth, Benjamin Brown, was found dead in the street from buckshot wounds, and two students received birdshot wounds.

On April 4, 1968, news of the assassination of Martin Luther King, Jr., triggered a rock-throwing demonstration on Lynch Street that escalated into looting of some white-owned businesses and the burning of an automobile. Police officers reported sniper fire and used large quantities of tear gas on campus to quell the disturbance. There were no reported injuries, but 15 students were arrested.

On the evening of May 1, 1969, rock-throwing began after a fight between students and nonstudents in which a black woman received a serious eye cut. A false rumor that four white policemen had gone into a bar and beat up black patrons increased tensions.

There had been no campus disturbances during the 1969-70 school year prior to the events of May 13. On May 7, three days after the shooting at Kent State, roughly 500 students attended a peaceful campus rally organized by student leaders to protest policies in Cambodia and Vietnam. In response to a call for a one-day boycott, a smaller number of students refused to attend class the next day.

The events resulting in the deaths at Jackson State College began on Lynch Street with another rock-throwing incident. They came to an end when peace officers discharged weapons at close range from Lynch Street into Alexander Hall and into a crowd in the vicinity of that dormitory.

EVENTS OF MAY 13, 1970

Disturbances began shortly after dusk on Wednesday, May 13. The triggering incident is undetermined, but by 9:00 p.m. rocks were being thrown at white motorists from a crowd of about 100 persons gathered on both sides of Lynch Street in front of Alexander Hall. Shortly thereafter, a Jackson City Police patrol car traveling west on Lynch Street was struck by a missile. By 9:45 p.m., there were approximately 150 persons, both men and women, in the Alexander Hall area. Most of them were students, and more than three fourths of those present were passive onlookers.

At approximately 10:00 p.m., Jackson City Police units established roadblocks on Lynch Street and on Pearl Street to seal off the campus. The rock-throwing stopped. But the number of persons in front of Alexander Hall continued to grow. A half block west on Lynch Street another larger group formed near Stewart Hall.

By 11:00 p.m. the number of persons in the street between Alexander and Stewart Halls would reach an estimated 700.

Members of Jackson State's eleven-man security force were harassed by small groups of students. Their attempts to quiet and disperse the growing crowds near Alexander and Stewart Halls proved futile. Jackson City Police made no attempt to enter the campus during the early stages of the disturbance.

At approximately 10:15 p.m. Edward Curtis, Dean of Men, accompanied by Sergeant M. P. Stringer of the security force, informed the crowd in front of Alexander Hall that President Peoples had imposed a 10:30 p.m. curfew. Some students went toward their dormitories, but many remained on the street. Little was done to enforce the curfew.

Jackson's Mayor Russell Davis spoke with the governor at about this time and requested that the National Guard be mobilized and the Mississippi Highway Patrol placed on standby.

At about 10:30 p.m. security officer George Jones was driving onto the campus in his pickup truck. A rock struck and shattered his left vent window as he passed in front of Stewart Hall, where about 200 persons were massed. Some in the crowd moved toward the truck. Jones fired three shots into the air with his revolver and then drove quickly to security police headquarters.

A little later, a group of perhaps a dozen corner boys and students broke out the rear window of a campus patrol car parked near Stewart Hall. They were attempting to turn it over when four security officers approached. The youths backed away when a security officer fired a shot into the air.

A trash trailer was pulled from behind one of the dormitories and into Lynch Street in front of the campus union. It was turned over and set afire. A second trash trailer was moved to the street in front of the east wing of Alexander Hall and set afire.

As the evening progressed, security officers increasingly heard reports that the students intended to march on the college ROTC building located some 150 yards south of Stewart Hall. At about 10:45 p.m. approximately 100 students and neighborhood youths broke from the crowd in the vicinity of Stewart Hall and moved toward the ROTC building. Dean Curtis and security officer Stringer went to the area, where they were joined by the commanding officer of the ROTC unit. With assistance from student leaders, they managed to quiet and disperse most of the crowd.

Stringer moved to another area of the campus but returned between 11:15 p.m. and 11:30 p.m. to find a small fire on the roof of a porch of the ROTC building and three black youths running from the area. After a bottle hit the gravel behind him, Stringer fired his revolver once into the air. He then smothered the fire with his shirt. He found two crude Molotov cocktails, one on the roof and one on the ground.

Around 11:00 p.m. TV newsman Bert Case was allowed to drive past the police barricades. His car was bombarded with rocks as he continued along Lynch Street through the campus.

Jackson City Police units manning the blockades on Lynch

and Pearl Streets were not released when their shift ended at 11:00 p.m. Shortly after the next shift of officers arrived at headquarters at 10:50 p.m., Dr. Peoples told Detective Chief M. B. Pierce of the march on the ROTC building. Pierce immediately ordered a squad under the command of Lieutenant Warren Magee to a police barricade northwest of the campus. Their instructions were to rendezvous with a unit of the Mississsippi Highway Safety Patrol and then to move onto campus to secure the area around the ROTC building.

Magee's squad moved toward the campus area, some of them in "Thompson's tank"—an armored vehicle designed for riot control and equipped to dispense tear gas. The custom-made vehicle had been ordered by Jackson's former mayor Thompson. The police have used the vehicle frequently on Lynch Street in the vicinity of the campus but nowhere else in the city.

Thompson's tank.

The city police and highway patrol units linked up before 11:30 p.m. They moved on foot to the ROTC building. As they passed Stewart Hall, the combined units were jeered by a crowd estimated at 250 to 300 persons. Rocks and other objects were thrown at them, but there were no injuries. Obscenities were shouted. There were statements that wives, mothers, and daughters of the officers at that moment were engaging in a variety of sexual relations with black men in dormitory rooms or at home.

Between 12:15 and 12:45 a.m. Magee's squad moved from the ROTC building east to the intersection of Rose and Lynch Streets to bar any attempt by the crowd to spread into Jackson's downtown area. The highway patrol unit remained at the ROTC building to secure the area. Magee avoided the shortest route, up Lynch Street through the heart of the campus, and chose instead to skirt the college. Sergeant Charles Lee, second in command of the police detachment, later testified that one reason for avoiding the campus was "not to harass or try to agitate in any way. I figured if we rode right back, all of these students out hollering and cutting up, that was just going to make the situation worse . . . ."

Police commanders were considering moving from the intersection of Rose and Lynch Streets onto the campus to clear Lynch Street. Some police assembled in formation. However, Thompson's tank had broken down and Magee held his men back. Mayor Davis arrived at the police barricade.

Martel Cook, a black reporter and part-time student at Jackson State, came from the campus area to the barricade. He informed the mayor that the situation was quieting down. Cook advised that there might be bloodshed if the police went in. Two other students also urged the mayor not to send the police back to the campus.

Mayor Davis conferred with Chief Pierce, who was at police headquarters, and with Magee about the advisability of ordering city policemen into the Lynch Street area of the campus. To some observers it appeared that police commanders wanted to move in. However, Davis and Pierce agreed to keep the police out.

Sometime after midnight, the crowd gradually began to

disperse. By the early hours of the morning the disturbance was over and the campus was quiet.

Around 1:00 a.m. Dr. Peoples met for more than an hour at his on-campus residence with about 25 students. They mentioned concern with the draft and the war in Southeast Asia but agreed that the rock-throwing had started without a specific reason. No serious grievances against the college were mentioned.

At about 3:00 a.m. the Adjutant General of Mississippi, Major General Walter Johnson, visited Dr. Peoples at his home and informed him that the Mississippi National Guard had been placed on alert. He told Dr. Peoples that tear gas probably would be used if disorders developed on the following day. Dr. Peoples was advised that gas masks would be brought to his home for him and members of his family.

During the disorder, security guards and some students reported hearing shots. Highway patrolmen heard shots fired while they remained at the ROTC building. At least four of the shots that were heard during the evening came in one burst when a black youth fired in the direction of a traffic light in front of Alexander Hall sometime between 10:00 and 11:00 p.m. Single shots were fired in the air by Stringer at the ROTC building and by another security guard while students were attempting to overturn a campus patrol car. Three shots were fired in the air by security officer Jones after his truck was attacked in front of Stewart Hall.

No law enforcement officer or security guard reported being fired on during the disturbance, and there is no indication that any city policeman or highway patrolman fired a weapon on May 13.

EVENTS OF MAY 14, 1970

There was some apprehension at Jackson State College on Thursday, May 14, but the campus was quiet and class attendance was normal.

At a 2:30 p.m. meeting with student leaders, Dr. Peoples stressed the seriousness of what had happened the night before and told them the National Guard had been activated and was being mobilized. They reported to him that the general feeling among students was that there would be no disturbance on Thursday night. The students were unable to explain what caused the previous night's disturbance and told Dr. Peoples they had no new grievances.

Dr. Peoples issued a statement that afternoon designed to shame the students who had participated the night before in what he called "the annual riot." He said Wednesday night's "riot was perpetrated by a faceless, mindless mob of students and nonstudents bent on doing violence and destruction to the college . . ."

Despite Dr. Peoples' request to Chief Pierce that Lynch Street be closed at dusk as a precautionary measure, police barricades were removed, and the street was opened to traffic.

City police had earlier received reports from "confidential sources" that trouble was expected at Alexander Hall. Dr. Peoples knew nothing of such rumors, nor did any of the students subsequently interviewed by members of the Commission's staff. The police did not check these reports with college officials but passed them on to the highway patrol commanders. Detective Chief Pierce explained that the reports reflected a fear that male nonstudents escorting girls to the dormitory might be a source of trouble. He viewed the reports as being based on rumor. At the time he assigned no special significance to them. However, some policemen later claimed that events had borne out the truth of this rumor.

At 7:30 p.m., a National Guard log recorded that 647 guardsmen were on duty and stationed at an armory in Jackson. The armory was more than a 20-minute drive from the campus.

Around 9:30 p.m., a small group in the vicinity of Stewart Hall began throwing rocks at passing white motorists. Lynch Street soon was sealed off as it had been the night before. The crowd swelled to between 100 and 200 persons, most of them onlookers who cheered the rock-throwers.

Around 10:00 p.m. an unidentified black man in a Volkswagen drove up to the crowd and announced—

falsely—that Charles Evers, mayor of Fayette, Mississippi and a civil rights leader, and his wife had been killed. Meanwhile, anonymous telephone calls to the same effect were made to several Lynch Street bars. Although many refused to believe this report, it spread quickly throughout the campus, and the level of tension rose.

Reports were coming in to the Jackson police department that the situation on campus was worsening. Around 10:15 p.m. a policeman gave a radio order: "Call that security guard out there at Jackson State and see if they can't scatter them niggers."

At the National Guard armory, an officer was monitoring the police radio reports. At some point between 10:30 p.m. and 11:00 p.m. he suggested to General Johnson that National Guardsmen be put on trucks, ready to roll onto the campus. After General Johnson listened to the police radio for a few minutes, he ordered the guardsmen to move to positions on Lynch Street near both ends of the campus. If called in, he wanted to be ready to move onto the campus

Dump truck burned in front of Stewart Hall.

at once. It was around 11:00 p.m.

Police radio reports were also telling of the movement of individuals from the Stewart Hall area to a dump truck at a nearby construction site. The truck was started; it jumped and sputtered and got as far as Stewart Hall, where the engine died. Then someone set the front seat afire. A nonstudent in the group pulled out a small pistol, knelt beside the truck, and began shooting at the gas tank.

At the other end of the campus, near the corner of Dalton and Lynch, two white newsmen were robbed and threatened by a gang of young Blacks. Martel Cook and two other students rescued the two reporters and recovered $90 for them. One member of the gang fled with a tape recorder and another took $20.

At city police headquarters, the 11:00 p.m. shift had begun to arrive. A few minutes after eleven, Chief Pierce ordered Lt. Magee to take Thompson's tank and a unit of 26 men to "clear the streets" on campus. On the way, they joined up with 40 highway patrolmen under the command of Inspector Lloyd Jones. The two police groups moved onto the campus, and officers formed a line in front of Stewart Hall between the burning truck and the crowd.

A fire station on Lynch Street, 1.3 miles west of Stewart Hall, had been called by their dispatcher and directed to send a fire truck to the campus. As police waited for the fire truck to arrive, they radioed that they were being fired on. The fire truck proceeded slowly, without sounding its siren or flashing its red light. It moved in behind the officers, and firemen began dousing the fire. There was no interference by the demonstrators, and the firemen were able to extinguish the fire, but not before the dump truck was severely damaged.

The crowd at Stewart Hall grew in size. Students from the dormitory joined the demonstrators in jeering and yelling insults and obscenities. They repeated the references to wives, mothers, and daughters of the officers made the night before. Rocks and pieces of brick were thrown, but there were no serious injuries to firemen or police officers.

Lt. Magee repeatedly told the crowd to disperse, but with

megaphone, also urged students to disperse and return to their dormitories.

Meanwhile, General Johnson had left the armory while the convoy of trucks was still being loaded with troops and equipment. He arrived at Stewart Hall ahead of the fire truck. A few minutes later, he rode through the campus on Lynch Street to the corner of Dalton, where a group had started a bonfire. He saw very few people on the street, but as he passed the front of Alexander Hall on his way back to the Stewart Hall area, his car was struck by a thrown object.

At 11:30 p.m. Chief Pierce called Mayor Davis to notify him that the situation on campus was worsening. The mayor asked that the National Guard be sent in before the highway patrol or the city police but was informed by Pierce that the patrol and police already were on campus. The mayor said he wanted the guardsmen to be sent in anyway. He drove to a barricade several blocks from the campus, where the convoy of National Guardsmen had taken positions. He was surpised to see them there rather than in the campus area.

Back at Stewart Hall, there was a barrage of bricks, rocks, bottles, and other objects, some of which came from

Window of room 421 of Stewart Hall facing alleyway showing buckshot holes.

dormitory windows. There were conflicting reports of small caliber gunfire from the area of Stewart Hall. Some highway patrolmen chased a group of persons into an alleyway adjoining Stewart Hall. Objects were thrown at them, and a patrolman fired a shotgun blast into a fourth-story window. No one was struck by the shot.

The gunfire from the highway patrol disturbed General Johnson, and he decided the National Guard should move onto the campus and relieve the highway patrol and city police. He conferred with Magee and Jones and told them that the National Guard was coming in.

Two blocks away, Mayor Davis had also decided the National Guard should move onto the campus. He informed General Johnson's assistant of his decision and the National Guardsmen began walking east on Lynch Street toward Stewart Hall, accompanied by the mayor.

Meanwhile, as the firemen moved away from the Stewart Hall area after extinguishing the dump truck fire, they received a call to go to the bonfire in the middle of the intersection of Dalton and Lynch, at the opposite end of the campus. They drove around the campus to avoid arousing the students, and as they rounded a corner one block from the blaze, they and others heard the sound of small arms fire. They quickly extinguished the fire while a small crowd watched quietly. As the fire truck turned around to leave, it was hit by a barrage of thrown missiles, one of which made a loud sound when it struck and dented the top of the cab. The truck proceeded rapidly from the scene; none of the firemen was injured.

Magee stated that before the fire at the corner of Dalton had been put out, he had been informed of a request for police protection for the firemen. Magee testified that as he looked eastward down Lynch Street toward the bonfire, he saw a crowd he estimated at 200 milling around in front of Alexander Hall, some 300 yards away. Led by Thompson's tank, the city police and state patrolmen began moving eastward. Several newsmen trailed behind them.

At that time, Johnson, Magee, and Jones each had a

different notion as to why police and highway patrol units were moving up Lynch Street. General Johnson thought the units were leaving the campus to permit guardsmen who were securing the perimeter on the east side to enter the campus. Johnson's opinion was based on his understanding of discussions held that afternoon with representatives of the police and highway patrol, which he felt had resulted in the decision that, once the Guard had moved onto the campus, law enforcement groups would move off and secure the perimeter areas. The police and patrol did not understand this to be their mission.

Lieutenant Magee, under instructions from Chief Pierce to "clear the street and restore order," ordered the tank and his men to move "up to Alexander Hall" to disperse the crowd that he had seen gathered in that area. He intended to disperse the crowd prior to relieving the Guard at the perimeter. Magee later testified that he also intended to provide protection for the fire truck at the Dalton intersection.

Inspector Jones at no time was under the impression that the patrol was to withdraw from the campus when the Guard moved on. When he ordered his unit to move from Stewart Hall eastward on Lynch Street, his intention was to proceed directly to the Dalton intersection to protect the firemen. He did not hear Magee's directive to the tank—broadcast on a frequency different from that of the patrol—to stop at Alexander Hall and therefore had no intention or expectation of doing so.

In addition to the confusion about objectives, there were crucial differences in procedure and training among the three law enforcement agencies concerning the use of firearms.

A basic policy of the National Guard is that no man can load or fire a weapon without an order from the senior commander. General Johnson believed that his men were well trained and well disciplined and would not load or shoot without an order. In the over six years he had served as their commanding officer—and in seven previous civil disorders—his men had not fired a shot. City policemen carried shotguns with shells in the magazine, but policy called for firing only upon order of the senior man on the scene, with the first shot over the heads of an advancing crowd and the second shot low and in front of the crowd. A separate order was required before each shot. The highway patrolmen carried loaded weapons and were authorized to decide on an individual basis if it was necessary to shoot to protect their own lives or those of other officers.

The National Guard was armed with special riot shotguns that hold seven rounds. The first four rounds are No. 9 birdshot, the smallest pellet used in shotguns, backed up by three rounds of double-O buckshot, the heaviest used in shotguns. City police carried shotguns loaded with heavy No. 1 buckshot. Most highway patrolmen were armed with shotguns loaded with double-O buckshot, others carried personally owned rifles or carbines, and two were armed with loaded submachine guns.

The National Guard and city police each had men specially assigned for antisniper duty, senior sharpshooters armed with rifles. Although the highway patrol manual indicates formal procedures for controlling sniper fire, Jones and a majority of his men considered each individual officer authorized to shoot any time he saw a sniper if he believed lives were threatened.

After reaching Alexander Hall, the tank stopped in front of or slightly east of the west wing. With few exceptions, the city police were in a line south and east of the tank, and the highway patrolmen were in a line north and west of the tank, nearer the crowd. There were highway patrolmen within 20 feet of the nearest member of the crowd, most of whom had moved behind a 3 1/2-foot high chain-link fence along a sidewalk.

Estimates of the size of the crowd range all the way from 40 to 400. Along the fence in front of Alexander Hall, a campus security officer was urging students to disperse. There were jeers, obscene epithets, and a chant of "Pigs! Pigs!" Many girls inside the dormitory watched from their rooms and from stairwell landings in the west wing. Behind the police—on the south side of the street—a smaller group of demonstrators and onlookers stood near Roberts Dining Hall behind a chain-link fence which runs on top of a concrete retaining wall.

Soon after the peace officers and their tank stopped, the insults grew louder. Two TV newsmen, Bert Case and Jack Hobbs, moved into the area of the skirmish line. Magee then stepped forward with a megaphone to tell the students to go to their dormitories. He ordered them to disperse several times, but many students claimed that his words had been drowned out by the noise. Two officers staggered when struck on their helmets by thrown objects; one of them stated he was knocked to the ground. Inside the tank, an officer was loading a short-range tear gas shell, anticipating an order to fire gas.

Lieutenant Magee and other officers state that the students backed away, but Inspector Jones testified that the students were advancing toward the officers.

Someone threw a bottle from the lawn behind the fence in front of Alexander Hall. Almost simultaneously, another bottle was lobbed from behind the retaining wall across the street, to the rear of the police line. One line of city police had turned to face that direction after some objects were thrown. A bottle shattered near the tank, and glass hit the ankle of the TV cameraman Jack Hobbs. Frank James, a student standing on the south side of Lynch Street across from the campus union, saw a rock almost hit the cameraman and strike the wall behind him. For his part, Hobbs stated that he heard a shot, then heard and felt an object, which he strongly believed to be a bullet, whiz by his left ear. He heard it ricochet on the wall behind him. An examination of this wall later failed to find evidence of a bullet mark there. Immediately thereafter, Hobbs heard shots fired by officers on his left.

Almost instantaneously, a general barrage of shotgun, carbine, rifle, and submachine gun fire began. Case, standing beside Hobbs, recalled that "the bottle crashed and the next thing I remember, they were firing."

Case looked toward the officers, saw their guns pointed

upward, and his first impression was that the officers were firing into the air over Alexander Hall or possibly shooting tear gas.

When Case heard the shattering of glass in Alexander Hall, he realized that the officers were actually firing into the building. To him, it appeared they "systematically" shot into the windows from the top floor down to the bottom.

A college official who was standing a block away later said, "The whole sky lighted up."

The students at first thought that blanks or tear gas were being fired. Those outside began running for the hallway entrance, then began diving for cover.

In the doorway in front of the officers, one student, then others, fell. The entrance was blocked, as students struggled to find shelter.

Phillip Gibbs, a married 20-year-old junior and father of an 18-month-old son, was struck by a shotgun blast about 50 feet east of the west wing doorway of Alexander Hall. One

Buckshot marks on Roberts Dining Hall and F.B.I. agent indicating where James Earl Green's body was found.

buckshot pellet entered his left underarm area and two more entered his head, one just beneath the left eye, fatally penetrating the brain.

James Earl Green was standing in front of Roberts Hall, across Lynch Street from Alexander Hall. A student saw him run to the side of Roberts Hall, stop suddenly, and fall. He was killed by a buckshot slug which entered his side and traveled through his liver, left lung, and heart. Green was a high school student.

Willie Woodward was wounded about 150 feet from the east wing of Alexander Hall as he fled toward the dormitory lobby door. Number 1 buckshot, probably fired by a Jackson city policeman, entered his chest from the back and collapsed a lung that filled with blood. Woodward, 31, was not a student; he explained his presence on the campus by saying he had driven a friend to the area to get a book.

Students Leroy Kenter and Vernon Steve Weakley were both struck in front of Alexander Hall. The large bone in Kenter's upper leg was shattered, and pellet fragments remain in his leg and pelvis. Weakley was knocked from his feet by a slug striking him in the lower right leg. He was attempting to run from the firing when struck.

Fonzie Coleman, a freshman, ran inside the doorway for cover. He tripped over a fallen figure, and then a bullet cut through his left thigh. He passed out. According to hospital officials, he almost lost his life from shock and loss of blood.

Sophomore Lonzie Thompson ran into the dormitory after the shooting ended and only then realized he had been struck in the right thigh. Andrea Reese, a junior, dived into the bushes for cover, no more than 40 feet from the firing officers. A buckshot pellet passed through her armpit, leaving both entrance and exit wounds. Redd Wilson, Jr., another student, was hit in the left thigh as he ran toward the west wing entrance and tripped over one of those who had fallen.

Inside the dormitory at the foot of the stairs, 19-year-old Gloria Mayhorn was struck by a pellet in the right shoulder and struck in the scalp and back by hot fragments from ricocheting bullets. Patricia Ann Sanders ran from the first floor entranceway to calm a near-hysterical friend and then realized from a wetness on her shoulder that a bullet fragment had struck her. This fragment still is lodged in her shoulder. Stella Spinks and Tuwaine Davis were wounded while in the dormitory stairwell. Miss Spinks was struck and burned on her back and arm by ricocheting fragments as she lay huddled on the landing between the third and fourth floors. Miss Davis was cut and burned by ricocheting bullets as she ran down the stairs from the fourth-floor landing.

Climmie Johnson was in the TV lounge on the second floor of the center section of the dormitory when the shooting began. She did not realize the officers were on Lynch Street until buckshot grazed her forehead.

Bert Case made a tape recording of the gunfire. The fusillade lasted 28 seconds.

Many of the officers emptied shotguns containing four rounds of buckshot. One patrolman, who fired four rounds, reloaded and fired four more, and reloaded and fired again. He told a Commission staff investigator he did not know "how many times" he reloaded and emptied his gun.

In all, more than 150 rounds were fired. Most were fired into the air, but FBI investigation showed that nearly 400 bullets or pieces of buckshot struck Alexander Hall.

The area of the south end of the west wing alone contained 301 separate bullet marks. The upper floor level was hardest hit, with 105 marks or bullet holes in the windows, panels, and wall. There were 83 separate buckshot or bullet marks counted in the fourth-floor area. There were 64 marks counted on the third floor, 36 on the second floor, and 13 separate bullet or buckshot marks in the windows, doors, and frames at ground level.

The glass in one of the doors to the ground entrance of the stairwell was splattered with blood. Blood stained the floor just inside the double glass doors of the entrance.

In addition to the firing at the west wing of Alexander Hall, shotgun blasts were fired into nearly every window in the first floor lobby of the center section of Alexander Hall. Windows in many student rooms in the center and east wings

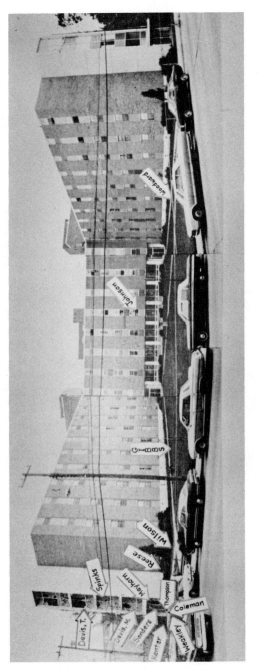

Composite photograph prepared by Commission staff indicating location of victims. Bullet holes in Alexander Hall have been marked for clarity.

West Wing of Alexander Hall viewed from the south side of Lynch Street.

of the dorm were also hit.

According to a highway patrol investigator, a "majority" of the patrolmen fired into the west wing of Alexander Hall. They used buckshot, rifle slugs, a submachine gun, carbines with military ammunition, and two 30.06 rifles loaded with armor-piercing bullets. Several city police officers also fired, although each denied doing so during a police department

Center and West Wing of Alexander Hall taken from south side of Lynch Street.

investigation that night and in subsequent interviews with FBI agents.

After General Johnson rushed down from Stewart Hall, he approached Inspector Jones and asked who had issued the order to fire. Jones said, "No one."

There had been no order to fire and no warning given to students that shooting was being contemplated. Shortly after the shooting began, Lieutenant Magee began shouting, "Cease fire! Cease fire!" Several other officers who did not shoot repeated the order.

Immediately after the shooting, highway patrolmen began picking up empty shell casings. They explained that this was their training on the firing range and that they turned in empty casings for reloading. The patrolmen also picked up empty shell casings of the city police.

At highway patrol headquarters, a patrolman made the following entry in the log at 12:11 a.m.:

Advise demonstrators threw rocks at them from a building. In return they tried to get them back into the building and they threw more rocks. Units had to hurt a few.

At the scene of the shooting, two newsmen recalled, the atmosphere among the officers was one of "some levity," and many officers engaged in casual small talk. Inspector Jones reported that two students were "10-7," radio code for "Out of Service." The radio tape continued:

Got one more female shot here—think it's serious.

A total of six injured there?

No, we got two more males, they say.

I think there are about three more nigger males over there, one of 'em shot in the arm, one of 'em shot in the leg, and one of 'em somewhere else. They ain't hurt all that bad. Them gals, it was two nigger gals, two more nigger gals from over there shot in the arm I believe. One of 'em is over there in the east end. I told . . . there two nigger females and three males we just discovered, that's a total of ten . . . . Here's another one, let me see what is this.

All persons killed or injured by gunshot were black.

FINDINGS

There are only a few disputes concerning the facts of what happened on the night of May 14 at Jackson State College. Here we address ourselves to the six most significant of these:

* Whether the crowd was advancing on the officers immediately prior to the shooting;

* The number of persons in the crowd at Alexander Hall;

* The amount of time that passed from the arrival of the officers in front of Alexander Hall to the shooting by the officers;

* The extent of verbal abuse directed at officers in front of Alexander Hall;

* The amount of debris thrown at the officers in front of Alexander Hall; and

* Whether there was shooting from the crowd while the officers were in front of Alexander Hall.

Was the Crowd Advancing?

Some highway patrolmen, including Inspector Jones, contend that just prior to the shooting the students were advancing on the law enforcement officers. Jones stated that the crowd was surging toward the officers and that the students were about to overwhelm the officers and cause them death or serious bodily harm.

This view is contradicted by the testimony of Lieutenant Magee and of all Jackson police officers interviewed by the staff, by the testimony of newsmen on the scene, by the statements of some highway patrolmen, and by the testimony and statements of students.

The crowd, with perhaps a few exceptions, was behind a chain-link fence which separates the grounds in front of Alexander Hall from the sidewalk and Lynch Street, where the officers were located.

No officer testified that he fired because the crowd was advancing. Each officer who fired stated that he did so in response to sniper fire from Alexander Hall.

The Commission concludes that the crowd in front of Alexander Hall was not moving toward the police officers just prior to the shooting.

How Big Was the Crowd?

The Commission concludes that the best estimate of the size of the crowd in front of Alexander Hall is between 75 and 200. This finding is based on the radioed estimate by Lieutenant Magee, on the published estimates made that night by newsmen on the scene, and on an evaluation of the estimates by numerous other persons present.

How Soon Did the Shooting Begin?

The Commission concludes that approximately five minutes elapsed from the time peace officers arrived at Alexander Hall to the time they began firing. The first police log entry concerning the firing was made at eleven minutes after midnight, immediately after the shooting. Bert Case testified that he arrived in front of Alexander Hall at approximately seven minutes after midnight.

Case recorded his departure from the intersection of Valley and Lynch, two blocks west of the campus, at 11:56 p.m. Subsequently he retraced his steps and determined that, at the pace he walked on May 14, it took 11 minutes to get to Alexander Hall. The police officers had been at Alexander Hall for approximately two minutes before Case arrived. Interviews conducted by Commission investigators confirmed that two other newsmen who retraced their activities the night of May 14 were in front of Alexander Hall at least three minutes prior to the shooting.

Most students and officers gave statements indicating their belief that less time passed from the arrival of the officers to the shooting. Inspector Jones, for example, testified the elapsed time "could not" have been more than "ten to fifteen seconds."

Farries Adams, a student, stated:

> It was spontaneous, you know. . . .It [the tank] stopped in front of the west wing almost and these people positioned themselves and what have you . . . the front line . . . knelt to the ground and there they kneeled and started to fire into the dormitory to the west wing first.

Some officers gave longer time estimates, as did some students. However, it appears to the Commission that these varying estimates are a natural consequence of the confusion that inevitably attends a dramatic, emotional experience.

Were Officers Verbally Abused?

While some students deny hearing any abuse directed at the officers in front of Alexander Hall, the Commission concludes that the police officers were subject to vile verbal abuse. Not only did students chant, "Pigs! Pigs! Pigs!" (as Miss Andrea Reese testified), but some crowd members screamed obscenities and racial and sexual epithets at the officers. Few individual words were discernible on Bert Case's tape recording, but the fact that vile and obscene screaming did occur is clear from that tape, and one particularly offensive obscenity—"motherfucker"—can be heard above the din.

Was Anything Thrown at the Officers in Front of Alexander Hall?

Earlier in the evening, a considerable number of rocks and other missiles were thrown at officers in front of Stewart Hall. There is conflict, however, over what, if anything, was thrown at officers in front of Alexander Hall.

Some students insisted in interviews with Commission staff members that there were no rocks, bottles, or other debris thrown at the police officers at Alexander Hall.

Some officers insisted there was a storm of debris. For example, Lieutenant Magee stated that when he was in front of Alexander Hall the debris "was coming directly in front of me, because I was having to dodge to keep from getting my brains knocked out." Inspector Jones testified that "bricks, bottles, rocks, and pieces of concrete . . . were thrown continuously from both sides of the street."

A tape recording that Bert Case made at the time of the incident has a sound that is unmistakably that of glass breaking near the tape recorder. Jack Hobbs felt shattered glass strike his ankle. Several students told Commission investigators that they saw a bottle thrown from the north side of the street, and it appears one was thrown also from the south side of the street. Frank James, a student from Vicksburg, saw a rock thrown near Jack Hobbs. Highway patrol officials recovered a brick that, laboratory examination proved, struck the helmet of patrolman William Turcotte. Jackson policeman Claude Gholson testified that a rock or brick thrown from the south side of Lynch Street struck his helmet and staggered him. Each of the four newsmen on the scene denies having seen or heard more than one or two objects thrown in front of Alexander Hall. The testimony of Bert Case is representative:

Q. Besides the bottle that you heard break in the street in front of you, did you see any bricks or other bottles flying through the air or striking the pavement?

A. The only thing I recall is the bottle breaking.

The city sent no special cleanup crew to the scene, and college officials responsible for keeping Lynch Street clean· recall no unusual amount of debris the morning of May 15.

Lynch Street in front of Alexander Hall the morning following the shooting.

The Commission finds that some members of the crowd did throw a small number of bottles, rocks, and bricks at peace officers in front of Alexander Hall. However, the Commission also finds that the missile throwing was far short of the "constant barrage of flying missiles" highway patrol investigators reported to Governor John Bell Williams.

Was There Shooting Just Prior to the Police Fusillade?

The most difficult factual dispute to resolve is whether

there was any shooting immediately preceding the firing by the officers. Clearly there was shooting on the campus while the dump truck was being burned. Frank James so testified, and other students have given similar statements. James also testified that there were shots fired while peace officers were in front of Stewart Hall. Police radio logs indicate two such incidents.

The evidence of shooting after the officers left Stewart Hall is much less clear. With one exception, only law enforcement officers state that they definitely heard shooting from the campus after the officers arrived at Alexander Hall.

A number of officials, including Mayor Russell Davis, Lieutenant Warren Magee, and General Walter Johnson, heard no weapon fire after the officers arrived at Alexander Hall, prior to the fusillade.

On the other hand, most officers stated that they did hear at least one shot from the campus before the officers' volley, and three of the four newsmen on the scene stated that they heard sounds that might have been shots. But two of them said the sounds they heard may have been firecrackers.

City policeman Charles Little told the Commission that from his position in Thompson's tank he observed shots . . .. being fired from the east side of a third-floor window of the stairwell:

> There was a colored male, ran to the window and . . . pushed the students in front of him away and apparently broke the window or a portion of the window with the back of his hand, or the butt of a weapon, I later found out, and it was a hand gun and I could tell when he stuck it out the window . . . He pointed directly at the men on the ground and fired it twice.

Little's testimony was corroborated by one highway patrolman who saw a gun at the third-floor window and by others who saw flashes or heard sounds they believed came from the third floor. Another patrolman told Commission investigators he saw a gun fired from a stairwell window but stated that it was on the west side of the fourth-floor window.

Stella Spinks, a junior at Jackson State, told the Commission that she was standing on the landing identified by Little as the source of the gunfire. She testified that she saw no one with a gun and heard no talk of a gun. She did not hear any glass break before the officers shot, and she heard no gun fired from that landing.

FBI agents who examined the third-floor stairwell window reported that all observable bullet holes in the window were made by shots from outside the building. A portion of the window is broken, a fact which offers possible corroboration of Little's tesitmony; but the broken area is very small, and examination of the glass indicates that the break was caused by incoming bullets or shotgun pellets.

TV cameraman Jack Hobbs gave the most persusive testimony of small arms fire from the area of Alexander Hall:

> At this point, a bottle shattered in the street just next to my foot, and I felt some pieces of it hit my ankle. At that point I heard a report, a bullet went past my ear and ricocheted behind me.

Not only did Hobbs testify that he heard shooting, but Bert Case's tape recording also reveals that Hobbs asked Case: "Did you hear that bullet?"

While at the scene, Bert Case did not believe he had heard any shots before the police fired. The tape recording, however, contains two sounds immediately before the breaking of the bottle that Case believes could be rounds of small arms fire. There are additional, less distinct sounds on the tape between the breaking glass sound and the first shotgun blast. FBI laboratory analysts were unable to determine whether any of these sounds were made by shots.

There is no physical evidence of small arms fire in the area around Alexander Hall. On the basis of Jack Hobbs' report that a bullet had gone past his ear and struck a white-painted concrete wall behind him, highway patrolmen searched unsucessfully with flashlights for a bullet or a bullet mark. FBI agents also examined that wall and found no evidence of any bullet having struck it.

Three .32 caliber cartridges and one .25 caliber cartridge were found on the south side of the chain-link fence. Because of the distance, it is unlikely that they were ejected from a weapon fired from Alexander Hall.

One unspent round of .22 caliber long rifle ammunition was found in the fifth-floor hallway of Alexander Hall approximately two feet from the door leading out to the stairway. The bullet was discovered the next day beneath a pile of clothing, books, and other material discarded by students who left the dormitory when the school was closed.

One patrol officer reported being hit by a lead fragment. In reference to this Governor Williams stated on June 4, 1970, that "one spent, mashed bullet" was picked up after the shooting and that it had not been fired from an officer's weapon. However, laboratory examination established that the lead fragment—the mashed "bullet"—was actually mashed buckshot. Apparently it was fired by a police officer and had ricocheted into the street.

No other officer was struck by gunfire. Thompson's tank was not struck by gunfire.

Sergeant Charles Lee, the Jackson police officer second in command and responsible for locating and controlling sniper fire, testified that while the officers were in front of Alexander Hall there may have been gunfire from another point on campus. He said he heard a shot that "sounded to me like it was more around the corner, which would be on the west side of the building. . . . I was more looking for flashes than anything else. . . . I never saw any."

It is significant to note that special agents of the FBI examined each of the rooms and stairs and stairwell landings behind the 24 windows and 18 metal panels into which shots were fired and found no evidence of shooting *from* any of these locations. The Bureau's agents reported that every bullet mark which they could identify in every broken window and in every defaced panel was made by a bullet or pellet fired from outside the building.

The Commission is unable to determine positively whether there was or was not gunfire from Alexander Hall prior to the fusillade. The most favorable reading of the evidence tending to support a finding that there was such gunfire indicates that at most two shots were fired from one window.

CAUSES OF STUDENT CONDUCT

Jackson State College is a black school situated in a white-dominated state. This is the starting point for analyzing the causes of the student disorders of May 13 and 14, 1970.

The stark fact underlying all other causes of student unrest at Jackson State is the historic pattern of racism that substantially affects daily life in Mississippi.

The National Advisory Commission on Civil Disorders emphasized that racism is a fact in American society. No state or community is totally exempt. What happened in Jackson could have happened on any number of campuses where black students are protesting—on white campuses as well as black ones.

Dr. Margaret Walker Alexander—poet, novelist, professor of English at Jackson State College, and a native black Mississippian—told the Commission at its hearings in Jackson:

> What is at issue is the issue of racism versus humanity. We have been educated for 350 years to think first in terms of race and property and almost never in terms of human lives. What is the value of human personality in this country? What would you give for a man's life? These two young men shot down, they could have been my sons. Of what value are they to the American society? Hundreds have been shot down. What does it mean? Is it tragic to other people, to anyone but the mother or the sister or the wife? What is the value of human life in America today?

It is important to emphasize that in any normal sense of the term, "student unrest" does not exist on the Jackson State campus. There is virtually no student movement as such and no deep or serious grievance expressed by students with respect to the administration of the school. This is not because Jackson State students are insensitive to the issues that concern students on other campuses in this country. On the contrary, roughly 500 students attended the student-organized rally on May 7 protesting the move into Cambodia by American troops and expressing their sympathy for the four students slain at Kent State.

The rally and a proposed strike were called by a group of eight students, seven of them newly elected student body officers. Their statement to the student body calling for a strike was phrased in language of restraint. It said:

> To those of you who are sympathetic to this cause, we ask for your support. However, any students who feel otherwise and who would like to continue classes, no hostile efforts will be made to prevent you from doing so.

Interviews with black students reveal that in general they take for granted that the United States should withdraw from Indochina, and that the social conditions which breed poverty and crime in this country should be eliminated. But Jackson State students do not agitate or protest or propagandize for these policies in any organized fashion.

There are three basic reasons why almost all Jackson State students are disinclined to participate in protest activities. The first is their feeling that protest if futile. In May 1970, shortly after the shootings on campus, Jack Hobbs interviewed Jackson State students. He testified to the Commission:

> Most students I talked to . . . their feelings was, as they said over and over, many of them, "Nobody cares about us, nobody gives a damn."

The students perceive that years of protest—by turns vigorous and muted—have not brought white Mississippians to respect the full human dignity of black people. It is a fact, for example, that Jackson State College remains a separate, black state school. To be sure, Jackson State is a source of pride, and it offers a possibility of restructuring education in terms relevant to Blacks. But its existence is also a reminder that the "separate but equal" spirit of 1896 is still a Mississippi reality.

Second, Jackson State students do not readily engage in protest activities because they cannot afford to, especially given their belief that the utility of such action is marginal at best. In their daily life in Mississippi, Jackson State students are too busy fighting for their physical, economic, social, and psychological lives to engage in protests. Many adopt a posture of apathy in an attempt to insulate themselves from the oppressiveness of daily life. Others have a singleminded purpose, often drummed into them from an early age by weary and all but hopeless parents: Get an education, learn a profession, and get out of Mississippi. An increasing number pursue that goal, but with a different purpose: Get an education and use it to serve the needs of the Black community today.

There is a third reason why Jackson State students do not readily protest: Southern black people as a group still believe that the American system will respond to their legitimate demands without the necessity of bringing to bear the pressure of protest activities. As Dr. Peoples put it: "I think one who is motivated to go to college, say in Mississippi, is one who would be highly motivated to try to make the system work."

Several Jackson State students and black community leaders stated that although their faith in America continues, it is on the wane and can be sustained for only so long. They also were emphatic in pointing out that the basis of that faith has never been confidence in either state or local government and that even the federal government is viewed more suspiciously today than in the 1950's and 1960's. Dr. Aaron Shirley, an advisor to the college's Committee of Concerned Students, expressed the view that the federal government indirectly contributed to the tragedies at Kent and Jackson by creating in the minds of both students and law enforcement officials a belief that dissent was no longer regarded with favor and that stringent measures to harness dissent were acceptable.

With hope waning and frustration growing, even those students who normally affect a pose of apathy sympathized with those few whose tempers had reached a boiling point. Many students said that onlookers, including some girls who were leaning out of their windows in Alexander Hall, cheered on those who were throwing rocks.

While the decline in hope and the rise in frustration help to explain why some students condoned or participated in the violent actions that occurred on the Jackson State College campus, they do not provide sufficient explanation.

We do not know the specific cause of the first rock-throwing incident either evening.

However, one force behind the student actions of the 13th and 14th of May was closely akin to spring fever. In the weeks before May 13, freshman girls had been jokingly asking their boyfriends when the "spring riot" would be. President Peoples testified that students "look forward" to the spring disturbances. But spring fever exists every spring.

It does appear that some people wanted to exacerbate the trouble once it had started. On May 14, a black man, about 45 years old, drove through campus spreading the false rumor that Charles Evers had been assassinated as his brother Medgar Evers had been several years ago. The same false rumor was telephoned to several bars frequented by corner boys. Both nonstudents and some students responded to the rumor.

A small group of students believed that it would help focus attention on student concerns to engage in violent action that would bring the National Guard onto the campus. One student said:

Some of the students wanted demonstrations on campus, not involving personal injury to anyone or extensive damage to property, but of sufficient magnitude to bring the National Guard on campus. It was felt that if the Guard came on campus, it would dramatize the students' position and create enough publicity to bring the matter to the attention of the President of the United States.

Spreading false rumors, urging rock-throwing, burning, and other violence, and taking violent action to focus attention on student concerns are deplorable and completely unjustified. Both false rumors and efforts to have the Guard called on campus contributed to the creation of a dangerous situation.

Before leaving the subject of the causes of student conduct on the nights of May 13 and 14, we reemphasize the central role of anger and frustration and the closely connected fact of racial antagonism.

One student, asked at the Commission hearings why the rock-throwing started, gave this response:

> I mean like some people say the Vietnam issue and, you know, it is a big thing on the campus, but I don't think that is true. I mean a lot of guys were upset, and, you know, something to the effect they wanted to step up the draft and there was a lot of—just a lot of tension.
>
> When you go to class every day and in overcrowded classrooms and it is hot and sweaty in there, you just get fed up with it and, you know, you should have had more classrooms and your classrooms should have been cool and you are sitting in a hundred degree classroom and that night it is the same thing, and you ain't got nothing to do. You just got to do something, and it is just one thing led to another, so that is the way it was.

Another student said:

> They throw rocks because they are angry. And they throw rocks at cars passing on Lynch Street, those cars carrying whites. Because, I guess, always in the back of your head you are thinking that somebody hasn't been

doing something right all along and if you can't get to
the source, get to the next best thing.... If you are
angry about anything that has political or social
overtones, and if you can't get to the politicians and the
government officials that are white here, and get them
to do a little better, then you go to the next best thing;
you get something that looks a little like them, I guess.

CAUSES OF POLICE CONDUCT

We have said it is impossible to understand the actions of
the students who participated in the events of May 13 and 14
without recognizing the central role of racial antagonisms.
That is equally true of the reaction of those peace officers
who fired their weapons at Alexander Hall.

Many white Mississippi law enforcement officers—and all
officers who fired were white—are afraid of what black men
may do to them in hostile surroundings. Whether that fear is
justified is of little consequence; the fear exists. That fear is
intensified enormously in a violent confrontation—one in
which foul language is made more threatening by thrown
bricks and bottles and by the knowledge that there are Blacks
with guns in the immediate area.

Moreover, many white police officers are influenced by
their disdain or hatred of Blacks. One officer characterized
the rock-throwing on Wednesday night as follows: "It's just
a bunch of damn niggers." And Bert Case testified:

I think that is probably the first time Mississippi
patrolmen and Jackson policemen had been confronted
at that close range with black people yelling obscenities
at them. This is enough to put them in an infuriated
mood, I am sure.

No white officer stated that he feels hostility toward
Blacks, but the chief highway patrol officer on the scene,
Inspector Lloyd Jones, acknowledged that he has used the
term "nigger" while on the job. He testified further that
there is no highway patrol regulation prohibiting the use of

such language.

We have previously quoted the catalog of injuries radioed by a highway patrolman shortly after the shooting. The attitude reflected in a statement of that type—"I think there are about three more nigger males over there, one of 'em shot in the arm, one of 'em shot in the leg, and one of 'em somewhere else"—is an attitude that Blacks are not fully human.

Racial antagonism is aggravated by the all-white makeup of the Mississippi Highway Patrol and the nearly all-white makeup of the Jackson City Police Department. The highway patrol's director of personnel testified there has never been a black highway patrolman. The Jackson City Police Department has 19 uniformed black policemen on a force of 279 members. No black policeman holds an officer rank. Of the 65 law enforcement officers in front of Alexander Hall, two were black; they did not shoot.

The Commission concludes that racial animosity on the part of white police officers was a substantial contributing factor in the deaths of two black youths and the gunshot injuries of twelve more.

One of the most tragic aspects of the Jackson State College deaths, however, is that—despite the obvious existence of racial antagonisms—the confrontation itself could have been avoided.

The Commission concludes that the 28-second fusillade from police officers was an unreasonable, unjustified over-reaction. Even if we were to assume that two shots were fired from a window in the west wing of Alexander Hall, the 28-second fusillade in response was clearly unwarranted. Peace officers should respond to sniper fire by taking cover and holding their fire. The Jackson City Police sniper team on the scene should have been used to deal with reported sniper fire. A broad barrage of gunfire in response to reported and unconfirmed sniper fire is never warranted.

Moreover, the Jackson City Police and Mississippi Highway Patrol lacked adequate planning, communications, training, and discipline—but not weapons—as they entered the Jackson State campus on May 14.

The confusion that existed at the moment the police and highway patrol contingents prepared to move east on Lynch Street from Stewart Hall reveals most dramatically the lack of adequate planning and communications. Each of the three chief law enforcement officers on the scene—Lieutenant Magee from the police department, Inspector Jones from the highway patrol, and General Johnson from the National Guard—had a different idea of the mission of the police and patrol contingents.

The FBI manual, *Prevention and Control of Mobs and Riots*, emphasizes that,

> No aspect of the program [for mob and riot control] is more important than planning. Unless the plan is organized . . . the operation will be doomed to failure.

Similarly, the Mississippi Highway Patrol manual for crowd control states, "Never move into action without a plan." Following this elementary principle of effective law enforcement action might have prevented gunfire and deaths at Jackson State College.

The National Advisory Commission on Civil Disorders also noted that:

> No matter how well trained and skilled a police officer may be, he will be relatively ineffectual in dealing with civil disturbance so long as he functions as an individual.

The policy of the Mississippi Highway Safety Patrol—that each officer may decide for himself when he should fire his weapon because of danger to his or another's life—is contrary to this principle. More than 20 highway patrolmen fired even though they had not received an order to do so. Later, each highway patrolman who fired told his superiors that he was firing in response to gunfire from one of two windows. The Jackson City Police Department has a standing rule that shotguns should be fired only upon the order of a commanding officer. Those city policemen who did fire were acting in clear violation of this rule. Sergeant Lee testified that immediately after the shooting ceased, he asked everyone, "Who gave the order to fire? Who gave the order to fire?" He said, "Nobody said anything." The only two city police officers who were assigned to respond to sniper fire, both of them armed with special rifles, did not shoot.

The FBI manual also states:

> Under no circumstances should firearms be used until all other measures for controlling the violence have been exhausted. Above all, officers should never fire indiscriminately into a crowd or mob.

Even if it is assumed that there was shooting from Alexander Hall, it is difficult to understand why officers fired "indiscriminately" into Alexander Hall. One officer who did fire told Commission investigators that if he saw a person in a crowd point a gun at him, he would fire his shotgun into the crowd in the direction of the gun. Each load of double-O buckshot contains an equivalent of nine .33 caliber bullets, each of which travels along a different trajectory and can be lethal for a distance in excess of 40 yards.

Lloyd Jones stated that had he not been occupied reaching for a tear gas canister and looking at a patrolman struck by a rock, he would have shot into the third-floor window:

> Q And in those landings were several people, students or otherwise and you could visibly see them, you said?
> A That is right.
> Q And you saw two flashes from the third floor; right?
> A Yes, sir . . . I told you I would have fired into the third story window. There [were] people in it. I couldn't tell who was doing the firing.
> Q But would you fire into a crowd of people?
> A I would have fired into that third floor window; yes.

Q Not knowing who was behind the window?
A That is right.
Q With a shotgun?
A Right.
Q With buckshot in it?
A Yes.

But the peace officers who fired that night did not shoot only into the crowds in the windows of Alexander Hall. Some fired at the crowds on the campus behind the fences on both sides of Lynch Street.

Law enforcement officers stated that they did not fire to disperse the crowd in front of Alexander Hall, but rather were responding to what they believed was a sniper located in the west wing. Every officer who admits firing stated that he fired either into the west wing or into the air. The physical evidence and the positions of the victims, however, indicate that the officers were firing indiscriminately into the crowd, at ground level, on both sides of Lynch Street.

Even though the officers did fire into the crowd, it appears that no one would have been killed if birdshot had been used rather than buckshot. The highway patrol was using buckshot because of a change in its policy concerning ammunition. Inspector Jones said:

Q In 1966 or '67, I believe you told me that the
   Highway Patrol used No. 9 birdshot and that you
   yourself fired No. 9 birdshot in the area of the
   Jackson State campus in 1967. Is that correct?
A Yes sir.
Q And you also used No. 9 birdshot at Alcorn College;
   is that correct?
A Yes.
Q What is the reason that the Highway Patrol now uses
   double-O buckshot, rather than No. 9 birdshot?
A I haven't been given a reason. We use what is issued
   to us. We were issued buckshot this last time.

This change in policy lends some support to the view,

widespread among Jackson State students, that police, particularly highway patrolmen, have become more hostile in recent years to Blacks and more inclined to deal harshly with black protestors. Some students say that national, state, and local officials have created a favorable climate for such police attitudes.

Finally, the Commission concludes that a significant cause of the deaths and injuries at Jackson State College is the confidence of white officers that if they fire weapons during a black campus disturbance they will face neither stern departmental discipline nor criminal prosecution or conviction.

This view received confirmation by the Mississippi Highway Safety Patrol investigation and by the report of the Hinds County grand jury. A federal grand jury was convened in late June to look into possible violations of federal law. It called some witnesses and obtained certain physical evidence for FBI examination. It has been in recess since that time.

The highway patrol investigation was conducted by a committee of three senior highway patrol officers who interviewed each highway patrolman who had been on the scene. Each patrolman was asked if he had fired his weapon. Those who said they had fired were asked where they had fired. All responded that they had shot either into the air or into the third- or fifth-floor windows of the west wing stairwell of Alexander Hall. When asked why he fired, each patrolman stated he had seen or heard shots from the third- or fifth-floor stairwell windows. The investigators examined no photographs or physical evidence and interviewed no witnesses other than highway patrol personnel. There was no transcript made of the interviews, no written statements taken, and no written report.

The patrol investigators made no effort to cross-examine any of the patrolmen or to examine their weapons or conduct any ballistics tests. The shotgun shells fired by the highway patrolmen were not available for ballistics tests. The empty casings had been picked off the street by the patrolmen and were either discarded or reloaded with buckshot. Although FBI agents found fragments of bullets fired from carbines and 30.06 rifles, the cartridges that held these bullets were not available for ballistics tests.

It seems reasonably clear that some highway patrolmen fired elsewhere than at the third- and fifth-floor windows, despite what they apparently told their superiors. Bert Case and Jack Hobbs saw what appeared to be systematic shooting by highway patrolmen into each window of the stairwell. Hobbs observed flame coming from the barrels of two shotguns that highway patrolmen were pointing straight ahead. In fact, it seems likely from the relative positions of state and city forces that highway patrolmen did most of the shooting into the west wing of the women's dormitory.

After the highway patrol had completed its interviews, it made an oral report to Governor John Bell Williams. Governor Williams told Commission investigators that he relied exclusively on the highway patrol's oral report in making his television report on the Jackson State incident to the people of Mississippi on June 4, 1970. In that address, he characterized the highway patrol's inquest as a "complete and impartial investigation." The governor explained the 28 seconds and 150 rounds of gunfire by saying that "the officers felt compelled in the interest of self-preservation to return the fire." The governor's chief conclusion was that "the officers . . . did not instigate the problem; they did not encourage it—the responsibility must rest with the protestors."

The report of the Hinds County grand jury was even more explicit in upholding the officers:

> We find that under the riot situation existing, the officers of both the Jackson Police and the Highway Patrol had a right and were justified in discharging their weapons . . . . [T]he officers used only that force that was necessary to protect themselves and to restore law and order on the campus of Jackson State College.

The conclusions of the grand jury are based on a number of inaccurate findings. For example, the report states that "three spent .32 caliber shell casings were found in the bushes in front of Alexander Hall by a member of the Mississippi Highway Patrol." In fact, Patrolman McComb informed a Commission investigator he found the shell casings on the sidewalk on the street side of the fence in front of Alexander Hall. The significance of the difference is that one could infer that spent cartridges in the bushes below the west wing stairwell were ejected from a weapon fired from that stairwell. No such inference can be made when one knows that the cartridges were found more than 20 feet from the entry to the stairwell on the other side of the fence.

The grand jury report further states that peace officer shooting was "at the area of the sniper." Photographs and diagrams presented as exhibits to the grand jurors indicate that there was shooting on both sides of Lynch Street and that shots on the north side of the street extended over an area more than 200 feet wide. Clearly the grand jury's conclusion that the officers "returned the fire" is a patently inadequate description of the extent of shooting that actually took place.

In the hours after the shooting and for months thereafter, the statements of some city police officers established a pattern of deceit. The night of the shooting, Mayor Davis and Chief Pierce decided to determine if any police officer had fired his weapon. Each officer who had been on the scene was interrogated and asked to turn in the ammunition he had been issued. Each officer replied that he had not fired a shot and returned the same amount of ammunition he had received. The following exchange occurred with Sergeant Lee during his testimony before the Commission:

> Q Just to clarify this point, afterward you checked each man, checked the amount of ammunition he turned in to you and asked each man whether he had fired; and you got the same [amount] of ammunition back

from each man, and each man told you he had not
fired; is that correct?

A That is correct, sir.
(It later developed that officers had obtained shells from
Thompson's tank to replace the bullets they had fired.)

The deception continued when, sometime later, agents of
the FBI interviewed each city policeman who was on the
scene. Each was again asked if he had fired his weapon, and
each repeated the denial he had made to Sergeant Lee.

Still later, policemen testified before a biracial lawyers'
committee appointed by the mayor that they saw no city
policemen fire. Newsmen testified to the same effect. While it
is now clear that the newsmen were not in a position to see
the policemen fire and that their apparent corroboration
was, in fact, meaningless, the committee concluded that the
officers had told the truth.

The highway patrol, which collected empty No. 1 buckshot shells on the street in front of Alexander Hall, did not
release these shells—or publicly announce their existence—
until required to turn them over to a federal grand jury. FBI
laboratory tests proved that these shells had been fired from
city police department shotguns. When confronted with this
fact, at least three city policemen admitted shooting. Even
now, those policemen who do admit firing claim to have shot
only up into the air. Ballistics tests show that at least two of
the victims, Green and Woodward, were shot with No. 1
buckshot. The city police used this type of ammunition in
their shotguns. The highway patrol was issued double-O
shells, though some of the patrol may have used other types
of shot.

Relying on the word of his police officers and the
conclusions of the biracial committee, Mayor Russell Davis—a
white Mississippi politician who urges whites and Blacks to
work together to improve Jackson—issued a public statement
to the effect that there was no evidence that any city
policeman had fired his weapon.

The reaction of the county grand jury to this chain of events was as follows:

It was most unfortunate that the Mayor of the City of Jackson saw fit to appear on television and make statements to the press to the effect that the Jackson Police Department officers did not fire their weapons at Jackson State College. This statement was absolutely false and the Mayor, in making it, has brought extreme and unwarranted criticism upon the Mississippi Highway Patrol and its officers. This action of the Mayor in the opinion of this Grand Jury is reprehensible and should not be excused or cannot be justified.

The county grand jury condemned the mayor for repeating what his officers had told him, but it did not suggest in any way that it had been improper for the police officers to lie. Instead, the grand jury report continues:

We feel strongly that insofar as investigations or other actions concerning statements that any of these twenty-two officers might have previously given be brought to an end with this Grand Jury report. We wish to make it clear that any future action of any kind against any of the twenty-two police officers involved by the Mayor of the City of Jackson or the Police Department of the City of Jackson would be unwarranted, unjustified and political in nature.

This Commission understands why both white officers and black people in Mississippi gain the impression that policemen need not fear official punishment—or even censure—for repressive action against Blacks.

We offer one final observation on the grand jury report. Its underlying philosophy is summarized in the following passage from the report: "When people . . . engage in civil disorders and riots, they must expect to be injured or killed when law enforcement officers are required to reestablish order."

That position, which the grand jury drew almost verbatim from grand jury charges by Federal District Judge Harold

Cox and State Circuit Judge Russell Moore, may reflect the views of many Americans today. It is a view which this Commission urges Americans to reject.

The Commission categorically rejects rhetorical statements that students must "expect" injury or death during civil disorders. Such statements make no distinction between legitimate dissent and violent protest. It is the duty of public officials to protect human life and to safeguard peaceful, orderly, and lawful protest. When disorderly protest exists, it is their duty to deal with it firmly, justly, and with the minimum force necessary; lethal force should be used only to protect the lives of officers or citizens and only when the danger to innocent persons is not increased by the use of such force.

CONCLUSION

There must not be a repetition of the tragic incident at Jackson State.

We are heartened by the stated determination of Jackson City Police and elected officials to take necessary steps to avoid the recurrence of tragedy at Jackson State College. It is imperative that this determination be reflected in action.

Mayor Davis described the first—and most difficult—task:

I know truthfully in Jackson we do have a problem that the whole United States has of race relations, and somehow the solution to that problem simply lies in the determination of the black people and the white people to get along with each other. This is what it has got to come down to if it is going to be solved.

City officials also state they will take specific steps to improve the capability of their police officers to respond appropriately to any further incidents of disorder at Jackson State. The City Council has approved an extensive police training program for handling problems of campus disorder. The police department has taken steps to reduce the necessity of using lethal force; it has obtained protective vests for its officers and a new, improved tear gas dispenser.

Chief Pierce has made it clear that the department policies with respect to the use of buckshot rather than birdshot will be reexamined. He also stated that the policy of using Thompson's tank on the campus will be reevaluated in light of its inflammatory effect on crowds. He was receptive to the suggestion made by a number of students that in the event of a disturbance campus security forces be supported by student marshals to minimize the need for city or state policemen. Finally, the chief testified that the police officers who lied to Sergeant Lee and to the FBI would be disciplined.

On the other hand, the reaction of the Mississippi Highway Safety Patrol to the deaths and injuries at Jackson State continues to be disturbing. Inspector Jones expressed the position of his patrol:

Q Do you have any recommendations to make to the Commission, particularly as it relates to command or control features for joint operation of law enforcement agencies, for this kind of thing if it should happen in the future?

A No sir; I don't.

Q Does your department plan to take any corrective steps in view of what happened?

A Not that I know of . . . . [There] was no doubt in my mind that some of us would have been killed down there if the volley of shots hadn't gone off and I see no reason for disciplining a man for saving his own life.

Q [D]oes your department . . . plan to take any corrective steps in the future to prevent this?

A Not that I know of.

Q How do you feel about it personally? Do you think they are needed?

A Not against any of our men, no, sir.

We urge a reexamination of this position. Every group or agency that participated in the Jackson State confrontation must learn from its errors of planning and judgment.

We are also concerned with the escalation of rhetoric on the part of certain Jackson State students. While we understand the profound emotional impact of the deaths and injuries of fellow students, we condemn statements to the effect that the next time something happens "all the pigs" will not walk away from campus or statements suggesting that students arm themselves because of anticipated future confrontations with police. We condemn any action on the basis of such statements even more strongly.

Andrea Reese, a student who sustained gunshot wounds on May 14, warned:

Unless somebody shows a little interest or a little common sense . . . looking at the whole problem of relationships between the white officers and the black people, if they can't establish some ground to meet on and to get a few things settled, it is going to happen again at Jackson State.

The Commission recommends that police and students commit themselves to end the hostility that presently divides them before it does, indeed, "happen again at Jackson State."

The Commission has devoted a considerable portion of its efforts to the investigation at Jackson State and the parallel investigation of the May events at Kent State, which are the subject of a separate report. The lessons of Jackson State and Kent State are reflected in many of the recommendations the Commission has made in the chapters of its report on campus unrest. The Commission believes that if those recommendations are followed, the tragedy of Jackson State is far less likely to be repeated. Indeed, we believe that no one would have died at Alexander Hall if those recommendations had already been accepted and acted on by police and highway patrol units.

Law Enforcement Officials

Even if there was sniper fire at Jackson State—a question on which we have found conflicting evidence—the 28-second barrage of lethal gunfire, partly directed into crowded windows of Alexander Hall and into a crowd in front of Alexander Hall, was completely unwarranted and unjustified. The appropriate response to sniper fire is set out in Chapter 5 of our report. The guidelines stated there were violated in every respect at Jackson State. The police officers did not withdraw and seek cover even though they had an armored vehicle which would have provided ample cover. The sniper team which was present at Jackson State did not fire single aimed shots at an identified sniper; instead, a large number of peace officers fired shotguns loaded with buckshot or rifles loaded with armor-piercing ammunition into a crowded dormitory and into a crowd of protestors. Indeed, the police sniper team did not fire at all.

The peace officers did not have a mobilization plan, nor did they have a tactical plan directly agreed upon and understood by all the units involved. They had no formal chain of command and no clear notion of who was in command among the various police and military forces present. They did not have a common radio channel for use during the disorder, nor did they have a central command post to provide liaison. The individual peace officers did not know, as they should, the destination and plan of their unit. Furthermore, there had been no adequate consultation with college officials before the law enforcement officers were sent onto the campus.

Most basically, there is no evidence that the police departments had appropriate training programs for disorder control or guidelines for the use of appropriate degrees of force to control a crowd. None of the police departments involved have sufficient community relations programs to insure that persons of all races are treated with respect. The Jackson City Police Department and the Mississippi Highway Safety Patrol should prohibit absolutely the use of the derogatory term "nigger" and should prohibit the derogatory use of such terms as "boy."

The community relations program should begin within the police departments. Law enforcement agencies and the National Guard must be racially integrated, not only at the lowest ranks but also in command positions. We have noted that there are no Blacks in the Mississippi Highway Patrol and only 19 Blacks in the Jackson City Police Department. The Mississippi National Guard, which has over 13,000 men, has only 21 Blacks and no black officers.

College Administrators

Jackson State officials must develop plans and procedures for dealing with campus disorders and for making prompt decisions if a disorder occurs. They should establish and maintain formal lines of communication with law enforcement agencies. The authority and responsibility of campus security guards at Jackson must be clarified. A rumor center should be established during periods of campus disorder where students can obtain authoritative verification or denial of rumored events. The Commission commends to the attention of Jackson State College administrators the many specific recommendations contained in Chapter 4 of our report.

Students

All students, and particularly elected leaders, have a duty to condemn absolutely and unequivocally the use of force and violence. The aura of respectability that appears to surround violent protest when those protests are made in support of legitimate grievances must be eliminated. Possession or use of weapons on campus by students should be strongly condemned.

Students should recognize that the use of obscenities and derogatory terms such as "pigs" and "honkies" during a demonstration may trigger a violent if unjustifiable response by peace officers and that the use of such terms in every day speech in the presence of police officers escalates tension.

Government Officials

The City Council of the City of Jackson has endorsed the goal of closing Lynch Street to the flow of major traffic through the campus of Jackson State College. However, there are substantial financial barriers to accomplishing that goal. We urge the appropriate federal and state agencies to assist city officials in obtaining all necessary funds.

The governor, the Mississippi Board of Trustees for Institutions of Higher Learning, and the Mississippi legislature should take whatever steps are necessary to insure that Jackson State College is developed rapidly to university status and that it becomes integrated.

The federal and state governments should provide long-term financial aid to Jackson State College—and to other predominantly black colleges—to insure that students attending these schools have opportunities equal to those available to students at predominantly white schools of comparable size.

The President should appoint a special advisor on black colleges. That advisor should prepare recommendations for specific federal action in such areas as financial aid to black colleges.

The President and the Department of Defense must bring about integration of the National Guard at all ranks on more than a token basis. They should consider creation of additional positions to overcome the effects of past discrimination.

The President should direct the Department of Justice to review whether it would be appropriate for the United States to intervene in pending litigation to integrate the Mississippi Highway Safety Patrol. In addition, the President should direct the preparation of any necessary legislation authorizing action by the federal government to integrate police agencies.

The Commission recommends that federal, state, and local officials take dramatic steps to reflect a commitment on the part of government to the protection of life and to the aggressive pursuit of equal justice—equal justice in the schools, in the courts, in jobs, and, most relevant of all to this investigation, equal treatment by policemen and just treatment of policemen. By "just treatment of policemen" we mean that policemen receive recognition for the difficult job they have, particularly during times of civil disorders, and that unfair vilification of them be ended. We also mean that when policemen willfully violate the civil rights of black or white citizens, they should be prosecuted vigorously and fairly by the government.

Bibliography

This bibliography is designed to serve two specific purposes. First, it furnishes some indication of the sources for the Report itself. Second, it offers a guide to representative literature on the subjects of campus unrest, higher education in general, and related issues. It includes significant scholarly works as well as those which, though written in a more popular vein, make a valuable contribution to the literature on campus unrest.

This bibliography is arranged in two parts. Part I corresponds to the chapters of the Report. A book or an article relevant to more than one subject area is listed according to its main emphasis. Part II is a selective guide to bibliographies on campus unrest, which the user may find helpful in locating more material on any phase of this subject.

The publications of three earlier Presidential Commissions—the President's Commission on Law Enforcement and the Administration of Justice, the National Advisory Commission on Civil Disorders, and the National Commission on the Causes and Prevention of Violence—were important to the work of the staff of the Commission. The staff also found valuable the continuing interest in campus unrest reflected in two journals, the *Educational Record* (published quarterly by the American Council on Education, One Dupont Circle,

Washington, D.C. 20036), and *Change in Higher Education* (published bimonthly by Science and University Affairs, 59 East 54th Street, New York, N.Y. 10022).

The Commission acknowledges the assistance of the George Washington University Library, the Howard University Library, the International Association of Chiefs of Police, the Library of the National Center for Higher Education, and the Library of Congress, particularly the Loan Division, Legislative Reference Service, and the General Reference and Bibliography Division.

Chapter 1: Student Protest in the 1960's

1. **Baker, Michael A., and others.**
   Police on Campus: The Mass Police Action at Columbia University, Spring, 1968.
   New York, New York Civil Liberties Union, 1969. 159 p.

   The authors present a chronological and analytical examination of the Columbia University crisis. Based on eyewitness reports by an independent group of scholars, the account describes the abuses in police action not as "the work of a few 'bad apples' ", nor as "the angry responses of men infuriated by physical threats or verbal provocation," but as "violence undertaken coolly—usually—and as a form of punishment."

2. **Bayer, Alan E., and Alexander W. Astin.**
   "Violence and Disruption on the U.S. Campus, 1968-1969." *Educational Record*, v. 50, fall 1969: 337-350.

   This statistical study of 382 institutions during the 1968-69 academic year relates campus unrest to certain institutional characteristics and discusses the relationship between institutional change and major campus protest.

3. **Becker, Howard S., ed.**
   Campus Power Struggle.
   Chicago, Aldine Publishing, 1970. 191 p.

   Popular sociological reports on undergraduate troubles, originally published in *Trans-action*, are brought together in this anthology.

4. **Bell, Daniel, and Irving Kristol, eds.**
Confrontation: the Student Rebellion and Universities.
New York, Basic Books, 1969. 191 p.

Student radicalism is described in this series of essays which range from descriptions of individual campuses (Berkeley, Columbia, Cornell) to more general and analytical discussions of student unrest. Most of the chapters were originally published in *The Public Interest* (summer 1968).

5. **Bolton, Charles D., and Kenneth C. W. Kammeyer.**
The University Student: A Study of Student Behavior and Values.
New Haven, College and Univ. Press, 1967. 286 p.

The results of this descriptive analysis of data concerning student behavior and obtained in 1962 at the University of California (Davis) indicate "that the informal peer-group aspect of student life does not generally support the intellectual-academic objectives" of the university.

6. **Boruch, Robert F.**
The Faculty Role in Campus Unrest.
Washington, American Council on Education, 1969. 28 p. (ACE Research Reports, v. 4, no. 5)

Faculty participation in student protest is documented and evaluated in this study based on administrator's responses to questionnaires mailed out in 1968 under American Council on Education sponsorship.

7. **California. Regents of the University of California. Special Forbes Committee.**
Report on the University of California and Recommendations. [Submitted by] Jerome C. Byrne, Special Counsel.
Los Angeles, 1965. 86 [18] p.

This report reviews the background of student unrest at the University of California before 1964, analyzes the causes of unrest, focuses on the Free Speech Movement crisis at Berkeley in the fall of 1964, and offers specific recommendations for changes in the public higher education system of California.

8. **Davidson, Carl.**
    The New Radical in the Multiversity: An Analysis and
    Strategy for the Student Movement.
    [Chicago] SDS Print Shop, 1968. 37 p.

    The author presents a new left analysis of institutions of higher
    learning, in which the current problems of the university are
    viewed as "firmly rooted in the American political economy."
    He outlines strategy for changing existent university structures
    and governance, and advocates the establishment of "an inde-
    pendent, radical and political Free Student Union" to work for
    political and social change.

9. **Fact-Finding Commission on Columbia Disturbances.**
    Crisis at Columbia; Report of the Fact-Finding Com-
    mission Appointed to Investigate the Disturbances at
    Columbia University in April and May 1968.
    New York, Vintage Books, 1968. 222 p.

    This official report—popularly called the "Cox Commission
    Report"—presents a thorough investigation of the facts per-
    taining to the events that took place at Columbia University in
    the spring of 1968.

10. **Feuer, Lewis S.**
    The Conflict of Generations: The Character and
    Significance of Student Movements.
    New York, Basic Books, 1969. 543 p.

    This provocative historical study of 19th and 20th century
    student protest movements in Europe and the U.S. explains
    student radicals in terms of a generation struggle.

11. **Foley, James A., and Robert K. Foley.**
    The College Scene: Students Tell It Like It Is.
    New York, Cowles Book, 1969. 187 p.

    Undergraduate attitudes toward current campus and national
    issues are explored in this volume.

12. **Foster, Julian, and Durward Long, eds.**
    Protest! Student Activism in America.
    New York, Wm. Morrow, 1970. 596 p.

    This up-to-date, comprehensive anthology on the student

protest movement in the United States includes: "the results of the only three inclusive surveys of the incidence of protest yet undertaken" (Part I); the activists' backgrounds, characteristics, world views, and organizations (Part II); case studies of protest movements at seven universities (Part III); student, faculty, and institutional attitude toward protest and change (Part IV); interpretations and commentaries (Part V).

13. **Goldsen, Rose K., and others.**
What College Students Think.
Princeton, Van Nostrand, 1960. 240 p.

This comprehensive study of student attitudes and values during the period of 1950-55 at 11 colleges is a forerunner of the studies of student behavior of the 1960's. It indicates that students tend, in terms of religion and politics, to take after their parents.

14. **Hayden, Thomas E.**
Rebellion and Repression: Testimony by Tom Hayden before the National Commission on the Causes and Prevention of Violence, and the House Un-American Activities Committee.
New York, Meridian Books, 1969. 186 p.

These edited transcripts of testimony by one of the leading spokesmen for the new left on the events at the Democratic National Convention in August 1968, reflect current radical thought on the draft, the peace movement, the Vietnam War, Black power, general student unrest, and the use of violence (in particular, guerrilla techniques).

15. **Jacobs, Paul, and Saul Landau.**
The New Radicals: A Report with Documents.
New York, Random House, 1966. 333 p.

This collection of essays and documents deals with the new left's origins, development, membership, factions, ideologies, and aims.

16. **Kelman, Steven.**
Push Comes to Shove: The Escalation of Student Protest.

Boston, Houghton Mifflin, 1970. 287 p.

A Harvard student describes the strike at Harvard in April 1969, and offers an evaluation of its causes and results.

17.   **Lipset, Seymour M., and Philip G. Altbach.**
"Student Politics and Higher Education in the U.S." In *Student Politics.* Edited by Seymour M. Lipset. New York, Basic Books, 1967. p. 199-252.

In a descriptive account of the student movement in the mid-1960's, which draws from many empirical studies of the subject, the authors trace the evolution and causes of student activism. This essay is the most important unit of a collection of essays, international in scope and concerned with student involvement in politics and higher education, with particular emphasis on the student movements in emerging nations.

18.   **Lipset, Seymour M., and Philip G. Altbach, eds.**
Students in Revolt.
Boston, Houghton Mifflin, 1969. 561 p.

This compendium of essays reviews the history and nature of various student political movements throughout the world since World War II, and speculates on their possible impact on international politics.

19.   **Lipset, Seymour M., and Sheldon S. Wolin, eds.**
The Berkeley Student Revolt: Facts and Interpretations.
Garden City, N.Y., Doubleday Anchor Books, 1965. 585 p.

In a comprehensive collection of documents and social science studies on the Free Speech Movement of 1964-65, the editors propose "to convey to a wider audience a sense of what took place and what the participants thought and felt. The articles, statements, and documents reflect the powerful feelings aroused by the events; even the editors of this volume were in disagreement."

20.   **Michigan State Senate. Committee to Investigate Campus Disorders and Student Unrest.**
Final Staff Report.

[Lansing, 1970] Mimeograph. Two parts.

The scope and degree of student unrest in Michigan colleges and universities is assessed in this report. Part I presents the staff's study findings and recommendations for legislation, governance, communications, academic affairs, coordination of programs, and campus security. Part II presents special task force reports on a chronology and forecast of student activism, legislative response to student unrest across the country, the creative arts on campus, mass media, college public relations, and campus security.

21. **New York State. Temporary Commission to Study the Causes of Campus Unrest.**
The Academy in Turmoil. First Report.
Albany, 1970. 197 p.

The report presents a preliminary study of the structure of higher education, and the nature and scope of campus unrest in New York State, together with specific recommendations for reforming colleges and universities.

22. *On Strike . . . Shut It Down! A Report of the First National Student Strike in U.S. History.*
Chicago, Urban Research Corp., 1970. 133 p.

The May student strike is presented briefly and is followed by short accounts of the incidents at Kent and Jackson, and by a state-by-state listing of protest activities at colleges and universities across the country during the early part of that month.

23. **Orrick, William H.**
Shut It Down! A College in Crisis: San Francisco State College, October 1968-April 1969. A Report to the National Commission on the Causes and Prevention of Violence.
Washington, U.S. Govt. Print. Off., 1969. 172 p.

This report presents a chronological account of San Francisco State College troubles.

24. **Sanford, Nevitt, ed.**
The American College: A Psychological and Social

Interpretation of Higher Learning.
New York, J. Wiley, 1962. 1084 p.

An extensive summary of all aspects of undergraduate education a decade ago is offered in this volume.

25. **Students for a Democratic Society.**
Port Huron Statement.
New York, Student Department of the League for Industrial Democracy, 1964. 63 p.

This is the constitution adopted by the Students for a Democratic Society (SDS) at the time of its 1962 reorganization convention in Port Huron, Michigan. It contrasts the ideals upon which this country was founded with those which seem to be guiding it today. This document reflects the spirit of SDS in its early stages.

26. **Teodori, Massimo, ed.**
The New Left: A Documentary History.
Indianapolis, Bobbs-Merrill, 1969. 501 p.

This volume assembles a comprehensive collection of documents on the new left, including a history of the movement written by a participant; it is focused mainly on off-campus developments.

27. **U.S. Library of Congress. Legislative Reference Service.**
The New Left: Students for a Democratic Society.
[By] Richard S. Jones.
Washington, 1969. 37 p. Multilith. (GGR 199).

This pamphlet offers a history of the rise of the new left, its relationship to earlier student and leftist groups, discussion of the political and social and university issues with which the new left has become involved.

28. ⊢—————⊣ .
Supplement. [By] Richard S. Jones
Washington, 1969. 20 p. Multilith. (69-251 GGR).

This supplement updates the developments in the SDS movement since the National SDS Convention in Chicago in June 1969; at that time the organization split into a number of different factions with significantly different goals and tactics.

29. U. S. Senate. Committee on Government Operations: Permanent Subcommittee on Investigations.
Staff Study of Campus Riots and Disorders—Oct. 1967-May 1969.
Washington, U.S. Govt. Print. Off., 1969. 52 p.

Disturbances which occurred on college campuses during the period under review are listed here in both chronological and alphabetical order.

30. Zinn, Howard.
SNCC: The New Abolitionists.
Boston, Beacon Press, 1965. 286 p.

Without attempting to give a history of the entire movement, the author describes the first four years of the Student Nonviolent Coordination Committee (1960-64), and focuses on the SNCC leaders, the freedom rides, and the early struggle for civil rights in Mississippi, Georgia, and Alabama.

Chapter 2: The Causes of Student Protest

31. Berger, Peter L., and Richard J. Neuhaus.
Movement and Revolution.
Garden City, N.Y., Doubleday Anchor Books, 1970. 240 p.

In their respective essays, the authors—a conservative and a radical—analyze contemporary youth culture, the new left (especially as it relates to the antiwar movement and the Black power struggle), and current revoluntionary consciousness in America.

32. Block, Jeanne H., Norma Haan, and M. Brewster Smith.
"Activism and Apathy in Contemporary Adolescents." In *Understanding Adolescence: Current Developments in Adolescent Psychology.* Edited by James F. Adams.
Boston, Allyn & Bacon, 1968. p. 198-231.

The authors review literature of student political activism up to 1968, and develop a typology of student political behavior ranging from apathy to radical activism.

33. **Farber, Jerry.**
     "The Student as Nigger." In *The Student as Nigger: Essays and Stories.*
     Los Angeles, Contact Books, 1969. 114-128.

     An ex-California State teacher describes and condemns education in the U.S. from kindergarten through the university as a master-slave relationship.

34. **Feldman, Kenneth A., and Theodore M. Newcomb.**
     The Impact of College on Students.
     San Francisco, Jossey-Bass, 1969. 2 vols.

     The influence of various colleges on the orientation and characteristics of American college students over a four-decade period is analyzed in this study. Volume 1 is an analysis of empirical data integrating a wide variety of studies conducted from the mid-1920's to the mid-1960's; Volume 2 contains summary tables of those studies.

35. **Flacks, Richard.**
     "The Liberated Generation: An Exploration of the Roots of Student Protest."
     Journal of Social Issues, v. 23, July 1967: 52-75.

     This is one of the first empirical studies examining the attitudes of both students and their parents. It shows that white activist students come from affluent backgrounds, are intellectually driven, and morally committed. This issue of the *Journal of Social Issues* contains a collection of articles under the general title, *Stirrings Out of Apathy: Student Activism and the Decade of Protest*, edited by Edward E. Sampson.

36. ├────────────┤ .
     "Social and Cultural Meanings of Student Revolt: Some Informal Comparative Observations."
     Social Problems, v. 7, winter 1970: 340-357.

     The author suggests that families of activist youth have instilled in their children certain humanistic values which are at variance with modern competitive-industrial society. These youth are compelled to self-expression and dissent, especially when they feel society is not living up to their expectations. In this respect the American student movement differs from student movements in other countries.

37. **Glazer, Nathan.**
Remembering the Answers: Essays on the American Student Revolt.
New York, Basic Books, 1970. 320 p.

This recent collection of essays written between 1961 and 1969 reviews selected aspects of the course of American student activism, its national implications, and the author's own changing relation to radical thought and action over the preceding decade.

38. **Gurr, Ted Robert.**
Why Men Rebel.
Princeton, Princeton University Press, 1970. 421 p.

This theoretical inquiry into the nature and sources of political violence makes use of most of the recent empirical literature on violence, and attempts to develop some typologies, propositions, and hypotheses.

39. **Haan, Norma, M. Brewster Smith, and Jeanne Block.**
"Moral Reasoning of Young Adults: Political-Social Behavior, Family Backgrounds, and Personality Correlates."
Journal of Personality and Social Psychology, v. 10, no. 3, 1968: 183-201.

Five types of young adults are examined in this study which points out some ways in which they differ. In general, students "of principled moral reasoning, as contrasted with the conventionally moral, were more active in political-social matters, particularly in protest . . . Perceptions of parental relationships suggest that little conflict or moral separation occurred in the families of the conventionally moral with more in those of the principled."

40. **Hook, Sidney.**
Academic Freedom and Academic Anarchy.
New York, Cowles, 1970. 269 p.

The author examines the sources of the freedoms to teach and learn, the assault on academic freedom and the democratic process in the university, and the issue of the university's political engagement in society. He asserts that "the primary goal of the university . . . is not the quest for virtue or power but the quest for significant truths, their transmission, and critical evaluation." Appendixes are included on the troubles at Berkeley, the SDS and its professorial allies, and the disturbances at the University of Colorado.

41. **Jencks, Christopher, and David Riesman.**
     The Academic Revolution.
     Garden City, N.Y., Doubleday, 1968. 580 p.

     This volume deals with the long-term "evolution" of American higher education. The authors describe the rise to power of the academic profession in America and the role it played in mass higher education and the spread of achievement-oriented values. Incisive treatment is offered of the development of graduate and professional schools, as well as denominational and black colleges.

42. **Keniston, Kenneth.**
     The Uncommitted: Alienated Youth in American Society.
     New York, Harcourt, Brace & World, 1965. 500 p.

     The author investigates the social and psychological roots of alienation in college youth and demonstrates how this alienation leads them to reject established American values and to adopt noncommitment as a way of life.

43. ⊢————————⊣ .
     "What's Bugging the Students?"
     Educational Record, v. 51, spring 1970: 116-129.

     Some factors contributing to student unrest are analyzed, and nine suggestions are offered for change in response "to the grievances of those who believe their interests have been neglected."

44. ⊢————————⊣ .
     Young Radicals: Notes on Committed Youth.
     New York, Harcourt, Brace & World, 1968. 368 p.

     A perceptive psychological analysis of radical youth involved in antiwar activities during the summer of 1967, this study was one of the first to claim that young radicals are not actually rebelling against their parents, but are trying to live what their parents preached.

45. **Kerpelman, Larry C.**
"Student Political Activism and Ideology: Comparative Characteristics of Activists and Nonactivists."
Journal of Counseling Psychology, v. 16, no 1, 1969: 8-13.

Activism can be left, middle, or right. So can nonactivism. This brief analysis focuses on the relationship between activism and ideology and searches for characteristics associated with each. "The results indicate the necessity of separating ideology from activism in investigations of student political activists."

46. **Marcuse, Herbert.**
One-Dimensional Man: Studies in the Ideology of Advanced Industrial Society.
Boston, Beacon Press, 1969. 260 p.

In a philosophical analysis of contemporary society, the author challenges the traditional notion of the neutrality of technology, and asserts that it has generated a tendency toward totalitarianism. This book has exerted great influence on the new left students' concept of political reality.

47. **Roszak, Theodore.**
The Making of a Counter Culture: Reflections on the Technocratic Society and Its Youthful Opposition.
Garden City, N.Y., Doubleday Anchor Books, 1969. 303 p.

Voicing a new left humanistic protest against the technocratic society, the author examines sources of the counterculture and suggests new modes of human creativity and community life.

48. **Schwab, Joseph J.**
College Curriculum and Student Protest.
Chicago, University of Chicago Press, 1969. 303 p.

The author examines the style, expression, and some of the content of student protest as it reflects curricular deficiencies. He surveys curricular resources for combatting these deficiencies and makes specific practical recommendations.

49. **Skolnick, Jerome H.**
The Politics of Protest. A report submitted by Jerome

H. Skolnick, Director, Task Force on Violent Aspects of Protest and Confrontation of the National Commission on the Causes and Prevention of Violence. Washington, U.S. Govt. Print. Off. [1969] 276 p., and New York, Simon and Schuster [1969] 419 p.

In his study of mass protest in America (viewed as a normal phenomenon), the author asserts that violence is not an essential concomitant of protest, but usually occurs spontaneously "out of interaction between protestors and responding authorities . . . . Recommendations concerning the prevention of violence which do not address the issue of fundamental social and political change are fated to be largely irrelevent and frequently self-defeating."

50. **Slater, Philip E.**
The Pursuit of Loneliness: American Culture at the Breaking Point.
Boston, Beacon Press, 1970. 154 p.

The author examines the assumptions and themes that shaped contemporary American culture and have now begun to split it apart, including the American addiction to technology and individualism as substitutes for human cooperation, and an eagerness to substitute fantasy for gratification.

51. **Susajima, Masu, Junius A. Davis, and Richard E. Peterson.**
"Organized Student Protest and Institutional Climate."
American Educational Research Journal, v. 5, May 1968: 291-304.

This analytic study represents an attempt to determine whether the degree and kind of student protest is related to college climate as assessed by the College and University Environment Scales (CUES). While CUES did not predict protest over campus problems, it served as a reasonably good predictor of student protest over off-campus issues.

52. **Watts, William A., Steve Lynch, and David Whittaker.**
"Alienation and Activism in Today's College-Age Youth: Socialization Patterns and Current Family

Relationships."
Journal of Counseling Psychology, v. 16, no. 1,
1969: 1-7.

This study, conducted at Berkeley, compares a group of student activists, a nonstudent sample, and a random sample of Berkeley students. "Both the activists and the nonstudents scored high on anomie; but, whereas the nonstudents were estranged from their families, the activists were not. Differences in socialization patterns, current attitudes and values are reported and discussed in terms of their relevance to the question of whether societal rejection takes the form of active confrontation or passive withdrawal."

53. **Westby, David L., and Richard G. Braungart.**
"Class and Politics in the Family Backgrounds of Student Political Activists."
American Sociological Review, v. 31, Oct. 1966: 690-692.

The data gathered from university student political organizations representing the far left and far right, suggest that leftist students come predominantly from upper-middle-class backgrounds, while those on the political right are more likely to be lower-middle-class or working-class in origin.

54. **Youth In Turmoil.**
Adapted from a Special Issue of *Fortune* [Jan. 1969].
New York, Time-Life Books, 1969. 159 p.

A collection of articles on young Americans explores a wide range of subjects—from their beliefs and ideals to their effect on American business, pop culture, universities, and political life.

Chapter 3: The Black Student Movement

55. **Baldwin, James.**
The Fire Next Time.
New York, Dial Press, 1963. 120 p.

In this influential essay the author warned white America of the pent-up fury among black Americans.

56. **Barbour, Floyd, ed.**
The Black Power Revolt: A Collection of Essays.
Boston, Extending Horizons Books, 1968. 287 p.

The editor has compiled an important collection of essays
dealing with Black identity and awareness and the history,
ideology, and implementation of Black power.

57. **Bayer, Alan E., and Robert F. Boruch.**
"Black and White Freshmen Entering Four Year
Colleges."
Educational Record, v. 50, fall 1969: 371-386.

In their comparison of black and white college students, the
authors examine data on recruitment, registrations, family and
educational backgrounds, aspirations, and suggest some
practical steps to aid disadvantaged students.

58. **Bennett, Lerone, Jr.**
Confrontation Black and White.
Chicago, Johnson Publishing Co., 1965. 301 p.

After analyzing the confrontations between black and white
Americans, the author argues that Blacks can no longer rely on
interracial civil rights movements to win their freedom and that
black leaders must now take the initiative to free the oppressed
and attain social justice.

59. *Black Studies: Myths and Realities.* Introd. by Bayard
Rustin.
[New York] A. Philip Randolph Educational Fund,
1969. 45 p.

This collection of seven essays explains the concept of Black
studies and explores the positive and the negative potential of
Black studies programs.

60. **Bond, Horace M.**
*The Education of the Negro in the American Social
Order.* With a new preface and an additional chapter
by the author.

New York, Octagon Books, 1966. 531 p.

First published in 1934, this is a comprehensive discussion of Negro education in the U.S. organized into three sections: (1) history; (2) geographic and socio-economic analysis of the education of Blacks in the North and South; (3) the problems and challenges in education facing Blacks, together with specific suggestions for change and improvement.

The current edition contains a new chapter, "A 1965 Retrospective of American Negro Education" (p. 464-494), which, following roughly the same divisions as in the original volume, updates the work to 1964. The author shows that educational success depends upon the degree of acculturation and assimilation to the larger mainstream culture. Social and educational changes thus must go hand in hand.

61. **Carmichael, Stokely, and Charles V. Hamilton.**
Black Power: The Politics of Liberation in America.
New York, Vintage Books, 1967. 198 p.

"T.C.B."—taking care of business, the business of Blacks—is discussed by analyzing the development of black and white power, especially Black economic power.

62. **Clark, Kenneth B.**
Dark Ghetto: Dilemmas of Social Power.
New York, Harper & Row, 1965. 251 p.

This influential study of the Negro ghetto (based on data from Harlem) deals with the social dynamics, psychology, pathology, educational system, and power structure of the ghetto. It pictures the combined problems of the slum and the Negro who "believes himself to be closely confined to the pervasive low status of the ghetto, and in fact usually is."

63. **Cleaver, Eldridge.**
Soul on Ice.
New York, McGraw-Hill, 1967. 225 p.

Notes and thoughts written in jail by a talented writer and leader of the Black Panthers.

64. **Commission on Higher Educational Opportunities in the South.**
The Negro and Higher Education in the South, a Statement.
[Atlanta] Southern Regional Education Board, 1967. 48 p.

The statement focuses on the predominately Negro colleges and the thorny problem of providing equal higher educational opportunities in the South. Several recommendations are urged pertaining to planning, mass educational opportunities, student progress, instruction, curriculum, inter-institutional cooperation and administration, and financial support.

65. **Cruse, Harold.**
The Crisis of the Negro Intellectual.
New York, Wm. Morrow, 1967. 594 p.

The author weighs the question of integration versus separatism and strongly advocates black cultural nationalism.

66. **Dollard, John.**
Caste and Class in a Southern Town. 2nd ed.
New York, Harper, 1949. 520 p.

In-depth report by a white social psychologist depicts the attitudes and problems of blacks and whites in a small southern town during the last years of Jim Crow.

67. **Drake, St. Clair, and Horace R. Cayton.**
Black Metropolis: A Study of Negro Life in a Northern City. [Rev. & enl. ed.]
New York, Harcourt Brace & World, 1970. 2 vols.

Two black sociologists present a detailed study of the Chicago ghetto in the 1930's. The first volume deals primarily with race relations; the second, with ghetto life. The authors cover almost every aspect of social life including politics, religion, and education.

68. **Edwards, Harry.**
     Black Students.
     New York, Free Press, 1970. 234 p.

     The history, characteristics, philosophies, and future of the
     Black student movement are discussed in this volume.

69. **Ellison, Ralph.**
     Invisible Man.
     New York, Random House, 1952. 439 p.

     This is an influential novel about the "invisible man"—the
     young Black whose existence is systematically denied by
     American society.

70. **Essien-Udom, Essien Uudosen.**
     *Black Nationalism: A Search for an Identity in
     America.*
     Chicago, University of Chicago Press, 1962. 367 p.

     This work by an African scholar studies the Black Muslims and
     other black nationalist groups in the United States.

71. **Fanon, Frantz.**
     Black Skins, White Masks. Translated by Charles Lam
     Markham.
     New York, Grove Press, 1967. 232 p.

     The author explores the dual role a black man must adopt in
     order to survive in a white Western society. He demonstrates
     that this dual role-playing is largely responsible for the
     distorted sense of identity and inferiority experienced by black
     people.

72. ┝─────────┥.
     Wretched of the Earth. Translated by Constance
     Farrington.
     New York, Grove Press [1965] 255 p.

     The author develops the concept of the Third World in this

volume and expresses the belief that a mental and spiritual revolution against Western values must precede the development of cultural identity and awareness by non-Western, formerly colonial, people. His justification for violence as a necessary liberating influence among ex-colonial peoples has influenced both black and white radical thinking on the validity of the tactical use of violence.

73. **Franklin, John Hope.**
From Slavery to Freedom: A History of Negro Americans. 3rd ed.
New York, Knopf, 1967. 686 p.

Written by one of the nation's most distinguished black scholars, this is a comprehensive history of Blacks in America.

74. **Frazier, E. Franklin.**
Black Bourgeoisie.
New York, Free Press, 1967. 264 p.

In a sociological analysis of the behavior, attitudes, and the values of the black middle class, the author attempts to assess the economic, educational, political, and cultural status of the black bourgeoisie and to study the "behavior and values of the isolated social world of this segment of the Negro population."

75. **Goodman, Mary Ellen.**
Race Awareness in Young Children.
New York, Collier, 1964. 351 p.

Causes and effects of race recognition among young black and white children provide the material for this psychological study.

76. **Gurin, Patricia, and Daniel Katz.**
Motivation and Aspiration in the Negro College.
Ann Arbor, Survey Research Center, Institute for Social Research, University of Michigan, 1966. 346 p.

This analysis, based on questionnaires and personal interviews, of the occupational aspirations of students in 10 predominately Negro colleges in the Deep South, takes into account students' pre-college backgrounds, occupational choices, and the influence on those choices of a variety of factors including sex differences; social class; family job, education, and income status; motivational characteristics; and the effects on the students of the institutions they attended. The research for this study was made possible by a contract with United States Office of Education.

77. **Institute for Higher Educational Opportunity.**
Special Financial Needs of Traditionally Negro Colleges: A Task Force Report.
Atlanta, Southern Regional Education Board, 1969. [14 p.]

This report studies the current financial needs of black colleges, which have always been underfinanced. It carefully evaluates the deficiencies of these schools and the costs of remedying them, suggests alternate forms of special funding required by public and private institutions and offers a rationale for providing special and basic operating funds to these Black colleges and universities.

78. **Isaacs, Harold R.**
The New World of Negro Americans.
New York, John Day, 1963. 366 p.

The author describes the influence of the newly emerging African states on the civil rights movement and Black nationalism in America.

79. **Keil, Charles.**
Urban Blues.
Chicago, University of Chicago Press, 1966. 231 p.

Focusing on the blues singer as a cultural hero, the author discusses some Black ghetto values—in particular, the basic male-female conflict of ghetto life, the concept of "soul" and its relation to the community's sense of solidarity, and the rejection of white values.

80. **King, Martin Luther, Jr.**
Where Do We Go from Here: Chaos or Community?

New York, Harper & Row, 1967. 192 p.

A long roster of failures, frustrations, and limited opportunities of the black man in modern society leads to a proposal of a society built on integrated equality, not Black power, and a consideration of methods for achieving economic power.

81. **Little, Malcolm.**
The Autobiography of Malcolm X. With the assistance of Alex Haley. Introd. by M.S. Handler. Epilogue by Alex Haley.
New York, Grove Press, 1965. 5 455 p.

Malcolm X's life story chronicles the evolution of one of the most influential black leaders in America in this centry.

82. **McGrath, Earl J.**
The Predominantly Negro Colleges and Universities in Transition.
New York, published for the Institute of Higher Education by the Bureau of Publications, Teachers College, Columbia University, 1965. 204 p.

This study analyzes the kinds of education available in Negro institutions and the numbers and typology of students enrolled in these programs, and it contains suggestions for extending and improving existing opportunities.

83. **McEvoy, James, and Abraham Miller.**
Black Power and Student Rebellion.
Belmont, Calif., Wadsworth Publishing Co., 1969. 440 p.

This compendium of historical narratives and empirical, analytical studies represents a broad spectrum of opinion on the meaning, origins, and possible future directions of current student unrest and the Black power movement on campus. Of special interest: "Negro Students and the Protest Movement" by Donald Matthews and James Prothro (p. 379-418), and "The Sources of Student Dissent" by Kenneth Keniston (p. 309-339).

84. **Myrdal, Gunnar.**
An American Dilemma.
New York, Harper & Row, 1944. 2 vols.

In what is perhaps the most influential book ever published on racial problems in America, Myrdal points out the contradiction between the stated egalitarian ideals of the United States and the existence of racial segregation.

85. **Robinson, Armstead L., Craig C. Foster, Donald H. Ogilvie, eds.**
Black Studies in the University: A Symposium.
New York, Bantam, 1969. 241 p.

This compendium of papers and discussions, originally presented at Yale in spring 1968, concerns the intellectual and political relevance of Afro-American programs.

86. **Silberman, Charles E.**
Crisis in Black and White.
New York, Vintage Books, 1964. 370 p.

This well-written account analyzes the racial dilemma in America in terms of its impact on black and white Americans. It is an unusually evenhanded and well-written study.

87. **Southern Regional Education Board.**
New Careers and Curriculum Change. Report of a Conference on Curricular Change in the Traditionally Negro Colleges for New Career Opportunities.
Atlanta, 1968. 61 p.

This study reviews "existing curricula as to their relevancy to and adequacy for manpower needs" and makes specific recommendations for accelerating curricular changes and additions.

88. **U.S. Federal Interagency Committee on Education.**
Federal Agencies and Black Colleges.
Washington, U.S. Govt. Print. Off., 1970. 45 p.

The final FICE report to the President deals with the current federal support offered to Black colleges and to white colleges by all government agencies with educational programs. The report points up the inequities in the amount given to Black schools (only 3 per cent of the total outlay to institutions of higher learning), offers specific short- and long-range recommendations; to appear also as a chapter in the forthcoming major study by FICE entitled *The Black Colleges: A National Resource* (publication pending). A revised edition containing data is currently in press.

89. Wilson, James Q.
Negro Politics: The Search for Leadership.
Glencoe, Ill., Free Press, 1960. 342 p.

A classic study of Negro politics in several major American cities, this volume remains valuable in describing black involvement in traditional party politics in urban areas.

90. *The White Problem in America.*
By the Editors of *Ebony.*
Chicago, Johnson Publishing Co., 1966. 181 p.

This collection of essays originally appeared in the August 1965 issue of *Ebony*, and examined various aspects of white American society. The essays argue that the causes of racial problems are rooted in white American society, and that the power and the responsibility to eliminate those problems are principally white America's.

91. Woodson, Carter G.
The Mis-education of the Negro.
Washington, Associated Publishers, 1969. 215 p.

First published in 1933, this is one of the earliest examinations of the inadequacies resulting from the exclusive adherence to traditional university curricula for black students. The author feels that the traditional approach miseducates the black man by forcing him to adopt foreign—i.e., white—values and ideals.

92. Young, Richard P., ed.
Roots of Rebellion: The Evolution of Black Politics and Protest Since World War II.
New York, Harper & Row, 1970. 482 p.

The essays in this collection have been selected with an eye to giving the reader "a broad view of the factors responsible for the growth of black frustration and militancy." Accordingly, they focus their fury on: the response to racism, the reality of the ghetto, the development of Black pride, Black politics and protest, and the evolving ideology and future of the Black revolution.

Chapter 4: The University's Response to Campus Disorder

93. **American Bar Association. Commission on Campus Government and Student Dissent.**
   Report.
   Chicago, American Bar Association [1970]. 36 p.

   This report, divided into two sections (the protection of freedom of expression and the maintenance of order with justice), attempts to formulate principles and procedures for open, free dissent within the university while maintaining the order necessary for the continuance of the educational processes for which the university exists.

94. **American Civil Liberties Union.**
   Academic Freedom, Academic Responsibility, Academic Due Process in Institutions of Higher Learning.
   New York, 1966. 17 p.

   "Principles concerning the civil liberties and obligations of teachers, and desirable procedures involving academic freedom in public and private colleges and universities" are formulated in this ACLU pamphlet.

95. **Bealle, J. Rufus.**
   "NACUA [National Association of College and University Attorneys] Report to the American Council on Education on the Use of Injunctions against Campus Disorders."
   College Counsel, v. 4, no. 2, 1969: 1-10.

   The use of the injunction is reviewed in this report and a survey made of institutional willingness or reluctance to use injunctions.

96. **Comment.** "Judicial Control of the Riot Curfew."
   Yale Law Journal, v. 77, 1968: 1560-1573.

   This note examines the nature and the use of the curfew,

positive and negative aspects of its use, the power to impose a curfew, its relationship to martial law and police power, particular issues involving preventive curfews, and curfews of limited geographic scope.

97.   **Fairlie, Henry.**
"How to Keep a Campus Together."
Interplay, v. 3, July 1970: 4-12.

A British reporter in residence at the University of Colorado at Boulder describes the disruptions at that campus during spring 1970 and analyzes the administration's tactics in handling these disruptions in a way that prevented the occurrence of serious confrontations.

98.   **Fischer, Thomas C.**
Due Process in the Student-Institutional Relationship.
Washington, American Association of State Colleges and Universities, 1970. 37 p.

Concerned only with public institutions of higher learning and addressed to university officials and responsible student leaders, this report presents "(1) a lay understanding of the *real* meaning of 'due process', (2) an appreciation of the current status of the academy before the courts, (3) the elements of fair and just dealing in student discipline cases which should meet the 'due process' requirements, (4) methods for initiating an adjudicatory system and procedures which will assure that these requirements are met," and other issues.

99.   **Georgia, University of. Institute of Higher Education.**
The Legal Aspects of Student Discipline in Higher Education.
Athens, 1970. 65 p.

The legal relationship between the student and the university, especially in the area of student discipline, is examined and documented.

100.   **Herman, Joseph.**
"Injunctive Control of Disruptive Student Demonstrations."

Virginia Law Review, v. 56, spring 1970: 215-238.

Some legal issues raised by the use of injunctions against campus disorders are discussed briefly but comprehensively.

101. **Holmes, Grace W., ed.**
Student Protest and the Law.
Ann Arbor, Mich., Institute of Continuing Legal Education, 1969. 403 p.

The full range of student, university, police, and court interrelationships, including the issue of the constitutional protection of protest on campus, is explored in this edited transcript of a Symposium on Law and Student Protest. Supporting documents include pleadings, injunctive orders, judicial guidelines, and student codes.

102. **Johnston, Orville W.**
"Amnesty vs. Order on College Campuses."
School and Society, v. 96, Oct. 26, 1968: 364-365.

This brief article urges administrative openness and willingness to cooperate in constructive change; and it contends that demands for amnesty after violent protest are self-defeating, because they prevent the inequities protested from coming to society's attention.

103. **Joughin, Louis, ed.**
Academic Freedom and Tenure: A Handbook of the American Association of University Professors.
Madison, University of Wisconsin Press, 1967. 343 p.

This important compendium presents cases and statements of AAUP regarding faculty and students' academic freedom.

104. **Lankes, George.**
"Campus Violence and the Law."
Police Chief, v. 37, Mar. 1970: 38-42.

Some incidents leading to the formulation and enactment of laws dealing with campus disorders and focusing particularly on the current status of the New York State law are discussed.

105 "Legal Aspects of Student-Institutional Relationships."
Denver Law Journal, v. 45, no. 4 (special issue) 1968: 497-678.

This collection of papers and prepared responses was originally presented at a conference in Denver, Colo., May 16-18, 1968, which examined the legal aspects of students' relationships to the university. Contributors include Logan Wilson ("Campus Freedom and Order"), William M. Beaney ("Students, Higher Education, and the Law"), Terry F. Lunsford ("Who Are Members of the University Community?"), Robert B. McKay ("The Student as Private Citizen"), William Van Alstyne ("The Student as University Resident"), William Cohen ("The Private-Public Legal Aspects of Institutions of Higher Education"), and Phillip Monypenny ("The Student as a Student").

106. **Momboisse, Raymond M.**
"Tactics for Colleges Facing Student Demonstrations."
College and University Business, v. 44, May 1968: 126-128, 131, 140.

This article outlines briefly the typical stages in the escalation of a protest, and suggests a number of practical responses for college administrators (and police, if necessary).

107. **New York University. School of Law.**
Student Conduct and Discipline Proceedings in a University Setting: Proposed Codes with Commentary and Bibliography.
New York, 1968. 36 p.

Student rights and responsibilities, the relationship between students and the university, and the rationale for student discipline are discussed.

108. **Rosenthal, Robert R.**
"Injunctive Relief against Campus Disorders."
University of Pennsylvania Law Review, v. 118, Apr. 1970: 746-765.

The author argues in favor of granting injunctions to colleges in the case of repeated trespasses on campus.

109. **Singletary, Otis A.**
Freedom and Order on Campus.
Washington, American Council on Education, 1968.
16 p.

The author treats the subject of students' rights and due process in a concise and thorough fashion.

110. **Williamson, E. G., and John L. Cowan.**
The American Student's Freedom of Expression: A Research Appraisal.
Minneapolis, Univ. of Minnesota Press, 1966. 193 p.

The authors present the results of a survey of 1,000 colleges in 1964, focusing on the questions of censorship, freedom of expression, and students' right to invite outside speakers.

111. **Wright, Charles Alan.**
"The Constitution on the Campus."
Vanderbilt Law Review, v. 22, Oct. 1969: 1027-1088.

The author's principal thesis is that "the full First Amendment, and not some watered-down version of it, applies on campus." He also examines students' procedural rights, concluding that courts will accept "any institutional procedure so long as it is reasonably calculated to be fair to the student involved and to lead to a reliable determination of the issues."

Chapter 5: The Law Enforcement Response

112. **Bayley, David H., and Harold Mendelsohn.**
Minorities and the Police: Confrontation in America.
New York, Free Press, 1969. 209 p.

The authors describe the nature of the relationship between the police and the community, especially minority groups; they analyze the factors which produce strain and suspicions; and make specific recommendations for improving police-community relations.

113. **Chevigny, Paul.**
Police Power: Police Abuses in New York City.
New York, Pantheon Books, 1969. 298 p.

In a case study of abuses by New York City police officers,

the author describes patterns of police conduct and indicates that abuse is likely to occur whenever police are allowed or encouraged to disregard professional standards of conduct by the department itself, by the courts, and by American society at large.

114.   **Coates, Joseph F.**
Nonlethal Weapons for Use by U.S. Law Enforcement Officers.
Arlington, Va., Institute for Defense Analyses, 1967. 125 p. (Institute for Defense Analyses. Study S-271)

The author examines situations in which nonlethal weapons are appropriate and discusses limitations on the use of such weapons.

115.   **Crockett, Thompson.**
Police Chemical Agents Manual.
Washington, International Association of Chiefs of Police, Professional Standards Division [1969]. 193 p.

This manual is intended to provide comprehensive and sound information relating to the use of chemical agents in the achievement of police objectives.

116.   **Drescher, Earl L.**
"Diary of a Peace March."
Police Chief, v. 37, Mar. 1970: 16-24.

The November 15, 1969, moratorium in Washington demonstrated that cooperation and careful planning between the protest organizers and the police can prevent major disorders.

117.   **"The Guard vs. Disorder."**
The National Guardsman, v. 24, June 1970: 2-7, 9-13, 40.

The role played by the National Guard in specific instances of campus, racial, and labor unrest during the stormy period of April 15-May 19, 1970, is reviewed state by state. The Active Army's "Rules of Engagement" are discussed and recommended as guidelines for the Guard's use when not in active federal service. Some guardsmen's reactions to the violence at Kent State are also included.

118. **Higham, Robin, ed.**
Bayonets in the Streets: The Use of Troops in Civil Disturbances.
[Lawrence] University Press of Kansas, 1969. 225 p.

In this collection of essays on the employment of military forces in civil disorders in the U.S., the following topics are discussed: the traditional conflict between the military and the liberal intellectual establishment; the numerous difficulties faced by the army in civil disorder control; the effectiveness of properly trained forces; and the nature of military professionalism.

119. **International Association of Chiefs of Police.**
"Campus Disorders." In *The Police Yearbook 1970: Containing the Papers and Proceedings of the Seventy-sixth Annual Conference of the International Association of Chiefs of Police, Inc., Miami, Florida, Sept, 27-Oct. 2, 1969.*
Washington, 1970. p. 46-58.

Prepared workshop statements on campus unrest and police response in 1969 by Chief William P. Beall, Prof. Herman Goldstein, and Mr. Henry S. Reith, Jr., are followed by an open discussion among the workshop leaders and participants.

120. **International Association of Chiefs of Police. Research and Development Division.**
Police Capabilities, Problems, and Needs in Dealing with Civil Disorders. A Report submitted to the President's Advisory Committee on Civil Disorders.
Washington, 1967. 99 p.

This preliminary report assesses the current capabilities of a sample of police forces in the planning, training, and actual handling of civil disorders. It points up tactical, legal, economic, political, media, and community problems, emphasizes the need for good communications among all levels involved in crowd control, and makes specific recommendations to enable police forces to remedy deficiencies in their handling of civil disorders.

121. **Marx, Gary T.**
"Civil Disorders and the Agents of Social Control."

Journal of Social Issues, v. 26, winter 1970. In press.

Breakdowns in police behavior in the midst of a racial disturbance have on occasion aggravated disorder. Some of the contexts in which this has happened are examined by the author. The last of the three sections discusses major causal factors of such breakdowns (inappropriate control strategies, lack of coordination among and within various control units, and breakdown of police organization), and suggests how they can be prevented.

122 . **Kobetz, Richard, and Carl W. Hamm, eds., with commentary.**
Campus Unrest: Dialogue or Destruction? Proceedings of the IACP Workshop for State Police Officials and Campus Security Directors, the University of Nebraska, Lincoln, Nebraska, May, 1970.
Washington, International Association of Chiefs of Police, 1970. 160 p.

These proceedings of a workshop for law enforcement personnel on the problems associated with campus unrest, disorder, and violence include papers on police relationships with the campus, the creation of a secure campus environment, psychological methods and considerations in police personnel administration, and the role of the National Guard in campus disorders. An appendix contains examples of campus regulations and disciplinary procedures and a statement of police responsibilities, attitudes, and guidelines for action.

123 . **Momboisse, Raymond M.**
Control of Student Disorders.
Sacramento, Calif., MSM Enterprises, 1968. 83 p.

Student activists and their tactics are described in this discussion of measures for dealing with disturbances, including the preparation of a flexible emergency plan.

124 . ├───────────┤ .
Industrial Security for Strikes, Riots and Disasters.
Springfield, Ill., C. C. Thomas, 1968. 496 p.

This volume presents information of value to campus police in the areas of communication, control of authorized entry, and in-transit security, and general aspects of maintaining an efficient guard force. It also considers the unique security and managerial problems that arise during a strike, demonstration, civil disobedience, and riot.

125.   ├──────────┤.
Riots, Revolts and Insurrections.
Springfield, Ill., C. C. Thomas, 1967. 523 p.

The emotional and psychological factors leading to the formation of crowds and mobs, the techniques of inciting a mob to riot, and the planning and organizational problems of the police and governmental agencies (as well as some guidelines) are included in this presentation of methods of controlling crowds, demonstrations, sit-ins, riots, and insurrections.

126.   **National League of Cities and U.S. Conference of Mayors.**
Street Crime and the Safe Streets Act: What is the Impact? An Examination of State Planning and Dollar Distribution Practices under the Omnibus Crime Control and Safe Streets Act of 1968.
Washington, 1970. 28 [1] p.

The processes developed by the states to allocate funds under the Safe Streets Act during its first year of operation are analyzed critically. The study indicates that state regional boards have generally failed to allocate proportionate funds to high-crime urban areas. Recommendations include a reorganization of the grant system with greater emphasis on urban areas and increased level of assistance under the Act and reduction of matching ratios.

127.   **National Urban Coalition.**
Law and Disorder II: State Planning and Programming under Title I of the Omnibus Crime Control and Safe Streets Act of 1968.
Washington, 1970. 43 p.

The administration of the Act is criticized because it has resulted in dissipating action funds for minor programs in low-crime areas. The failure of federal and state leadership, the operation of state agencies, and the planning process are studied. The report also presents a state-by-state breakdown of allocations (as of mid-March 1970), and makes specific recommendations for improving the Title I program.

128.　Note. "Riot Control and the Use of Federal Troops."
　　　Harvard Law Review, v. 81, 1968: 638-652.

The role of federal troops in civil disturbances in the past and the policies governing their use are examined in an effort to determine whether the standards are still applicable today.

129.　**Rosenthal, Carl F.**
　　　Phases of Civil Disturbances: Characteristics and Problems.
　　　Washington, American University, Center for Research in Social Systems, 1969. 66 p.

The author studies the phases in the social process that culminate in a civil disorder, indicates the most important problem areas in maintaining law and order during each phase, and suggests some effective countermeasures to civil disorders.

130.　*Some to Demonstrate, Some to Destroy.* (Motion Picture)
　　　Washington Metropolitan Police Dept. Made by Audio-Visual Specialties. Released by International Association of Chiefs of Police, 1970: 23 min. sd. color. 16 mm.

This excellent presentation of police tactics in handling demonstrators was filmed during the November 1969 Moratorium Weekend in Washington. The movie focuses on the minimal use of force and tight police control during the march. It explains the principle of leaving avenues of escape open to demonstrators, and the correct use of tear gas.

131.　**Smith, R. Dean, and Richard W. Kobetz.**
　　　Guidelines for Civil Disorder and Mobilization Planning.
　　　[Washington] International Association of Chiefs of Police, Research Development and Planning Division, 1968. 77 p.

This booklet is a comprehensive planning manual for police departments.

132. **Trickey, F. David.**
      "Constitutional and Statutory Bases of Governors'
      Emergency Powers."
      Michigan Law Review, v. 64, Dec. 1965: 290-307.

      In this study the author attempts to evaluate the sources,
      scope, and limitations of governors' emergency powers. He
      focuses primarily on "the extreme breadth of executive
      emergency authority and in particular, upon the power to use
      military force during times of public emergency."

133. **U.S. Army. Military Police School, Ft. Gordon, Ga.**
      Riot Control. Special Text.
      Ft. Gordon, Ga., 1964. 273 p. (ST-19-180)

      This special text provides law enforcement personnel with
      concepts, procedures, methods, and techniques which can be
      used in planning for peaceful assemblies, prevention of civil
      disorders, and restoration of order.

134. **U.S. Army.**
      Civil Disturbances and Disasters.
      Washington, 1968. [150 p.] (FM 19-15)

      Guidelines (policies, legal considerations, operational tech-
      niques and tactics) for preparing for and controlling civil
      disturbances and the support of disaster relief operations are
      provided in this comprehensive field manual.

135. **U.S. Federal Bureau of Investigation.**
      Prevention and Control of Mobs and Riots.
      Washington, U.S. Govt. Print. Off., 1968. 111 p.

      This manual, based on the Army's FM 19-15 (No. 134),
      emphasizes the need for prevention of violence; highlights
      some factors contributing to civil disturbances, and outlines
      legal and tactical procedures in preparing for and controlling
      riots.

136. **U.S. President. Commission on Law Enforcement and
      Administration of Justice.**
      Task Force Report: The Police.
      Washington, U.S. Govt. Print. Off., 1967. 239 p.

      All aspects of police structure, organization, management,

coordination and consolidation of services, policies and decision-making, internal and external controls, police-community relationships, professional standards are reviewed in this thorough analysis.

137.   **U.S. Task Force on Law and Law Enforcement.**
Rights in Concord: The Response to Counter-Inaugural Protest Activities in Washington.
A staff report of the National Commission on the Causes and Prevention of Violence [submitted by Joseph R. Sahid].
Washington, U.S. Govt. Print. Off., 1969. 120 p.

The cooperation between political leaders, police, and protestors in planning a demonstration is shown to be effective. Tight control by D.C. police prevented violence.

138.   **Walker, Daniel.**
Rights in Conflict: The violent confrontation of demonstrators and police in the parks and streets of Chicago during the week of the Democratic National Convention of 1968.
A report submitted by Daniel Walker, Director of the Chicago Study Team of the National Commission on the Causes and Prevention of Violence.
New York, New American Library, 1968. 324 p.

The author indicates that the actions of political leaders in refusing to cooperate with the protest leaders in the planning of protest events eventually resulted in trouble.

139.   **Wilson, James Q.**
Varieties of Police Behavior: The Management of Law and Order in Eight Communities.
Cambridge, Mass., Harvard Univ. Press, 1968. 309 p.

In an in-depth study of eight cities, the author relates the police style and the political style in each city. The problems faced by city mayors in dealing with police policy are examined, as well as the difficulties of police administrators in formulating that policy.

Chapter 6: University Reform

140. *Agony and Promise: Current Issues in Higher Education, 1969.* Edited by G. Kerry Smith.
San Francisco, Jossey-Bass, 1969. 282 p.

This collection of essays, addressed to some fundamental issues facing current higher education, suggests that it is no longer possible for the problems of academia to be considered apart from those of society at large.

141. **American Association for Higher Education.**
A Productive Voice for Students: A working paper on campus governance prepared for the National Summer Conference for Academic Deans, July 31, 1967. [By] Morris Keeton.
Washington, 1968. 10 p.

Some factors to be considered in choosing a particular form of shared responsibility for the governance of a college or university are discussed.

142. **Barzun, Jacques.**
The American University: How It Runs, Where It Is Going.
New York, Harper and Row, 1968. 319 p.

In a somewhat traditional fashion, the author analyzes the present and future of American higher education and offers numerous suggestions for the future of the educational enterprise. The concluding chapter, "The Choices Ahead," proposes in entertaining fashion many choices that the author believes a university must make if it is to determine what its fundamental purpose and philosophy are and if it is to reflect these in all its activities.

143. **Caffrey, John, ed.**
The Future Academic Community: Continuity and Change.
Washington, American Council on Education, 1969. 327 p.

This represents some recent thinking among university administrators, students, and professional educators on what is happening in the university today and how it will affect its future.

144.   "The Embattled University."
Daedalus, v. 99, winter 1970: 1-224.

The transition from class-based to mass education, the idea of university as a community, the design for the university, and issues of governance and dissent are among the subjects included in this series of essays on the major shifts in contemporary higher education.

145.   **Flack, Michael J.**
"Innovation and the University in Crisis: Three Proposals."
Educational Record, v. 49, summer 1968: 347-349.

The author suggests three innovations—appointment of an ombudsman, establishment of an all-university council, and setting up of a "hearings" panel—all of which could profitably be used to improve communications, widen responsibilities, and check growing polarization on today's campuses.

146.   **Hazen Foundation. Committee on the Student in Higher Education.**
The Student in Higher Education.
New Haven, 1968. 66 p.

This critical examination of higher education presents a perspective on the various social and psychological influences which shape the interests, attitudes, and activities of students; and it suggests some alternative ways in which the college can create a situation facilitating the intellectual and emotional growth and maturation of the student while fully respecting his freedom. The report contends that such alternatives do exist, and that "given the size and complexity of American higher education and the inarticulate restlessness of its students, the alternatives have ceased to be optional."

147.   **Hodgkinson, Harold L.**
Institutions in Transition: A Study of Change in Higher Education.

Berkeley, Carnegie Commission on Higher Education, 1970. 169 p.

The first of a two-part study presents a statistical analysis of qualitative and quantitative changes in 1,230 institutions of higher learning during the last three decades. (The second part, not yet published, will be more general and interpretive.)

148. **Jaspers, Karl.**
The Idea of the University.
Edited by Karl W. Deutsch. Translated by H.A.T. Reiche and H. F. Vanderschmidt.
Boston, Beacon Press, 1959. 135 p.

The concept of the university is submitted to a challenging examination in three parts: the first deals with the intellectual life in general; the second, with the objectives which a university must have; and the final section, with the basic requisites for the existence of the university. Jaspers believes that academic teaching, scientific and scholarly research, and a creative cultural life are inseparably linked to each other. Moreover, the university is the place where man must be allowed the freedom to search for and profess truth.

149. **Kerr, Clark.**
The Uses of the University.
Cambridge, Mass., Harvard Univ. Press, 1963. 140 p.

The author describes changes that have occurred in universities during the past 20 years and the development of the "multiversity." He views institutions of higher learning as the keystone of the "knowledge industry" and asserts that they will continue to be required to respond to society's need for information and expert capabilities.

150. **Kline, Stephen J.**
Principles and Procedures of Campus Government.
Stanford, Calif., Council for the Academic Community, 1970. 58 p.

Some ideas and experiences relating to problems and changes in university governance are presented, including sections on information flow on campus, grievance procedures, legislative and judicial procedures.

151.   **Lee, Calvin B.T., ed.**
Whose Goals for American Higher Education?
Washington, American Council on Education, 1968.
241 p.

This compendium of essays, first delivered at the ACE's 50th
meeting in October 1967, analyzes basic conflicts of function
and goals in higher education today, focusing on areas such as
teaching-learning-research responsibilities, town-gown relationships, university governance.

152.   **Martin, Warren B.**
*Alternative to Irrelevance: A Strategy for Reform in
Higher Education.*
Nashville, Abingdon Press, 1968. 160 p.

This is one of the most thoughtful—and least circulated—
analyses of the present crisis in higher education. Martin sees
the division in the academic community as an essentialist-
existentialist confrontation. It describes well why essentialists
(Dewey, James, Hegel, Kant, Mill, etc.) tend to be against
educational innovation, while the existentialists (Buber, Sartre,
Camus, Kierkegaard, etc.) are inclined to change. The book
concludes with numerous practical suggestions for reconciling
the two views within the university setting.

153.   **Mayhew, Lewis B.**
Colleges Today and Tomorrow.
San Francisco, Jossey-Bass, 1969. 255 p.

This well-written book, especially useful for those outside
higher education, surveys the present state of higher education
and suggests some possible future developments. The main
concerns are government-university relationships, student complaints and protest, and curricular reform.

154.   **Mayhew, Lewis B., ed.**
Higher Education in the Revolutionary Decades.
Berkeley, Calif., McCutchan, 1967. 476 p.

This anthology of essays is concerned with developments in
higher education since 1945. It examines some of the radical
changes that have taken place in society and the impact those

changes have had and may be expected to have on the objectives, governance, student attitudes and dissent, reform, and research and teaching obligations of the university.

155. Nisbet, Robert.
The Degradation of the Academic Dogma: The University in America, 1945-1970.
New York, Basic Books, in press.

A study by a distinguished sociologist (to be published in 1971) voices concern with the post-World War II developments that have transformed the university from an institution in which knowledge was pursued as an end in itself to one in which knowledge is sought as a commodity for resale to the society at large. The author's fundamental thesis is that the modern American university has betrayed its own central purpose: the pursuit of knowledge. Outside claims for services cannot and should not divert the university from its primary mission—scholarship.

156. Ortega y Gasset, Jose.
Mission of the University.
Translated with an introduction by Howard Lee Nostrand.
Princeton, Princeton University Press, 1944. 103 p.

In a philosophic scrutiny of the university system in Spain and elsewhere in Europe, the author discusses what a university ought to be and what it actually is. Of central concern are the nature of the relationship of the university to external constituents (society, governments, etc.) and the problems of politicization.

157. "Rights and Responsibilities: The University's Dilemma."
Daedalus, v. 99, summer 1970: 531-714.

The issue is devoted to an appraisal of the contemporary state of higher education. The crisis of academic authority, changing aspects of policymaking, institutional responses to change, the roles and critique of learning, and the political relationship between state authorities and state universities are among the problems discussed.

158. **Robinson, Lora H., and Janet D. Shoenfeld.**
Student Participation in Academic Governance.
Washington, ERIC Clearinghouse on Higher Education, 1970. 29 p. (Review No. 1)

This review includes an annotated bibliography of selected literature on student participation in governance and a compendium of recent changes.

159. **Roszak, Theodore, ed.**
The Dissenting Academy.
New York, Vintage Books, 1968. 304 p.

Noted new left scholars in the humanities and social sciences admonish the academic community. The essays in this collection, though differing in emphasis, all express the conviction that public examination of the moral quality of human life is the primary obligation of the academy.

160. *Stress and Campus Response: Current Issues in Higher Education, 1968.* Edited by G. Kerry Smith.
San Francisco, Jossey-Bass, 1968. 297 p.

This compendium of essays deals with five broad areas: the severe dislocations of society at large, which have left an impact on higher education; analyses of various aspects of student unrest; dysfunctions in institutional organizations and governance, and suggested remedies; changes toward increasing curricular relevance; and prospects for the future.

161. **Wallerstein, Immanuel.**
University in Turmoil: The Politics of Change.
New York, Athenaeum, 1969. 147 p.

A historical analysis of the nature of the Western university, and particularly the contemporary American university, provides a springboard for a critical examination of its purpose, internal structure, role, and impact on society. In his discussion of the use of violence as means of achieving social change, the author offers some useful insights on attitudes and actions of ethnic minorities.

162. **U.S. Office of Education. Subcommittee on Easing Tensions in Education.**

Report [submitted by] Gregory R. Anrig, Chairman. Washington, 1969. [155 p.]

Major factors contributing to student unrest are briefly reviewed. The Subcommittee concludes that changes must take place in both the educational system and the society at large to reduce the ideological, radical, and institutional tensions of which campus unrest is symptomatic. The report makes 18 specific recommendations to the Secretary of HEW concerning ways in which he can positively encourage and assist in achieving needed change, and lists 11 negative responses that should be avoided.

163. **Wolff, Robert Paul.**
The Ideal of the University.
Boston, Beacon Press, 1969. 161 p.

In this inquiry into the nature of the university, with emphasis on the development and present state of U.S. higher education, the author presents an insightful analysis of the grading system, questions a number of myths by which universities currently operate, discusses issues related to university governance, and suggests some practical proposals for reform.

Chapter 7: Government and Campus Unrest

164. **Association of American Universities.**
Survey Report: Status of Reserve Officer Training Corps Programs at AAU Member Institutions.
Washington, 1970. 19[14] p.

Factual report of the general trends in ROTC programs at AAU member institutions is presented herein.

165. **American Civil Liberties Union.**
Statement on ROTC and Educational Institutions.
New York, 1970. 2 p.

This brief statement reaffirms the ACLU policy recommending that "if ROTC programs do exist they should be separated to the maximum extent feasible from academic institutions"; and suggests standards with which such programs should comply.

166. **American Association of State Colleges and Universities.**

ROTC Programs at State Colleges and Universities.
Washington, 1970. 30 p.

The report presents a study of approaches to ROTC programs at State colleges and universities: it describes enrollment and officer production trends; reviews policies regarding ROTC supervision and staffing; and discusses some of the issues surrounding the program. At state schools where ROTC is a major campus issue, its compulsory nature is the source of contention; they tend to favor continuation of ROTC as a voluntary program.

167. **Chambers, Merritt M.**
Freedom and Repression in Higher Education.
Bloomington, Ind., Bloomcraft Press, 1965. 126 p.

The effect of government-university ties on quality of education is examined and analyzed. The author disputes the assertion that our universities suffer from a lack of centralized planning, and calls for greater flexibility and variety of opportunity for individuals and institutions alike.

168. **Eberly, Donald J., ed.**
National Service: A Report of a Conference.
New York, Russell Sage Foundation, 1968. 598 p.

This series of papers and summaries of workshop discussions deals with the concept of national service for youth, proposals for the organization of National Service, areas in which it could be utilized, and related issues.

169. **Lyons, Gene M., and John W. Masland.**
Education and Military Leadership: A Study of the ROTC.
Princeton, Princeton Univ. Press, 1959. 283 p.

The authors make an inquiry into the history, nature, and rationale of ROTC programs, examine the relationship of higher education to the national defense, attempt a clarification of the objectives of the ROTC program, and suggest directions for organizational and curricular change.

170. **Orlans, Harold.**
The Effects of Federal Programs on Higher Educa-

tion: A Study of Thirty-Six Universities and Colleges.
Washington, The Brookings Institution, 1962. 361 p.

In this study the author examines "the effects of federally supported research programs upon selected departments of science, social science, and the humanities at 36 universities and colleges." The volume is divided into 3 parts: Part 1 deals with the effect of federal programs on quality of education; Part 2, with the question of whether present funds should be more widely dispersed; and Part 3, with experience in administration of federal programs.

171. **U.S. Congress. Joint Economic Committee.**
The Economics and Financing of Higher Education in the United States: A Compendium of Papers.
Washington, U.S. Govt. Print. Off., 1969. 683 p. (91st Cong., 1st sess. Joint Committee print.)

This anthology of essays deals with the structure, growth, and financing of higher education. It should be particularly valuable for the reader interested in university relations with state and federal governments.

172. **U. S. Dept of Defense. Special Committee on ROTC.**
Report to the Secretary of Defense.
Washington, 1969. 61 p.

Known as the Bensen Committee Report, this study includes a brief history of ROTC and a factual description of current programs, an evaluation of alternate methods of providing professional training for officer candidates, an examination of the validity of various criticisms of ROTC programs, and a list of recommendations to strengthen ROTC programs.

173. **U. S. Office of Education.**
How the Office of Education Assists College Students and Colleges. Compiled by the Bureau of Higher Education of the Office of Education.
Washington, U.S. Govt. Print. Off., 1968. 41 p.

This report includes a history of all major aid programs for the support of institutions, facilities, and equipment, programs for disadvantaged students, general student aid, research and community activity.

174. **U.S. President. Commission on an All-Volunteer Armed Force.**
The Report of the President's Commission on an All-Volunteer Armed Force.
Washington, U.S. Govt. Print. Off., 1970. 211 p. and New York, Collier Books, 1970. 218 p.

The Gates Commission recommends the elimination of conscription and the return to an all-volunteer army in order to "minimize government interference with the freedom of the individual to determine his own life in accord with his own values." It includes sections dealing with objections to an all-volunteer force, recent foreign experience with such a force, alternatives to an all-volunteer force, and recommendations of the committee for increasing the efficiency of the Armed Forces' utilization of manpower.

Special Report: The Kent State Tragedy

175. **Kent [State] Chapter of the American Association of University Professors. Special Committee of Inquiry.**
Report.
[Kent, Ohio] 1969. 74 p.

Report on the investigation of an SDS protest demonstration on Apr. 16, 1969, at the Music and Speech Building attempts to assess the meaning of the incidents "in the context of academic due process . . . and to report its findings to the full membership." The report is also known as the Rudrum Report.

176. **U.S. House of Representatives. Committee on Internal Security.**
Investigation of Students for a Democratic Society: Part 2 (Kent State University).
Washington, U.S. Govt. Print. Off., 1969. p. 475-642. (91st Cong., 1st sess.)

The hearings were conducted into "the origin, history, organization, character, objectives, and activities of the Students for a Democratic Society at Kent State University." Testimonies include those of KSU president Robert I. White, student Margaret Ann Murray; KSU Police Lieutenant Jack Crawford, and others.

Part 2

Selective Guide to Bibliographies on Campus Unrest

This guide is intended for those readers who want to concentrate on the specific topic of campus unrest and go beyond the titles suggested in the preceding bibliography. Simple lists of books or magazines which merely repeat the contents of *Books in Print* have been omitted as have experimental automated bibliographies which do not, as yet, provide adequate subject classifications.

I. Monograph-length Bibliographies

1. **Altbach, Philip G.**
   Student Politics and Higher Education in the United States: a Select Bibliography, Prelim. ed.
   Cambridge, Harvard Center for International Affairs, 1967. 36 p.

2. **Altbach, Philip G.**
   Student Politics and Higher Education in the United States: a Select Bibliography. Introd. by Seymour M. Lipset.
   Cambridge, Harvard Center for International Affairs, 1968. 86 p. $2.

   The preliminary edition (No. 1) lacks the introductory essays but does contain entries on doctoral dissertations and unpublished papers which were dropped from the published bibliography.
   Altbach first compares several national student movements, then develops a bibliographic essay which takes the place of annotations. Works of major importance are starred (*) in the body of the bibliography.
   The 1968 edition of this bibliography is considered definitive in the field of student activism. It is divided into nine major subject categories with 49 subheadings. The principal divisions are: General Material; the University in Society; Sociological Aspects of Student Activism; Psychological Aspects of Student Activism; Radical Student Politics; the Civil Rights Movement; Other Student Organ-

izations and Movements; Non-political Aspects of Student Life; and Journals.

It includes material of historical as well as current value. Articles from anthologies are entered under the relevant heading. Some published material which was considered to be of only peripheral interest has been excluded from the bibliography.

Materials of particular use to administrators can be found under: Civil Liberties and Academic Freedom; Legal Aspects of Student Activism and Discipline; and Administrative Response to Student Activism and Disruption.

These editions of Altbach's bibliographies are not to be confused with his 1967 *A Select Bibliography on Students, Politics, and Higher Education,* which deals with student activism outside the United States.

3. **Aptheker, Bettina, comp.**
    Higher Education and the Student Rebellion in the United States, 1960-1969: a Bibliography.
    New York, American Institute for Marxist Studies, 1969. 50 p. $1.

    Miss Aptheker writes in her introduction that, although the "Liberal Establishment" is represented in her sometimes annotated listing, "greatest emphasis was given to the Left, and especially to the critiques of the rebels themselves. Special attention was given to black students and the crisis in Negro higher education."

    Although her "Books" category is useful, the major contribution of this bibliography is in its "Pamphlets," "Periodicals," and "Continuing Sources of Information: Magazines, Newspapers, Organizations, Films" divisions where the author's knowledge of the student left is brought to bear on the description of their own publications. The section on "Continuing Sources" keeps this essay from becoming outdated. It is not organized by subject, concentrates heavily on the students themselves, and develops in depth student activities in California.

4. **Mayhew, Lewis B.**
    The Literature of Higher Education, 1967.
    Washington, American Association for Higher

Education, 1968. 57 p. $2.

5. **Mayhew, Lewis B.**
The Literature of Higher Education, 1968.
Washington, American Association for Higher
Education, 1969. 74 p. $2.50.

6. **Mayhew, Lewis B.**
The Literature of Higher Education During 1969.
Washington, American Association for Higher
Education [One Dupont Circle, Suite 780, Wash.,
D.C., 20036] 1970. 80 p. $2.

Only a small section in each of these critically annotated
annual bibliographies is devoted to student unrest. His
subject categories change from year to year but his
annotations and comprehensiveness remain valuable. Books
about higher education in all countries are included in this
compilation. Recent volumes are indexed.

This is an important series for the field of higher education
in general but Altbach (No. 2) remains the key list devoted
principally to campus unrest.

II. Pamphlet-length Bibliographies

7. **Dunlap, Riley.**
*A Bibliography of Empirical Studies of Student
Political Activism.*
Eugene, Univ. of Oregon, Dept. of Sociology, 1969.
Mimeograph. 5 p.

This represents an attempt to consolidate the rapidly
growing body of empirical literature now available on
student activism. It is limited to papers which have been
published or delivered at professional meetings. It covers
the period from 1961 to 1969 and is valuable in that it
identifies many unpublished papers.

8. **O'Brien, James.**
A History of the New Left, 1960-1968.
Boston, New England Free Press [791 Tremont St.,
Boston, Mass., 02118] n.d. 32 p. $0.50.

O'Brien writes, "As originally conceived, this article was to be strictly a bibliographical essay, in which I would point out some books and articles helpful in explaining what the New Left is and how it developed. It became clear, however, that I would have to write it as a narration, with bibliographical notes . . . . The bibliographical references are handled in an arbitrary, if not actually a whimsical, way, some of them being incorporated into the text and others being relegated to a long footnote section at the end; the only criterion was whether they tended to interrupt the narration."

The essay is organized chronologically and the footnotes almost constitute an independent annotated bibliography.

9.   **Segal, Patricia.**
     Annotated Bibliography on Student Rebellion and Revolutionary Movements.
     Claremont, Calif., Claremont Graduate School, 1970. Mimeograph. 9 p.

     The annotations on the 23 books included herein are excellent one-paragraph summaries of their contents. This bibliography does not make an original contribution to the compilations extant in this field, but it would be of use to a reader wishing to familiarize himself quickly with this topic.

10. **Shulman, Carol.**
     Governance.
     Washington, ERIC Clearinghouse on Higher Education, The George Washington University [One Dupont Circle, Suite 630, Wash., D.C., 20036] 1970. 23 p. (Compendium Series of Current Research Programs and Proposals, No. 1.) Single copies free upon application.

     Although primarily devoted to the problems of governing a university, this well-annotated list does describe many projects which study governance from the student point of view in general and the position of the student protestor in particular.

III. Bibliographies Contained in Other Works

11. **Foster, Julian.**
"Student Protest: What is Said." In *Protest! Student Activism in America.* Edited by Julian Foster and Durward Long.
New York, Wm. Morrow, 1970. p. 27-58.

This chapter is divided into nine categories which summarize existing knowledge and sometimes indicate areas which need further investigation. Foster discusses the differences in approach to student activism between the professors of humanities and the behavioral scientists, and between the conservatives, liberals, and radicals. Included are categories such as: Events on Particular American Campuses; On Student Politics and Protest in Other Countries; and Studies of Protest Action: Strategic, Theoretical and Predictive.
This chapter is a good starting point for a researcher new to this topic or for a worker who needs a concise summary of research in this area as of early 1970.

12. **Merideth, Robert.**
"The New Left: An Introductory Bibliographical Commentary." *Radical Amerikan Studies.* v. 1, May 1970: 3-8.
Available from Robert Sklar, Dept. of History, Univ. of Michigan, Ann Arbor, Mich., 48104.

Prof. Merideth is a member of the Radical Caucus of the American Studies Association and writes dogmatically from the radical point of view.
This essay updates O'Brien (No. 8) and is intended for an outsider who wants to learn about the new left and counterculture movements among the young in our society. It is not organized by subject but does give valuable insight into which radical publications, newsfilms, and organizations are of major importance for an understanding of the contemporary radical movements in this country.

13. **Michigan State Senate, Committee to Investigate Campus Disorders and Student Unrest.**
Final Staff Report.

[Lansing, 1970] Mimeograph. Two parts.

The bibliography is given in the last chapter of Part Two (p. 150-180). It contains much material of use to college administrators and is oriented toward their point of view. It is not annotated, but is divided into several useful categories. Section Two is devoted to general legal questions. Section Six is on Speaker's Policy and Use of Facilities. There is also a section on Freedom in the Arts. It fails, however, to distinguish between books and pamphlets in its entry format. Some citations appear to be inaccurate.

A condensed version of this bibliography has been published by Higher Education Executive Associates of Detroit, Michigan.

14. **Skolnick, Jerome H.**

The Politics of Protest. A report submitted by Jerome H. Skolnick, Director, Task Force on Violent Aspects of Protest and Confrontation of the National Commission on the Causes and Prevention of Violence.

Washington, U.S. Govt. Print. Off. [1969] 276 p.

The appended bibliography (p. 267-276) is concerned exclusively with literature on the protest movements of the 1960's. It is partially annotated. The subject categories on The Racial Attitudes of White Americans and The Police in Protest are particularly extensive.

IV. Work in Progress.

Starting in the fall of 1970 a computer printout of abstracts of 1967-69 journal articles relating to the Student Power movement will be available at no charge from: National Institute of Mental Health Information, 5454 Wisconsin Avenue, Chevy Chase, Md., 20014.

Commission Hearings and Investigations

COMMISSION HEARINGS AND INVESTIGATIONS

The Commission held its first Executive Session on June 25, 1970 in Washington, D.C. During the next three months of its operation, the Commission held fifteen executive sessions and thirteen public hearings.

The President announced the appointment of Wm. Matthew Byrne, Jr., as Executive Director of the Commission on July 7, 1970. Mr. Byrne hired and headed the Commission's staff, which included a total of 147 members.

The Commission received and solicited a variety of papers from scholars and other experts on subjects concerning campus unrest.

In addition Commission staff members conducted extensive research and prepared studies for use in writing this report.

The Commission held public hearings in Washington, D.C., and Los Angeles, California. The witnessess were chosen to provide a cross-section of opinion regarding campus unrest. Testimony was taken from the following persons:

Washington, D.C.

William P. Beall, Jr.	Coordinator of Police Services, University of California, Berkeley
J. Otis Cochrane	National Chairman, Black American Law Students Association
Bruce Dearing	President, State University of New York, Binghamton
Robben W. Fleming	President, University of Michigan

S. I. Hayakawa	President, San Francisco State College
Denis Hayes	National Coordinator, Environmental Action
Sidney Hook	Professor of Philosophy, New York University
Eva Jefferson	Student Body President, Northwestern University
David A. Keene	President, Young Americans for Freedom
Steven Kelman	Student, Harvard University
Kenneth Keniston	Associate Professor of Psychology, Yale Medical School
Edward M. Kennedy	United States Senator, Massachusetts Majority Whip of the U.S. Senate
Henry W. Maier	Mayor, Milwaukee, Wisconsin
Charles F. Palmer	President, National Student Association
Nathan M. Pusey	President, Harvard University
Robert Rankin	Vice President, Danforth Foundation
Robert D. Ray	Governor of Iowa
Charles Rogovin	Former Director, Law Enforcement Assistance Administration
Granville M. Sawyer	President, Texas Southern University

Hugh Scott — United States Senator, Pennsylvania, Minority Leader of the U.S. Senate

Harold E. Sponberg — President, Eastern Michigan University

William A. Steiger — Member, U.S. House of Representatives, from Wisconsin

Edward Teller — Professor of Physics, University of California

William Sullivan — Assistant to the Director, Federal Bureau of Investigation

Jerry V. Wilson — Chief of Police, Washington, D.C.

Winston P. Wilson — Maj. Gen. U.S. Air Force, Chief, National Guard Bureau

Los Angeles, California

Jesus Chivarria — Assistant Professor of History, University of California, Santa Barbara

Steven Cooley — Past President, Associated Students, California State College, Los Angeles

Richard Flacks — Associate Professor of Sociology, University of California, Santa Barbara

David P. Gardiner — Vice Chancellor, Univeristy of California, Santa Barbara

Harold Hodgkinson — Project Director, Center for Research and Development in Higher Education, University of California, Berkeley

Louis B. Lundborg	Chairman of the Board, Bank of America
William J. McGill	President, Columbia University, Past Chancellor, University of California, San Diego
Thomas Norminton	Past President, Associated Students, UCLA
Jerome Richfield	Past Chairman, Academic Senate of the California State Colleges
Robert Singleton	Former Director, Afro-American Studies Center, UCLA
S. Alex Stalcup	President, Associated Students, University of California, San Francisco Mecical School
James W. Webster	Sheriff-Coroner, County of Santa Barbara

The Commission and members of the staff participated in a one day seminar with the following law enforcement officials:

William P. Beall, Jr.	Coordinator of Police Services, University of California, Berkeley
W. Wade Bromwell	Director of Security, University of Virginia
Dale Carson	Sheriff of Duval County, Jacksonville, Florida
Frederick Davids	Director of Michigan State Police, East Lansing, Michigan

Edward M. Davis   Chief,
Los Angeles Police Department

Charles R. Gain   Chief,
Oakland Police Department

Bernard L. Garmire   Chief,
Miami Police Department

James J. Lison   Adjutant General,
Wisconsin National Guard

Frank B. Looney   Commissioner,
Nassau County Police,
New York

John C. Marchant   Director of Security,
University of Massachusetts

Donald D. Pomerleau   Commissioner,
Baltimore Police Department

Thomas Reddin   Chief,
Los Angeles Police Department
(Retired)

Charles L. Southward   Commanding General,
District of Columbia National
Guard

Quinn Tamm   Executive Director,
International Association of
Chiefs of Police

Jerry V. Wilson   Chief of Police,
Washington, D.C.

Staff members interviewed administrators, faculty and students at the following colleges and universities:

Brooklyn College
City College of New York
Colorado State University
Emory University
Morehouse College
Southern Illinois University
Southern Methodist University

State University of New York at Buffalo
University of Denver
University of Illinois (Chicago Circle Campus)
University of Maryland
University of Michigan
University of Oregon
University of Texas
Virginia State College
Washington University
Wayne State University
Wiley College

Staff members were sent to Jackson, Mississippi to investigate the events of May 12-14, 1970 at Jackson State College. Another team of staff members went to Kent, Ohio to investigate the occurrences of May 1-4, 1970 at Kent State University. Reports of the Federal Bureau of Investigation and other relevant materials were reviewed and analyzed. Students, faculty and administrators of the colleges, law enforcement officers, government officials, and townspeople were interviewed.

The Commission held public hearings in Jackson on August 11-13, 1970. The following individuals testified:

Farries Adams	Student Jackson State College
Margaret W. Alexander	Professor of English, Jackson State College
Gregory Antoine	Student, Jackson State College
Warner Buxton	President, Student Government Association, Jackson State College
Bert Case	Television Newsman
Martel Cook	Part-time student and newsman
Russell Davis	Mayor, Jackson, Mississippi
James Downey	Newsman

Claude Gholson   Patrolman,
                        Jackson State College

Jack Hobbs   Television newsman

Frank James   Student,
                        Jackson State College

Walter Johnson   Adjutant General,
                        Mississippi National Guard

Lloyd Jones   Inspector,
                        Mississippi Highway Safety Patrol

Charles E. Lee   Sergeant,
                        Jackson Police Department

Charles Little   Patrolman,
                        Jackson Police Department

Gene Livingston   Staff member,
                        President's Commission on Campus Unrest

Warren Magee   Lieutenant,
                        Jackson Police Department

John Peoples   President,
                        Jackson State College

M. B. Pierce   Chief of Detectives,
                        Jackson Police Department

Andrea Reese   Student,
                        Jackson State College

Aaron Shirley   Pediatrician,
                        Jackson, Mississippi

Charles Snodgrass   Administrative Assistant,
                        Mississippi Highway Safety Patrol

Stella Spinks   Student,
                        Jackson State College

M. R. Stringer   Jackson State College
                        Security Patrol

Public hearings were held in Kent, Ohio on August 19-21, 1970. The following individuals testified:

Meyer Alewitz	Student, Kent State University
Doris Amick	Co-founder/Portage County Citizens for Law Enforcement
Robert H. Canterbury	Assistant Adjutant General, National Guard
John Carson	Former Mayor of Kent
Sylvester Del Corso	Adjutant General, Ohio National Guard
Dennis Durand	Student, Kent State University
Glenn Frank	Assistant Professor, Sociology
Barbara Knapp	Student, Kent State University
Jerry M. Lewis	Associate Professor, Geology
Donald Manley	Major, Ohio State Highway Patrol
Robert Matson	Vice President, Student Affairs, Kent State University
Craig Morgan	Student, Kent State University
Robert Pickett	Student, Kent State University
Howard Ruffner	Student, Kent State University
Leroy Satrom	Mayor, Kent, Ohio
Steven Sharoff	Graduate Student, Kent State University
Robert Stamps	Student, Kent State University
Robert C. Terko	Student, Kent State University

Roy Thompson	Chief of Police, City of Kent
Stephen Titchel	Student, Kent State University
George Warren	Staff member, President's Commission on Campus Unrest
Robert I. White	President, Kent State University
Chester Williams	Safety Director, Kent State University
James Woodring	Student, Kent State University

Staff members accompanied a panel of Commissioners to Albuquerque, New Mexico to hold informal interviews on incidents involving University of New Mexico students. The Commissioners also gathered information relating to problems of Mexican-Americans and American Indians. Other staff investigators went to the University of Kansas, Lawrence, Kansas to study the tensions arising from the off-campus killings of two former students. They reviewed investigative materials, conducted interviews, and circulated 2000 questionnaires, approximately 500 of which were returned and analyzed.

Staff members conducted interviews with government and university officials, law enforcement officials, faculty, students and others relating to the bombing of the Army Mathematics Research Center, Madison, Wisconsin and prior disruptions at the University of Wisconsin.

Through the Urban Institute, the Commission conducted a national survey of college presidents, faculty senate chairmen, and student government presidents at every accredited institution of higher education in the country. The Institute (1) developed and distributed 8,100 questionnaires to approximately 2,700 colleges and universities throughout the United States; (2) coded and tabulated closed and open-ended attitude responses; (3) performed tabular and computer analysis; and (4) reported their findings in the form of a research monograph, which is published as a separate Commission document.

Official Documents

EXECUTIVE ORDER OF JUNE 13, 1970 ESTABLISHING THE PRESIDENT'S COMMISSION ON CAMPUS UNREST

By virtue of the authority vested in me as President of the United States, it is ordered as follows:

Section 1. *Establishment of Commission.* (a) There is hereby established the President's Commission on Campus Unrest (hereinafter referred to as the Commission).

(b) The Commission shall be composed of a Chairman to be appointed by the President, and of so many other members as the President may appoint.

Sec. 2. *Functions of the Commission.* The Commission shall study dissent, disorder, and violence on the campuses of institutions of higher learning or in connection with such institutions, and report its findings and recommendations to the President. The duties of the Commission shall include, but not be limited to, the following:

(1) Identifying the principal causes of campus violence and the breakdown in the process of orderly expression of dissent on the campus.

(2) Suggesting specific methods and procedures through which grievances can be resolved by means other than the exertion of force.

(3) Suggesting ways to protect academic freedom, the right to obtain an education free from improper interference, and the right of peaceful dissent and protest.

(4) Proposing practical steps which can be taken by government at all levels, by the administrations of institutions of higher learning, and by students, through student governments or otherwise, to minimize dangers attendant upon expressions of dissent.

Sec. 3. *Staff of the Commission.* (a) The Commission shall have an Executive Director, appointed by the President in accordance with law.

(b) Subject to law, the Commission is authorized (1) to appoint such additional personnel as it deems necessary and fix their compensation, and (2) to obtain services in accordance with the provisions of 5 U.S.C. 3109.

Sec. 4. *Expenses.* Members of the Commission shall receive compensation of $100 per day when engaged in the performance of duties under this order and shall be allowed travel expenses, including per diem in lieu of subsistence, as authorized by law (5 U.S.C. 5703) for persons in Government service employed intermittently.

Sec 5. *Cooperation by executive departments and agencies.* (a) The Commission, acting through its chairman, is authorized to request from any executive department or agency any information and assistance deemed necessary to carry out its functions under this order. Each department and agency is directed, to the extent permitted by law and within the limits of available funds, to furnish information and assistance to the Commission.

(b) The General Services Administration shall provide administrative services and support for the Commission.

Sec. 6. *Report and termination.* The Commission shall present its final report and recommendations to the President not later than October 1, 1970, and shall terminate thirty days after the presentation of such report.

Richard Nixon

STATEMENT OF THE PRESIDENT UPON ESTABLISHING THE COMMISSION. JUNE 13, 1970

The United States has the greatest system of higher education ever developed by man. But in the past academic year, the integrity of this system—involving more than 2,500 colleges and universities and nearly 8,000,000 students—has been threatened. While the overwhelming majority of those who live and work in the academic community are dedicated to nonviolence, there have nevertheless been over one hundred campuses on which violent acts have recently occurred. The tragic results have included loss of life, vast property damage, and serious disruption of the educational process. This situation is a matter of vital concern to all Americans.

Today I am appointing a Commission on Campus Unrest to study this serious situation, to report its findings and make recommendations to me. William Scranton, the former Governor of Pennsylvania, will be the Chairman.

The following are among the purposes of the Commission:

—To identify the principal causes of campus violence, particularly in the specific occurrences of this spring.

—To assess the reasons for breakdown in the processes for orderly expression of dissent.

—To suggest specific methods and procedures through which legitimate grievances can be resolved.

—To suggest ways to protect and enhance the right of academic freedom, the right to pursue an education free from improper interference, and the right of peaceful dissent and protest.

It is my hope that the Commission will help us discover what practical steps can be taken by all levels of government—including law enforcement agencies—to alleviate the dangers involved in this situation. I hope, too, that the Commission will explore ways in which university admininistrations and student leaders can contribute more effectively to the control and elimination of campus violence. There is nothing that any of us can do now to restore the lives that have been lost or to undo the other effects of past campus violence. But the Commission can help us to avoid future incidents of the sort which occurred this past spring, the most appalling of which were the tragedies at Kent State University in Ohio and Jackson State College in Mississippi.

The Commission will receive assistance and support from its own staff and from the investigative facilities of the various Federal departments. I will ask the Congress to provide the Commission with the power of subpoena.

I have asked the Commission to begin its work immediately and to report to me before the beginning of the coming academic year.

JOINT CONGRESSIONAL RESOLUTION GRANTING
VARIOUS POWERS TO THE COMMISSION

Joint resolution authorizing the President's Commission on Campus Unrest to compel the attendance and testimony of witnesses and the production of evidence, and for other pruposes

Resolved by the Senate and House of Representatives of the United States of America in Congress assembled, That (a) for the purposes of this joint resolution, the term "Commission" means the Commission created by the President by Executive Order 11536, dated June 13, 1970.

(b) The Commission, or any member of the Commission when so authorized by the Commission, shall have power to issue subpenas requiring the attendance and testimony of witnesses and the production of any evidence that relates to any matter under investigation by the Commission. The Commission, or any member of the Commission or any agent or agency designated by the Commission for such purpose, may administer oaths and affirmations, examine witnesses, and receive evidence. Such attendance of witnesses and the production of such evidence may be required from any place within the United States at any designated place of hearing.

(c) In the case of contumacy or refusal to obey a subpoena issued to any person under subsection (b), any court of the United States within the jurisdiction of which the inquiry is carried on or within the jurisdiction of which said person guilty of contumacy or refusal to obey is found or resides or transacts business, upon application by the Commission shall have jurisdiction to issue to such person an order requiring such person to appear before the Commission, its member, agent, or agency, there to produce evidence if so ordered, or there to give testimony touching the matter under investigation or in question; and any failure to obey such order of the court may be punished by said court as a contempt thereof.

(d) Process and papers of the Commission, its members, agent or agency, may be served either upon the witness in person or by registered mail or by telegraph or by leaving a copy thereof at the residence or principal office or place of business of the person required to be served. The verified return by the individual so serving the same, setting forth the manner of such service, shall be proof of the same, and the return post office receipt or telegraph receipt therefor when registered and mailed or telegraphed as aforesaid shall be proof of service of the same. Witnesses summoned before the Commission, its members, agent, or agency, shall be paid the same fees and mileage that are paid witnesses in the courts of the United States, and witnesses whose depositions are taken and the persons taking the same shall severally be entitled to the same fees as are paid for like services in the courts of the United States.

(e) (1) Whenever a witness refuses, on the basis of his privilege against self-incrimination, to testify or provide other information in a proceeding before the Commission, and the person presiding over the proceeding communicates to the witness an order issued pursuant to paragraph (2) of this subsection, the witness may not refuse to comply with the order on the basis of his privilege against self-incrimination; but no testimony or other information compelled under the order (or any information directly or indirectly derived from such testimony or other information) may be used against the witness in any criminal case, except a prosecution for perjury, giving a false statement, or otherwise failing to comply with the order. The term "other information" includes any book, paper, document, record, recording, or other material.

(2) The Commission may, with the approval of the Attorney General, issue an order requiring an individual who has been or may be called to testify or to provide other information to give any testimony or provide other information which he refuses to give or provide on the basis of his privilege against self-incrimination: *Provided*, That the Commission may issue such an order only if in its judgment (i) the testimony or other information from such individual may be necessary to the public interest, and (ii) such individual has refused or is likely to refuse to testify or provide other information on the basis of his privilege against self-incrimination.

(f) All process of any court to which application may be made under this Joint Resolution may be served in the judicial district wherein the person required to be served resides or may be found.

Sec. 2. The Commission shall have power to appoint and fix the compensation of such personnel as it deems advisable without regard to the provisions of title 5, United States Code, governing appointments in the competitive service, and such personnel may be paid without regard to the provisions of chapter 51 and subchapter III of chapter 53 of such title relating to classification and General Schedule pay rates, but no individual shall receive compensation at a rate in excess of the maximum rate authorized by the General Schedule. In addition, the Commission may procure the services of experts and consultants in accordance with section 3109 of title 5, United States Code, but at rates not in excess of the daily equivalent of GS-18. The Commission is also authorized to enter into contracts with Federal or State agencies, private firms, institutions, and individuals for the conduct of research for surveys, the preparation of reports, and other activities necessary for the discharge of its duties.